Rilke
in the Making

Rilke
in the Making

A Comprehensive Study
of His Life and Work
from 1897 to 1926,
in Three Volumes

John O'Meara

HcP
Ottawa
2023

HcP
Heart's Core Publications
447 Clarence Street E.
Ottawa, Ontario
K1N 5R9

Library and Archives Canada Cataloguing in Publication

O'Meara, John, 1953- author.
Rilke in the making : a comprehensive study of his life and work
from 1897 to 1926, in three volumes / John O'Meara.
Includes bibliographical references.

Canadiana 20230498817 | ISBN 9780992097189 (softcover)

LCSH: Rilke, Rainer Maria, 1875-1926. | LCSH: Rilke, Rainer
Maria, 1875-1926—Criticism and interpretation. | LCSH:
Andreas-Salomé, Lou, 1861-1937. | LCSH: Novalis, 1772-1801. |
LCSH: von Thurn und Taxis, Marie, Princess, 1855-1934.

LCC PT2635.I65 Z6357 2023 | DDC 831/.912—dc23

La Famille des Saltimbanques, by Picasso,
National Gallery of Art, Washington, DC.

Interior Design:
Aline Francoeur

Cover Design:
Tom Tassel

Contents

*The reader will note that pagination begins where the body-text for that Volume begins, each beginning preceded by front matter that includes the Main Reference Works for that Volume.—*HcP*

Also by
John O'Meara

The Way of Novalis

Remembering Shakespeare

Publisher's Note

The avid reader of this book will discover that it consists of three volumes, each of which will require particular attention, as the reference system in each case is internal to itself. Originally the intention was to offer this study in the form of three separate volumes. The first volume had, indeed, already appeared on its own, in 2017. Subsequently, however, it became clear that the second and third volumes connected too closely to the first to warrant separate publication in those cases. They have consequently been brought together with the first volume and are here published in one book—one book, with a reference system unique in the case of each volume. To have sought to render the referencing uniform across the three volumes, after the enterprise was well underway, would have entailed a mammoth remaking of the second and third volumes which would not have been in any reasonable sense practicable. Let the reader, therefore, be advised, proceed accordingly with due allowance for the limits of human endeavour, and settle at last into the happiness of knowing that all is yet well in hand here.

HcP

Author's Summary

This book takes the form of a close, exegetical commentary on all the major poetry Rilke wrote, and, equally, functions as a running biography of his life with immediate applications of that life to Rilke's developing artistic work. It is intended for a reader who will, therefore, be prepared to enter into a very close study of Rilke's life and work, and who will be ready to consider, more intimately than is usual, the many particulars of his poetic- and life-expression, which more than in the case of most poets, were virtually one and the same.

Two major theses are put forward, the first touching on Rilke's well-known relationship to his lover and mentor, Lou Salomé, which is understood to have been far more problematic and more crucial than we had supposed, the second touching on an equally crucial and at some point, indeed, saving influence on Rilke from the literary sphere, which is shown to be that of the great visionary poet who went by the name of Novalis.

Volume 1 focuses primarily on the *Book of Hours* and the first period of his life as a major poet, after meeting Lou and through his subsequent separation from her through 1905. Volume 2 continues from the moment of the reconciliation between Rilke and Lou in 1905. In the period that follows this reconciliation, for the first time Rilke is writing with a new freedom, filling out an initial body of work composed in the background of their turbulent former time. The result, after expanding on this work, will be the wondrously crafted, personal collection of poems, *The Book of Images*, published in 1906. A still more intensely independent period follows upon this, undertaken in the shadow of Rilke's new mentor Rodin, which bears fruit in the two volumes of *New Poems* published in 1907 and 1908.

Over these years of astounding new production, Rilke had only put off coming to terms with the complications in his nature that had been exacerbated by the troubles with Lou. Seeking at last to resolve these complications through his novel, *The Notebooks of Malte Laurids Brigge*, published in 1910, Rilke is only drawn deeper into the disturbing nature of his own and world-existence. In the two years that follow, for the first time he suffers a complete creative breakdown, until the sudden miraculous emergence of the famous consolatory *Elegies* begun in 1912 when at Duino. How he arrives at these poems is closely linked, as throughout these volumes, with Rilke's deep, ongoing, problematic relationship to Lou, which grows ever more decisive, but perhaps still more crucially in the end with his deep relationship to the creative inspiration of Novalis, with whom he is subconsciously linked from very early on.

Volume 3 completes this wide-ranging commentary on the life and work of Rainer Maria Rilke. Apart from a few incidental poems over this period, including the Fourth Elegy composed towards the end of 1915, 1914 through 1921 sees Rilke at a virtual standstill in his production. The problematically displaced and involuted relationship between Rilke and Lou continues, and its effects are compounded by the still more crippling distress of the war years. Then, half-way through the war, Rilke reaches a resolution with himself; the end of the war finds him shoring up against the ruins, until, in the winter of 1922, once again he is visited, not by the Angel of the Duino moment but, this time, by his new Master, Orpheus. He discovers an utterly fresh centre of creative life that forms the basis of a new Orphic creation, illustrated in *The Sonnets to Orpheus*, and this becomes, in turn, the impulse that brings the *Elegies* to completion. Behind the grand story of Rilke's final poetic emergence lies the fundamental and long-standing reality of his repression by Lou and what that would sow, paradoxically, by way of a sublimated achievement as sublimely poignant as it is finally tragic. All is brought into being by the fact that behind the scenes Rilke had at last found resolution through his perversely sustained love of Lou, his lost Eurydice…

JOM

All heirs bear their deceased fates like jewelry.

—Rilke

for

A.F.
always

Volume 1

A Poet's Fall from Grace
(1897-1905)

Contents

Acknowledgments

Thankful acknowledgments are duly rendered to the several presses cited throughout this book for the possibility of further extending the study of Rilke to English readers who are without German. Thankful acknowledgments, especially, to the translators of many of these materials, who, by their work, have greatly advanced the study of Rilke in English.

Main References and Abbreviations

GRN   *Letters of Rainer Maria Rilke 1892-1910*. Tr. Jane Bannard Greene and M.D. Herter Norton. New York: Norton, 1969.

HSTN   Rainer Maria Rilke. *Auguste Rodin*. Tr. G. Craig Houston. Mineola, NY: Dover Publications, 2006.

MCHL   Lou Andreas-Salomé. *Looking Back: Memoirs*. Ed., Ernest Pfeiffer. Tr. Breon Mitchell. New York: Paragon Press, 1991.

RANS   *Rainer Maria Rilke's "The Book of Hours"*. Tr. Susan Ranson. Rochester, NY: Camden House, 2012.

SN   Rainer Maria Rilke. *Diaries of a Young Poet*. Tr. Edward Snow and Michael Winkler. New York: Norton, 1998.

SN   *Rilke and Andreas-Salomé: A Love Story in Letters*. Tr. Edward Snow and Michael Winkler. New York: Norton, 2008.

Author's Note

Not all endnotes are meant to be consulted by the reader, but some turn out to be indispensable reading if the full contours of an author's argument are to be seen. For reasons of symmetrical form, because it would overwork an exposition to incorporate into it any further material, sometimes the full implications of an argument must be pursued in the notes. In the present case the reader is exhorted to consider especially those endnotes that elaborate on Rilke's primordial link to Novalis and the originally repressive effects of Lou's dealings with Rilke.

Preamble

By 1905, when he was not yet thirty, Rilke knew what direction his work as a poet would have to take. He knew also what the work he had already done was worth—"everything about me is unfinished, insufficient" he complained at this time, a judgment that extended surprisingly, but properly as we shall see, also to his composition of *The Book of Hours,* which by then was behind him. He knew very clearly by this point what he had made of himself, what of himself he had had to leave behind, and what he was also destined to be. He knew all this better, by then, even than his great lover-mentor, Lou Salomé, in spite of her greater experience and riper years. She had been the prime mover in his more significant life as a poet from the time he met her some eight years earlier, but after four years of separation from her (over the last two of which they had resumed relations through an intense correspondence only—intense certainly on his side), he had become his own mover. Even at the time he contacted Lou again after their separation and they began their correspondence, in 1903, he knew better than she did what he was now all about.

All this to redress our received understanding of the relations between Rilke and Lou. For in the critical literature on Rilke we consistently find an almost unqualified deference about Lou, as if, not only in the beginning but throughout his life, she knew Rilke better than he knew himself. In fact, Lou ceased to understand Rilke fully only one year into their relationship. This was at the time of Rilke's trip to Florence in 1898, which ironically she had prescribed for him. Lou begins to display a stubborn blindness to Rilke's deeper personal evolution from this time onwards. There is, first, a deliberate refusal to open herself to the extraordinary new depth of inspiration Rilke acquires when on his own in Florence. This we gather from the response, or failure of response, he gets from her about this when he returns. A deep rift opens up between them at this time; currents of disillusionment and dismay are engendered in Rilke that will, from thereon in, substantially undermine relations between them, until, in the summer of 1900, on their second trip to Russia, their relationship would reach a breaking-point.

By then, Rilke had already written the first part of *The Book of Hours*, "the Book of Monastic Life", a work he looked upon as a great act of rapprochement between them inasmuch as it showed him fully taking on what Lou had had to offer him. Well over a year after Florence, Rilke had surrendered himself to Lou's notions of what he required for his development, in spite of the very significant perceptions *he* reserved about how his development might have proceeded. He had very consciously taken the decision to defer to Lou—this when he saw her intransigence about his own notions for his development. His decision had borne fruit: he had been drawn into an experience of Russia that he would never forget, even if it came to haunt him to his disadvantage as a poet later. Rilke had become Lou's poet as well as his own: a dramatic balance had been struck between them, and yet expressions of her indifference to him continued. Tensions spilled over again on their second trip to Russia, this time more seriously, since Rilke could no longer be denied his own identity, even if he continued to vacillate over this. Once again he was sent to be on his own, this time to Worpswede where he would encounter numerous kindred souls, among whom were two women of his own age, Paula Becker and Clara Westhoff. He would make a great deal of these two in his personal life at this time.

However, characteristically for this period, Rilke cut short his stay in Worpswede at the very height of yet another round of inspirations of his own as to how he should be developing as a poet. Ambitiously—blindly and desperately—he wished to bring all of this back to bear on the progress he had already made in another kind of development, equally if not more importantly, with Lou and in his relationship to Russia. Once again he met with dumb resistance in Lou and indeed opposition to the further interests and scope of experience he had recently privileged while in Worpswede. The effect on Rilke this time was a depth of depression unlike anything he had known before. This depression seemed to confirm for him that he would never be free to rise above the condition of self-division and self-doubt with which he had been grappling since early childhood. Rilke could only envision the prospect of overcoming this condition if Lou had been ready to integrate into their relationship his own deepest longings, the full happy life he could see them coming into by satisfying him in his own inspirations also.

But the "happiness" he had experienced when in Florence and again in Worpswede—a happiness that could only be, finally, fulfilled with Lou, who held the other half of him—all had come to naught. He knew himself now destined for self-division and so also for those darker dimensions of life that included deep depression. That he knew himself now destined for self-division explains why in spite of the now total impasse experienced with Lou at this time Rilke continued alongside her for another four months. He had already entered into his difficult new life, and it was only when he could see that Lou was on the verge of separating from him, unable herself to bear with Rilke's deepening ambiguity about their relationship, that he took steps to prepare a *ground* for his new life. Worpswede had afforded him that one mercy: that he could counterbalance his despair with the prospect of married life—with Clara; *she* would restore him at least to a relationship to happiness. In this Rilke pre-empted Lou's own resolve to separate from him. Ironically, his choice of another brought home to her her own significant inadequacy with him, forcing her to face up to the fact that it was she who had failed him.

Thus the unity by which their relationship had been marked from the beginning seemed to her suddenly something *she* had thrown away, and separation was to bring on as much sorrow for her—a sorrow she had not counted on—as there was sorrow for him. In this way the tragedy of their separation had become their shared destiny. What this meant was that all that Rilke was later to contend with, by way of difficulty with himself as a consequence of their separation, now became something she would have to bear also and would wish to bear, since separation had become a matter of managing her own tragic feelings, about failing that special unity that had once existed between them. That original unity of which she herself had made so much, she realized, had slipped away from her, and she found her idealizing notions of health of soul, by which ironically she had condemned Rilke, accordingly compromised and freshly challenged. (She herself would fall mysteriously ill from that time onward.) A restored unity with Rilke could only come now from a reconciliation to tragedy that was as much her responsibility as it had become, more frighteningly, his, since it is he who would now have to make as much sense as he could of the self-division that seemed forever established in him.

***

There are many reasons why this particular undertow to the story of Rilke's relations to Lou will have escaped the attention of critics and biographers of Rilke. For one thing, there is the almost complete absence in what Rilke wrote of any criticism of Lou, with the one exception of the last part of the Florence Diary where his criticism of her is barely kept within bounds. *From* this account, the whole of our knowledge of the underlying impulse to their relations proceeds that leads to their separation.[1] Contrasting with the lack of any further evidence from Rilke, Lou put out memoirs of their time together, a few years after his death, which purport to explain, in some detail, how their separation came about. It is the version of their relations that critics and biographers have adopted. In this version it is Rilke who is made responsible for their separation, because of the episodes of nervous breakdown and melancholia to which he was prone. There is no doubt that these "episodes" took place, though they are unlikely to have been as numerous as critics and biographers suppose. Moreover, the last part of the Florence Diary is an instance of such a breakdown, and clearly in this case it is Lou who brought it on. What is left out of the account in Lou's version of their life is the fact that she herself contributed significantly to the recurrence of these episodes. Lou knew of Rilke's tendency to breakdown (it originated from childhood from the sense of his difference and unacceptability to others), and yet she continued to comport herself in a way that fired it up. She *kept* him in his inherited condition, when she could well have supported him in his attempts to forge his way out of it. On each occasion when Rilke comes through with a new vision of himself that points him beyond his inherited condition, Lou *fails to respond* to what he has successfully managed or is on the verge of making of himself. Very simply put, she was bent on her own ways and on her own ideas for him, without regard to how he was otherwise *also* meant to develop both as himself and a poet. The *full* complexity of what he was about she was not ready to see, let alone absorb into their relationship. A full responsiveness Rilke naturally expected of them as a couple and continued to hope for. In the meantime he was absorbing all of the lessons she was providing for him.

Lou's version of events is, in fact, disingenuous to this extent: that she "knew" herself responsible for the breakdown in their relationship, without, however, being able to confront and accept what she knew. There is that amount of *un*consciousness in her about this relationship, ironically even while she allows herself to continue to psychoanalyze Rilke, right through to the point of her memoirs after his death.[2] On his side Rilke *had* the full consciousness of how the story of their relations had unfolded, but *he* does not speak about it, except in the one case of the "episode" after Florence. That the thread that runs through their relationship is not picked up from this episode by critics and biographers is explained by the insouciance with which Rilke's early Diaries have been received, in comparison, for example, with almost everything Rilke wrote after *The Book of Hours*. The critical history on Rilke is peculiar in this respect: conditioned by the version of events Lou later provided, critics and biographers have failed to give due recognition to the full scope of Rilke's experience as his Diaries reflect this, wherein much that turns out to be problematic between himself and Lou *is* explained in fact. In what follows, I have tried to show precisely how critics and biographers have failed in their reading of these Diaries. Another symptom of the general critical deference to Lou is that *The Book of Hours* is seen almost entirely as the outcome of *her* beneficent influence on Rilke, when this (highly) elaborate work betrays, on the one hand, a great deal of *his* conceptions initially, and, on the other, an uneasy condition of backward–looking subjection to Lou in the later books even after he had separated from her and was by then well-established with Clara, the sign of an influence that had also been experienced as oppressive: his own conceptions in the case of "The Book of Monastic Life", a regressive subjection to Lou in the case of "The Book of Pilgrimage" and "The Book of Poverty and Death". I demonstrate both of these matters below. Critics and biographers have generally paid only lip service to *The Book of Hours*: extended critical analysis of this work is not a salient feature of the file on Rilke, and I have sought to correct that deficiency in the following pages, which are to a great extent devoted to such an analysis. It is especially in *The Book of Hours*, along *with* the Diaries—the Schmargendorf and the Worpswede Diaries quite as much as the Florence Diary—that the true story of the relations between Rilke and Lou in this period finds its fullest and most complex expression.

In the end, what makes a full and proper narration of the relations between Rilke and Lou especially awkward is a still more baffling paradox: namely, the undoubted fact that Rilke *intended* the story of his deference to Lou for posterity. He had good reason for this, for Lou had been, and remained to the end of his days, the principal reference-point in his life, holding the key to his destiny as a man and a poet. This is to come back to a significant implication in my exposition above, that while Rilke as a poet might, in the profoundest sense, have gone quite another way, it was his destiny to go the way he did, even if all *is* due to Lou's interventions. It is for this reason, I believe, that *he let things stand* as they have come down to us on the surface. Profoundly unstable as this could make him, his tendency to "episodes" of melancholia and despair became an intrinsic part of what went into making him as a man and a poet, and who else but Lou had been in the position to highlight these episodes? One cannot help seeing a form of parallel with the case, in England, of D. H. Lawrence and John Middleton Murry. It is Murry who served in the role of bringing out the chronic tendency to another depth of dark melancholia in Lawrence, and indeed as a fulfilment, as Murry shows, of Lawrence's own secret wish that Murry should do so.[3] Similarly, Rilke, I believe, wanted his own complex of melancholia to be made into an explicit feature of his life, and for the same reason. It was his special destiny as an author to have to confront such darkness in himself and to deal with it also, fully and completely, in relation to everything else one naturally and positively hopes for by way of "happiness". In the meantime, to attribute the very complex motive to Rilke that I have as to his intentions for posterity, in regard to his share in such darkness—intentions that are hardly out of keeping with the sheer depth of his subtle ways, is to accept that things have come down to us in the fashion they have. It is how Rilke *wanted* the story to come down to us, and one is accordingly *bound to* the narrative Lou provides, even if the undertow to this narrative, implicating Lou, inevitably becomes an aspect of our conscientious reading of

Rilke and must be made room for. It comes into the narrative precisely as an undertow, and I have accordingly proceeded by focusing initially on the narrative as it has come down to us. Only by hints along the way, hints that are forced upon as we proceed, do I lead the reader to the actual undertow to this story which necessarily forms part of our understanding of "Rilke in the Making". It is in keeping with this procedure that the third Part to the present Volume, "Rilke's Defeated Hopes After Florence", thus acquires the function of an appendix to the other two. To speak faithfully of Rilke in the process of making himself at this time, one has to include an exposition of this story's undertow: the full story of his making cannot be properly grasped otherwise, though the larger part of Rilke's preoccupations at this time concerns what he had desperately to make of himself *given* the condition he had inherited. This is to see Rilke in the process of making himself in the more immediate terms of this time.

It was, to put it bluntly, a matter of survival. It is not just that Rilke had to work things out with himself; he had to do so also in a relationship to Lou, for the not so simple reason that it was a matter of *their* shared destiny—*their* happiness, and the unity that had once bound *them*, which had been displaced. One must bear in mind that, by virtue of this formerly experienced unity, the experience Rilke and Lou shared remained, through the whole of this tragedy, the main concern to each. In one sense, they had given up everything in giving up each other, and this effect is only highlighted the more when Rilke, too aware of Lou's intention to separate from him, at last turned his energy and focus to his future wife, Clara. In this respect, the great symbolic association of Clara and Lou in the progression of Rilke's story cannot be overstressed, and, among other things in this first Volume, I have sought to re-instate Clara's own extraordinary role in this story. She has been almost grossly under-represented, in large part because of another seduction to which the critical literature on Rilke has succumbed. This has to do with the additional role of Paula Becker in the story, who has been, I believe wrongly, made into Rilke's other great love at this time (apart from Lou). Without meaning to degrade Paula's quite special relationship to Rilke, which as an exquisite friendship represented for him a great ideal of its own, it is rather Clara who, after a period of seemingly equal association with one and with the other, came primarily to engage Rilke's admiring attention. It was she who was, by far, more fitted to become his wife. Her superior qualities impressed themselves upon Rilke from the first, not the least of these being her own remarkable strength as an artist, which suffered in the shadow of Paula's more glowing ways. This artistic strength Rilke could see was linked to a profoundly unique strength of character as well as a power of insight into life's paradoxes that, as we shall see, finally outdistanced Paula's. In seeking to give a faithful account of Rilke in the process of making himself—in this early, tumultuous, and most decisive period of his development as a poet and a man—one would do ill to overlook the utterly crucial role played by Clara who very much helped to lay a bridge over the abyss that Rilke was destined to cross.

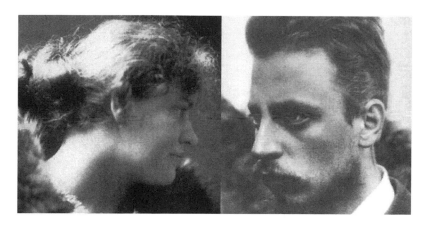

Rilke and Lou Salomé

I
Ascension of the Work:
Rilke's Return to Lou to 1905

I
A Poet's Fall from Grace

The love-bond between Rainer Maria Rilke and Lou Andreas-Salomé would last, in fact, all their lives, and it is a famous case. The love-affair between them was precipitous. They became lovers less than a month after they first met, and this in spite of Lou's stubborn-minded abstinence from sex until that point that had involved her in the rejection of several men over years, including her own husband. It was a totally unlikely affair, between an established literary woman of thirty-six who was by then famous in Europe and a fledgling, virtually unknown poet of twenty-one who, in spite of a few "dream-crossed" publications, had nothing but himself to recommend him. However, the bond between them would appear to have been complete already at their first meeting, and it seems almost to have been preordained. As Lou would put it, remembering it all years later:

> We were **not** two halves seeking the other: we were a whole which confronted that inconceivable wholeness with a shiver of surprised recognition ...
>
> (MCHL 85)

From the time they met, they already belonged to each other in a way that was not, and would never again be, possible with anyone else.

Sexually, their relationship is explained by a condition in Rilke that Lou had not come across in another man: "body and man indivisibly one", as she would put it years later. There was about Rilke "a type of manliness" that spoke to her by its marvellous subtlety: he had "his own style of gentle but inviolable control and dominance" (MCHL 69). According to her, he possessed "what we call 'manly grace' to a high degree, uncomplicated in its gentleness", and what was especially important for her, "in imperishable consonance with all the expressions of his being". *Spiritually*, they were both profoundly committed to the idea of "God-creation" (about which more below)—a total concept that originates with Lou but the experience of which they shared. They felt that, together, they embodied this experience in themselves. Insofar as it concerned *him*, the fruit of their collaborative participation in this experience would be Rilke's "Book of Monastic Life", completed about a year and a half into their relationship, this after a long and intense period of shared study of Russian things followed by a trip to Russia. Rilke had brought to Lou all the enthusiasm of his youthful spiritual-poetic self-searching, in which she saw a perfect integrity of body and soul, and she had brought to him her experienced knowledge of the form a spiritual-poetic training should take. His enthusiasm brought *her* more deeply in touch, among other things, with her own deepest yearning, which she had not been able to share with any man hitherto: to re-connect with herself through a re-acquaintance with her Russian origins.

Things altered for ill, however—even these lovers were to fall out of their paradisal idyll—from the time Rilke became more anxious about his calling as a poet. As a poet, he *would* at some point have felt the need for a more appropriate corresponding *poetic* form for his God-creating, beyond the spontaneous "praying" (and talk with Lou about "praying") that he had been doing until then, only in part through verse.[4] The problem was that *there had been* a breakthrough, in "The Book of Monastic Life". As Lou was to put it in her *Memoirs* some years after Rilke's death, addressing Rilke directly:

> *The most difficult aspect of the matter was that the poetic breakthrough, which led to such a direct confrontation with the immensity of its subject, forced you simultaneously to find a corresponding form of technical mastery ...*
>
> (MCHL 90)

A very large form of poetic mastery had been imposed upon Rilke, and his failure to meet this suddenly huge demand would occasion an immense struggle in him greatly disturbing to their relationship:

> *But now a gradual change occurred ... related to the conflict be-*
> *tween hymnic experience and its expression in creative form. It*
> *was accompanied by anxiety, almost states of terror, in which*
> *the two competing claims could not be brought into balance, but*
> *instead became a ghostly tangle.*
>
> (MCHL 89)

The state of mind into which Rilke fell on these occasions is closely described by Lou:

> *It was not disappointment, self-accusation, and depression which*
> *set in (as with the average, normal man), but an explosion of*
> *feeling which soon became immense, monstrous, as if you felt*
> *compelled to let yourself be overwhelmed, almost as in that bless-*
> *ed state when you were writing.*

Looking back on these devastating developments, Lou would lament the necessity of that singular fate reserved for Rilke that would displace the astonishing harmony that first brought them together:

> *How little we cared at first whether the impulse to give creative*
> *form might come in conflict with total receptivity to that which*
> *was to be expressed! Does someone praying worry about whether*
> *his prayer might seem more perfect if he has his hands folded*
> *correctly?*
>
> (MCHL 88)

Torn by these developments, Lou was still able to recognize that Rilke would have to go his own way. The arc of his development as a poet, all of which lay before him, was too large for her to support from where she was, already well on in years and with her own ongoing development as a thinker and as a writer to attend to:

> *It had never been so clear to me at what profound depths your*
> *development to full maturity would occur.*
>
> (MCHL 90)

In fact, Lou would look back on these times with some pride in the decision she took to encourage Rilke along his own path, which would have to mean away from her:

You had never seemed to me greater or more admirable than at that moment. I was drawn to you by the inner problematic which was weighing you down, and this effect never lost its force. Now it was necessary for you to enter into open spaces and freedom as quickly as possible, to develop everything within you fully.

Here, at any rate, is the official version of the main developments as declared by Lou in her *Memoirs* more than five years after Rilke's death, with the advantage by then of her knowing the whole pattern of Rilke's life. Naturally, the reality was far more comprehensive than this. It involved, besides the studied generosity Lou continued to profess towards Rilke when sorting himself out, also an immense resentment, at having to continue to support him through his episodes, in large measure because of the continuing demands of her own burgeoning work. A very large part of the problem was that there was hardly a dividing line between Rilke's devotion to God and his devotion to her, a fact that took startling expression at one point in a poem Rilke originally wrote for Lou that would eventually find its way into *The Book of Hours*, Rilke's long work devoted to his God, of which "The Book of Monastic Life" was the first part:

Blot out my eyes: I'll still see you
Stop up my ears: and yet I'll hear you
Without feet I'll find my way to you
Without a mouth I'll still implore you
Tear off my arms: I'll seize you
With my heart as if it were a hand
Tear out my heart: my brain will beat
And if you throw a torch into my brain
I'll bear you still upon my blood.[5]

Significantly, it was Lou who proposed that Rilke include this poem in his *opus* to God, because she felt that the real subject of this poem *was* his God. Confusion of this sort no doubt exacerbated the intense pressure and indeed suffering Lou experienced in dealing with Rilke during his episodes. However, Lou was herself guilty of encouraging such idolatry in Rilke, by the completeness of her own involvement with him—"I could have said the same to you", she remarks years later:

*was there not, whispering in **both** of us, something which eluded
our grasp, yet which we 'bore upon the blood'—and experienced
to the depths of our physical being ...*

(MCHL 86)

In their developing circumstances, this mutual experience, as Rilke
continued to live this out, would become too much for her, especially
when, on their second trip to Russia, Rilke wrote to her, in frustration
(the following is her paraphrase) about how "depraved" he was feeling
because his "prayers [to God] had become so presumptuous" (MCHL
90). The real frustration in this case was Rilke's resentment that on
this trip, which they had taken alone, Lou could spend so much time
away from him as she saw to her social life elsewhere, while in the
meantime his creative life had relapsed. Rilke's emotional demands
on Lou had indeed become suffocating to her, but a life alongside Lou
was, in any case, not the direction Rilke seemed meant for. Without
his wishing to admit this, the depth of his own personal ambition
would not have tolerated a state of continual immediate reference to
Lou's own creative and social situation, a state that amounted, as we
shall see, virtually to subjection; it menaced Rilke with the repression
of his own deepest drives. Such a life is not what he could possibly be
seeking, and he knew it, clamoring, fruitlessly, on behalf of the only
life that could accommodate them both, which would have needed to
make more room for them also as a couple.[6]

Thus an estrangement set in between Rilke and Lou that would
grow more and more, in spite of all of their past triumphs. By the end
of 1900, some four months after their second trip to Russia, Lou was,
as usual, deep into her own work and social associations in Berlin; in
the meantime, Rilke had just returned from a two-month stay on his
own in Worpswede where he had made the acquaintance of several
male and female artists, sculptors and painters. Rilke and Lou continued, well into the new year, to be loosely associated, as if their lives
could still carry on together because they were still bound to each other.
But Lou had reached her wits' end with Rilke, while he, aware of the
signs, was secretly, even to himself, preparing the ground for the new
life he saw coming, apart from her. Then, in late February of 1901,
Rilke announced the news of his engagement to Clara Westhoff, and
all came to an end. Responding to this amazing announcement, Lou
insisted on a complete break between them and that, moreover, they

should destroy all letters that had passed between them. There was, however, one last letter Lou wrote Rilke after they had parted, from which it would appear that she expressed herself at their parting, in fact, in joy of the freedom she had come into, explaining to Rilke that she herself was in need of connecting to a new part of herself, having only now come into her unlived youth, as she put it to him, which she felt she would in any case have to explore for herself.

For his part, Rilke could not be as happy with the break-up as Lou appeared to be, in spite of the new life he had committed to. It was only when he could see that their relationship looked fated to end, after being back again with Lou for four months, that Rilke finally committed to his engagement. In fact, he had returned to Berlin from Worpswede prematurely, fearing that his involvement there was taking him away from the life he had known with Lou, by which, in spite of everything, he continued to define himself.[7] Still, he had been wise enough to carefully lay the ground, over this time, for the move he was finally forced to make. There was, in fact, a very real basis to the marriage between himself and Clara Westhoff, and a very fine tenderness and care would grow between them that would last for years, in spite of Rilke's need for a free lifestyle during their marriage. However, despite the closeness of his relationship to Clara, long after the separation between himself and Lou Rilke brought himself to act on his idea of a reunion with her. That was when things were really beginning to look bad for him again and in the knowledge that only Lou would know what all of that was about. Rilke's fresh overture to Lou was not as obvious as it might appear, for a long time had passed since they had parted, and Lou had in her final letter to him also demonstrated a decidedly alienating haughtiness about his emotional dispositions. Behind this we may assume, paradoxically, her bitterness over their break-up. It is typical of Rilke's way of dealing with the conflict between them at this point that there is, on the contrary, no evidence of any haughty or defensive response from him, though deep down his own bitterness must have been as great. Still, they were bound to be in communication with each other again at some point, since Rilke had left the manuscript that would become "The Book of Monastic Life" behind with Lou. And so, in spite of an appearance of final separation at the time, this was not to be the end of the story of Rainer Rilke and Lou Salomé...

II
Getting in Touch With Lou Again

On June 23rd 1903 Rilke got in touch with Lou again by mail, in a very short letter proposing that they meet again. This was after a separation that had lasted for well over two years. Over that period there had been no communication whatever between them, and inevitably Rilke's letter bears all the marks of officiousness and trepidation.[8] No doubt his fear was that Lou might simply ignore his overture, or what is worse rebuff him in the same overbearing tones with which she had finally left him. Back then, they had already been drifting apart; Lou had even encouraged him to seek his own adventurous life away from her, packing him off to an artists' colony in Worpswede: she was fully bent on separating from him in time ("To make Rainer go away, *go completely away*", as she puts it in her diary[9]). However, nothing had prepared her for the amazing news she received from Rilke, some four months after he had returned to Berlin, that he had become engaged to a young female artist he had met while in Worpswede and that he was planning to marry soon.

With the announcement of this engagement, Lou insisted that they disassociate completely, and they had already parted when she wrote him that one last letter, famously entitled "Last Appeal"[10]. Ostensibly, Lou was writing out of concern for the person Rilke had now committed to. He must understand, for one last time, what it was about himself that had made it impossible for her to remain by him in their own relationship. Lou's descriptions of the anxiety attacks that regularly came over Rilke, which had made things impossible, are graphic and unsparing:

> *Again the sluggish resolve alongside the sudden, nervous eruptions of will that tore through your organic being, gave in to every suggestion, and did not descend into the fullness of the past in order to assimilate things healthily ... Again the wavering uncertainty alongside the loud accents and strong words of protestations, manic compulsions without the compensating drive for truth!*

(SN, *Rilke*, 41-42)

Her concern, she claims, is also for him: she claims to have received clinical confirmation that these attacks could lead to either serious physical illness or "insanity". Her "last appeal" to him is to embrace, once and for all, the path that she has taken, which is to obey "the great plan of life" (SN, *Rilke*, 42). She had accepted that it was for her to embrace the eluded "youth" she had recently come into, driven thereto by the call of healthy psychic self-encounter. He should do the same: it was for him now to heed the "dark god" who, she said, was his real guide and who seemed to be demanding that he take charge of his experience for his own health. His tendency was, rather, to let himself be overtaken; because of this they were breaking up for good. However, Lou would appear, on re-living these matters, to have been moved enough to offer the afterthought that, should he ever reach what would appear to him to be "the worst hour" (SN, *Rilke*, 42), there would always be a home to count on, with her and her husband, for relief and comfort. This offer Lou had hastily scribbled down at the last moment on the reverse side of Rilke's bill for milk deliveries, and she had enclosed this note with her letter.

Thus Lou had left a "door" open, and over two years later Rilke was taking her up on her offer. His point in his overture is that, in that "worst hour" that still threatened him, he might not have the self-possession to be *able* to come to them. Things were suddenly at this moment foreboding enough for him to wish to call on their hospitality for a visit, if only for a day. In writing to Lou in this way, Rilke was playing directly into the judgment she had so sternly expressed about his neurotic disposition when they parted, and he must have felt all the more downtrodden by appealing to her so weak-mindedly now. Remarkably enough, she replied more than fairly to his overture, even if she was very brief, proposing, however, that they "first reunite in writing" (SN, *Rilke*, 44). The door to "reunion" had thus been opened, although reunion in the physical sense would not take place for another two years.

How Lou could have allowed Rilke access to her again in spite of all that she knew about his disposition, and especially as he was writing now in his difficulties, can be explained. Theirs had been a union of souls of great depth, and Lou herself had suffered badly from their separation. There is evidence of significant distress in her over the years during which they were separated.[11] There is also her own moving testimony, written several years after Rilke's death, about her despair at the time of their separation, in spite of her assured exterior when they parted:

And yet—and yet wasn't I being torn from you at the same time? From the reality of our beginnings, in which it had seemed as if we were but a single person. Who can fathom the darkness of our ultimate distance, our ultimate intimacy! ... How many times I held my head in my hands back then, struggling to understand it myself.

(MCHL 90)

Rilke may have become literally impossible for Lou at some point, but she could not forget the great depth of personal beauty in him that had made him otherwise so complete a person, to others as well as to herself:

That which rose in you, almost without intention, as "prayer" ... enveloped any person with whom you came in contact; it remained corporeal, disclosing at your touch how it partook of the divine; and the childlike, unselfish way in which you accepted it so trustingly ensured each day, each hour, its intimate perfection.

(MCHL 88)

There would inevitably be a deep nostalgia about their time together before division came into the whole; Lou would speak of an "attitude" in Rilke, before the tragedy, that

*unified his spirit and his senses, allowing them to commingle ... No matter what part of him was stirred—it was a single emotion, which could not even conceivably be split, and which **knew nothing of** internal doubt, hesitation, or second thoughts, except in the still restless development of his own poetic gifts.*

(MCHL 69)[12]

This knowledge of his capacity for a marvellous wholeness, in spite of his trying neurotic tendencies, must have given Lou reason to believe that re-connecting with Rilke was still very much worthwhile if not inevitable. Her deeper knowledge of him was an essential ingredient in her extraordinary personal attachment to him. In the meantime, Lou had not committed to actually seeing him, and this had left her with a protective distance from those typical states he would appear to have gotten into again. He and Lou could not take up with each other in the same way again, but she could be safely there for him as his knowing confidant, as the one who, alone, could really know what it was he had to be dealing with personally.

On his side, it might appear equally strange, at least on the surface, that Rilke should be turning to Lou again after she had virtually condemned him to his emotional problems, and especially as he had fared quite well in his production in the long interval away from her. Seven months after his marriage, he would complete "The Book of Pilgrimage", the second part of his long work to God that he ultimately entitled *The Book of Hours*. Another nine months later he would put out his first significant mature collection of poems, the first edition of "The Book of Images". Within six months of that, Rilke would produce his superb monograph on Rodin, which the latter described as the best book written on him. Four months after the monograph, Rilke then completed the third and what was to be the last part of *The Book of Hours*: "The Book of Poverty and Death". And yet only two months after this latest production, in a long line of freshly accomplished work, Rilke felt desperate enough to feel he had to turn to Lou again.

He had moved to Paris in September of 1902, commissioned (by a German publisher) to write the monograph on Rodin. There he had experienced at first hand Rodin's heroic creative genius, but at the same time he had been exposed to all the appalling squalor and chaos of the Paris of that era. Rilke puts it in this way in a letter around that time[13]:

> *Paris ... is a difficult, difficult, anxious city. And the beautiful things there are there do not quite compensate ... for what one must suffer from the cruelty and confusion of the streets ... something unspeakably dismaying ... lost ... utterly ... like a star off its course.*
>
> (GRN 93-94)

To this he adds that:

> *To all that, Rodin is a great, quiet, powerful contradiction.*

Having completed the monograph, and because of the herculean effort he had put into writing it while fighting the difficult circumstances of life in Paris, Rilke fell ill and then into a depression that did not lift even after he settled in Viareggio in the spring to recover. While in Viareggio, for a brief period he was to have a breakthrough ("[o]nce I did succeed" (SN, *Rilke*, 56) he later tells Lou): the "prayers" that would later constitute "The Book of Poverty and Death" emerged. However, immediately on their completion Rilke was compelled to return to Paris, in part from the astonishing notion, in spite of his illness, that this city still held the key to "one more work" (GRN, 105)[14]. It was on his return to Paris at this time that he fell into the still more disturbed state of mind that desperately drove him to reach out to Lou again.

Paris was the immediate cause of his disturbance at this time, but it was also a terrible agency: it brought back symptoms of a fearful anxiety Rilke had known in his youth. He describes what the experience has been like recently in his first long letter to Lou:

> *I feel thrust out of a world where everything is familiar and close and meaningful into another vague, inexpressibly fearful world ... as if I wouldn't recognize anyone who might enter my room and as if I in turn would be a stranger to everyone who might see me ... And the fear arose in me that **my worst hour** might lie in that other world from which I can come to no one.*
>
> (SN, Rilke, 46)[15]

When this experience comes on, he says, he is in dire need of something in the real world that can be as strong, as support against the surge of the experience:

> *When it comes, I would like to cling to some one, real thing; but nothing is real enough, everything withdraws, gives me up, goes away ...*

He had been especially overwhelmed by this experience the night before he wrote Lou again; he wrote her because only she could offer the support he needed, because "only you know who I am. Only you can help me" (SN, *Rilke*, 47). The experience brought with it the sense that he might merge in it beyond recall, and it was Paris especially that had brought it on again through the frightful unreality of its daily life.

That life, Rilke says, opened up to him a world in which all that was recognizably human seemed to vanish into a perpetuated anonymity of lost souls who carry on unregarded in their sordidly alienated sphere:

> *[W]hat people I have encountered ... Ruins of caryatids upon which an entire suffering still rested ... beneath which they lived slowly like tortoises ... passers-by among passers-by, ignored and undisturbed in their fate ... as if there was still something to wait for ... Pieces, pieces of people, parts of animals, remnants of things that once functioned, and all of it astir ...*
>
> (SN, *Rilke*, 51-52)

Rilke felt especially sensitive to this sordid world partly because he himself was materially downtrodden and close to the hopeless squalor that characterized this world, living for the most part sporadically off meagre literary commissions and, so, easily taken over by the impression this world gave of general disinheritance. In addition to this, the extraordinary susceptibility of his mind, which would be abnormal perhaps in another but was the whole basis of his creative intensity as a poet, drew him irresistibly into this world, which he had no trouble living into mentally. Such mental identification with this world he could only see as a grave threat to himself because his creative-poetic powers were as yet no match for this world, as he properly recognized:

> *Had I been able to **make** these fears I underwent, had I been able to shape things out of them, real, steadfast things that are bliss and freedom to create ... But these fears ... stirred a hundred other fears ... I became creative for them; instead of making them into things of my will ...*
>
> (SN, *Rilke*, 56)

Thus, even before he was to hear from Lou in any substantial way about this[16], Rilke was already trying to grab hold of the possibilities such an experience offered to his creative genius. To an extent, he had managed some success in this regard. He had fled Paris for a time for Viareggio, where he had a momentary breakthrough: "The Book of Poverty and Death". But this effort to come to terms had left him unsatisfied; he knew there was much more to make of his experience:

at least "one more work" to come out of it, as he had said. However, returning to Paris, as he laments to Lou, he found to his great dismay that, in this sphere, the man remained very much less than the poet, and that he could not take control of his experience:

> *What should he do, Lou, who grasps so little about life, who must let it happen to him and comes to realize that his own willing is always slighter than another great will into whose current he oftentimes chances like a thing drifting downstream?*
>
> (SN, *Rilke*, 60)

Once Lou had received Rilke's first detailed account of his life in Paris, she was quick to see that, in spite of his challenging disquietude, here was a new Rilke who had at least begun to outgrow that "old self"[17] Lou feared she would be hearing from again. His letter about Paris, by the sheer strength of his description, she said, was already proof that he had reached a new phase of his creative life, one that would allow him, in time, to take full charge of the experience he claimed to be submerged in. Lou saw the real possibility of "health" for him for the first time by virtue of the mental strength he was showing, paradoxically in being able to describe his experience with such conscious power:

> *That something could so continually oppose you without eventually breaking you down is testimony to the heightened resistance of a united, concentrated sensibility ...*
>
> *I felt that odd process of "ensouling" that can emanate even from impressions of misery when they come not just straight from life but channeled through the life of the person creating them ...*
>
> *... That one "most real thing" ... you already have it inside you ... You have never been closer to the health that you wish for than now!*
>
> (SN, *Rilke*, 58-59)

Lou was insisting, as she always had, on her favorite category of experience ("health"), but there was still a good deal of wishful thinking in her about this, or so one can imagine Rilke thinking. Her words must, nevertheless, have served as a great balm to him, both as a man and as a poet. It is indeed the paradox of Rilke's creative life that the

path he was taking *had* to expose him to the depths of the experience
he would so often lament in his letters. How else was he to make of
himself the poet who was to become the poet of his time, the poet of
our whole experience? Without knowing what he was asking for, he
had wished this himself, addressing his desired God in this way, in
"The Book of Monastic Life":

> *You see, there is much I want.*
> *Perhaps everything*

> (RANS 17)

His present experience was, still, a far cry from the satisfying life with
God he had counted on. His God's creation was turning out to be a
far deeper and a more oppressive problem than he had anticipated,
and he did not now feel equal to the task of continuing to create
alongside his God.

One cannot underestimate the almost insuperable power Rilke's
depressive experience generally had over him. It had a power over
him that even Lou much underestimated, for all of her prognostica-
tive insight. Only in the semi-autobiographical *Malte*, completed a
full six years hence, would Rilke begin to show any command over
this experience, and even so, the generally depressive content of *Malte*
would leave him wondering if it had not in fact gotten the better of
him.[18] It must have seemed to him a dismally long and frightful path
ahead, in spite of Lou's best expectations about this, which she was
already expressing now. After faithfully acknowledging Lou's generous view of his incipient powers, "[b]ut it was only a letter" Rilke
reminds her in response: "as yet nothing has taken shape from it, as
yet no one thing stands there and testifies on my behalf" (SN, *Rilke*,
59-60). From these words, we can infer that even *The Book of Hours*
had been no real success for him. He was conscious of not having
as yet achieved much at all: "almost nothing in me has reached frui-
tion" he says in this same letter, and it was a view he would continue
to hold about himself a full two years beyond the present exchange
with Lou: "everything about me is unfinished, insufficient", he laments, which he is still linking to the same problem: "What event in
life, what actual happening was there that didn't force this realization
upon me?" (SN, *Rilke*, 143). Rilke was only twenty-seven at this time
of his renewed exchange with Lou, and yet he understood already

that he was destined to watch his life-experience getting the upper hand, falling too deeply into him as he says, so deeply and burden-somely in fact it would not allow him to feel that enough time could be allotted him that would permit of its transmutation into the art for which he was made:

It is as if whatever I truly receive falls too deeply into me, falls, falls for years, and in the end I lack the strength to lift it out of me. And I walk about fearfully with my heavily laden depths and never reach them. Yes I know ... those ... transformations that take their course in darkness ... But life moves on and is like the day and whoever wished to be patient would need a thousand such days, though perhaps not even one is given him.

(SN, *Rilke*, 60)

In the meantime, Rilke had sent Lou his monograph on Rodin, which she had received with much enthusiasm: "the most valuable of your published works" (65), as she put it. The monograph also held for her the key to Rilke's present anxious condition. What it showed, in her opinion, again was how far Rilke had evolved creatively, even if he could not come into his new creative powers as yet. His commit-ment to his study of Rodin's art and "the pure human intimacy" to which this study bears witness—"you gave yourself to your opposite, your complement, to a longed-for exemplar" (SN, *Rilke*, 67)—had drawn Rilke out of his own personal world and had brought about a "psychic re-orientation" in him even if he was not yet in the position to act on it, since work on this new basis only lay "before" him:

Perhaps only after many years will some of the most sublime truths about yourself arise in you as if in memory of these very hours, and reveal to you the deep logic that holds the man and the artist, life and dream together.

This may not have been what Rilke wanted to hear, since the whole basis of his anxiety in this period lay in what he could proceed to do now, though he seems to have accepted that, in the long run, what Lou was saying must be fundamentally true. Lou also saw in Rilke's new condition an explanation of the bodily symptoms of his anxiety. Rilke, in immersing in Rodin's example, had opened himself, in the case of sculpture, to a form of art radically different from his own as a poet, and this, according to Lou, had engendered conflicting impulses in him:

> *The sculptural urges ... unable to find satisfaction through the poet's means, had to turn their energy against your own self, had, as it were, to hold in thrall **your own body** like a vampire.*
>
> (SN, *Rilke*, 66)

But a compensating process was at work:

> *Everything assailing you during that work, along with all the after-effects attendant on it, seem as nothing compared to the psychic re-orientation it entailed.*
>
> (SN, *Rilke*, 67)

Thus on the basis of Rilke's letter addressing his experience in Paris, and now his monograph in which Lou saw the same new capacity to stand in an objective strength apart from the experience that was reaching him, Lou was convinced that Rilke was at bottom possessed, in the midst of even the most difficult experiences of life, of that in-alienable "centredness" that for her alone justified life's re-creation as art. The practice of art would always be for her a question of proceeding, in health, in relation to "the difficult mysteries of living and dying", and she now saw in Rilke, as never before, an ally in these mysteries. This understanding ("now I understand, understand everything", she is happy to say—SN, *Rilke*, 65) moved her to a final, irreversible affirmation of partnership with him: "From this moment on you can count on me" (SN, *Rilke*, 68). These words, with which Lou ends her second letter to him about these matters, would fall upon Rilke's ears as a balm from heaven, for he could be sure from now on that, no matter how "assailed" he might be, she would always be there for him.

   It is one of the curiosities of the correspondence between Rilke and Lou at this time (making for significant confusion in the long run) that before he received this account by Lou Rilke had already sent off a letter of his own in which he goes more deeply into his relationship to Rodin and what he has derived from it as a concept of creation for himself. Rilke's own account moves in a very different direction from that charted by Lou. In the comparison with Rodin, Rilke could only put one question to himself: "where is the handcraft of *my* art?", an invidious comparison, to say the least—inasmuch as Rodin was well on in the maturity of his art, being a full thirty-five years older than Rilke—and yet a real comparison for Rilke. The question he throws out circles back upon his one great theme at this time: namely, his inability to dissociate himself sufficiently from the flux of daily life (most importantly in his mind) in order thereby to find himself in his art. This Rodin *was* able to do magisterially. Of Rodin's work, Rilke says: "this work could only have come from a workman":

> *His very work has sheltered him ... then his house with all its constant noises seems something trivial and irrelevant ... His daily life and the people who are part of it lie there as an empty riverbed through which he no longer flows; but there is nothing sad in that: for nearby one hears the great roar and the powerful flow of the stream that would not divide into two arms ...*

> (SN, *Rilke*, 71-72)

Then follows the conclusion that would so rankle with Lou, since it seems to affirm what she so forcefully rejects on principle: an artistic work-ethic that would wilfully separate art from life:

> *And I believe, Lou, that it must be so; this is one life and the other is a different one, and we are not made to have two lives...*

Rilke considers that he falls well short of this ethic:

> *But I still lack discipline, the capacity and **compulsion** to work ... Do I lack the strength? Is there something wrong with my will? ... Days pass and I sometimes hear life going by. And still nothing has happened ... and I keep dividing and flowing in all directions ...*

> (SN, *Rilke*, 73)

Replying immediately in turn to this letter, Lou would seize upon Rilke's idea of "handcraft" quite literally, as inappropriate to his poetic art, which was not like sculpture, thus coming back to the point of her previous letter to him, to which he had not yet responded. Sculpture, she implies, gives the impression of assimilating life all too easily, since it immediately satisfies our sense of the reality of life by giving over "from one's hands a thing", and so more obviously communicating the sense of "handcraft" than does the art of the poet

(SN, *Rilke*, 74). But Rodin, no less than any other artist, had first to assimilate his life, to settle his relationship to it in just the way an artist must who does not want to be undermined by influences from that life that have not been addressed, this effort being as much a part of the artist's vocation as the effort to be put into the art itself. Thus, in Rodin's art, it only appears as if life were left out (SN, *Rilke*, 74). However, "handcraft" Rilke had, in fact, intended only in a metaphorical sense, to import the effort he would have to make to work effectively at *his* art. There was never any question for him of mistaking the sculptural effort for the poetic. This he clarifies in the letter that eventually served as a response to the first of Lou's successive letters relating to Rodin (see p.26). He must "follow" Rodin, Rilke says:

> not by a 'sculptural' alteration of my work, but by an inward ordering of the creative process; it is not shaping things that I must learn from him, but a deep collectedness for shaping's sake ...
>
> (SN, *Rilke*, 76)

It is then only officiously that Rilke hears out Lou's account of the impingement of Rodin's sculptural art on his own in the sense she intends: that Rilke's intimate closeness to Rodin's sculptural art during the time of the monograph had overwhelmed his own artistic world as a poet, and that it is this that had effected the blockage that had imprisoned Rilke in a world of anxious fear and ailments.

This is not, however, how Rilke had seen it and continued to see it. The blockage for him, it is clear, came from his peculiar inability to stem the tide of daily life. That life oppressed him all the more just because of Rodin's example, who himself had attained the power to manage this perfectly. The achievements of Rodin's art had accumulated over the years to become a firmer and firmer buttress against life's power to overwhelm from its own insistent source. In this sense the successful practice of his art had become its own defense against the continued onslaughts of daily living:

> until he himself seemed to stem from a dynasty of things: that is the source of his quietness and his patience, his fearless ongoing old age, his superiority to those who move about so much, who vacillate, who keep shifting the balances in which, almost unconsciously, he rests.
>
> (SN, *Rilke*, 76)

Rilke, so young himself by comparison, was still very far from such a condition, which yet had become the ideal according to which he sought to make himself. This experience of creative disparity, just because it was so huge, could only intensify his longing to overcome his own characterological deficiencies and to get on better. He was continuing with his own account, elaborating further on his deficiencies and indeed with an over-compensating passion that comes, ironically, from feeling free to talk about it:

> *perplexed and burdened with things that are completely irrelevant ... without the composure for reception ... everything races straight through me, what is vital along with what is least significant ... I am merely a passageway instead of a house ...*
>
> (SN, *Rilke*, 77)

Rilke's purpose would necessarily have to be to fight against this constitutional tendency, by finding himself in regular artistic work:

> *for this reason it is so frightfully necessary for me to find the tool of my art ... my hammer, so that it might become master and grow beyond all noise. There must be a handcraft in this art also: a faithful daily labor that utilizes everything ... everything would suddenly be far away ... and even what was set against me would weave its way into this work as loud sounds enter a dream ...*
>
> (SN, *Rilke*, 78)[19]

When Rilke finally received Lou's first and second letters relating to Rodin (the one in response to the book and the one on art and life; see, in the latter case, pp.27-28), Rilke's tone inevitably altered. On receiving the first letter, he was, naturally, overwhelmed by Lou's declaration of faith in him and her promise of a permanent devotion: "calmness and confidence [come] to me from my faith in all your words". He was, at the same time, conscious of the irony in the way he had gone on about himself before receiving Lou's letters: "How impatient ... I must seem to you in my letters". Also, it could not be his purpose, he says, to "sunder art and life; I know that sometime, somewhere, they must agree". But he is still maintaining the same position as to his predicament, in spite of Lou's more generous idea about it; he would have to maintain that position, paradoxically, *in order to* get on:

But I am all thumbs at life, and that is why ... it so often turns
out to be ... a delay that causes me to lose so much ... And in truth
life does go by and leaves no second chances for things missed and
the many losses; especially in the case of someone who wants to
have an art ... And how should one not be afraid, Lou, when one
rarely enters art's sanctum because outside in recalcitrant life one
gets caught in all traps ...

(SN, *Rilke*, 80)

This was Rilke's second and last letter in response to Lou's own about Rodin. A third letter would follow in which he goes on at even greater length about the peculiar challenge of his constitution. What is remarkable about these three letters is the evidence they give of Rilke's having *in fact passed on from Lou*, and become a guide to himself.

It is significant in this respect that from the time Rilke is responding to Lou's views and carrying on with his own position, Lou drops out of the conversation on these themes. While she made sure that Rilke's letters would reach her (for these were now catching up to her, just as her original letters had been running after him), she would not respond any further to the position Rilke was taking about himself. In fact, from this point onwards Lou would write Rilke only about every two months. She would retreat into the role of audience to him and a distant support. As an immediate influence on him, Lou had been displaced, her position as mentor having been taken over in the meantime by Rodin especially. This is not to say that Lou did not remain absolutely indispensable to Rilke, both psychologically and creatively, as the key person he needed to depend on for most of his life. His "confessions" to her about his struggles, which would continue for years, are what, in a very significant if ultimately an indirect way, allowed him to repeatedly overcome himself. Shrewdness in observation and "a clear-eyed intelligence"[20], in her support of Rilke in his troubles, have always been remarked of Lou in accounts of their relationship. But what has not been stressed is how shrewd Rilke was himself, not least in knowing how much he still needed Lou and finding ways to keep her alongside him. He was more than shrewd in knowing also what he needed generally. This included the position he was taking about himself now, which he was pursuing independently of Lou's own rationally-based conceptions about it. Lou could not, in fact, have any real idea of what Rilke was engaging in himself, or why this engagement with himself was inevitable. Here was a deeper wisdom at work in him (the wisdom of his own destiny) that finally explains why he could go so far in his accomplishments. For in spite of all of his deep troubles, it was his very openness to life and the submergence in it that constantly threatened him as a result, that would, when he manages to take charge of this, make him into the very great poet he would become. And for the moment, though he could not *fully* know it, he "knew" better than anyone what it was in himself that he must come to terms with for better or for worse, though he was more than intent on it being for the better...[21]

III
The Shadow of Rodin

Rodin's influence on Rilke in this period of his life was as crucial and decisive as Lou's had been in their time. It is, indeed, one of the peculiarities of Rilke's development, as a poet and as a man, that he should have come very early under the influence of people who, because of their greater age, were already well on both in their creative lives and in their conceptions of themselves. This would not make it very easy for Rilke who, as we have seen, developed consequently an acute sense of wasted time and how urgent every moment must be for him. Equally, he had his own very peculiar vulnerability and openness to life to deal with, what he now felt was his great weakness but which would turn out in time to be his strength. For nothing in life would, along the way, fail to affect him, and with his ever-growing control over himself, which would not be without its deep paradoxes[22], he would consequently become one of the most comprehensive poets of human experience we have known. He was now, however, only at the starting-point, and among other things it must have been especially difficult to support the scope and depth of Rodin's artistic achievement, in which he had become immersed, when he compared all this with where he was with his own power and ability to "work".

This would have to be the case especially as what Rodin had achieved spoke so nearly to Rilke's experience of himself. One would have to make a thorough study of Rodin to be able to conclude that his life embodied so entirely the happy terms that Rilke ascribed to it. What is clear is that Rilke was only too ready to see in this life the mirror-image of his own best aims, which *he* was falling short of. Seeing Rodin as possessed from early on of all that he was destined for artistically, Rilke projects the case of someone who *because of this* was capable of dealing with all the natural trials life threw his way:

> *And when beset by doubts and uncertainties, by the great impatience of conscious immaturity, by the fear of an early death or by the threatened lack of daily necessities, he met these things with a quiet, resolute resistance, a defiance, a strength, a confidence, all the unfurled flags of a great victory.*

(HSTN 8)

All the trials, that is, that Rilke himself felt beset with. More significantly, in Rodin Rilke saw the artist who, more than any other perhaps, had come to terms with "the life of the modern man" (HSTN 21), the very life Rilke was now struggling with on the streets of Paris. Behind Rodin's great capacity for address in this regard lay the still greater ideal Rilke ascribed to him that would go far in characterizing Rilke's own artistic end, namely that "none of the drama of Life" should remain "unexplored" (HSTN 19). This extends even to the idea of "the burden of all vice" and "all lustful sins" as rooted, by a tragic paradox, in "longing" gone wrong, as in Rodin's massive work the "Gates of Hell" (HSTN 20-21). Rodin's depictions had expanded (with a somewhat different emphasis) on the very real impressions Rilke's life in Paris was presently making on him:

> *He imparted to hundreds and hundreds of figures scarcely larger than his own hand the life which is in all passion, the florescence of all desire and the burden of all vice. He created bodies touching at all points and clinging together like animals at deadly grips with one another, falling into the depth as one single object; bodies which were like listening human faces and like arms about to strike; chains of bodies, garlands and tendrils, and figures like heavy bunches of grapes, into which the sweetness of sin rose from the roots of pain ... figures flinging themselves into the abyss in order to escape from the thought of the great woe ...*

(HSTN 21-22)

In this context we can understand why Rilke was so eager to share with Rodin his own impressive poem, entitled "The Last Judgment".[23] Amidst so much that would have mesmerized Rilke at this time, one could single out works such as Rodin's *Danaide*, his *Illusion the Daughter of Ikarus*, and his *Thought*, where we find depicted respectively a "face losing itself in the stone as in a great weeping", "that dazzling embodiment of a long, helpless fall" and another "face rising out of the heavy sleep of inanimate continuity" (HSTN 23-24).

What a burden, as well as an inspiration, all this must have been for Rilke: Rodin had already accomplished so much, while he, Rilke, had yet really even to begin. Moreover, Rilke did not lighten the burden for himself: his idea was that Rodin had succeeded at what he did because already from the beginning, from childhood, he was destined for such an accomplishment; he had been in touch with the wellsprings of the life that leads to it: that perfectly borne life to which the creative imagination rises beyond all flux and vicissitude, turmoil, or tragedy. It is only from such a life, Rilke believes, that the creative imagination derives its indomitable power of inspiration:

> It is a life in which nothing has been lost or forgotten, a life which as it passed was stored up ... a life in which everything is present and alive and nothing past ... rising with constantly renewed inspiration to works which are sublime.
>
> (HSTN 1-2)

Of this life especially Rilke says that it is in need of being properly conceived or "invented":

> The time may come when the history of this life will be invented, its ramifications, its episodes, its details. They will have to be invented ... from the days of his boyhood will be dated some episode containing a promise of future greatness ... in the days of his beginnings ... was what he sought: the grace of great things.
>
> (HSTN 2)[24]

It is the life that Rilke at once idealized and felt estranged from. For his had been, in respect of this idealized life, in fact a *counter*-life: an intensely problematic childhood that had given birth, among other things, to the terrible anxiety to which he became prone again with his new experience of life in Paris. It had bred an oppressively para-normal disposition in him which was the exact opposite of that free, commanding power over life he attributed to Rodin. Consequently, Rilke felt that he was not just, potentially, the hopeful depictor but himself like one of those depicted in Rodin's art. The paradox of Rilke's later achievement, one could say, lay all in this terrible oppos-ition between the ideal and this reality. This opposition he would only manage to transcend, if he ever does, towards the end of his poetic career, and perhaps only with the end of his life.

In the meantime, a very long road lay ahead, and Rilke too, like Rodin, would have to find the "handcraft of his art". When Rodin found it, he would never be diverted from it, by any of the obstructive realities that an anxious and wasteful social life confronted *him* with. Such "handcraft" was to be the antidote to Rilke's fear of collapsing under the weight of life's daily invasions both on a smaller and a larger scale. The secret, as Rilke shows, lay in Rodin's discovery of what he called the *modelé*: the secret of that surface-point and texture at which the inner life of the human being is fully manifested outwardly. It is possible that when Rilke presented this idea he was already thinking of a similar "surface" achievement transposed from sculpture to the medium of words. Rilke's *New Poems*—published some four and five years hence—would at least appear to fulfil this project. Certainly Rilke says of his aim:

> *I too must discover that smallest basic element, the cell of my art,*
> *the tangible immaterial means of representation for everything.*
> (SN, *Rilke*, 78)

But this was not, for him, a matter of preconceiving any special "tech-nique" of art, rather of finding, first, that self-directing impulse that would allow him to work on a daily basis starting from the minutiae of words and of stored knowledge as he found them[25], from which the "technique" of his art would naturally emerge. Once it did, he would, like Rodin, be established:

> *Then the clear strong consciousness of the enormous task that lay*
> *before me would drive and bend me toward it; then I would have*
> *so infinitely much to do that one workday would resemble an-*
> *other, and the work I had would always succeed because it would*

start out with things attainable and small and yet all along be involved in things great.

(SN, *Rilke*, 78)

In a letter written to Lou some three months after initiating a correspondence with her again, Rilke would still be saying:

my time and my strength, as things stand with me, can have but one task, this task: to find the road that will lead me to quiet, daily work ...

(SN, *Rilke*, 88)

The problem was that regular daily work at his art was not, and had not until then been, Rilke's practice or a possible mode of life, as his words imply: "as things stand with me". All was of a piece in this regard: his personality, as well as his art as he had managed it until then. His inclination was to be possessed of the whole of an experience all at once; experience for him always started from that one point: "there is always only *one thing* in me" (SN, *Rilke*, 84), and he was, as a result, already absorbed and immersed in everything before he could break it down, had already reached the "end", as he calls it, without consciousness of the stages of the "way" that had led there. This inclination would spill over into his social relations, with the result that he would, as he puts it, "unload everything" on others at once, experience after experience, without discriminating even between one experience and another. It was an inclination of personality that inevitably isolated him further from others, for:

no one can reciprocate me, since I give ruthlessly and brutally, without regard to others, unloading everything now at one place, now at another, instead of offering, of showing and bestowing things chosen considerately from an ordered store.

(SN, *Rilke*, 84)

In this same letter, among his most revealing, he articulates the problem still more pointedly:

It is a defect of my nature to forget all paths taken ... I fly straight to so many destinations (or reach them walking blindfolded), so that I am given the end but not the way that led there ...

(SN, *Rilke*, 83)

He is acutely aware of what this inclination of personality, or orientation of his being, imports also for his relationship to his art:

*All my creative work ... bears ... this tendency, which shows in
the extremely unscientific developments any material or cause for
work undergoes in me ... the last and most distant thing appears
as the point of origin, from which, proceeding backward, I must
invent paths ... initiated only into the goal, into the final concluding summation and apotheosis.*

(SN, *Rilke*, 85)

This had been Rilke's way of working in the case of *The Book of
Hours*, especially "The Book of Monastic Life", but this tendency of
his being brought with it an attendant problem inasmuch as it could
also put off creative work indefinitely. Left, as we have seen, at the
mercy of the depth of his experience, he had, for creative purposes,
to rely on this experience sorting itself out far beyond his conscious
ability to follow the process, a process that, moreover, took its own
unpredictable time:

*This defect is the source of my continual poverty ... the empti-
ness and inactivity of many days: for since I carry nothing in
me but some last-acquired product, while the reckoning itself ...
takes place illegibly inside me, waiting period after waiting period
appears to intervene between one result and another.*

(SN, *Rilke*, 84)

Once again Rilke shows here a preternaturally clear consciousness of
his own workings, something made possible, no doubt in large part,
by the special opportunity being in touch with Lou again provided for
articulating his deepest concerns. Here was a truly faithful account
of why it was he had succumbed so often to those anxious feelings
of being lost, even of being lost for good, by which he was especially
oppressed, to the point of burdening Lou at one time beyond hope of
their remaining together:

*And this ignorance of the path, this certainty only of the last
and most distant thing, the point at the end of it all, makes all
proceeding difficult for me and scatters over me all the sadness
characteristic of those who have become lost—even if I am on the
way to finding myself.*

(SN, *Rilke*, 85)

IV
Rilke on the Way

Rilke would, for years to come, continue to deal with this fundamental condition of his being before which he was, naturally, left in great dismay. However, he would also have success in countering it, according to his intentions, at least in the short term. Already in the fall of 1902, not long after meeting Rodin, Rilke had composed "The Panther", the most well-known of his poems from his *New Poems*, a large collection that he would begin to put out five years or so hence. It is almost certain that he did not have, over this period, a very clear conception of what this collection would be about or that any particular collection was even taking shape, though he was already working towards it. Here was a case of forging a "path" step by step without an already formed notion of the "end", a case of getting down to "working" at the "handcraft of his art" primarily, thus offsetting his former practice of waiting for it all to come at once. This was not exactly daily work, but it was a different way of working, born of Rilke's need to counterbalance his constitutional tendency to remain, for long fruitless periods, in final things. Similarly, in February of 1904, while in Rome, some six months beyond his succession of initial letters to Lou, an attempt was made to put down in writing some of those disturbing impressions of life on the streets of Paris that he had had so much significant trouble with. This was the genesis of *The Notebooks of Malte Laurids Brigge*, though Rilke hardly knew this at the time. He would continue to chisel away at this work, sporadically and yet consistently, over the next five years. He had put down these first impressions, in fact, in the context of another project he had deliberately conceived, an extension to an early prose work, *The Stories of God*, which he had published in 1900.[26] As it happens, Rilke could not see this new project through; it fizzled within a month, bringing back all the anxieties about being unable to carry through systematic work on his art. In fact, he had momentarily gone back to his former expectation of having it all come at once, only to discover that he could no longer work in this way either. His predicament seemed to him thus only to have intensified, caught as he was at this juncture, in a generally unstable relation to his work, as he reports to Lou:

> *It became apparent that my mode of working (as well as my more receptive way of looking) had changed, so that I would probably never again be able to write a book in ten days (or evenings), would need for each new one a long and uncalculated time ... an advance towards that state of continual work I want to achieve ... But this change brings with it a new danger; fending off all external disturbances for eight or ten days is possible—: but for weeks, for months? This fear oppressed me ...*
>
> (SN, *Rilke*, 106)

Rilke, in fact, came very close at this time to falling back, as a result of this impasse, into that experience of paranormal anxiety that had initially prompted him to get in touch with Lou again.[27] Somewhat prophetically—since the writing of *Malte* would, especially in its last stages, captivate him to the point of breakdown—in his first attempt at formulating his Paris impressions Rilke became absorbed in his writing to the point of overexertion, and he had begun to feel ill.

Fortunately for him, at this very time, he received unexpected invitations to stay in Sweden and in Denmark on the basis of the enthusiasm for his early published work expressed by Ellen Key, an influential writer and lecturer in that part of the world, of whom Rilke had until then known nothing. Proceeding to Scandinavia, Rilke was in this way brought into contact with the environment and culture that was eventually to serve as the dynamic setting for *Malte*. Even before he had received the invitations, Rilke had expressed his resolve to apply himself more strenuously to a program of work that would involve "appropriating" to himself "a little of the historian's craft and the archivist's patience" (SN, *Rilke*, 118); "without some acquisition of this kind", he adds, "I will be unable to take my next forward steps". He appears to have entered this program of work already when in Rome (where he had been staying before his visit to Scandinavia) with his new study of antiquity. This is judging by two great poems he wrote back in January, "Orpheus, Eurydice, Hermes" and "At the Tombs of the Haeterae", both of which would find their way into *New Poems*. He was also determined to extend his effort of work in this regard to a closer study of nature:

> *How life originates, how it functions in the lower creatures, how it branches and spreads, how life blossoms, how it bears fruit: I need*

to learn all of that. To bind myself more firmly to the reality that
so often denies me, by taking part in all that lives—to be there,
not just in feeling but in knowledge ...

(SN, *Rilke*, 117)

Already we can divine in these various intentions the basis of work that underlies the great range of creation that we find in *New Poems*. Especially in this collection, though also in *Malte*, we are given the direct fruit of Rilke's deliberate plan of "work", even if this was work from day to day on another level that did not involve the regular daily artistic practice he had associated with Rodin as a great example. In fact, one can speak of such regular practice only in the case of three periods associated with the *New Poems*: the summers of 1906, 1907, and 1908, when almost all of the poems in that collection were produced except for some thirty odd poems already written (the collection containing near on two hundred poems). In the meantime, Rilke had also produced, more incidentally, the new poems that would be added to *The Book of Images*, which would go through a second printing in 1906. In this second printing Rilke would radically re-arrange his original sequence of poems to bring them into a firmer relationship to the new. This additional collection, which has been treated merely as a miscellany but only gives the appearance of one, is no less an editorial masterpiece than the *New Poems*, or *Malte*, or for that matter Rilke's monograph on Rodin which itself unfolds with a masterly sense of progression and overall design from one section to the next. In his general editorial effort over this period we find still more evidence of the fruit of the deliberate "work" to which Rilke had committed from the time of his life-altering "apprenticeship" under Rodin.

All of this, moreover, showed something more essentially new that Lou would summarize years later, especially in connection with *Malte*, in her analytical memoir specifically devoted to Rilke:

An indescribable clarity with which the poet is able to penetrate reality marks the changing psychic strata in which Rilke now lived.[28]

It is the new power Lou could already see developing in Rilke from the time of his first letters to her when he put himself in touch with her again. As for the "path" to his "end", his "way" to "himself" so to speak, which he was now so desperately trying to "find", this new power was what he had to go by, and he was in the process of developing it to great sophistication, extending himself as it were as far as reality would allow. Rilke's "end" as he puts it above, had always been and could only ever be one thing: to gather all things to his God, in Whom he had begun, as in "The Book of Monastic Life". In his fresh resolve to commit to daily work when in Rome, he was primarily led back to his *Stories of God*. This had been until now the main line of his work, starting from "The Book of Monastic Life", and carrying on with "The Book of Pilgrimage" and "The Book of Poverty and Death". Even his first attempts to set down in writing some of his impressions from Paris life were developed in the context of extending his *Stories*. But he was to be subverted by these attempts; they had, in fact, put an end to fresh work on the *Stories*. For the import of his creative life had shifted radically: from the God Who had formerly "embraced" him in every step Rilke took creatively, to a new world of "God-forsakenness" in which he was virtually at sea, except for that "indescribable clarity" of mind he had developed since leaving Lou and which was, in her view, such a welcome, if still largely an unrealized, acquisition.[29] How far should Rilke go in capturing this new world of "forsakenness" that threatened to annihilate him and yet seemed, even to him, to be where his "path" was leading? When *Malte* was finished at last, Rilke would remark about it, when still overcome:

> For the longest time ... "Malte Laurids Brigge" seemed to me not so much a downfall, as a strange dark ascent into a remote and neglected part of heaven.
>
> (SN, *Rilke*, 176)

By a deep paradox, Rilke's path back to God would be *by* such a "dark ascent" whose fortunes he would be unable to gauge with any confidence, in fact at any stage of his experience. It was also as a pure dark mystery that he was to be taken up by the visitation he famously experienced at Duino and which gave rise to the first of his Elegies, some two years after *Malte*, and after much aimless wandering from the time *Malte* was published.[30] As his writing of *Malte* developed, he had once again submitted to that inherited condition of his being in which everything tended to seep down deep inside him (see above p.25)—a condition over which he had little control, and about which he otherwise complained in loud dismay. But perhaps he did know, somehow: that this could only *be* his way. Life had confronted him with the whole reality of alienation from God, in which he had immersed, and in *Malte* he was now living this out as far as clarity of mind would allow. He was facing the worst of his own self, the full impingement on him of what was "unreal" in the world at large, almost ready, as it were, to live into these things paranormally, for such too was the scope of the world's reality by which his God was to be measured. To this compulsion of his being in the case of work on *Malte*, his more deliberate work towards the *New Poems*, steeped as this collection is in the many discrete revelations of history and of nature, must have seemed a necessary ballast, a way of keeping sane and in control, at the complete opposite pole from *Malte*. Only by looking into these many paradoxical developments will we be able to fathom the deeper sense in which Rilke may be said at this time to have been "on the way", as he puts it to himself. Another form of shrewd understanding was at work in his compulsively comprehensive range of engagement with his experience—shrewd, on this level, to the point of genius. It is another way of seeing his idea of the "work" he so felt was necessary to lead him on in the "progress" he was looking for both in the short and the long term.[31]

When Rilke returned from his six-months stay in Scandinavia in December of 1904, the need to "speak" to Lou in person, on which he had been harping for over a year, had grown more urgent and was now more overtly expressed in his letters to her. This may well be because Rilke had grown clearer after his trip about what the scope of his new work would be in the case of both *Malte* and the *New Poems*. Not that he envisaged anything approaching the final form these works would take, but that he felt clearer in himself about his purposes generally, and he knew all this would clarify further in Lou's presence: "There is much, so much to discuss" (SN, *Rilke*, 143), he insists. There was the strange, if not so surprising, assertion that his future would somehow only open up through a reunion with Lou, and that Lou herself knew this:

> *a reunion with you is the single bridge to my future—you know that, Lou.*

I have been feeling for years: that all my next advances are in your
hands ...

(SN, *Rilke*, 143-144)

By March of the new year, it had become clear to Rilke that it was
time to proceed to the publication of *The Book of Hours*, and sometime after mid-April the full manuscript was once again in his hands.
Its first part, "The Book of Monastic Life", especially absorbed him
at that time as the work in which he had first found himself so profoundly:

To hold the old black book in my hands again, that was the true
reunion ... like a heightened presentiment of that other reunion I
keep thinking of ...

back then I was the tower whose great bells began to peal ... trem-
bling so far down ... reaching so far out ... so passionately toward
you.

(SN, *Rilke*, 148)

He was, in short, re-discovering himself, and this only strengthened
his sense that he was approaching the new turn Lou had prophesized
for him:

I still have not ... taken that turn that is supposed to come now.
But it must come; I am more firmly convinced of this than ever.

It must have seemed to Lou a very good time to finally allow
Rilke to visit her—after he had pleaded with her so much, to know
him still so full of devotion to her and with more confidence than had
been that he was truly on the verge of advancing with himself. After
two years of faithful correspondence, their reunion took place at last,
at Pentecost in late May of that year. We cannot know how much was
discussed between them at this time, but it seemed to Lou, as she put
it in her *Memoirs*, like an "ascension" of the "work" in him, which
Lou explicitly sees by then as "an expression of your destiny, which
was not to be denied" (MCHL 91). A form of mutual comprehension
had been created between them, if with much of the tragic undertow
to their relationship still left unnoted. Certainly from this meeting
onwards, Rilke's work took off and was both profuse and virtually
non-stop until the end of 1909 when *Malte* was at last completed.

Paradoxically, through the greatest part of this period, from 1905 to 1909, there would be no need for Lou and Rilke to continue to write each other much, for they had, from the time of their reunion, been linked indissolubly. As Lou puts it memorably: "I became yours again in a second way—in a second maidenhood". And it was *The Book of Hours* that had been, as she formally notes herself, the catalystic occasion for this.

II

Looking Back on *The Book of Hours*

I

"The Book of Monastic Life"

The question thus arises: in what sense precisely can we say *does The Book of Hours* represent Lou and Rilke over this period? No analysis could properly do justice certainly to "The Book of Monastic Life", the first of the three parts that comprise *The Book of Hours*, especially when one looks back on this first part from the point of view of Rilke's disturbed concerns in the period we have just traced, from the spring of 1903 to the spring of 1905. In contrast with the deep uncertainty of his present development at this time, "The Book of Monastic Life" represented for Rilke a ringing symbol of the very certain power he had at some point achieved before his separation from Lou: "back then I was the tower whose great bells began to peal ... trembling so far down ... reaching so far out" as he put it, so wistfully. "The Book of Monastic Life" was certainly a high achievement, to be followed by some very noble, if uneven, attempts to continue in this direction with the second and third parts, after Rilke's separation from Lou. However, the facts behind the case of "Monastic Life" run far deeper than a simple achievement. Rilke had looked back wistfully on "The Book of Monastic Life" before. This was on his return from their second trip to Russia where tensions with Lou had reached a breaking-point. In the first of his entries in the Schmargendorf Diary when in Worpswede, Rilke laments the fact that he was recently unable to write in spite of the many occasions on which he felt he could have been writing:

as was the case with so many on this trip ... [c]ountless poems

> *I failed to hear ... Everything that arrived found me locked up.*
> (SN, *Diaries*, 142)

This contrasts, dramatically, with the steady flow of creative work that followed the writing of "Monastic Life" a year earlier, over the course of the many months that preceded this second trip, as the Schmargendorf Diary also shows.[32] Tensions with Lou were high: he was not a full month beyond writing that "ugly letter" to her in which he had broken down over Lou's long period of time away from him[33], and confronted now—at a distance from her in Worpswede—with his creative failure during their stay in Russia, naturally he looked back on what he had achieved in "Monastic Life", which had been written after their monumentally successful first trip to Russia:

> *The tremendous is still somewhere inside me. I did experience it all. I was surely not dreaming. If it would only somehow come back to me.*
>
> *I have such a longing for what has passed.*
> (SN, *Diaries*, 142-143)

Rilke made this entry in the form of a direct address to Lou, and without his fully realizing it perhaps, he was yearning for the power he had come into as a poet that had at last justified him with her. Here we enter the additional *psychological* situation behind the obsessive quest for poetic form that Lou would later say was the cause of their eventual separation. The power Rilke had exercised in this poem had given him at last a certain leverage with Lou; it had established him, as it were, as an equal in her company, at least in his mind. With this creative success, repressed feelings of rivalry with the ever-dominant Lou had been satisfied, but these had been newly aroused as a result of Lou's insistent absence from him and with Rilke's failure to create during that summer. All this had led to a climactic flare-up in their relationship that must have seemed to Rilke to forebode sadly the separation that was shortly to come ("I have such a longing for what has passed", he says, looking back from Worpswede): "Monastic Life" was, after all, a symbol of what had kept him together with Lou beyond the competitive tension that had begun to creep into their relationship[34]. This poem, along with its sequel in the other two parts written after their separation, must thus have represented a very complex symbol to both Rilke and Lou at their joyous reunion in 1905, their "Pentecost"[35], as Lou would put it later. *The Book of Hours* was at once a symbol of what had united them in their creative life together (among many other influences, the idea of visiting Russia, which had been decisive in the production of "Monastic Life", had been Lou's), *and also* what had separated them drastically. It was over this production that they were now being brought together again, and again it was over the recurring sense in Rilke that he could not quite find his way. In the meantime, they had learned (no doubt from what it had cost them) what it meant to pretend not to be in need of each other.[36]

Rilke's deep conflict with himself, stemming from his repressed rivalry with Lou, is already reflected in "Monastic Life" itself, in its strangely overloaded structure as we proceed through it. In a sequence of poems of this great length, and especially if there are no sectional breaks, an impression of unimpeded continuity is of the essence. However, twice in "Monastic Life" we are jarred out of this continuity: poems appear that are not properly assimilated into the sequence. There is the first case of the poem that introduces the voice of a young monk into the sequence (RANS 27), one of only two[37] dramatizations in the sequence, the poem that begins: "Trickling, trickling, I run like sand". This poem sticks out like a sore thumb here and tears apart the continuity of the piece up to this point. Later in the sequence there is another poem in which the young monk speaks that is no less out of place at that juncture, and this in spite of the narrator monk's deliberate attempt at this point to make room for the issues raised by the young monk's strange interjections into the sequence. I will come back to these 'young monk' poems below. The other case of ill-fittedness, a more revealing one for our immediate purposes, concerns the transition from the poem that begins "With a bough so unlike that other, God the tree/arrives" to "I cannot think that little figure Death/.../will be our forced fate" (RANS 39, 41). The effect is a shift to an altogether distinct theme to which no bridge of any kind, thematic or artistic, has been offered. As with the introduction of the initial (as well as the later) poem spoken by the young monk, there is a complete disjunction or seismic fault in the text at this point.

"With a bough so unlike that other" relates itself, in fact, to what precedes it in a direct contrast: the period of the Renaissance had *its* way of relating to God, but this has been not only superceded but improved upon and rounded out in the later period in which Rilke was now living. This greater potential for knowing God in his time Rilke identifies with the land of Russia. However, even in the context of this contrast, the shift into a proclamation of the greater destiny of this later time is precipitated awkwardly. One feels this all the more as this proclamation, as its own distinct theme, is not elaborated on beyond itself, while the period of the Renaissance has just received as many as four poems dedicated to it. This series of five poems would have served more fittingly as a Prologue to the sequence as a whole; as part of such a Prologue, the singular proclamation which the fifth poem represents ("With a bough so unlike that other") would then have stood up well, since the sequence as a whole is intended to be its demonstration. At the same time, we would have no trouble moving from this Prologue to the first poem in the sequence as it now stands: "Bright with metallic strike the hour/tilts and touches me" (RANS 3). Likewise, the new transition, created with the extraction of these five poems from the poem that precedes them that begins "Those were the days of Michelangelo" (RANS 33)—the transition from that poem to "I cannot think that little figure Death", is easily assimilated. The shift from the theme of the first of these two poems, that "only God confounds his [Michelangelo's] will's control" to "I cannot think that little figure Death/.../to be a serious threat", explains itself. [See Appendix II for a full diagrammatic breakdown of the revised sequence I propose.]

The highly disjunctive awkwardness with which Rilke introduces the contrast between the Renaissance and his own time in "Monastic Life" is all to the point. This is the very theme Rilke had elaborated on in his Florence Diary that had made so small an impression on Lou it brought on a major breakdown in him, since he could not at the time see (or accept) that this theme, in the intense form in which he (as the great aspiring new poet) had lived it, could be so casually regarded.[38] Rilke could not help but bring this greatly cherished theme of his into "Monastic Life", but he does so stealthily, without grace or, as one would expect, the freedom to elaborate on it. This most cherished theme of his, the one he had especially prided himself on, ought to have been trumpeted in the form of a Prologue to "Monastic Life", but there could hardly have been any possibility of that after the poor reception this theme had received from Lou and the very painful crisis this had brought on, as we shall see (in Part 3).

On that occasion Rilke stood on the very verge of a final separation from Lou that he himself was almost ready to initiate. Rilke's blunted and gauche *re*-presentation of his cherished theme in "Monastic Life" reveals him as still in conflict with himself one full year later. He did not wish to alienate Lou again or bring up too boldly out of himself the material issue that had caused him so much pain and both of them so much turmoil. He was by now primarily committed to Lou, in spite of the residual effects of his subjection to the programme of work *she* had conceived for him. This had included the trip to Russia that had transformed him at last into the poetic genius he was destined to become.

The effect of Rilke's conflict with himself over Lou can be seen, in fact, through the whole period of his work on *The Book of Hours*. There is a very peculiar failure of editorial intervention in the case of *Hours* as a whole, when one compares this work with everything else Rilke wrote beyond it when he was finally fully separated both from Lou and that work itself. All of his later work is submitted by Rilke to his very remarkable editorial capacity. We cannot feel that any of the later poems (or prose pieces in the case of *Malte*) are out of place in the larger works to which they belong. To re-arrange there would be to destroy the fabric of these works; the effect is perfectly streamlined and, indeed, seamless. This is not the case with *The Book of Hours*, which ought to have been submitted to further editing but was not, very simply because this collection, precisely in the spontaneous form in which it was produced, and with all the imperfections it might contain, was a sort of sacred scripture for Rilke, something that expressed the very way in which his relationship with Lou had been lived, which made this work untouchable. *The Book*, left to stand as it is, is evidence of how faithful Rilke was to all that he had shared with Lou that had so defined his life; it is evidence *also* of how subjected and repressed he had been and remained right up to the time of their reunion. In the second half of "The Book of Pilgrimage", Rilke, as we shall see, finds himself looking back to where he had been with "Monastic Life", turning back anxiously, and regressively, to the favorite themes he had treated there, when the whole thrust of the first half has been towards a *re*-making of his relationship to God, brought on by his newly alienated circumstances and geared necessarily towards the future. Likewise in "The Book of Poverty and

Death", we find an inability to move further into the future, in that Book's second half, in this case because Rilke had still not worked out his relationship to the disturbing new theme of (his) spiritual poverty. It is clear that only in a healed and restored relationship to Lou and a newly shared understanding of the effect their falling out had had would the freedom to move forward and to be on his own creative way come to him at last.

The actual starting point of "The Book of Monastic Life" takes us back, in fact, to the great personal revelation about the Renaissance and its further relation to his time that Rilke had had while in Florence, a full account of which is to be found in his Florence Diary.[39] The five poems couched away inside the "Monastic Life" that properly form a Prologue to this piece distil this revelation to fine effect. In the first line from the first of these poems we are brought back dramatically to where Rilke's breakthrough-revelation began:

> *The bough of the tree that is God, that overhangs Italy,*
> *has dropped its blossom.*

(RANS 35)

In humankind's long relationship to God over time, Renaissance Italy had at last reached spring, though it was destined to live in "celebration" (37) of its own "blossoming" or "flowering" (35) only. The possibility of its "fruiting", or coming to fruit, lay beyond this epoch; the epoch was "burden"-ed by its flowering to the point of "exhaust"-ing itself in it. What "came to completion" was, therefore, "only God's spring/only his son, the Word", in the first instance to a great extent as the Christ-Child, "the shining child" (of the Nativity) who was "followed" (in the case of the Magi) by "[g]ifts from the world" and who was "s[u]ng" of by "all the world like cherubim" (as in the scene of the choir of angels that appeared to the shepherds). In the second instance, God came to partial completion in the form of the Son as a grown Man, He Who "walked without let/mantled in metamorphosis", which is to say, without obstruction from either human or spiritual adversaries, superordinately as it were, as if in His case there could only be "metamorphosis" from one condition to an-other, this God being beyond the reach of either deep human tragedy or spiritual devastation. It was a concomitant of this view of the Son that the Mother of this God should be celebrated as the great mediating force in this "spring" of a new revelation, as in the poem that follows: "In those days they loved her too, the Maid" (37). "Sought and awoken to the fruitful", She Herself, nevertheless, embodied but the "spring-flowering". Such flowering held potentially more—the elaborate "fruiting" of the whole process, but all this would remain in the end "hidden" within the seemingly endless possibilities of "flowering". Representations of the Virgin Maid at this time expressed a flowering that Rilke characterizes as a case of being "consummate by the One". A certain complete grace already lies over the story of the Redeemer as if the flowering of His Being in Mary had been the whole that had carried Him through His Passion and Death.

In his Florence Diary, Rilke notes that "the gestures of the figures" of this art "are all consecrated by longing" (SN, *Diaries*, 36); "the discoveries they [painters and others] made in their own depths ... they lifted ... into the light ... [that] then was", in its own way, "full of God" (SN, *Diaries*, 20). There could not be anything more essential for Rilke, both at this time and in the long run, than this longing for God—"longing" being the most often used and the most representative term in Rilke's experience at this time. Eventually, from within the culture of the Renaissance, the hint of a great intuition emerged that more was bound to come, inasmuch as the gestures of that time "nowhere venture all the way to the borders" (SN, *Diaries*, 37). "Longing" would have to embrace more of both the human and the spiritual realities involved in the story of Christ's Redemption, with the result, as in the next poem, that:

> *the Virgin now, in a different hour,*
> *undelivered of a burden more solemn,*
> *turns to the pains to come.*

(RANS 37)

Most prominent among the artists who did at least venture to the borders, according to Rilke, was Michelangelo, whose Madonnas, however, betray their failure to integrate experience at those limits by their "hard and unfeminine" pose, arriving merely "at a kind of defiant heroism", so that "[o]ne could *almost* believe them—that they had given birth to the Redeemer in grief and labor-pain" (SN, *Diaries*, 62). More representative of Michelangelo and his time is his early *Pietà*—though Rilke does not explicitly comment on this work. Here one notes the muted bafflement and clueless incomprehension of this strangely young Mother who is too young to have a son of this age. Viewed symbolically, she holds the defeated body of her dead Son as if in this fate He lay beyond the time in which grace and beauty were alone the reality.

For Rilke, it remained rather for Botticelli to express the deepest urge towards the farther reality that was making itself felt at this time. For Rilke, this urge appears naturally out of the "longing" (RANS 39) for God of that time. However, Botticelli knows that the Virgin of this time cannot yet bear this farther reality or, as Rilke puts it in his poem, that "the greatest is not yet born of her" (37).[40] It is precisely the limitation of the Virgin of this time that she has given birth "without suffering" (SN, *Diaries*, 55), that "the fruit simply fell into [her] arms", the end having been conceived before the process of suffering that leads to this end has been lived. The fullness of the revelation she bears could only be properly known through a further engagement with this suffering. (Here a curious parallel suggests itself between the Renaissance's pre-emption of "the way" and Rilke's own inveterate tendency (fully addressed later in time) to project himself into the end of an experience, thus bypassing the way to it, as discussed above—p.35ff.) In this regard it is a sombre urge that makes itself felt in Botticelli. In a dramatic reversal of the customary iconography, before the unknown prospect that Botticelli's Madonna forecasts "angels do not comfort her/but stand, dread, forbidding, alien, round her"—RANS 37 (see, e.g., his Corsini Madonna). In another highly expressive reversal, it is not Botticelli who, in these circumstances, turns inwardly to the Mother but rather she who now turns towards Botticelli as the artist who knows. She thereby finds for the first time "the common pain of humanity" (RANS 39) with which the religious longing of this time had yet to contend and out of which Botticelli wished to be lifted through his longing.[41] Only in this way could the "fruit" of this longing be, at last, fully comprehended. In this respect Botticelli is unique for the completeness of a life that was committed to the farther reality that was tragically beyond the reach of his time, and for the hopeful realization of which he suffered:

> *He spent his life in a long flow of tears*
> *that struck home into his own hands.*
> *And as the finest veil before her pains*

he clings to her anguished lips, and closely bends
over them almost melting to a smile—

Through this profoundly plumbed experience while in Florence, Rilke in fact discovered three principles that would serve as the hall-marks of his life's work as a whole. Primordial in this account is the principle of "longing" that is inseparable from an experience of God; this is where or how it all begins: *You must have your longing over you*, he counsels everyone in his Diary (SN, *Diaries*, 38). This is the first principle of any process of faithful discovery—the very longing that the Quattrocento itself could boast of and that those of Rilke's time were bound, as he thought, to re-connect with and to build on. Those of his time, he notes in his Diary, had already an affinity with such longing: "It is not chance and whim and fashion that lead us to those who pre-cede Raphael. We are the distant heirs whom destiny appointed in the interest of the many legacies"—(SN, *Diaries*, 38). In the meantime, as he acknowledges, "We have lived through centuries since then" (37), and these have put up formidable "barriers" to this longing. From Rilke's association of these "barriers" with "a cramped finality", he clearly understood by the challenge of his own time far more than simply "the common pain of humanity" to which the Renaissance Madonna could hardly reach. This still deeper embroilment in real-ity, deeper than was forecasted, is a consequence of the fact that the Renaissance "spring" could not turn into full summer, and so "[t]he great spring gradually became a wilderness". There is however, for Rilke, no choice in the matter but to contend with our common pain, however distorted this struggle had become from the deeper material entanglements brought on over the course of the centuries—for, if we are to have the full experience of reality, *We must be human* (SN, *Diaries*, 37): this Rilke adds as a second principle. We are, at the same time, aided in this struggle by the fact that, rather momentously, "we now grasp ... again" (37) "that innermost beauty" that was experi-enced so marvellously by the Quattrocento. In this way we are made ready to act on Rilke's third principle, for, in addition to the other two facts of life, *We need eternity*, quite apart from what the material civilization of Rilke's own time was, for the most part, saying. In con-trast with this civilization that had become a wilderness, knowledge of this whole process had in the meantime made a "solitary" (RANS 39) of the one who knows.

Out of this long process a new age had at last arrived "as the announcer of the summer"; this is how Rilke puts it in the last poem from our Prologue. As it happened, this new age was being heralded in by the Russian people in his time, or so Rilke was by then disposed to see it. His trip to Russia, one year after Florence, had exposed him to another extraordinary culture in which God took existence not from an already perfected model of the One Being in Whom He had manifested Himself, after the image of the Quattrocento, but rather from the manifold groping revelations that came diversely to a whole people, each one among whom had been made in the meantime into a solitary like Rilke himself. It was out of *such* a culture that God manifests in Rilke's own time; God does so now all the more fully inasmuch as "more is given to many of a kind/if they are alone, than to a mere one" (RANS 39). In this way God reveals Himself in the ubiquitous form that is more truly expressive of His omnipresence; He appears as the One *in* the Many, even if this experience *will* put a strain on the individual's sense of coherence potentially (which explains why the individual in this experience can be brought "close to despair"). It is, still, One God Who so powerfully manifests in the Many. This Russian experience is seized upon as a fresh model of 'openness' to God, and Rilke describes this way of seeing and reaching out to Him as "the last of the last prayers/visionaries shall celebrate". It is an experience that is about embracing everything that could possibly manifest God, and this embracing of comprehensiveness explains what will otherwise strike us as glaring presumption in the poet: "You see, there is much I want./Perhaps everything"— (RANS 17). Here is an openness to the experience of God that contrasts with the impulse to bring Him into that sharply defined "light" of discrete artistic accomplishment that had characterized the Italian Renaissance. God is to be found quite as much, and indeed more essentially, in the "dark" spaces that, from within, empower those manifestations in the "light", which, in comparison, only bear His reflected existence. His actual existence is what the artist of Rilke's time was committed to, and this would require his "draw[ing] near" to "the stiller time" (39) that would open the artist, beyond the finished form of art, to the world's dark depths out of which God reveals Himself through all things.

The four poems that open "Monastic Life", as this sequence

presently stands, immediately elaborate on Rilke's view of a cultural evolution. After noting, in the first poem, how everything comes alive and is completed in its divine form only when the artist himself awakens and lives into things, and that there is nothing in this respect "too small" for the artist's "love" (RANS 4), the poet goes on, in the second poem, to wonder projectively if he will ever be able to "complete" God in the "last" sphere of His existence. The poet then gives us the basic cultural opposition: unlike his Italian "brothers" (5) to the South, the Russian painter-monk who is the sequence's narrator distinguishes himself from their own impulse to "draw Madonnas to the life" and otherwise to fix both the Madonna and the God She serves to the "glorious" finality of their artistic forms. Contrastingly, the narrator-monk's "God", he says, "is dark"; "so arbitrarily", he goes on to say about the Italian achievement, "we may not paint you". God's image cannot be so fixed, and it is rather a case of fashioning the kind of art that will not come between God and the devotee in any way, letting Him reveal or announce Himself through a seemingly more imperfect and yet more actual way of representing Him, by invoking in the "heart" of the devotee His actual presence rather than any graven image. Here Rilke was drawing symbolically on the practice of Russian iconography, which had, for centuries, borne this vision of the religious artist's role—"a bough so *un*like the other" (39), as Rilke puts it, even if *this* bough does spring from the same "tree" that is God working through the centuries.

How very startling, we must feel, was this plunge from the Catholic Italian Renaissance, which only a year before Rilke held so dear to his heart, suddenly deep into a Russian Orthodoxy so new to him he could not possibly have belonged to it to the extent he wished to proclaim. We know that Rilke embraced his Russian experience with a passion that was dramatic and nearly absolute. Over a year later he was still appearing, even in European settings, dressed in the garb of the Russian folk, to the point where Lou, and others, thought his comportment even weirdly excessive. But could the orthodox Russian experience in its *own* terms have possibly constituted the evolutionary fulfilment Rilke was counting on finding and embodying in his own art after the direction set prophetically by the Catholic Italian Botticelli?—"a bough so *un*like the other", as Rilke himself acknowledges. A very huge gap remains between the Catholic Italian and the Russian Orthodox cultures, and it has not been filled; it is, in fact, a case of Rilke stepping out of one tradition in the West suddenly into another very different one in the East. Very strangely, when one considers all that Rilke had made of him in his Diary, and continues to make of him even in "Monastic Life", Botticelli is simply left behind, as Rilke 'progresses' now to the Russian experience. Precisely *what* was meant to come to fruit from Botticelli's struggle in later ages Rilke does not pursue because he had now stepped outside the tradition in which Botticelli had developed.

The direction from Botticelli should have landed Rilke else-where, within a continuum, still within Western tradition, that did begin to find dramatic expression later—in the work of Novalis. Significantly, one could fit Novalis directly to Rilke's descriptions of Botticelli in *his* tragic struggle:

> *He spent his life in a long flow of tears*
> *that struck home into his own hands.*

The focus is on the Virgin Mother:

> *And as the finest veil before her pains*
> *he clings to her anguished lips, and closely bends*
> *over them almost melting to a smile—*

Like Botticelli, Novalis also spent his life in this tragic way from the time of Sophie's death, and the end result of *his* struggle was to sur-pass Botticelli in mediating at last the Virgin's power to bring in a new age. Novalis would speak of an angelic "brother" who "is the heartbeat of the new age" and who "has made a new veil for the Holy Virgin" [42]:

> *The veil is for the Virgin ... her indispensable instrument whose folds are the letters of her sweet Annunciation ... For me her singing is nothing but the ceremonious call to a new foundation gathering, a mighty beating of the wings of an angelic herald who is passing. They are the first birth-pangs, let everyone prepare for the birth!*

By the time Rilke had begun to live with *his* angel, after Duino, a whole other path had been walked that would not make relating to this angel as straightforward a case as the one Novalis had proclaimed was now possible. Yet very early on, in the Florence Diary, Rilke had put his prospective vision for the Western artist in the same terms as had Novalis:

> *We shall be like mothers ... let it be known: we shall be like mothers ... You must learn only to believe; you must become pious in a new sense ...*
>
> *As pure as each loved one was in the Renaissance-spring: so holy shall each mother be in the summer we inaugurate ...*
>
> (SN, *Diaries*, 38-39)[43]

In "Christendom or Europe" Novalis had written:

> *All these things are still only hints, disjointed and rough, but to the historical eye they betray a universal individuality, a new history, a new humanity ... Who does not feel the sweet shame of being with child? ...*[44]

The impending event Novalis could only conceive of as happening on the basis of a prior experience of Christ's Redemption (as I show fully in Appendix I).

On the basis of what Rilke had presented in considerable depth in the Florence Diary, and again aphoristically and so memorably in "Monastic Life", it is very likely that Rilke was himself meant to go a way roughly similar to the one Novalis went. However, he was diverted from this path and, as it were, cast from it—this after Lou's indifferent response to his Florence-experience forced him to give this path up. Instead Rilke was directed towards Russia after Lou's own heart, and in the meantime his vision for Western experience had been forced underground. It would re-appear in his later work (from Duino onwards) after a long period of repression, very significantly altered, almost in ruins—and yet grandly so, for Rilke had in the meantime kept the dream alive through all the odds that had been laid against him.[45] For now, he had embraced quite another direction, almost without reserve, so given was he to what life had to offer him he felt sure he had found his God in these new terms. Rilke had been repressed in his own experience, going now another way, one in which the actual extent of God's presence in the creation had become his focus beyond the question of this God's work of Redemption—a question that, in the meantime, had been begged.[46] Rilke's path had gone from Botticelli's anguished longing, the longing that would embrace the full process of Christ's Redemption that escaped him, to the Russian's already created, working, and omnipresent God. In the meantime, what Rilke had come into was an apparently unreserved openness to experience that left no room for doubt in him that the gates to life—to "everything"—*had* opened. This is what, without her being quite fully able to anticipate this, Lou had made possible for him by the direction she had prescribed.

***

Rilke's sudden new experience of God was made possible through the depth of a "pure longing" (RANS 47) of a significantly different sort from the "longing" he had conceived in the Florence Diary. The new "longing" is already implied in the fifth poem from the sequence, in "I *cherish* my mind's hours of the dark" (7). Rilke's need to highlight this ground-impulse of his creation is what explains the otherwise improperly assimilated poems which bring in the young monk and his interposed complaints about the many sensual urges he feels (likewise as an icon-painter) that are threatening to tear him apart (27). These urges the narrator monk condemns (several pages later) as arising from "the glow and beat of the blood" (45) and "your blind blood". This issue, which was to concern Rilke so troublingly later in the Elegies, is here categorically resolved: it is not for the young monk to express himself in his art through a sensual longing; this threatens, in the end, to stifle his spiritual will, as "the pallid faces of the shrine/flush and flicker with alien fires—/and .../your serpent-senses dance". One must understand that underlying the natural forces of the blood is something deeper that links one spiritually to God, the "longing" precisely that has freed itself from the sensual need to grab hold for oneself which paradoxically will only leave one dispossessed:

> But there are night-alley rumours sourced in **God**
> That run unquenchably in your dark blood.
>
> (RANS 45)

Of himself, the narrator-monk says:

> *my blood*
> *rushes on, full of its murmurings*
> *but in my substance I am pure longing.*

(RANS 47)

All this is well-taken, but the point could easily have been made without the uncalculated intrusion of the young monk, and *is* made, both elaborately and extensively, in the rest of the sequence. The issue of the "blood", is, in any case, a non-issue for Rilke at this time, unlike in the rest of his *oeuvre* where it will take on a decidedly sombre cast, both in its sensual and sexual significances.[47] In the present sequence Rilke's focus is on another area of pretense to direct knowledge, or another misguided kind of impulse to grasp, which takes the form of ecstatic flight. He is especially intent on resisting the notion that God can be known in this way: God is not even in the transcendental light through which He can reveal himself but rather stands behind this radiated light as its originary source. Projecting his own "longing" for God in the form of an "angel", Rilke says of this angel that "He wants nothing of unbounded flight" (RANS 31), even though Rilke is himself disposed to such flight. Speaking in a sort of Miltonic self-take—"I return from my swinging pulse, where/I had lost myself' (61)—Rilke is conscious of taking stock of himself, "returning" from flight to work deliberately at being "serene again", aware as he is of the limits to God's revelation through the light:

> *I was as far as angels are,*
> *high, where the emptying light runs thin*
> *but God deep dark*

It is the great temptation of his time, Rilke notes, to project oneself into the role of "angels" who "believe more in the light than in their far/God's sombre might" (63). Rilke equates this temptation to make everything of the light, predictably, with Lucifer, but Lucifer as he appeared in Rilke's time, in the guise, e.g., of Nietzsche, of whom so much was mistakenly being made just because of his wilful struggle to continually even everything out, quite impossibly:

> *He is the shining god of our time,*
> *waking it with a shout,*
> *and, for he often **cries in pain***

> *and laughs in pain again,*
> *it* ['the time'] *calls all blessings on his name*
> *and hangs hard on his might.*

The contrast between the nature of Lucifer's might and of God's might (as above) will be noted. However, any ultimate cultural achievement in any period of time is, in the end, simply "discarded" by God in "fatigue" or weariness of its limitations. God is rather *continually* in the process of revealing Himself; He is doing so out of those dark depths of our existence that transcend every cultural achievement and every period of time. To grasp *this* is to understand *how* we are involved at last in "completing" God and how He "completes" Himself. On the basis of this understanding, Rilke, through his narrator-monk, thus boldly invites God to "come/at last to the peace of your completion" (RANS 29). There will be an end to the pretension to "reach" Him in any grasping, formal way, artistic or otherwise, and a real effort, rather, to gather Him continually in one form of manifestation or another, from one period of time to another. In our very "wrestling" with Him, Rilke adds, He will be "ripening us as we wrestle". Thus the continual attempt to help God into manifestation *is* the way to complete Him. This requires, at bottom, that typical Rilkean disposition of "openness" to experience that Rilke presents here as a case of God "foregathering" all experience, great and small: "Desire him or not/God foregathers" (19). At the same time, none of this "foregathering" becomes reality for us without the knowing mediation of the artist, or any such representative human being, who must first offer himself as the space through which alone God can reveal Himself today. And so we find Rilke, in the guise of the narrator/monk/painter, equally insisting, in a bold claim of worthiness: "*I am* your space" (21)[48]. Quite as much depends on the human I making itself properly available for God's revelation as it does on His own readiness, at all times and in all places, to reveal Himself—always assuming that circumstances can be propitious for this profound ongoing dynamic. As Rilke especially was to discover, circumstances could radically undermine such a dynamic, even positively militate against any creative "opening" for us. But at this particular moment in time, clearly the circumstances became uniquely right for him, and, as a consequence, Rilke, the great poet, had arrived.

However, we need to note, for our understanding in the long run, that in experiencing life and the world in this way, Rilke was now working *outside* the process of Redemption that had become his focus in his Florentine experience. Over a year later, we find him suddenly catapulted, as it were, into what is, contrastingly, a direct I-Thou relationship with God. In this relationship God is both a given and a total fact: "Let everything happen to you" (RANS 79). The human I, for its part, is made suddenly worthy of mediating Him by itself, so long as it understands that God reveals Himself in a continual state of becoming through every one of His manifestations in turn: "from recurrence to recurrence" (55). That Rilke finds himself working outside the process of Redemption at this point is signaled to us by the fact that it is not God Who redeems him but he, Rilke the representative artist, who redeems God. This new understanding is impressively represented in the following lines:

> *And on the void we lie like balm*
> *to veil your gashed, broken places*
> *your boundless wound, the void, cooled*
> *by application of the world,*
> *and here imperceptibly, healed.*
>
> (RANS 49)

In fact we find God in no other way than out of the "darkness" (13), the dark "unknown", from which we issued from Him—Rilke sounding here very much like the Novalis of *Hymns to the Night*:

> *Darkness of night, out of which I came,*
> *I love you more than the flame*
> *that circumscribes the world*
> *by lending gleam*
> *Darkness confines all things*
> *I believe in the night.*

In spite of the similarity in expression, however, it is quite another condition out of which Rilke proceeds inasmuch as this darkness *includes* that fallen condition Novalis had himself transcended by the time *he* is invoking the power of the Night.[49] It is the great paradox of Rilke's idea of God in these poems that, by offering ourselves to

Him out of this darkness that includes our fallenness, we actually help to complete God as well as ourselves, inviting Him to "suffer the dark/the dark we do to you" (29). It is a function of this fallenness that Rilke and his God are not always there together; God and the human I must both reach out from where each finds Himself/himself. However, a baptismal event has already bound us together with God;

> *I inclined my head*
>
> ....
>
> *and saw you (as it was later told)*
>
> ....
>
> *above me and the world.*
>
> (RANS 53)

In the general fate, Rilke found himself straying for a time, until he was again suddenly surrendered to his God out of his fallenness. Upon this surrender, there followed a shared darkness with God in which they found themselves mingling very uncertainly:

> *a little struggle, and I gave.*
> *Your long darkness wraps round*
> *your velvet victory.*
>
> *You have me now, not knowing me,*
> *For your extending senses find*
> *just that I have darkened.*

In this paradoxically tense association, Rilke finds himself, still, close to his God, insisting on their inevitable rapprochement and ultimate identification with each other. It is the dominant emphasis in these poems, one in which Rilke appears very much like John Donne of English tradition, though without Donne's additional mocking irony or anxiety about this situation. There is every manner of reminder that creature and Creator are indissolubly linked. Thus, filling out the view that "I am your space" (RANS 21) are the added comments: "I am what you dream" and "I am your will" (23). Like Donne, Rilke insists on an existence of his own that is yet indissociable from his God: "*I am*, you Anxious One" (25)—the anxiety, about a rapprochement between them, being in this case reversed, not associated with humankind but projected rather onto God.[50] Separate yet indissociable, Rilke, like Donne, is ready both to admit to his pride and to integrate it into his proceedings, so long as the force of Rilke's will, which is all he has to drive him, is directed to an audience with his God:

> *Overweeningly proud? Be it so, for my prayer's sake*
> *standing now so wholly alone*
> *and solemn at your clouded brow.*
>
> (RANS 13)

> *I need my will, to go with it as it drives.*
>
> (RANS 15)

It is as if only a thin wall separated Rilke from God, composed merely of an insubstantiality in their relation to each other: "[b]etween us only an insubstantial wall" (7). And there seems to Rilke no point otherwise to their existence if it is not to know each other at firsthand: "for who am I and who are you/should neither know the other's face?" (65). And rather more like Shakespeare in his Sonnets appealing to the revelation of his God, the God of his immortal beloved, Rilke sees no point to failing each other while he is still alive since his death will only put away forever the chance of God's knowing him:

> *What will you do, God, when I die?*
> *Your glance ...*
> *... will lose me, seek me—*
> *and settle ...*
> *into some lap of alien stone.*
>
> (RANS 43)[51]

The potential parallel with Donne, as well as with Shakespeare, is some measure of the large extent to which Rilke writes in these poems as a Western European, far removed from the more natural assumption of a fully established relation with his God typical of the Orthodox Russian with whom Rilke only appears to be aligning himself. The Russian devotee Rilke has in mind never did feel the distance from his God that Rilke often feels about his. The Russian context of these poems, including the use of an icon-painter from that tradition as a narrating framework for the poems, has been greatly over-emphasized both by critics and by Rilke himself. Apart from the narrator/monk/painter who technically narrates the whole, there are comparatively few references in these poems to the Russian context that is invoked[52]; as for the rest of the poems' material, this could be referred to almost any Western European cultural context and for the most part is frankly revealing of Rilke's own experience. Rilke would, later in life, famously say that at the time "Russia was reality" but it would have been truer of him to say that Russia happened to be how and where Rilke found *his* reality.[53] The narrator/monk/painter is generally a mere mask, a persona that allows Rilke to give expression to, by Western standards, a somewhat more unconventional idea of the experience of God. Over the course of *The Book of Hours* as a whole this narrator/monk grows thinner and thinner as a presence, turning at some point beyond "Monastic Life" into a mere metaphor, until in the last of the three books he fades completely out of view. Hence, my assumption that it is Rilke himself who is always speaking in these poems even when there is the slight and in fact only occasional suggestion of the dramatic mask speaking. What certainly impressed Rilke about the Russian religious devotee was his sense of the constant presence of God, a God who, it seemed, could be concretely invoked at any time and without any great concern otherwise that He should have to reveal Himself dramatically. This was, in turn, not a Western attitude. Thus, the poet can also fall back on the view that

> *I need not know your whereabouts;*
> *speak from the world around*
> *... I at least can always approach you*
> (RANS 65)

Here, then, is the other main tendency in Rilke's rather mixed approach to his theme. Fallen yet potentially redeeming, in close proximity yet separate, Rilke is in the end also content with being simply ready—to sense, here and there, the "trace" (27) of his God's presence quite apart from any incidental points of direct experience of his God. These latter appear, in fact, very rarely in this work. In an early poem he claims "in a dream" (19) to

> *... have overseen*
> *your gilded space,*
> *from its deep foundations*
> *up to the highest golden groin.*

Speaking more openly through the consciousness of his narrator-monk, Rilke refers to the many drafts the monk has attempted all of which in their unsatisfactoriness of expression "sickened and spoiled" (59):

> *... until there sprang from deep*
> *inside me, with a leap*
> *out of the sure to the unknown,*
> *the holiest of forms.*

There is also a strong intention to represent God directly through the forces at work in Nature:

> *I want to narrate you ...*
> *... with ink of apple-tree rind*
>
> (RANS 81)

This intention extends to this God's tendency to manifest Himself through the "gentlest gesture" (87) of Nature, as in the "twilight and its tender extents" (87). Primarily, however, Rilke's natural God manifests directly as the profound rhythmic force of Rilke's own poetry, which is explicitly recognized, for example in the following lines:

> *... an impulsive*
> *energy takes me ...*
> ....
> *With this flowing out and issuing*
> *wide-armed to the open sea,*
> *with this filling surge of returning,*
> *I shall announce and honour you more*
> *than any before.*
>
> (RANS 13)

In this "flowing out and issuing" (to a great extent as the peculiar force of his insistent rhyming) Rilke can even lose himself as we have seen:

> *I return from my swinging impulses, where*
> *I had lost myself. For there*
> *song was my name—and God the rhyme*
> *rushes still in the ear.*
>
> (RANS 61)

However, Rilke is equally conscious of stemming this massive tide, to allow for a proper manifestation of his God Who *will* be seen flowing through it:

> *In the mind's eye often I see*
> *your ubiquity slipping part from part*
> *as you pass across ...*
>
>   (RANS 55)

> *... all your deeps*
> *pass me unstopping as they rise.*
>
>   (RANS 79)

In the seventh-to-last poem of this highly varied and eclectic sequence, Rilke invokes the Last Judgment as the hour when God will take back into Himself His own image, until then largely "unfinished" (83). The longstanding efforts of cities and even of churches to ape His greatness, Rilke says, God will have patiently borne with, giving these one or two more hours to blazon themselves, while to those who are, contrastingly, "redeemed" He will be granting several more "hours" of necessary, additional "struggle and toil" and, to the highest among these more, "work on the soil", the soil in which *they* can actually commune with God. Rilke has, throughout "Monastic Life", offered a whole history of human and religious endeavor, in one way or another associated with a consciousness of God. Thus, among the many "builders" (RANS 29) are the ancient monks and folkloric pagan peoples (81), theologians (71), tsars (67) in their church-building, painters and sculptors—including Botticelli (39) and Michelangelo (33); poets, girls, youths (71), simple praying folk (51), and among the genuine "workers" (31) apprentices, journeymen and masters: the whole gamut of both misguided and genuine seekers after God who will have appeared since the first crime against Abel was committed (13, 25) when the possibility of a direct communing with God was first taken away. Counting himself confidently among the redeemed, or rather the redeeming, Rilke now asks for yet seven more "hours" for himself to add to his work. These are the seven last poems of his sequence.

Thus would Rilke put off the Last Judgment, in order, once and for all, to prove himself in the power "to love each thing like no-one before" (83). The Last Judgment he projects as "the hour of inconceivable fear", and it is "after the night, after fear" (85) that, in the poem that follows, he "wake[s]/... in the assured grace/... that I shall see your face". This "night" of "fear", which is to be distinguished from the "night" out of which Rilke emerged from his God at birth and once again at the time of these poems, is an indication that all is not well in the world of the poet's imagination, in spite of a successful show of association with his God in the rest of the sequence. The poet's formal acknowledgment of "fear" towards the end of the sequence is a far cry from the Faust-like confidence with which Rilke enters the sequence, as where he had boasted: "Your whole heaven turns to listen to me/for in your presence I muse wordlessly" (21). Rilke, like Goethe's Faust, is now momentarily undone but will soon be speaking of *recovering* his confidence (again like Faust on "waking"[54]), and final efforts on behalf of the completion of his God follow in the last six poems. The process of recovery at this point is revealing as Rilke finds himself once again riding the tide of his fluidic capacity to be with his God:

> *So I wake full of a child's trust,*
> *in the assured grace*
> *after the night, after fear,*
> *that I shall see your face.*
>
> *Measuring you, I am aware*
> *how deep, long, wide—*
> ....
> *I thank you, energy profound,*
> *for your handling of me ...*

(RANS 85)

In those last two lines, recovery is explicitly related back to the "impulsive energy" (13) or "will" ("will" in quite another sense than the Western "will") that the poet had noted "drives" (15) his fluidic creation. Such fluidic creation is more nearly recognized here as a case of being directly "handled" by his God.[55]

Along our way through this sequence, we will have noted how underlying the poet's effort of association with his God, if only as a barely hinted concern, is his awareness of the subversive power of time. Earlier, the poet had considered specifically the menace of an untimely death, which, Faust-like, he had grandly dismissed.

Considering Death, the poet had boasted:

> *I cannot imagine him a serious threat;*
> *I am alive, have time to build; my blood*
> *is red for longer than the roses are.*
>
> (RANS 41)

The thought of death can take the form of the fear of non-being, but this additional potential menace the poet had likewise put away from himself with the thought that, just because death signifies non-being, God cannot afford, for his completion, to do without the poet remaining alive; God would have everything to lose by the poet's untimely death:

> *What will you do, God, when I die?*
>
> (RANS 43)

Nevertheless, thoughts of non-being and the possibility of being undermined by time have, in the last part of "Monastic Life", come suddenly closer to the poet. He is more concerned now about the time that remains to him to pronounce on the required work of completion. (Here Rilke's own personal anxiety about time becomes obvious.) The need for completion, as well as the potential for it, suddenly looms larger than ever in his consciousness, especially as human efforts to reach God have over the centuries grown progressively weaker and weaker, leaving Him virtually alone in His element today:

> *That some time ago I was not, are you*
> *aware? ... If I ask*
> *release from haste, if I can slow,*
> *I shall hold out against the past.*
>
> *For I am more than dream in dream*
> *... [or] the reachers after borders*
> ....
> *... following their freedoms;*
>
> *The dark is left you, yours alone,*
> *and into the further empty span*
> *arose a world history*
> *built of an ever blinder stone.*
>
> (RANS 87)

This situation seems to the poet to be all the more urgent as God seems otherwise to have been always so ready and so willing to manifest, having done so especially "in the old familiar signs" of religion:

> *You willing, full source: your grace was always*
> *manifest in the old familiar signs*
>
> (RANS 89)

In the last two poems or "hours" that are left to him, in the broad testimony he would offer, the poet seems especially intent on properly rounding out his audience with God. He contemplates this task so as to clear the ground for continued work on His completion in the future:

> *One hour from the end of day,*
> *and the land is prepared for what comes.*
>
> (RANS 91)

From out of the "night" that is coming, he declares, a singer will be brought forth to show the way. Rilke here brings forward his monumental figure of the Ancient who himself abides in this "night" whence He is pictured blindly throwing out his songs to an unresponding world. He, the poet Rilke, on the other hand, has heard the Ancient's songs, the songs he has made his own, which is to say those he has so far preserved. These songs now "run back" (93) to the Ancient in an established circuitry of inspirational collaboration that the poet feels will more than likely secure the opening to God's world that he intends for the future, in the time, that is to say, that will remain to him, having successfully negotiated with God for time, at least up to this point:

> *And yet it has happened to me*
> *as though each song I heard*
> *I saved and hid for him.*
>
> *He* ['the Ancient'] *is silent behind his beard,*
> *eager to flourish again*
> *in his melodies.*
> *Then I approach to his knees:*
>
> *and his songs run*
> *rushingly back to him ...*

And so ends, for now, Rilke's monumental project bearing on the ongoing "completion" of his God. Grandly overextended as we will feel "Monastic Life" is, it is very unlikely that Lou would not have recognized in this extraordinary sequence of poems not just the promise of greatness in Rilke but a suddenly already realized capacity for it, all the more astonishing in a young man who, at the time, was not yet twenty-four. Even so, we have noted Lou's insistent distance, a strange degree of indifference in her to the full depth and scope of Rilke's poetic undertaking, not to mention the comprehensive originality of his vision. On the other side of the elusive equation between them, Rilke had for his part come a long way to meeting Lou, for one thing in the "God-creating" she had impressively championed for years; Russia, also, had been Lou's gift to him. But there had been more to Rilke's achievement in "Monastic Life" than Lou's "God-creating", which was for her a purely subjective creating, however much one's own creating of God had the "back-effect" of suggesting a God of objective presence.[56] For her this was only ever the illusion of an objective presence, whereas it seems fairly clear that, in spite of his own highly deliberate effort of God-creating in "Monastic Life", Rilke's God is quite His own Being, occupying His own sphere and waiting to be met on His own terms. There is, additionally, Rilke's historical notion of "completing" God, which likewise goes beyond the repertory of Lou's ideas about God-creating, since God-creating in Lou's conception simply repeats itself in different forms from age to age, without teleology. Likewise does Rilke's notion of "God-redeeming" extend beyond the range of Lou's God-creating, especially when this is seen in conjunction with the notion of "completing" God. There was thus already, even for Lou, much to engage Rilke over and much to learn from him at this time, and yet Lou's range of concerns had passed much of this over, at least sufficiently to have added to Rilke's sense of being demeaned, and he was understandably resentful for this generally.

What he had repressed of his own rivaling spirit, as we have seen, at last came to the fore, bringing on what was to be the decisive crisis between them on their second trip to Russia in the summer of 1900. Almost a full year had passed since Rilke had composed "Monastic Life", and he was, no doubt, feeling the pressure of the lull. This profoundly problematic situation we have already covered (see above pp.13-15, as well as p.46): Lou was, for a significant part of that second trip, in fact both physically and mentally inaccessible to Rilke. It was in quite another mood and on the basis of quite another relationship that Lou and Rilke would meet again over Rilke's extension of his work on God, after a long tragic separation, about five years later. Again one can only wonder at what would have come of a more equal and more grounded relationship between them of the kind Rilke had always hoped for and was still hoping for as late as the time of that second trip. In Lou and Rilke, two cultural periods of time, the nineteenth-century and the modern, had touched borders, but there was to be no real interassociation between them, until each had experienced the loss of the other. Even so the relationship between them, after they were re-united, was to be more along the lines of an *emotional* understanding in Lou, without any specific commitment on her part to Rilke's own programme of ideas. Nevertheless, such understanding was offered now on the basis of a more genuine recognition that Rilke, the great poet and mind, had indeed arrived, and that the "ascension of the work" had at last gotten the better of the romantic tangle that had so tragically embroiled them to the great pain of each for a long period of time.

II

Worpswede and After

In spite of the grand style in which he had finished off "The Book of Monastic Life", as if proclaiming a life-long commitment to his mission of "completing" God, Rilke would not carry on with *The Book of Hours* until a full year after his second trip to Russia, which is to say two years after finishing "Monastic Life". Rilke's long frustrated struggle with Lou had brought them to a real breaking-point, and by the time he felt he could return to *The Book of Hours*, his life had changed radically. In the meantime, Rilke had separated from Lou, had suddenly married Clara Westhoff, and a child by this marriage was expected. Thus very much had happened to Rilke in the interval between the time "Monastic Life" was written and "The Book of Pilgrimage", the second part of *The Book of Hours*. There had been another case of a romantic tangle that would leave Rilke in a still more complicated state of suspension than he had been with Lou. In addition to the difficult position Rilke was in with Lou, while at Worpswede Rilke had met, along with Clara, Paula Becker with whom he would also develop an intense relationship. Both Clara and Paula were Rilke's contemporaries in age, and, for a while, he had some form of romantic feeling going with both. Rilke would eventually marry Clara, but it is his relationship to Paula especially that has whetted the interest of critics because of the comparatively greater attention he would appear to have given to her. Some have gathered that Rilke was quite smitten with Paula and that he was (at least speculatively) concocting plans for them, and that he regretted never proposing to her as he might have.[57] It has also been thought that Rilke left Worpswede one morning without goodbyes, after developing a very close relationship to the whole Worpswede group, because he had learned that Paula had been engaged for months to another painter in the Worpswede school, named Modersohn.[58] Whether this was the case or not, the reasons Rilke gives Paula for absconding from Worpswede, in a letter he wrote some two weeks after leaving, were that he had to get back to his own world and his own studies, which he could not continue to neglect and which he continued to see in association with Russia and, of course, Lou.

The irony of this step back to Lou was that Rilke had already, in a shockingly sudden way, passed on into a whole new world and a whole new life from which there would be no return. One could say that this new world had opened up to him from as far back as the time he completed "Monastic Life". It was already being prepared when, in his assurance of the powers he had achieved with "Monastic Life", Rilke threw himself into the many diverse poetic explorations that dot the Schmargendorf Diary between the time of that achievement and the time of the second trip to Russia. Still, the fact that he suddenly found himself powerfully drawn into quite another world at Worpswede must have been shocking to him and finally very disconcerting. In little more than a month, he had plunged into relationships with two serious-minded young artist-women of his own age, and he had learned from them, and from their group, a whole new way of looking at the world that would greatly deepen especially his lyrical powers. The entries in the Schmargendorf Diary for this time are highly revealing of his development in this respect. It is a poignant experience to watch him slowly warming to the Worpswede group, whom he would come to feel suddenly so intensely close to, from an initial attitude that was quite distant and less than admiring. He was still steeped at this point in Russia and, despite their antagonisms, in Lou, and initially it is Nature at Worpswede that absorbs Rilke's attention rather than the Worspwede group itself, whom he critiqued for their indulgence in their raw pleasures. Until one night, withdrawing into his room as host to the party (in the Master Vogeler's place), and with his door left open and now at his open window (see SN, *Diaries*, 156-157), Rilke was joined in his landscape-watching by Paula and Clara who were transformed by the scene. Suddenly he was watching Nature also through these young artists' bewitched eyes; his window had suddenly opened out onto a whole new world for him.

He would learn a great deal from the special insightful "looking" of these girls and the Worpswede group generally, painfully aware, in comparison, of the inadequacy of his own looking, which had become an issue lately, after his second stay in Russia:

> *The Russian journey with its daily losses remains for me such painful evidence that my eyes haven't ripened yet: they don't understand how to take in, how to hold, nor how to let go; burdened with tormenting images, they walk past things of beauty and toward disappointments.*
>
> (SN, *Diaries*, 195)

Contrastingly, he was now in the company of such as made looking, in the form Rilke felt was his great need, into their way of life. Against the burdensome pressure of merely inward images thrown out from himself without regard to the reality of things outside him, and so potentially disillusioning, Rilke could now oppose images that were constantly impressing themselves upon him from the world around:

> *I am gradually beginning to comprehend this life ... this thousandfold seeing and seeing always **away** from oneself ... this being only eye ... because something always is happening. ... How richly these people must travel! ... what a wonderful language they must possess, what images for everything experienced! Then they must confide themselves the way landscapes do ...*
>
> (SN, *Diaries*, 162-163)

Ten days later his experience had already grown out immensely, and he could allow himself still broader generalizations:

> *Almost all observations confined to a small area can, if they are only undertaken seriously and diligently enough, be understood as a symbol for something larger, as images for vast processes and relations that configure themselves a thousand times within smaller dimensions.*
>
> (SN, *Diaries*, 180)

And while on a visit of several days to Vogeler in Adiek, Rilke could not help already feeling homesick for Worpswede, especially:

> *for its high, rapturous skies beneath which the shadows of so many images and gestures and objects also are constantly moving.*

Needless to say, it was the whole group of Worpswede artists who had opened Rilke's eyes to the world's phenomena, but notably Paula and Clara, especially from the time of their transformation on that night. Suddenly these "girls" had made an especially deep impression on him. A few days before he had already noted Paula for her "seriousness" and Clara for her "dark vitality" (SN, *Diaries*, 146); on the night of their landscape-gazing, Rilke takes note more particularly of Clara's "beautiful dark face" (SN, *Diaries*, 155). Even so, the poet remained aloof: impressed upon as he was by the "girls", through whom the being of things is known, or so he implies in a poem Rilke wrote just then, yet "[n]one may ever give herself to the poet" (SN, *Diaries*, 157), for, in order to create, the poet must remain "alone in his garden", given up to the dark depths of his creative calling, and with "no whiteness beneath the dark birch trees". It is also with regret that the poet must let go of these "girls" whom he poignantly remembers after they pass back into the social spheres that degrade his purpose and vocation. Thus of the more mature men, including those of the Worpswede group, who threaten the purity of the young poet's experience and motivation, even of those whom the poet considers "like-minded" (SN, *Diaries*, 159), the poet asks:

> *Who muses on things the same as he?*
> *Who stands bowed over God?*
> *Who keeps silent?*
> *And where*

> *might **that one** be found*
> *who fled from the garish feast of men?*

Rilke writes here still very much in the mode of "The Book of Monastic Life", where he had proudly claimed "purity of longing". There is, in fact, an especially strong sense in Rilke of being sustained in his vocation by "that one" whom he continued to celebrate even beyond the writing of "Monastic Life", on whom he continues to rely for supporting inspiration, and who cannot be known while oneself is drawn away into "the garish feast of men". As to that other kind of life, with which Rilke at first associates the Worpswede group, one month after completing "Monastic Life" he had put it this way:

> *How will you usher into this night*
> *That one person, the very One*
> *Whose single glance transported you*
> *To ecstasy or tears ...*
> *..................................*
> *where will you go with this one person*
> *if you've used up your night?*
>
> (SN, *Diaries*, 119)

It is all the more telling, then, to watch Rilke slowly weaned from his high-minded aloofness, sufficiently to acknowledge the wonderful power of selfless "looking" that otherwise animated the Worpswede group in their serious work. In only a few days Rilke would be singing the group's praises (163); over the course of only one week already his appreciation had grown exponentially, sparked by additional meetings with Clara and especially with Paula ("How much I learn in watching these two girls, especially the blond paint-er", i.e., Paula—173). This alteration in Rilke's experience had much to do also with the special capacity for "listening" he found in these "girls", which they displayed notably on those party-nights when he read out his poems, but also generally. All this was enough to take Rilke away from himself and to transport him to a brave new world where he more easily found acceptance; "images" that came from him also seemed to find a rich correspondence now with the world, where before they were but dream-laden:

> *My whole life is full of the images with which I can talk to them*

... new material, simple material, those nuances of feeling that had previously been bound up in overly complex concerns.

(SN, *Diaries*, 173-174)

It was just the sort of listening that Lou had not been able to offer Rilke, and it once again points to the idea that his difficult bouts of resentment and depression while with Lou had much to do with a failure of intuitive comprehension in her that rendered her deaf to the more lyrical basis of Rilke's sensibility, which could not be repressed. Into the fourth week of his stay at Worpswede, Rilke had begun to forget this oppression and could see clearly for himself what an emancipation of his poetic sensibility had come already from his short time among the "girls". In his Diary he adds, with further reference to his recent time in Russia ("the grand tour"):

Here [in Worpswede] *I have no memories. My eyes won't let themselves close...*

Here I can once again simply go along, become, be someone who changes.

On the grand tour it was a great burden to have to be someone who is firm, someone who stands, someone who remains immovable in the face of the profusely fleeting, the always unexpected ...

At Worpswede Rilke could at last be listened to because he was among those who, as well as looking, like himself had made a life of listening. Rilke had already noted this of Clara on that night of transformation:

Every time I looked at her this evening she was beautiful in a different way. Especially in her listening, when that aspect of her face that is sometimes too strong is bound up in something unknown. Then the rhythm of restrained, listening life imprints herself on her figure, softly as among folds. She waits, completely given over, for whatever she is about to experience ...

(SN, *Diaries*, 155)

Then there is that extraordinary moment shared with Paula, some four days later, when Rilke visited her at her studio, returning a previous visit of hers to him about a week before:

We made our way towards each other through conversations and

silences. It was a very quiet occurrence, as if the world were turn-
ing more softly by several degrees of nuance. It was a shared hour
or a shared moment at the edge of that hour when I said: "... de-
siring the right thing ... one suddenly feels oneself to be devoutly
continuing, across all the intervening years and inner chasms,
one's childhood ... So often lately I've had the feeling of interlock-
ing with that place ..." And in this confession we were one. Knew
ourselves in what is past and what is to come ... Had suddenly
heard one another ... On a long road whose end no one could fore-
see we arrived at this point of eternity. Surprised and shuddering
we gazed at each other like two people who stand unexpectedly
before the gate behind which God has already arrived ...

(SN, *Diaries*, 169)

Episodes and comments such as these have led critics to suppose
that Rilke was growing amorous of Paula but, if he was, the irony at
his expense was great. For if Paula appeared to him so transfigured
in these moments it is because she was basking in the radiance of
her joy at being now engaged to Otto Modersohn, the engagement
having taken place only the day before the episode recorded above.
Then there is the famous scene in the barouche one week later during
the Worpswede group's journey to Bremen. Otto Modersohn himself
was in the barouche along with Rilke and Paula. The barouche itself
had been filled with flowers, as in the meantime Rilke held in his
hands an elaborate wreath of heather that Clara had artfully woven
together and given to him:

So I rode holding Clara Westhoff's large heather wreath, and
across from me the blond painter sat ... In her lively brown eyes
I saw much of the agitated, wandering land ... and ... [e]ven as
I write this I can feel again her eyes, whose dark cores were so
smooth and hard, slowly unfolding, how like ripening roses ...

(SN, *Diaries*, 182)

Yet even in this episode we note a degree of interest in Paula and in
Clara that seems almost perfectly balanced:

Thus I savored the strength of the one girl with my propped-up
hands, and out of the dear face of the other something gentle
came towards me from which all humility takes heart.

Even as great listeners, along with Rilke, the two were hardly to be distinguished:

> *Slowly I place first one word, then another, on the delicate balance of their two souls ... And ... my ... words ... play, without either pan ever dropping, within the two shores of equilibrium.*
>
> (SN, *Diaries*, 174)

In fact, as one critic has duly noted[59], quite as much attention is given to one as to the other in Rilke's Diary entries generally, in spite of the apparently greater intensity of Rilke's encounters with Paula. From the time of that overwhelming impression she made that first night, Clara was growing on Rilke in every way as much, only differently, through narrations of her experiences that were no less captivating. What very much impressed him about these was the evidence they gave of Clara's great capacity for self-sacrifice, her ability to give herself with a complete generosity to everything and everyone outside herself. Several such narrations are given in Rilke's Diary. The most striking concerns the time when at the very moment she was about to leave for the adventurous life she was looking forward to in Paris, she was asked to stay behind to sculpt her father's mother, in this way sacrificing her own desires, but not for this any less devoted to the task she had been asked to perform. Rilke would make very much of this story later, as we shall see. An essential difference between Clara and Paula is tellingly revealed in another episode with Paula that paints Clara more advantageously, even if the qualities to be compared between them are superior qualities each in its own right. Paula had commented to Rilke on Clara's disposition in words that he transcribed:

> *'It often moves me to watch how Clara, whose instincts as a sculptor are so strong and monumental, will cup a single flower in her hands, a single flower, or apply to some small object all the kindness and fullness of her broad being ... so that it almost collapses under the weight of love. Watching this makes me melancholy. Watching how she contracts herself, withdraws herself from her own dimensions ...'*
>
> (SN, *Diaries*, 203-204)

To which Rilke's response, as he writes in his Diary, is:

> *You blessed girl, you see such things in your friend and see them and say them so beautifully. And don't know what greatness and good fortune it is to become so selfless and dedicated in the context of another's life.*

Yet Paula had her own degree of deep "kindness" (206), as yet another entry on this same day records.

Certainly what Paula offered Rilke was a more richly inward experience of communion with the world, though one that Paula experienced very much in herself, and in any case on grounds quite different than Rilke supposed, whereas Clara lived things out more outside herself with a strong, if only somewhat less subtle, inward intensity all her own. It is an even bet what captivated Rilke more between these two women, but such a complementary combination of superior qualities, especially as shared with him, was enough to make Rilke feel quite blessed and more than ready to stay on at Worpswede, so integral to the Worpswede group as a whole and so appreciated did he feel in this totally accepting company. He had felt this especially on his return to Worpswede after their recent, long and successful group excursion to Hamburg:

> *And how they love me here. How good our time together was in Hamburg. How they responded to me as a counselor and helper. How requisite I was to them. And how I grew strong enough under the shelter of their trust to be everything they needed ... All strengths rise in me. All life gathers in my voice.*
>
> (SN, *Diaries*, 195)

It is as if the old confidence Rilke had felt about himself two years before when in Florence was returning to him, and indeed over the week that followed this pronouncement, feeling now fully one amongst them all, and after deciding to rent his own place in Worpswede, Rilke only grew more and more in confidence. Numerous fine poems punctuated a sudden fresh surge of enthusiasm in him—including the poem famously written in honour of Paula to be later titled "The Singer Sings before a Child of Nobles"—on "[t]hese days so rich with gifts" (215) as he puts it in an entry for the 3rd of October. On that same day at another group gathering in Paula's studio, Rilke had once again read from his poems with the same effect he was accustomed to, and then remarkably rich and involved "conversations" (221) had ensued, with Rilke very much at the centre of these, about God and about Christ and how the tragic sadness of "every past" will shed "its heaviness" and become "brilliance" and about how "All heirs bear their deceased fates like jewelry" (222).

And then, so suddenly as it seems, the bell tolled. Astoundingly, the morning after Rilke set down these entries in his Diary, which is to say on the morning of the 5th of October, he was gone from Worpswede, not to return. More than one commentator has speculated that at this point Rilke received a summons from Lou, in no uncertain terms to leave Worpswede and to report to Berlin. According to this view, Lou would appear to have known what was going on at Worpswede (one cannot think she would have warmed to the glowing eulogies that Rilke offers in his diary on Worpswede and especially the "girls", Clara and Paula), and it is easy to imagine her stepping in at some point to put an end to the direction Rilke was taking, which, quite explicitly as we have seen, was away from that fundamental experience of his that he himself symbolically associated with Russia and with Lou. We cannot know if a summons from Lou is the reason why Rilke left Worpswede. We remain in the dark likewise in the case of the optional theory that he left Worpswede because he was utterly distraught to hear suddenly of Paula's engagement. Only two days before, he had written that famous poem on Paula:

> *Your life is so inexpressibly your own*
> *because it is laden with so many.*
>
> *... things trivial and difficult took place*
> *Only to give you ...*
> *a thousand great similes and likenesses.*
>
> (SN, *Diaries*, 214-215)

which makes of her a symbol comparable to what Shakespeare makes of the young man in his Sonnets: "What is thy substance, whereof are you made / That millions of strange shadows on you tend?" If, on the basis of this idealization of Paula, Rilke had had any designs on her so deep into his time at Worpswede and if he had had no idea that

Paula was engaged, then to hear of her engagement suddenly would certainly have driven him away in utter dismay. What we *do* know is that some portion of Rilke's Schmargendorf diary was torn out between the time of the 4th of October, which was Rilke's last entry while at Worpswede, and the 21st of October when Rilke's diary-writing resumes. A few highly expressive and deeply melancholic poems appear just before the entry of the 21st that may have been written close to that date, or not. We can only say that "at least one sheet [two pages] of the diary"[60] was removed, but there might, in fact, have been many more discarded scribblings in the period of over two weeks about which nothing remains to shed light on Rilke's thoughts or feelings at this time. Commentators who work from the theory of Rilke's dismay over Paula will assume that the lost pages held the key to his feelings about *this*, but it is just as possible that these pages bore testimony, as of old, of renewed disturbed frustration with Lou on returning to Berlin. Who knows if Rilke did not, at this point, go through yet another crisis, something along the lines of what he suffered on returning from Florence two years previously? because he was, after all, returning to someone who was not a listener in his terms, or open to the directions in which he himself was being drawn and which had lately taken him so deeply into his Worpswede experience. All this would apply whatever the reason may have been for Rilke's departure from Worpswede, whether this is taken to be from a broken heart or the sense of betrayal having to do with Paula or as the consequence of a summons received from Lou to return to the business of his self-development, as she saw it.

It is my own view that Rilke left Worpswede, as it appears to us so suddenly, because he had once again come powerfully into his God, the God of *The Book of Hours*, paradoxically just when it seemed that he was giving himself to a whole other world productive, among other things, of the poems that were to find a home in *The Book of Images*. Rilke's diary-writing at this time continues to give evidence of a strong undertow of God-directed purpose. Rilke was still ensconced in his God when he first made his appearance in Worpswede, submitting the social scene he encountered there to his characteristic God-based critique: "Who muses on things the same as he? / Who stands bowed over God? / Who keeps silent?" The Worpswede group, notably Paula and Clara, would soon convince Rilke that they could be quite as "silent" as he, and quite as wonderfully given over to God's world, if far less given to God in Rilke's specific terms. In fact, Rilke's God never leaves him during his time at Worpswede, and it is all to the point that when he finally indicates just how much at home he has become in Worpswede—"How they love me here ... And how I grow strong ... All strengths rise in me. All life gathers in my voice"—Rilke should refer this developing situation directly to his God, punctuating this moment of fresh homecoming with a typical "Prayer" as of old:

> *And again my deep life rushes louder,*
> *as if it moved now between steeper banks.*
> *Things seem ever more akin to me,*
> *all images more intensely seen.*
> *I've grown more at ease with the nameless,*
> *with my senses ... I reach*
> *into the windy heavens ...*
> *and into the small ponds' broken-off day*
> *my feeling sinks ...*
>
> (SN, *Diaries*, 196)

Rilke's image-seeing ability was growing, and it is here associated also with "things" his famous concern with which, usually linked to his *New Poems*, begins, in fact, as early as in "The Book of Monastic Life".[61] Both "images" and "things" are in turn further referred to Rilke's "deep life" with God, which Rilke describes as becoming "louder". He had thus continued in a relation to his God, and suddenly this relation was intensifying again powerfully. Four days after recording these impressions, Rilke had a tremendous religious experience while on a trek through the moors with the Worpswede group, which included on this occasion their founding father, Mackenson, newly arrived to their large company. The landscape, as it appeared to Rilke then, had literally become God's landscape:

> *The distances were ... simply: the earth ... over which the nations*
> *were scattered like dust in a storm ... too vast for man ... the earth*
> *which God still holds in his hand.*
>
> (SN, *Diaries*, 209)

Then Clara stood still, though it might have been anyone else, and suddenly all of them stood still in the midst of this landscape, themselves become things among all the rest of God's things:

The heath stood there dark and insensible ... and for a moment
Clara Westhoff's light, reed-green slenderness stood out against
the landscape with gray twilight air surrounding it, so ineffably
pure and great that we all grew solitary and each was completely
held in awe ... [T]hat impression ... removed me from human be-
ings and set me down in the object world, where the things mutely
endure one another's presence ...

(SN, Diaries, 209-210)

Focusing further on his company, Rilke having stepped back at some
distance from the rest as they now meandered on into this landscape,
he notes:

I began to experience them as more and more image-like, more
and more beautiful, more and more like landscape ... the figures
simply let ['the winding trail'] *take them along with it ... all of*
them lost in thought, oblivious to one another, striding ... against
the wind's resistance.

At this point, Rilke conceives of them as so many pilgrims, as depicted in one of the many devotional paintings he had seen at first
hand during his days in Florence:

This is how that rich wandering and aimless strolling of hu-
man beings ... entered the landscape ... in the background of a
Madonna ... small and moved to praise her rich, peaceful stature.

Only the day before this, at one of their regular Sunday gatherings, Rilke had had a similar epiphanic experience. It had struck
him with intensity how very blessed their group was to have each
other—"we all felt how beautiful it was and how fortunate we were to
have one another's company", and then Rilke suddenly heard voices
who were singing God's praise:

Now everyone was out on the dark forecourt ... [a]nd suddenly—
or is the wind deceiving me?—voices ... in the midst of a song
that is always in progress ... and I hear: "Praise be to God on
high..." And then I knew that this song ... is always present, and
that we become aware of it when we view singing profiles before
starry nights ... the voices had risen like fountains ...

(SN, Diaries, 216)

On this occasion Rilke had just made an impression on the group with a reading of one of his poems (on Paula and on Clara, most notably), and in a similar way, three evenings later (two evenings after the landscape experience) Rilke's reading would open up a whole discussion about God initiated principally by Paula who spoke up in reaction to Rilke's God-experience. It must have seemed even to the group that his God-experience had been growing while Rilke was amongst them. Rilke recorded what then took place one evening later, the evening before that fateful morning when he suddenly left Worpswede. In his entry he congratulates himself for speaking up on his God's behalf, first in a poem that recalls the idiom of "Monastic Life": "I spoke of You .../I named You .../... for whom I'm dark and still .../... in whom I've never erred .../Your growing now goes on beyond me" (SN, *Diaries*, 219).

Then Rilke records the exchange that took place principally between Paula and himself. It is more than unlikely that the conversation took the exact form of Rilke's entry. He was re-writing their exchange the following day in his own language, as where he ascribes this statement to Paula:

> *'I also lacked the intellectual distance to take all miracles, which worked so variously and at such great remove from one another, and sum them up into a single, emanating will—and even if I could I would have no name for this unity ... All the same it would be comforting to believe in a personality around whom all circles close ... '*
>
> (SN, *Diaries*, 220)

Then there is the following statement, which Rilke is maintaining was what he actually said to Paula:

> *Whatever we do bears on him once we have found ourselves.*

If Rilke spoke up in precisely this way, it must have come across to Paula as a case of someone with whom it would have been very difficult to be amorous, for there would have been strong competition for Rilke's attention from his God. It is very possible that the difficulty Rilke sensed that evening of meeting with Paula over his God would have added to the impulse that had, more or less consciously, been forming in him to leave Worpswede: he had once again his relationship to God to prove to himself. Paula's position as expressed that evening, as Rilke transcribed this, is a moving testimony. She had never thought of relating to the name God, among other things because she could not accept all the cruelties He had allowed to take place in the world even with the few simple miracles of life she had personally experienced. She could not bring all this diverse matter into a whole around any "God" who was for her otherwise but a name. The only power she could recognize was what was life-creating, and this she associated rather, and very simply, with "Nature":

> *'No, it would all be foreign doctrine, for me God will be 'she', Nature'.*

In response Rilke had argued that that was just the point about God, that He was "not finished yet", that He had not had the time to *become* because man had wanted Him forcefully to *be* before His time, and it now devolved upon the strong individuals of their day (over and against all the cruelties) to help God more fully into becoming the great God He is and is meant to be. A further passage from Rilke's entry gives even more strongly the impression that he was carrying on the conversation they had had with himself:

> *And this most gives me the heart for life: that I must be great to benefit his greatness, that I must simplify myself in order not to complicate him, and that somewhere my seriousness connects with the seriousness in his being ...*

Rilke records maintaining other typical views of his in their exchange at that moment: for example, that Christ in fact diverts from a proper relationship to God by encouraging, especially in young people, the false notion that God can ever be known through "human means and measures" (SN, *Diaries*, 221):

> *They pamper themselves with the human and later freeze to death in the bleak summit-air of eternity. They wander back and forth between Christ, the Marys, and the saints: they are adrift among figures and voices.*

Rilke goes so far as to note also, in what are now clearly his comments to himself, that the idea of a decisive relationship to his God was already gestating in him back in his Florence days. (Significantly he paints those days as the "remote, perhaps already deceased *mother* of my feeling" (221), thus returning to the metaphor of child-bearing that had very much dominated his thoughts in those days. He had by now, however, wilfully reneged on what such "child-bearing" then implied; it was clearly serving now the broader view of his God that he had since adopted in deferring to Lou's notions of the path he ought to be taking, as we have seen (above, on pp.57-58). However, even in his account here Rilke recognizes the wonderful power of those days that he now mis-represents to himself—on which more in Part 3: "and I still know exactly what she looked like, and that she was beautiful"—speaking of this deceased mother.) Finally, as if he were, on that evening with Paula, having an unconscious premonition of his departure, Rilke would appear to have spoken also of things past as if it were only a good thing that things turned into the past:

> *And earlier I said ... 'There comes a time when every past sheds its heaviness ... And the darker and more colourful our various pasts were, the richer the images will be ... All heirs bear their deceased fates like jewelry. Dead eyes full of lament have been transfigured into precious stones, the gesture of a great leave-taking repeats itself, scarcely noticed, in an inconspicuous fluttering of their garments'.*
>
> (SN, *Diaries*, 221-222)

That last main clause must surely have been written self-consciously; they are the last words Rilke would set down before his departure from Worpswede the following morning.

It is my view that, in spite of the arrangements he had made to settle there for the winter, Rilke suddenly left Worpswede because he had been feeling, for some time, the oncoming once again of his great God-experience as recorded in "The Book of Monastic Life", and that by that last evening all this had come to a head. I believe he felt very strongly, and was even sure, that he was on the verge of a new moment of poetic creation comparable to that which had occasioned the writing of "Monastic Life". It would have been a different kind of creation, a still more comprehensive creation, inasmuch as he had in the meantime progressed significantly in relation to the image-making power he was now also looking for:

I'll not rest until I've reached that one goal:
to find images for my transformations.
The spontaneous song no longer will suffice.

(SN, *Diaries*, 194)

Rilke had given himself a more embracing goal, inclusive now of both sound and images, not to mention the further reference to God's things. There had been the "spontaneous song" of "Monastic Life": such spontaneous singing would, of course, continue, but buttressed now more firmly by all that he had learned about making imagery while at Worpswede. There was, among other possible kinds, the very abundant imagery of the Worpswede experience itself to draw on poetically. These were days "so rich", as he puts it, in poetic "gifts" (215), especially over his last week at Worpswede. The moment was as ripe as it could be, and it was converging once again on his God. What he needed was to be alone again in order to work devotedly as the poet of God (or as he puts it to Paula, His "priest"—220). He could hardly have had the kind of space to rise to this greater work while the Worpswede society continued around him, drawing him continually into its own peculiar, if rich, level and rhythm of life. Rilke left Worpswede because he felt the need to prepare for the coming on of poetry-writing that augured to be as grand as the poetry of "Monastic Life". Everything in the rhythm of his experience over his last days at Worpswede points in this direction *even as* he was settling more deeply into his experience there. He was carrying it all away with him. The ongoing work he had been looking ahead to (now with images included) was at hand, and at this point Rilke withdrew to see this work through. In the meantime, he was taking all of his experience at Worpswede away with him at what was in fact perhaps just the right point.[62]

Rilke's return from Worpswede to Berlin and to Lou at this juncture is so uncannily like his return from Florence two years earlier. Just as in those days, Rilke was imbued with the power of an astonishing new vision that he seemed so ready to see through and to act upon, but just as in those drastic former days, he was again utterly stymied, returning to find Lou as *she* always was and, moreover, highly critical of what seemed to her his latest pretensions. Just as after Florence, I believe there was another, and very likely this time more serious, disaster. The pages Rilke tore out of his Diary that correspond to the time of his return to Lou have been referred back to his situation in Worpswede with Paula, as if he were by this gesture coming to terms with a form of betrayal either of her or by her, but it is far more likely that these pages had to do with his return to Lou, who after all remained, in spite of the superb time he had had in Worpswede, still the chief person in his life, the source, he continued to think, of all his being. Because of Lou's more than indifferent reception this time, there was to be no great poetry-writing as anticipated. Instead, the materials that do survive, in the form of fragments leading up to the next entry in his Diary two weeks later, give indication of the depths of desperate solitude into which he had then fallen. These materials read like shadow copies of the depths of solitary encounter with his God that he had looked forward to. To be with his God, as he had been with Him in "Monastic Life", Rilke required such depths, and he had returned to them, only to find himself again betrayed in his efforts and soon left only with himself. The themes of these materials consistently announce as much: "Whoever walks now anywhere out in the world/...walks toward me"; "Soon I will be as if the first of all"; "I am growing more alone"; "In the faded forest there is a birdcall"; "I am a picture.../...My life is: the stillness of final form/...gesture's beginning and end" (SN, *Diaries*, 222-223).

What had sent Rilke back to Berlin was the hopeful prospect that had opened up of those "great connections" (234) with his God that he had counted on finding again but which had now reverted to being again a wish only rather than the actual event coming upon him that he had expected. His commitment to such "connections" remained right through this latest setback, and he felt sure he could best maintain his resolve about them, in spite of everything, from where his life continued, in Berlin. Letters from Paula and Clara soon followed him to Berlin. As for his reply to Paula two weeks later, we have no reason to think that Rilke was misrepresenting himself where he explains that he left Worspwede because he needed to remain in his own writer's environment where the things that counted most for him were to be found, what he calls

*the everyday, the enduring, the path on which I return from every
flight, the life above which one can raise oneself only when one*

has and rules it, the stillness and the shore of all my waves and
words.

(GRN 45)[63]

In a letter to Otto Modersohn, Paula's fiancé, four days later, Rilke notes, gratefully, how fully he was taken with the sketch-pages Modersohn had once exceptionally shown him, since these had inspired in Rilke the desire for a similar achievement as a poet:

> *So in every page there was that warm and eternal quality, that atmosphere which is about young mothers in the evening. That most peaceful thing in the world, that one thing which is not chance, that moment of eternity about which everything we think and do circles like birds about clock towers ...*
>
> *Then I thought: sometime I would like to have hours like these pages ... Now I know that I am living toward such hours, toward such poems ... I have only been as pious and reverent as before your little pictures two or three other times in my life ... And is all that so easy?*

(GRN 49)

Thus Rilke had courageously looked ahead again to what very nearly materialized for him, had it not been again for the alien reception he received from Lou when back in Berlin—about which more below.

Rilke was, in the meantime, in a regular correspondence with both Paula and Clara, both of whom continued to cling to him as he now clung to them. We are mistaken, however, in ascribing any greater power of attraction to Paula; it was attraction of a different kind, in both cases a powerful attraction. Moments shared with Paula give the impression of something more intimate and interpersonal only because more is suggested of an almost physical bond between them in the episodes we hear of. Contrastingly, Rilke's relationship to Clara is conveyed to a great extent through the narratives she offered of her experiences, including those surrounding her Paris period. Nevertheless, we see quite as much that was grand about Clara from these narratives, and, as it happened, these turn out to be a measure of the greater possibilities that were in process of being created between Clara and Rilke. From the episodes with Paula as described in Rilke's diaries we deduce about her an exquisite inner depth that was capable of awakening the grandest idealism in Rilke, precisely of the kind that his exceptional poem about her, later given the title "The Singer Sings Before a Child of Nobles", reveals. We know that they shared a moment of deep silent communion with each other early on during Rilke's stay at Worpswede, and another moment of intense silent communication when in the barouche, where deep knowing glances were exchanged between them. However, in both instances Paula was caught up in her feelings for another, feelings that were spilling over to Rilke primarily as to a confidant who was being let into the mystery of those feelings. As for the object of these feelings, Rilke does not appear to have known at the time, although Paula thought he "knew".[64] In any case, Paula became for Rilke, more than the person for whom he felt an obviously deep affection. Primarily she was an object of intense admiration and of fascination, a symbol of artistic inspiration, all of which made her potentially his very close friend especially as she was a fellow artist possessed of a comparable depth; she might also in other circumstances, have become Rilke's lover, but he very likely saw that she was probably not made to be his wife.

The very strength he marvelled at in Paula was also a menace to his own self-freedom. Her power of self-possession and her confidence in herself came with a limitation brought out, e.g., where she discusses Clara with him. There Rilke could see from her inability to fathom Clara's disposition to serve the purposes of others and of other things even where these did not suit her purposes, a limitation in Paula's capacity to give of herself. Likewise in her deep scepticism about God Rilke will surely have discovered a significant limitation as far as his own purposes went. There is no sign of any such scepticism in Clara, and what's more a decided capacity in her to forget herself with others that made *her* someone whom Rilke with his own strong purposes, which would have needed some primacy, could have to wife. We find another significant difference in Clara's favor reflected in the different relationships Paula and Clara possessed in relation to the natural cycle. Imagining already for himself the "sadness" of the dying and dead seasons in Worpswede, Rilke remarked to Paula that there had to be, therefore, something especially "cheerful" about the coming in of spring in comparison. To this Paula responded "Cheerful? Poignant would be more like it" (SN, *Diaries*, 151-153), thus expressing a limitation in her acceptance of the cycle, a lingering scepticism in her world-view. Clara, contrastingly, displays to Rilke a capacity for total acceptance of the cycle, in a show of great depth in her own kind. Such acceptance Clara had already demonstrated in her youth when she insisted to her parents on knowing the full range of the yearly cycle at their country home, having until then only ever been allowed to stay the summer. Rilke would make very much of this narrative, so expressive as it was of Clara's own exceptionally strong disposition, when he writes her from Berlin:

> *And you were to see suffering where until now was only rapture and anticipation ... And you were to behave like the grownups who all at once may know everything ... [H]ow simply and well you endured ... So great was your love that it was able to forgive the great dying ... all coming to an end seemed for your feeling only a pretext under which Nature wanted to unfold beauties yet unrevealed ... [S]o without concern you saw in the dying earth the smile and beauty and the trust in eternity.*

(GRN 52-53)

Rilke had the sense that Clara could, by her own power of spirit, go farther with him, penetrate as it were more fully into the whole reality of life and death that he, perhaps still only half-consciously, sought to know himself, and would certainly be destined to know.

For the longest time, and indeed through at least most of his time while at Worpswede, Rilke saw in his relationship to Paula and to Clara a situation of remarkable complementarity and, indeed, of equality: Paula because of her superior inner depth and capacity for "gentle"-ness (SN, *Diaries*,182), and her selective, sceptically qualified "kindness" (206) that yet could inspire so much idealism; Clara because of her superior outer strength, her capacity for self-sacrifice and total submission to life, all the while reserving her own intense depth as a remarkable artist in her own right, so that Paula could wonder at how she could forget herself. Yet contrary to what is generally thought, it is in fact Clara who was slowly winning Rilke over in the real terms of any possible shared life, a situation reflected also in the way he refers to each. Not once does he refer to Paula by name in his diaries but always at some distance as "the blond painter" or with reference to his visiting her studio, "the studio with the lilies" (219) as he puts it as late as the night before he left Worpswede—all of this a measure of Rilke's ongoing idealization of Paula. Clara, contrastingly, is for the most part "Clara Westhoff" until she eventually appears in the last week of his stay at Worpswede, more intimately and suggestively, simply as "Clara" (SN, *Diaries*, 216-217). Even so, during his whole time at Worpswede and indeed far beyond this, it is primarily as the great poet he aspired to become that Rilke responded to his experience of his "soul's sisters" (227)—as he would put it in a poem composed from Berlin equally for them both. Commentators forget that Rilke remained through the whole of his time at Worpswede, by a far, far stretch, more the poet than he was the man. This is how he thinks of himself from the very first period of his stay—"None may ever give herself to the poet"; "Let him be alone in his garden" (157), and this would remain his position right through his deepening intimacy with both women. In fact, especially when his relationship to these women was intensifying, as Rilke was nearing the end of his stay in Worpswede, one remarkable poem follows upon another poem with mounting intensity, because he was giving himself more and more to the dramatic re-appearance in his experience of his God. He then leaves, as a poet, to be alone in his garden, as he would have to since another powerful inspirational God-drive had come upon him. In this drive, he was bringing the whole of his Worpswede experience along with him. All of this then gets dramatically squelched, and we find him two weeks after his return, as in the post-Florence days, once again picking up the pieces of his shattered hopes and aspirations. The damage, we feel, must this time have been all the greater, since so many more feelings and experiences were at stake, including those related to Paula and to Clara, both as dear friends and as deep symbols. Beyond the epiphanic vision of historical artistic progress with his God, which of course Rilke continued to have to heart, there was also all of this additional matter, of considerable intensity, that would in some way have also shattered for him, and not just in relation to his artistic purposes.

The only other option for explaining the disturbance we associate with the torn-out pages from Rilke's Diary would have to do with Paula, but there is nothing in Rilke's Diary that would suggest that he was involved with her to that extraordinary point where disillusionment on such a grand scale would follow. To the very end of his stay in Worpswede, Paula has undoubtedly the most remarkable, but yet still a clearly delimited, significance for Rilke both as an aspiring artist and as a man. At the same time, one could just as easily argue, on the basis of this Diary, a deeper involvement developing with Clara. Commentators, perhaps naturally, look back from Rilke's torn pages to what had recently taken place in Worpswede instead of looking forward to Lou to whom he had returned, she who was still the first person in his life and on whose approbation or disapprobation he continued to depend. It is only too easy to imagine Lou disapproving of what Rilke was making of the two Worpswede women certainly.[65] If Lou did read his recent Diaries, as critics assume, then she would hardly have taken to his vivid descriptions of his all-embracing "happiness" while at Worpswede or the depth of his admiration, in so many places, for those to whom he had grown so close there, and especially Paula and Clara. Lou had other ends for him in mind. Once again what was so clearly to Rilke a positive path through his life and had even become inextricable with his more recent God-drive (a further association that had compelled him back home)—all this was very simply negated by Lou. What followed naturally in Rilke was disturbance on a scale that was the equal of, and indeed likely greater than, his disturbance after Florence, the other main evidence we have, from Rilke's life, of disturbance on this scale (apart from the "ugly letter" he also wrote Lou while in Russia, which has not survived[66]). That Rilke's disturbance after leaving Worpswede had to do, in fact, with Lou strikes me as an unavoidable conclusion, also from other extensive evidence.

There are at least two very dark poems Rilke wrote within a month of his leaving Worpswede that can only point to disturbance about a life of some duration. He can hardly have been thinking of his recent time at Worpswede in the poem that begins "O How everything is far off/and long deceased" (SN, *Diaries*, 225), written on the same day an appreciative poem went out to his Worpswede friends, the first after leaving them. Also, we do not have those torn pages for evidence of Rilke's disturbance at this time, but we do have the poem "Fragments from Broken-off Days". In this poem Rilke runs through a whole catalogue of metaphors for a tragic misery that could only bear on a form of disillusionment based on long experience. Rilke was addressing, in tragic even rebellious tones, the torment of his ongoing frustration at Lou's hands. There were the sad effects of the disillusionment he continued to feel after being displaced from his grand designs on returning from Worpswede; the poem puts it in this way: "The earth sucks out.../the brave memory of every/great thing that happens high up," (SN, *Diaries*, 231). Rilke senses a horrible power behind this repeated experience of debacle: "something outside is huge and incensed,/...outside Power stalks, a fist/that would strangle" (SN, *Diaries*, 232). Every form of analogy is then cited for the deeper repercussions of this experience: "Like long nights in faded bowers/that have been ripped open on all sides"; "like old men who curse their race"/"like an earth that cannot orbit":

> *...many a day's hours were like that,*
> *as though my likeness, clay-grey, lay somewhere*
> *in hands that tortured it dementedly.*
> *I felt the sharp pricks of their playing,*
> *as though a long rain fell on me*
> *in which all things slowly changed.*
>
> (SN, Diaries, 233)

Critics automatically assume that what this describes is Rilke's own "illness", the very "illness" with which Lou would charge him when she finally breaks off with him. In his Florence Diary Rilke himself acknowledges his disposition to this so-called "illness", but he *also* indicates there, as we shall see, that he knows what it feels *to have overcome* it. What critics strangely overlook was that Rilke's fortunes lay in Lou's hands; much depended on how she related to his own hopes and aspirations. After Florence he again becomes what she calls "ill" only because she throws him back into "illness", and so again after Worpswede, when *with her proper attention to the progress he was making* with himself he could easily have overcome. Rilke shows no sign of instability at all, and every sign rather of mounting confidence and growing happiness when away from Lou in Florence, and again in Worpswede. Such experiences only reinforce the view that it was Lou who made him "ill" on returning to her. Nothing else will explain the abyss of despair into which he was thrown once again on this occasion.—Why would Rilke think of going back to her, given his mounting good fortunes at Worpswede? from a stubbornly insistent hope that was, paradoxically, past hope. One of the first letters he wrote Clara after the most recent debacle sadly explains his move, drawing on a parallel from her life that she had narrated to him. Clara had spoken of that time when she had put off going to Paris at the last minute in order to comply with her father's request that she sculpt the face of his mother:

> *You told me then about those days that piled up before your journey to Paris ... you had to delay your departure ... Instead of your art, thirsty for the friendly strangeness of new things, your human feeling ... your love gathered itself ... I was so struck then by your humility: suddenly your eye ... goes about ... over ... a long dead experience and ... has forgotten the world, and has no world but a face.*

(GRN 42-43)

After speaking of the great temptation of Worpswede, and implying that he might well have stayed on, Rilke says he realized that he too had a duty to perform:

> *Your home was ... simply ... the first home in which I saw people living ... and rich enough to love me too and to uphold me ... So I all but forgot it, the quiet face of life, which waits for me and which I must shape with humble, serving hands. I was all the time looking out beyond it into radiance and greatness and am only now accustoming myself again to the near and solemn sternness of the great face which must have been shaped by me before I may receive something more distant, new.*

The point of view is complex, as Rilke was characterizing his decision to move back to Berlin *after* the debacle. Nevertheless, clearly Rilke saw it as a case of an unfinished life that he had to see through, and he must have guessed that his relationship with Lou was coming to an end (consider "a long dead experience"). However, Rilke was bound to want to continue to honour this relationship: it was on its basis that he had won through to everything that had concerned him until then, not least the "great connections" to his God that had come from persisting in this relationship. These "connections" he continued to associate, naturally, with the memory of his experience of Russia and with Lou. Though his choice of life pointed to the death of his relationship with Lou, this he would *have* to experience simply because it *was* his experience. It is as if he had accepted that happiness was not in the cards for him, that what these reserved was rather the greater knowledge of the tragic life for which he was destined. That too would have to be brought within the purview of a great poet's vision. There was, in fact, something premonitory in what he additionally says to Clara: "I shall perhaps have to work for years before I may devote myself to something which deep down is friendly." This comment points to another more far-reaching sense to Rilke's remarks to Paula (also voiced after the recent debacle) that he was bound to stay on in Berlin in order to embrace "the everyday, the enduring". For now, despite the depths of humiliation that had attached to his latest setback with Lou, Rilke continued to honour the pattern of life he was still living out with her. He had gone back to his Russian studies, was contemplating another trip to Russia, perhaps with the hope that another trip would open up another chapter in his great ongoing poem to God; he even went so far as to try his hand at several poems in Russian to impress Lou with his resolve. It is as if Rilke were playing out his life with Lou to the end in order to see *all* that would come of it, all that would have to be known (also in the long term) by way of tragedy, understanding that he was no longer destined for happiness.

Over his last four months with Lou, Rilke continued in a deep relationship to Clara and to Paula. They break into the life he had resumed with Lou repeatedly, offering occasions, among other things, for many rich poems written in response to their presence. Among these poems is one of very special note. It is the poem he wrote for them three weeks beyond his departure from Worpswede: "I am there with you, you Sunday-evening ones" (SN, *Diaries*, 225-227). In that poem he celebrates them equally as "sisters of my soul" (227); his "soul" is the "Soul of song" (226), and *they* have become the pre-eminent "listeners to that sound". They know his soul, in fact, better than he does himself (227) because from his perspective, things being what they are, his soul lies behind a wall "in uncomprehended sadness". But the sound, the music, the song in the meantime ring out and are "collect[ing] what is scattered in the great hour" (226). For this role he must at the same time remain distant: "so that I can be with you as I am, far off". Perhaps it is this sadly distant relationship to Clara and to Paula that the poet has specifically in mind where he speaks in "Fragments from Far-off Days", written three days later, of "happy hands that/grow hesitant, because in the full chalice/things are mirrored that are not near" (231). Rilke had chosen his fate; he had fallen in with Lou's notions of what the graver subject of his poetic life-longing should be, even though, without realizing this herself, though I believe Rilke knew, to walk this road he would have to continue to risk the very "illness" that became the cause of her leaving him. Still, positive intimations would now and again emerge from Rilke's subordination to his destiny, and so "Fragments" is followed in his Diary by "In the Music Hall", a poem in which Rilke describes how his "fear" is momentarily "put to rest", and: "A longing came forth in the violins,/And it carried something infinitely craved/... making straight for me/... the Strongest" (SN, *Diaries*, 233).

Ten days beyond this point, in the next entry in his Diary, in "Memory of the Sinding Concert", sounding like T.S. Eliot's Fisher-King Rilke paints himself precisely as he was in this period:

> *I, far from the others, mused days on end*
> *on the identity of what survives*
>
> (SN, *Diaries*, 234)

In search of "what survives", as he will be in the deepest sense from hereon in, to the end of his life, the poet inquires further:

> *Whether one has to say or to paint it,*
> *or whether it's just part of life?*
> *Whether it resembles happiness or grief*
> *and whether ...*
> *our life's frame doesn't wish to teach us*
> *to select quietly and seriously*
> *from all we love that one thing most eternal—*
> ....
> *woven into the great connections,*
> ....
> *...what centuries have bid us honor*

Here we meet in a first expression Rilke the great poet of the tragic whole, whom we will fully come to know in time. It is in the same far-reaching spirit that he comments on his experience of Maeterlinck's *The Death of Tintagiles* two days later.[67] Of this play Rilke notes how as "in a dream everything takes place on *one* stage, *one* feeling stretches out" (235); so, he adds, is the world "constituted" out of "fear" and "joys", "blissfulness" and "sadnesses". Of this "*one* feeling" in Maeterlinck's play he notes further that it takes the form of "a great gray fear that manifests itself as the eternal vis-à-vis all events" (236). Surely Rilke would have seen in this representation a reflection of his own condition of mind at this time and, what's more, a model for that broader view looking beyond tragedy that remained his only hope if he was to justify his experience in the long run.

It was on the very day of these comments about Maeterlinck's play that Rilke heard from Paula formally announcing at last her engagement to Otto Modersohn. Rilke responded to the announcement with a poem written down two days later. The poem takes the form of a blessing, and in it Rilke has managed to work himself up to the point where, assuming the "countenance" (SN, *Diaries*, 237) of a wise, quiet, and deep God, he can bestow upon Paula the kind of blessing in marriage that would keep her fully safe through the "storm" of life. He has succeeded in living into this persona starting from his "hands" which he has lovingly placed inside her own; until the occasion was given for this act of blessing, he says, his hands were "empty"—empty from his dispossessed condition, until "someone, close beside You, placed/such splendid things into these poor vessels" (238). This "someone" is that same "One" on whom Rilke had been continually attending in his idea of a rigorous life set apart for His visitations (see above, p.75). After "days that whisper, shiver, rain", has come at last a "twilight" that, inspiring this blessing, looks ahead, as in "spring", to a revelation of life that will be both great and magical, at least for the one who is blessed—such is the generosity Rilke displays, in spite of his own condition at this point. How significant that in the meantime Paula should be addressed here as an idealized (capitalized) You, a designation that Rilke had formerly reserved for Lou alone. One notes that he had used this same privileging designation for the first time also in addressing Clara in a poem written to her one week before ("On Receiving the Grapes from Westerwede"—SN, *Diaries*, 230). In contrast with such usage, Lou is addressed once through the familiar use of "you" (260); she otherwise appears at only one other point, very remarkably, in the third person simply as "L." (258). In the preceding Schmargendorf Diary, begun as long before as after Florence and in which Rilke was still writing in the first stage of his stay in Worpswede, Lou had appeared only once, where Rilke (from Worpswede) writes in response to her news that Tolstoy has become seriously ill (170). Her appearance at that point is startling, and a measure of his alienation from her over a long period of time.

"Blessing for a Bride" was accompanied by a whole spate of poems that were written down that same night and the following day. Among these the most impressive is the first poem that was put down, which would find its way into *The Book of Images* under the title "About Fountains". By these fountains, Rilke has specifically in mind the various occasions of his own tears. The unhappy condition of life this poem reveals makes his poem of blessing to Paula appear all the more generous and courageous. It is as if Paula's announcement of her engagement had stirred in Rilke thoughts of what might have been with Lou. In short, "About Fountains" constitutes his attempt to come to terms with the history of his own disillusionment and tragic sadness over Lou. In this poem Rilke argues himself into believing that he is ready to accept his dark fate. In the first place, he revives in himself the view that "heavens" do "reach hands ... into this commotion" (SN, *Diaries*, 238); in this way he calls upon a direction of thought that, without any clear anticipation of this at the time, will come to a climax when he will describe his dark explorations in *Malte* (years later) as: "not so much a downfall, as a strange dark ascent into a remote and neglected part of heaven" (SN, *Rilke*, 176). Negative copies of real experience are themselves, paradoxically, real and themselves membered into the whole of what humankind knows. In his tears he at least "came alive" (SN, *Diaries*, 239), in comparison with the emotional sterility that could also be the effect of impasse. And although these tears have plunged him into nether worlds that could only bewilder by their negative reflection of what is real, still their positive counterpart, that for which humankind supposes it is really made, can be measured there. Thus his glimpse in these "waters"

> *of evening skies, that from charred western forests*
> *shrank back totally bewildered,*
> *arched differently, darkened, and acted*
> *as though this were not the world they had supposed ...*
>
> (SN, *Diaries*, 239)

Recognition between beings, he implies, can only come from the experience of separation and tragedy;

Could I forget ...
That worlds in space only recognize each other
as if through tears?

This forebodes the direction that his relationship with Lou will actually take, but for the moment Rilke fantastically imagines a world beneath our own in which other beings might, like ourselves, be fruitlessly and tragically looking up to a god in *our* sphere:

... whom they envision
in our heights when they weep alone,
whom they believe in and whom they lose,
and whose picture, like a gleam from their
seeking lamps, fleeting and then gone,
passes over our scattered faces ...

This account amounts to an acknowledgment of God-forsakenness and how it feels before any recognition from God will come again. It is the area of experience into which Lou was driving Rilke without her knowing this, though it is she who would later come to see his fate in those terms. There is a sublime gesture of recovery from "Fountains" in the poem that follows, in which Rilke asks, just because of the acute loneliness *he* feels, to be the one who may "sing someone to sleep"—anyone: in his knowledge of affliction, he would protect from affliction:

... go with you to and from sleep.
I would like to be the one in the house
Who knew: The night was cold.

(SN, *Diaries*, 240)

Another way Rilke chooses to dramatize his experience of dispossession is to see himself as inheriting "homeless"-ness, as in the next poem (the third in this series), which would appear as "The Last of His Line" in *The Book of Images*. In this condition of homelessness, everything the poem's persona attempts, as the last of his line, to "put away / into the world—/ *falls*; / as if I'd placed it / on a wave" (241). Clearly the *Malte*-mood of extension in the negative life is here already foreshadowed. An experience of God-forsakenness is alluded to in the last lines of "Fountains" (also in the "sing to sleep" poem—

at night, the poet says, "one sees to the bottom of time"). Such for-sakenness calls forth in Rilke despair that he is actually made for the God-creation he has been privileging up to now. In the last from this series of poems ("In hours when I am full of images") he confesses that: "I don't live the life that's deep inside me", and he has come to the point of believing: "*Mine* never was that life inside me", meaning by this his "deep life" with God. What he *can* continue to depend on is the image-making that he has newly learned and especially the sound of his verse that carries these images and that had always been his strong-point as a poet. He otherwise feels dissociated from his deep life with God. And in a dedicatory poem intended for a reader for her copy of one of his early books, Rilke speaks of "unknown chasms" that "plunge" (242) where "only sounds / walk safely across string-playing"; in the meantime, that poem says, "*We* stand behind at the chasm's edge, alone". This last line is the first indication we are given of that fundamental dissociation in Rilke that would turn out to plague him to the end of his life. He feels that *he*, the man, has been left behind, that from this point onwards he will not be able to carry *himself* into his creation, that his life and his creation will from henceforth stand dissociated one from the other. The one chance he had to bring life and work together has, in fact, been squandered, his hope in a full association of life and work with Lou defeated, and he can only move forward now in disjointed half-measure. Significantly, Lou will speak of this essential division in Rilke in her critical mem-oir of him years later without any recognition, even by then, that she was the reason why he would remain divided. We can say that at least two parts of himself had been left behind, after Florence and after Worpswede.[68]

Rilke's direction in deepest melancholy at this time found fur-ther expression in a letter he wrote to Clara only four days after send-ing Paula his blessing. It is in this letter that he returns to Clara's narrative about that time in her youth when she insisted to her parents on staying in the country beyond summer, in order to witness the whole progression of the year in that place for herself: "And you were to see suffering where until now was only rapture and anticipation" (GRN 52). Perhaps Rilke already saw then those qualities in Clara that would make her an ideal companion for someone whose own life now certainly implied a great dying and whom only a higher destiny could save from despair:

> *And you, Clara Westhoff, how simply and well you endured ...*
> *So great was your love that it was able to forgive the great dying ...*
> *all coming to an end seemed for your feeling only a pretext under*
> *which nature wanted to unfold beauties yet unrevealed. Just as*
> *the eyes of angels rest on a dying child ... so without concern you*
> *saw in the dying earth the smile and the beauty and the trust in*
> *eternity.*

(GRN 52-53)

Rilke had received news of the sudden death of Clara's young friend, Greta, and this became the occasion for a new poem entitled simply "Requiem", written within a week of "Blessing for a Bride". The poem has been seen as more evidence of the deliberate "illness" that it is thought would understandably alienate Lou from Rilke more and more.[69] However, an unprejudiced reader will find in this poem, in which Clara is the speaker, in fact a moving and profound expression of imaginative empathy with the dead one. At issue is imagery that Rilke was, clearly, especially intent on developing, as the prose section that precedes the poem in his Diary bears witness (SN, *Diaries*, 245-246). In the poem Clara imagines an ivy wreath she has woven together and laid over her dead friend's thin coffin with its own weight breaking into the coffin, spreading over her dead friend's body, and even entering into her friend's inwards through her congealed blood to mingle and unite at last with her heart: by this point her friend's heart will have opened itself to the wreath. Such a development of imagery will strike the reader as morbid if considered in the abstract, but in the context of the rhythmic development of the poem it expresses ideas of astonishing originality. The poem ends with Clara musing over the fact that she has had the "strength" (SN, *Diaries*, 251) to work the wreath into a shape that reflects her will, that this strength now lies woven into the wreath, and it is as a further expression of this strength that the ivy wreath finds its way in her imagination into the body of her friend, among other things, in order to console her.

Death imagined even in this form, Rilke assumes, is part of what a human being must come to terms with as an essential, tyrannizing aspect of his or her experience deep down. We know of Rilke's vivid struggle with his consciousness of death from the time of early

childhood. The poem at some point reflects something of his own
early experience:

> *Was its coming-near fearful, dearest playmate?*
> *Was it your enemy?*
> *Did you weep yourself to its heart?*
> *Did it tear you out of the burning pillows*
> *Into the flickering night*
> *In which no one in the whole house slept?*
> (SN, *Diaries*, 247)[70]

Denied the chance of happiness, Rilke would be returned to his fears.
Life had suddenly laid this challenge once again at his feet, but this
time he has risen to the occasion; he has had the strength, along with
Clara, to come to terms: one cannot emphasize enough that it is
Clara's own natural strength of character that has given him the courage of this imagination. It is all the more remarkable a feat, coming
as it does at a time when Rilke was himself gripped by despair. It is
a measure of Clara's potential value for him personally. It is also a
measure of his tremendous resilience and the readiness he reserved
as a poet through every sort of affliction. At the height of the poem's
imagination, prayerful comfort is extended to the dead one even in
the sphere of its remains where it lies in the darkness of God and
no longer resists reality: "into your heart, which, completely silent, /
darkened, to all stands open" (SN, *Diaries*, 249). To the extent that he
has had his imagination of his dark God but feels presently alienated
from Him or forsaken, this is Rilke heroically imagining beyond himself. It is to reach with the imagination as far as is humanly possible,
and as such the feat is a form of negative triumph. In this respect, the
dead have a decided advantage on the living: "because you know the
path" (248). Earlier in the poem it is said that Greta knew that her
life was "not the *whole*", leading to the further question, "Life", then,
"is a part ... of what?" The speaker, being alive, is unable to say, but
Greta would be able to say. Death was a choice she made, or that was
made for her on behalf of a knowledge of the whole, and Clara and
Rilke remain behind to make sense of this.

The details of Rilke's own life are projected onto Greta's: her
case is dramatized as if she had experienced what he experienced
when he travelled to the South (247-248):

beauty so infinite
that only the blissful lips
of blissful pairs can speak it—two together
*with **one** world and **one** voice ...*
... not tempted by the blood

Shall we not see in this dramatization a memory of where Rilke stood potentially with Lou at the time of his visit to Florence? That situation has here been re-envisioned inasmuch as Greta is imagined finding life, even in this blissful form, unacceptable, inadequate because it could only be one half of a whole that also encompasses death. Rilke, in other words, has accepted his fate, intent on re-creating himself in relation to that former life and hope of his:

For you were not happy in all that brilliance,
every color lay on you like guilt.

(SN, *Diaries*, 248)

Rilke had to be knocked out of his hopes after Florence, likewise his hopes after Worpswede, because his concept of life, however grand and inspired this may have seemed at the time, had not reached out to the blighting power of death as known by many, and a form of which Rilke was dealing with now.

In this re-envisioning of himself, Greta becomes Rilke's way of seeing a humility before life *and* death that is greater than the grandly happy hopes he had brought back with him, both on his return from Florence and more recently on his return from Worpswede:

O how the infinitely grim
touched your infinite humility!

Greta's destiny (which the poem has depicted as fated from the first—246-247) betokens the new model of comprehensiveness that Rilke now felt compelled to look for. There is, yet, an attempt to bestow upon Greta what is still due to her from life: the wreath of flowering ivy that has been woven for her and that will now follow her into death. Some form of recognition from life or from those in life is still due to her, so the poem assumes. At the same time it is said that "all" who are dead being "as one"—one also with the continuity of Nature's process—this wreath is bound, through the force of this unity, to reach Greta, even if she is powerless to take this wreath herself. Remarkably, the facts of decay and the form of reality death takes are never compromised, even when Greta continues to be addressed in the terms of life:

> *Are you afraid, too, Gretel?*
> *You can no longer walk now,*
>
> ....
>
> *Do your feet hurt you?*
> *Then remain where all are as one now,*
> *they will bring it to you tomorrow, my child,*
> *through the leaf-stripped avenue.*
> *They will bring it to you, wait with good cheer,*
> *they will bring you that and more,*
> *even if tomorrow it storms and rages,*
> *the flowers will scarcely be affected.*
> *They will bring them to you. It is your right*
> *to have them as your very own, my child,*
> *and even if tomorrow they are black and spoiled*
> *and have long since perished.*
>
> *Don't be frightened, you won't distinguish*
> *any longer what rises from what sets,*
> *all colors are closed, all sounds are empty,*
> *and you won't even be aware*
> *who brings you all those flowers.*
>
> (SN, *Diaries*, 250)[71]

Life (the life that remained unlived) retains its own claims in this tense account of the relationship between life and death. It is, in short, a stupendous imagination, and who knows if the dead do not require or take consolation from this form of additional gesture towards them? One way or the other, the human imagination of death has been grandly extended and an additional form of power in relation to death achieved, both for the living and the dead. This in the poet who would no longer shy away from all that there was to be humanly imagined.

One is much struck by the spirit of initiative Rilke was demonstrating at this time when he was grappling with a deepening despair. It might, however, be truer to say that in the face of the menace of despair, he was simply continuing, as he always had, in his initiative both as a poet and as a man, and it is almost as if he had accepted that despair had become his life. Connected with this "acceptance" is the fact that he has no thought of leaving Lou at this time in spite of all the threatening signs of breakdown between them. On the very day of his Diary entry for November 20th, having considered precisely what image he would wish to develop in a Requiem conceived in response to the news of Greta's death—"I would like to write a requiem around this image" (SN, *Diaries*, 246), Rilke proceeded to do just that. Earlier in his entry for that same day, he had been considering other projects—"I would like to inscribe a drama into the space of longing. It would have to be called: *The Blind Woman* ... Or the drama *Fire!* ... Worldfire ... A drama shaped inside terror" (244-245). Rilke would never get down to either of these dramas, but he did, not long after, manage a poem on the fire-idea (even if this was not quite the large-scale "worldfire" he had conceived); it is a poem that eventually found its way into *The Book of Images* (as the third part of the sequence "From a Stormy Night"). As for "The Blind Woman", while a full-scale drama did not materialize in this case, Rilke did produce a "Fragment" on the theme, in the form of a dramatic dialogue, five days later. As in the case of "Requiem", one easily reads his own life-situation into the details of this production. It is true that in these works Rilke's interest is in the close realistic presentation of his themes, and so in "The Blind Woman" we have the actual feel of what it would be like to wake up one day suddenly totally blind—the terror of that experience; and how, also, it would feel to have made, with time, a virtue of an ineluctable fate. However, the thoroughness and depth of this realism only lend the more power to the way the poem additionally bears on Rilke's life. Dramatizing so thoroughly the effect of suddenly going blind, Rilke was all the more seriously coming to terms with the severe disjunction that had taken place in his own life. His refreshed hope in God after Worpswede had been no less suddenly subverted, and we are brought back to the "tears" about which the poem "About Fountains" also speaks:

> *My whole body was a wound.*
> ....
> *and I lay*
> *like churned-up earth, and drank*

> *the cold raining of my tears,*
> *which out of dead eyes ceaselessly*
> *and softly streamed, the way the clouds fall,*
> *when God has died, from empty heavens.*
>
> (SN, *Diaries*, 253)

At the time of the Florence Diary Rilke had dramatized his relationship to Lou as that of a child to a mother:

> *I was like a child who was hanging from a precipice. It is reassured when its mother grasps it in dear, quiet strength, even if the abyss is still below it ...*
>
> (SN, *Diaries*, 38)

But in "The Blind Woman" the point is made that

> *Death severs even the child from its mother.*
>
> (SN, *Diaries*, 253)

Fate had in the meantime intervened between Rilke and Lou, and there is a hint of what the mother would also be bound to suffer in this case—a premonition perhaps of what Lou, the mother, herself was bound to suffer?

> *For a while it was silent,—*
> *and I felt my pillows turned to stone;*
> *then I saw something that seemed to flicker:*
> *it was my mother's woeful weeping,*
> *about which I no longer wish to think.*
>
> (SN, *Diaries*, 253-254)

There is a still more far-reaching premonition of that vast world of dispossession that looms fearfully as a consequence of Rilke's life-tragedy:

> *But is it you there, Mother?*
> *or someone else? Who is that on the other side?*
> *Who stands behind the curtain? Winter.*
> *Mother? Storm, Mother? Night, tell me!*
> *Or else Day? ... Day!*
> ***Without me.** How can it be day **without** me?*
> *Am I missed nowhere?*

Does no one ask about me?
Are we entirely forgotten?
We? ... But you're there.
You still have everything, no?

(SN, *Diaries*, 254)

In spite of the veritable horror inscribed into this account, which stands as a symbolic projection of what Rilke theoretically was facing, there is a marked tendency in him nevertheless to want to think the best even of his situation at this time. And so at the end of the poem he can still project hopefulness:

Everything in my heart went away.
....
But then I found them all there;
all my feelings, all that I am,
....
All my led-astray feelings ...
....
... they all came back broken
....
That's when the path to my eyes grew over ...
....
Now everything walks about within me;
....
my feelings walk, enjoying the stroll
through my body's dark house.

(SN, *Diaries*, 255)

This account can be taken either as a dramatization of a future hope, *or* of Rilke's hopefulness even in his present debilitated condition. He is ready to accept and to live with his life's imposed burden, and it is in this spirit of wishful acceptance that Lou's comments on God are taken the very next day(!) in a conversation among friends. In his fundamental readiness to meet Lou in her thoughts, Rilke considers that her comments are said "very beautifully": Lou had remarked that the idea of God is needed especially as "an audience for those events and destinies that no one sees ... things nowhere spoken of" (258). There is a strangely glaring irony to this pronouncement inasmuch as Lou was herself at this time oblivious to the negative effect she had had/

was having on Rilke. But the irony is countered no less strangely by Rilke's own readiness to think that this is the very kind of experience that should be suffered if one is know life in all its completeness:

> *Things without end are being endured, things without name are being suffered, and this at heart is what we need to experience in order to assess life and its values properly.*
>
> (SN, *Diaries*, 258)

However, so telling of Rilke's situation at this time and a measure of his widening distance from Lou, is his further remark that

> *We don't really need God at all for this, since I know of a person whose best and deepest-seated faculties include finding, viewing, and loving that which doesn't put itself on show.*

By this person it is likely Rilke meant Clara (the only person who in his life at this time fits his description), unless he was, in fact, speaking about himself. Immediately following this comment, in an entry on this same day, he takes up directly with Clara, the photographs of whose statuettes he had just received. On one of these statuettes, a male figure, Rilke comments that "He is Clara Westhoff through and through; likewise everything quiet and soft that she says: it could be sung by choirs and received by vast countrysides" (259).

Yet another detail pointing to Rilke's disposition towards Lou, in spite of growing developments that were only creating more distance between them, are Rilke's Russian studies, which continued, seemingly without break, after his return from Worpswede. At the time of these remarks about Lou's God, he was reading in the letters of Alexander Ivanov (250). Here again Rilke's life-situation obtrudes itself, as he cannot help empathizing with Ivanov's own "despair", noting how "time weighs him down with a load of pasts that cripple him. And all this year after year!" We have said that Rilke also went so far as to try his hand at some Russian poems with some intention of pleasing Lou over this effort, although these poems themselves betray a covert absorption in the impasse of his life, it would appear in this case without his having quite noticed this. There is a bizarre congruency with the pattern of the life he had known with Lou in the themes featured in these poems, which have the effect almost of a mini-history of that life. First, the relationship of child to mother and how the child had to be helped through "nothingness to life, to long existence" (260); then the memory of his first encounter with Russia when he passed beyond his Florence experience (which he otherwise presents as "the great days") into what he felt was the truer reality:

> *And how far off from me now are the great days by the southern sea, and the sweet night of May sunsets; there everything is emptiness and merriment—and here: God darkens ...*
>
> (SN, Diaries, 261)

The third poem, written down six days later, is as a memory of the decisive breakdown on his second trip to Russia when he felt, more clearly than before, unjustly neglected by Lou, and he saw, as it were, the writing on the wall:

> *The solitary house had locked itself up, the garden tossed and turned: it couldn't sleep after the rain. The boy looked out into the night and fields ... Suddenly he felt: Fire far-off! Even the sky aflame! And thought to himself: Life is hard! Is there no salvation?*
>
> (SN, Diaries, 264)

The fourth poem is like an account of how, in spite of where things stood with Lou and after coming away from Worpswede, Rilke picked himself up again for what he continued to maintain was his primary work on God:

> *And now we must begin. What will transpire? Don't concern yourself and don't fear perishing; even death is only a pretext ... we shall be and God shall be.*
>
> (SN, Diaries, 265)

In the fifth poem Rilke re-visits the depth of his commitment to his God-efforts; this had always entailed a solitary, almost puristic focus on work and prayer (*ora et labora*): "my hands ... by day ... would close around work, at night ... would fold into prayer ... the eternal face of labor" (266). This is the attitude that brought "The Book of Monastic Life" into being, and it is the standpoint Rilke continued to believe he could reach again on leaving Worpswede. But his efforts were to no avail. This is reflected in the sixth and last of these poems. In the context of "the soft crying of the weeping child" and a sleepy "old man" at his stove (pointing to an ever-ongoing cycle of unrealized promise), there is an acknowledgment of failure to rise to the (historical) task (of completing God):

> *Already his blood is turning dark, and that sweet, noble love has moved about in his breast for more than a thousand years and has found no lips for itself, and it understood again that there is no salvation, that the poor flock of tired words passed by like a stranger into the light.*
>
> (SN, *Diaries*, 267)[72]

These poems were purportedly dedicated to Lou as a form of acknowledgment of what they shared by way of their Russian experience, but is it any wonder that only a few days after Rilke's composition of these poems he would fall into a still deeper depression?

> *What good are the efforts one makes ever more sluggishly, ever more wearily, ever more laboriously ... One's will is there ... but it is like a piece of conduit that had hit rock. One tries: uprisings, ascents ... and it all comes to this: one lies down, lies down ... humble to the point of baseness. Humble like a dog with a guilty conscience. Flat, without feeling and filled only with fear, fear of everything that does and does not happen, of what exists and of any change in what one can scarcely bear.*
>
> (SN, *Diaries*, 267-268)[73]

What is especially remarkable is how fear emerges from Rilke's deepening experience of alienation; here is that distressing condition developing in Rilke over which Lou would finally leave him. But what was to blame for it? Quite understandably when we look into the abuse he received in his early life[74], Rilke had brought the disposition to this condition with him from childhood. However, Lou's wilful resistance to the needs of his development as he saw this also *kept* him in this condition and repeatedly drove him back into it. Rilke's unreal idea of carrying on with Lou and continuing at least to make poetry out of their situation, not just in spite of but to a significant extent out of his despair, had its grave perils, and these now begin to get the better of him. Not only were things now going nowhere between Rilke and Lou, their relationship threatened to drag him down into Hamlet-like depths of stagnation and self-disgust. Snatching at any, even the slightest, prospect of hope, he is inevitably deceived, and disturbed, by the unreality of what comes to meet him that is so out of tune with his needs:

> *Out of distrust one flatters. Crawls before every accident of the day, receives it like a guest one had been expecting for weeks, praises it, disappointed by its scowl, seeks to hide the disappointment, seeks to erase it inside oneself, to deny it to oneself, deceives oneself, while one has already been deceived as it is, digs oneself deeper and deeper into confusions ...*
>
> (SN, *Diaries*, 268)

A veritable hell opens out from here that makes one understand why Rilke would be so disturbed later by the plight of the oppressed populations of Paris, seeing, as he would, the menace of his own psychological breakdown in theirs. Rodin himself would not have had a greater hold on what hell is:

> ... [one] *judges the value of everything now like a child by its golden glitter, now like a whore by profit and pleasure and night—is invaded by everything that happens, is screamed at by all the trivialities and obscenities of the day as by drunken gendarmes ... goes soiled in the company of cherished memories ... takes things that piety has kept untouched into one's sticky, sweaty, swollen hands ... Pasts fall into impure fire, futures consume themselves in the womb of ill-used hours ... Deluge and sin's malediction ... [a]nd not to think about the fact that it will all lie before you again the very moment you have overcome it ...*
>
> (SN, *Diaries*, 268)

God, Rilke says, has no power over this condition, and by the time we reach the following details in Rilke's account, which generalize his condition, one reads with his own tears:

> ... *only heartbeats of unspeakably sorrowful hearts suspended high up and frightened, unaware of one another, deprived of all relations and connections, switched off, without meaning, their beatings possessing as little truth and reality as the royal proclamation delivered by a lunatic in a straightjacket ...*
>
> (SN, *Diaries*, 268-269)

So much pain, so much bitterness is written into these lines, and clearly such power of knowing would prepare Rilke for the task that would later devolve on him to represent all who are at the mercy of this condition:

> *Such stretches of hopelessness, such gaspings of the soul. And should they once not recede, not come to an end ...*
>
> *if one had to name all this "I", this unspeakably disconnected, helplessly isolated consciousness that ... falls into itself as into an empty well ...*
>
> *What is one then? Who knows how many afflicted with this in-between existence live in lunatic asylums and die there?*
>
> (SN, *Diaries*, 267)

Rilke ends this awful rendering of his experience with the words: "This had to be written as a sign for myself. God help me" (SN, *Diaries*, 269). Rilke's effort of resolve and initiative in the face of his greatly desperate condition, however slight this effort might appear in these words, is yet ominous. Just when it seemed he was being defeated in some frighteningly final way, after giving himself to his dark descriptions, he inscribes into his *Diary* a poem he had composed earlier that day that gives the lie to his despair. After this poem, he adds a comment that may well have been meant metaphorically: "After many incredibly heavy and vague days, today I experienced an hour of sunshine in the woods" (270). The moment of "sunshine" he experienced earlier in the day may well have been this poem. In it Rilke re-affirms himself in the power of the creative life he has stood by until now—this life that, he insists, will remain his focus, however afflicted he might be. Dedication to his poetic destiny had entailed until now that characteristic puristic openness of his to all that makes for creative readiness: a proper way of living out his evenings and his days, pen at hand, and accompanied as always by the "One" Who alone can ensure that he has the space to properly mediate his life. Rilke projects the prospect of a return to this life here, which involves:

> *broad nights, not tired, full of gestures,*
> *early mornings bathed in sun*
> *and daytime hours close to earth*
> *and in relationship to shape and stone.*

A craft sufficent to fill the hands
and One who keeps me veiled
so that I can be unnoticed and alone
and far apart and his and mine.
And simple fare: greens and meal and bread
And unassuming sleep, dreamsoft, close to death,
And good exhaustion, and after sunset,
To end each day, a prayer, ...

(SN, *Diaries*, 269-270)[75]

It is as if Rilke were here applying a balm of his own making to himself, to heal his mind, and he is in the end returned to the making of "prayers". In this case they are "prayers" that unfold towards a future that Rilke, at this moment, so much needed to re-envision:

And not one prayer like any other;
each one new, distilled from each new day,
imbued with new objects,
rich in some new degrees of love,
the day's fruit, which, without wind, grasped
only by its own fully ripened weight,
breaks off and falls and falls
until God stretches out beneath it
like a rolling meadowland ...

It is out of such a world as this, freshly envisioned, that Rilke will find again the focus he needs to apply himself creatively as much to those directions in "darkness" (269) that life will now have in store for him as to the directions in "light" which he says he has unduly privileged at the expense of "darkness" (which was the case at Worpswede). The same poetic "hands", he reminds himself, will apply themselves in each sphere, however opposed each of these spheres appears to be at present, as the first part of his poem elaborates.[76] In the meantime, the "in-between land" (267), as Rilke calls it, of universal depression, which is not to be confused with the "darkness" of "night", the creative "night" of his God, is another world still. This *essentially* dismal world, which he says is *not* presided over by his God (267), this world of hell, Rilke has in the meantime, by the stratagem of his poem, managed to slip away from, but it will return to menace him again more than once in his lifetime.

Sometime between his composition of his second and the last four of his Russian poems, Rilke was introduced, through his continued association with Lou, to Gerhard Hauptmann, a writer of considerable fame and reputation in Germany at that time. Some two weeks after writing the Russian poems and a week after recording those intervening days of deepest depression, Rilke found himself sitting in a theater with Lou at a dress rehearsal of Hauptmann's play, *Michael Kramer*. The play, on its own merits, is of considerably less significance than what it represented to Rilke as a symbol; it is unlikely that he did not get seriously caught up in the uncanny applications of this play to his own life. For a start there is the character of Lachmann, a former devoted pupil of the painter Kramer, who at the time passed up the chance of marriage to Kramer's daughter, Michaeline. Marriage between Lachmann and the daughter seemed inevitable, even an intrinsic part of his developing life as an artist, but he balked before the prospect:

> *The latter's daughter ... was woven wondrously for him into everything that was on its way. But what was on its way never came and didn't reciprocate when Lachmann approached it. Perhaps he never seriously gave it a try—who's to know? And it doesn't really matter now, now that nothing in his life will ever change again ...*

(SN, Diaries, 272)

It is difficult not to project into Rilke's account here his own thoughts about the direction he might have taken (i.e., his own "way") after Florence and again when in Worpswede: Lou would be the daughter in both cases, while Kramer stands in for God. Lachmann, after this, goes the way of conventional ease and adaptation, which was not to be Rilke's choice of life: Lachmann takes to wife someone of whom Rilke says that she is "the visible sign of that great resignation with which he has taken upon himself ordinary life in all its smallness and almost comic mediocrity" (271).

Lachmann represents precisely the type of capitulation that Rilke would have abhorred, but it is nevertheless Lachmann who is present when, towards the end of the play, Kramer speaks of what he has learned about his genius-artist son who, at the other extreme, has committed suicide and whose coffin now stands before them both.

Thus just as the Lachmann option of proper marriage did not materialize, so too the artistic promise of the son. Gifted as Kramer's son was, he faced obstacles to his life too hard to overcome, obstacles the play dramatizes as related to a condition of physical deformity. It is hard to believe that the son was not taken by Rilke as a version of his own youthful promise that likewise had been wasted. The effects of depression in Rilke point to an experience of feeling at some point trapped inside his body—a further aspect to his tragedy that is, uncannily, reflected in this drama's details. Rilke knew too well what all this felt like:

> *This life, which wants to be open and carefree and beautiful, involuntarily becomes a lie inside this twisted body ...*
> (SN, *Diaries*, 275)

Indeed now that his own fate was sealed, Rilke would continue to experience such symptoms repeatedly over the course of his life. Suicide, however, would not be Rilke's way either, anymore than he would have allowed himself to succumb to conventional ease, but from Hauptmann's play he gathers that all is otherwise inevitable: that the youthful Rilke has had in some sense to die, because only beyond this death could the real effects of the genius he reserves begin to come into view. The following are the relevant lines from the play:

> *What now lies open on his face—all that, Lachmann, has been lying inside him. I felt, I **knew** it was inside him, and yet I couldn't raise it, this treasure. And look: now Death has raised it.*
> (SN, *Diaries*, 297)

It is said[77] that both Rilke and Lou saw in this play the obvious applications to Rilke's own troubled youthful condition, but, as I have shown, Rilke must have seen this condition quite differently from Lou, even if in his characteristic far-sightedness he was at last ready to accept all that had happened to him. This was now driving him towards a different future than the one he had once anticipated and hoped for. But whatever that future might hold, Rilke would appear to have been more confirmed than ever in the thought, which this play also voices (275), that what he reserves as promise is an inherent good that will remain, no matter what fortunes might befall him, and that if not in him than in another who is to come that promise will be fulfilled:

> *the face of his boy lies opened like a book and he reads in it—*
> *reads word for word the confirmation that **it exists**, the thing ...*
> *now ... present only for someone who will sooner or later arrive to*
> *take it in hand ... Everything is as it should be; it **exists**. And we*
> *must continue on ... precursors of the one who is on his way, who*
> *will not arrive in vain, the treasure seeker, the finder ...*
>
> (SN, Diaries, 275)

In any event, Rilke, following the lesson of the play, knew that he would certainly be

> *incapable of ever again experiencing anything petty, insignifi-*
> *cant, or fortuitous after* [viewing] *something so triumphant, so*
> *immense.*
>
> (SN, Diaries, 276)

And a final lesson is drawn from all this:

> *Whoever understands and honors Death correctly, grants Life*
> *greatness.*

And thus ends (on December 23rd) the Worpswede Diary, the third and last of Rilke's early diaries. It is an ending that, typically, rounds out the main theme of this diary, for it was also Rilke's purpose, through all the trials and tribulations of his life that are recorded there, to bring out in each of these diaries, artist as he was in all things, its distinctive theme. His great, stubborn artist's hand would have to lie over this material also.[78]

Towards the end of this year (1900), almost unthinkable as this would seem, Rilke would spend "a Russian Christmas"[79] with both Lou and her husband in their home, and he and Lou continued, right through early January, in "their old routines", which included "their customary long walks together in the woods".[80] Lou's diary through this time inevitably records "her growing disaffection with Rainer from day to day"[81] but, though it is clear that "she wanted to have done with him", yet she "could not cut herself off".[82] Rilke likewise, though "only too aware that she was lost to him in the way he needed her"[83], could not conceive of breaking it off with her, and he was ready to suffer extremes of humiliation if this had to be. Fate would have to intervene. In mid-January Paula came to Berlin for reasons of her own and, of course, was often in Rilke's company. That relationship continued magically intimate: her first visit to his rooms left him basking in the afterglow of her intense presence, and he did not for a time alter any trace of herself that she had left behind. On this visit Paula also shared the diary of her early youth with him, and he responded to it by letter. There is a strangely over-rationalizing excitability to this letter marked as it is by elaborately involuted expressions of admiration and praise for Paula in seeing her personal purposes through (GRN 53-56).[84] Paula would be nearly as effusive with Rilke in *her* response to the gift he would send her on her birthday, which she celebrated with him in Berlin: "I was inundated with love today" she said.[85] But it was rather Clara who stole the day after she joined them in Berlin some few days before Paula's birthday. Significantly, it was Clara whom Rilke had written back in December when he had fallen into his deep depression, imploring her not to stop writing to him.[86] Less than two weeks after her arrival in Berlin, he and Clara became engaged, and they announced their engagement to Paula. It was at this time that Rilke announced the engagement also to Lou.

Rilke could see there was no going anywhere from here with Lou—in his shrewdness he would surely have seen that she had plans to break off with him at last. In the meantime, a profoundly serious and tender love, based on many sound and intimate experiences, had emerged with Clara. Even so, it must have taken much courage to confront Lou with his decision. For her part, Lou had wanted Rilke to make a fresh start on his own, but she had never bargained for a move such as this. She had, as it were, been outflanked, and she clearly was very hurt, never expecting to be hurt when the break-up with Rilke she so longed for would come. Paula was no less shocked by the news, declaring to Rilke "a great sadness" on hearing it, though she finally came around to wish Rilke and Clara well.[87] Lou insisted that there should be a complete break between herself and Rilke, which he in turn did not expect; "the sharing of their thoughts would end, they would not even write"[88]. Rilke responded with three poems that he wrote to himself in which we note his experience of a new degree of "death"[89] and other details that elaborate on the stupendous paradox and frightful range of his relationship to Lou:

You were the height that gave me blessing—

> *To become the abyss which swallowed me.*[90]

Nevertheless, Rilke's experience on this hand did not stop him from re-affirming to Clara the very next day the wonderful hopes he now entertained with her:

> *My life till now was something uncertain, but now all is reality around me ... everything becomes straightforward ... and I want to stay with my feet on the ground, the earth on which our home will stand.*[91]

Lou's parting from Rilke had not been enough for her. Ten days later she would send him her famous "Last Appeal" or "Final Call or Warning", a message of great emotional complexity, in which her old warmth and tenderness for him inevitably seep through. Nevertheless, there is something patently *dis*ingenuous about this message, if only in that Lou pretends not to have been hurt by the way events have unfolded but is rather, now that she has been set free, "standing in pure sun and stillness", "the fruit of life having grown perfectly round and full" for her (SN, *Rilke*, 41). In the meantime, her purpose in writing is to let Rilke know that *he* faces in himself a chronically neurotic condition that could, potentially, lead to nervous disease and even to insanity. What a message to be sending him just as he was about to embark on his new life with his young vibrant wife! Having withdrawn from him so categorically and insisting now on letting him know how sick he was, Lou was crippling him before he could make a fresh start. Why, especially, insist on making it sound as if he were lost to his condition far more than he was or had to be, which was precisely the route she was saying he should not take, going into his condition not once but twice in this letter in the same insistently dramatic tones:

> *Again the sluggish resolve alongside the sudden, nervous eruptions of will that tore through your organic being, gave in to every suggestion, and did not descend into the fullness of the past in order to assimilate things healthily, to digest them, to build up from the ground! Again the wavering uncertainty alongside the loud accents and strong words and protestations, manic compulsions without the compensating drive for truth!*
>
> (SN, *Rilke*, 41-42)

All of this sounds very much like the behavior of one who was acting out of being hurt, and who was, also, anxious for herself. What was Lou's outcry, her last appeal, if not some version of the classic break-up case: "*You* are the reason why things failed, not *me*"? How little Lou could have endured knowing that it was her ways that had repeatedly driven Rilke back into himself. Lou must surely also have been feeling the threat of an invidious comparison with Clara. Could Lou have endured the thought that Rilke might, in fact, turn out well in his new life with Clara? What would Lou then have thought about the effect *she* had had on him?

Between the time of Rilke's and Lou's last meeting and her one last effort to communicate her "appeal", all in a matter of ten days, Lou had entered into a sexual relationship with her psychiatrist-confidant, Pineles, and it was from a discussion with the professional Pineles that she could confirm that Rilke's symptoms did indeed threaten him potentially with insanity. But in spite of her citation of a "clinical diagnosis" of Rilke (which reads like a form of triumphant gambit) and her euphoric claims about herself, we know that, after separating from him, Lou herself fell into a depression which was to last for years, at least until she and Rilke were re-united four years later. Deep down Lou knew that she had failed him, but she did not have the frame of mind to be able to face up to herself sufficiently to see how she was to blame. Only one thing could cure her of her part in this failed relationship: the prospect of a re-union with him and the reconciliation that would follow upon this that was made possible two years later. Even so, it would take Lou another two years to decide that she was ready to see Rilke again, two years of careful, elaborate correspondence after he first broaches the idea of their seeing each other again. Over the years Lou had wanted a simple, straightforward case of health between them, Rilke a full harmonious relationship fully responsive to the inspirations of each other. Instead they had inherited their own special destiny. For Lou this meant living with guilt, very largely without her knowing this, and with a form of depression, including a heart ailment, that was psychosomatically connected with this guilt. There was guilt and anxiety for herself; she was also hurt: there was the sense of having been defeated, contradicted, even outmanoeuvred. For Rilke the destiny they inherited meant freedom at least from the form of despair he had been floundering in while still connected to Lou, though he had now inherited a new despair from the final separation Lou had arbitrarily imposed upon them. In the meantime Rilke had also come to know again the depths of depression he had so hoped he could leave behind him, and he must surely have been wondering if he would be giving way to them again.

He had put his hopes in his well-founded relationship to Clara, and they were great hopes. Letters and poems to Clara "showed clearly how complete was his confidence in their future together. No longer mere clay in another's hands, he could be his own master now"[92]. Having grown sensitive to any obstruction of his hopes for himself, it is understandable that, with the sudden news of Clara's pregnancy, the dread of these additional, unanticipated limitations on his new life, so soon after the recent turmoil, should expose Rilke to physical illness. He contracted scarlet fever some few weeks before the wedding. However, on recovering from this and now married, Rilke resumed, with great pleasure, the task of establishing his new home-life with Clara. This was to be out in the great open spaces of Westerwede, and "their euphoria lasted well into the autumn"[93]. Through much of this time, Rilke was trying to win professional contracts for his critical work, also producing and publishing poetic work in (for him) a small way, while Clara became very productive with her sculpting[94]. By September, he was at last ready to plunge into some major work dedicated once again to his God. In a single week, he wrote out the more than 30 poems that constitute a sequel to "The Book of Monastic Life", which he would entitle, fittingly for this new stage of his life, "The Book of Pilgrimage". By Christmas, their daughter Rose now born, Rilke could write to a friend: "Life has suddenly become quite new, richer by a new future!"[95], and looking back on this period in later life, he would see himself at this time like "a seedling ... taken out of his pot ... and planted into my proper station ... into the great, real, whole earth itself"[96]. One of his biographers has summarized what Rilke was feeling at this time in this way:

> *In his simple country surroundings Rainer felt he had at last **made his own** the secret of the life of the Russian peasants, their sorrows and joys "linked in some way with God, ... led by some hidden impulse to a wise selection of realities" ...*[97]

Rilke had for now, so he believed, become the master of his own destiny, but he had not reached this point by any easy route, for he had still had much to contend with by way of an after-effect of all that he had been through.

III

"The Book of Pilgrimage" and "The Book of Poverty and Death"

Thus, in the first line of "The Book of Pilgrimage" Rilke speaks anew of a "storm" that, after a short period of connubial respite and freshened hopes, is now up and again "raging" (RANS 95). Finding himself, at this point, beyond the fruitful "summer" of his home-making, and with the coming in of fall, he is returned to the terms of his personal tragedy—to all, that is, that he had suffered so intensely through the many difficult episodes that preceded and surrounded his engagement to Clara, and to the repercussions of this tragedy on his uncharted future. The storm first appears in the poem as a natural image whose power to outstrip all human intentions is very carefully described:

> *The trees flee. Their flight beats out*
> *avenued strides.*

However, this image is very quickly appropriated into a *symbolic* representation in which the wind (which underlies this storm) takes shape more meaningfully as the difficult personal destiny in which Rilke remains caught. For a time Worpswede had been the experience of a perfectly fruitful, happy life—that life of the happy man Rilke might well have thought himself meant for. But now he is returned to the greater reality to which even a culture as fine as this must submit:

> *Midsummer force was tangible*
> *as fruit in your grasp,*
> *but now reclaims the ineffable,*
> *and you—are again the guest.*

In Clara the spirit of Worpswede had been carried further, directly
into their life together:

> *The summer has been your own house*
> *and your life's drift stayed;*

but that extended reprieve has also had to give way:

> *now you must travel out to your heart*
> *as across the plains.*
>
> *The enormous solitude begins*

Rilke was now returning to himself but, as in his farther past,
also with the old faith that "Heaven watches", the "heaven" that, in
spite of the depths of alienation he has recently known, he says he
"owns", inasmuch as his identity was once, and so still is, bound up
with "heaven". He remembers himself as the one who even "devised"
(RANS 99) his God in his power to "create" him, and he knows that
in the last analysis:

> *... you are still the wave that passes*
> *over all things that have been.*
>
> *There **is** no more.*

It is to his God that Rilke now brings the memory of his still fresh experience of intense personal degradation. He has had the experience
of falling through *depths* of spiritual disability. Such depths were all
the more horrible given the role of God-watcher he had once fulfilled
so magisterially. We have looked closely at what he underwent in this
regard, which continues to be echoed here:

> *From ends of waste and old glass,*
> ....
> *I pieced myself in shabby yards,*
> *stammered at you semi-dumb.*
> ....*my hands....*
> *half made, pleading for my eyes*
> *wordlessly, to have them again,*
> *my watchers of your ways.*
>
> (RANS 97)

Rilke's account here echoes the desperate metaphors of his diaries: "I was a house swept by flames", "I was a city by the sea / overrun by pestilence"; most to the point, he remembers, "I was a stranger to myself, like any stranger" (97). In this last condition, Rilke sees himself as working "to my young mother's hurt / as she carried me": one of his deepest metaphors for the prospect of his creative life, which at that time lay in ruins. We find here, in fact, an irrepressible insistence on his degraded condition that compares directly with that entry in his *Diaries* in which he reports his "infinite humiliation" after Worpswede and before his engagement to Clara:

> *In disarray and thrown about,*
> *offered piecemeal, robbed of my whole*

So poor was his condition at this time, Rilke felt he was worth even less than those who make a joke of living, especially sensitive as he could be to the decadent social life that surrounded him continually and that is assumed by others simply as a matter of course:

> *dear God, the scoffers have laughed me out*
> *and drinkers drunk my soul.*

He has succeeded, he says, in re-making himself even through all this, and so he can assume that his God will offer to restore him in His sight as the one He once knew, on the assumption that, in spite of all appearances, he (Rilke) remains "as one / indivisible single thing" (99). In this sense, Rilke says, he requires a "bond" (98) of "understanding" (99) with his God and needs too "your heart's great hands / (oh, if they could so far extend)"—the parenthetic structure here continuing to express the painful distance Rilke still feels from this God to Whom he is appealing for a renewed life.

"I am the same", Rilke otherwise insists; "I am the very one... / who often asked who you might be" (RANS 101)—"scared" and "orphaned" though Rilke is at this moment and only "pallidly yielded to the All" Who is his God. As his God is "the All", Rilke *should* be the complementary "One" (99) who is associated *with* Him, but he has come to know his subjection to another "All", the "All" of "Everyone" who is "washed in tears", making of God now the complementary "One" Who surely, Rilke maintains, "hears" their cries (this is the elaborate way in which Rilke's language operates here). Out of this "storm" that continues to "toss" both Rilke and, he feels sure, many others, all of whom are similarly crying out to God so that His attention must be too diffusely portioned out, Rilke insists on being heard for *his* "song", which speaks *on behalf of* Everyone.[98] Already in the *Diaries* he had reached the point of universalizing his own experience of degradation, and here he reviews that experience, speaking for all who are morally defeated, blighted, and without a way through in spite of their most heroic efforts:

for those whom sin and scandal blight

..

.....................lives given up for dead,

..

The past stands before, unspent,
and in the future corpses lie;

..

..............driven by fear............
They tear great doorways through walls—
Then come interminable halls
And no gates that open out.

(RANS 101)

"[S]omeone", Rilke insists, "is always there" desperately searching for God's help though it seems as if their efforts only carry them in an opposite direction: "On staircases twisting *down*".[99] Rilke's God is the only One they can call upon because He alone abides at a depth that lies beyond all degrees of depression and despair:

Whom to call,
if not the one darkest of all,
more night than night?

(RANS 103)

Here Rilke is ready to believe once again, certain that the one world of night (the world of universal depression) is, in fact, subordinated to the other (the world of God's all-encompassing life). This is in spite of the fact that Rilke had at some point seen the two worlds as radically separate (see above p.114), the former world belonging to an "in-between God" of nondescript and essentially extraneous significance, this God being one who presides over a sort of Heideggerian outer-world in which one is simply "thrown out". Now Rilke attests to another, hoped-for experience: the one "All" of "Everyone" would give way, through Rilke's desperately intercessional appeal, to the God Rilke feels he knows is the veritable "All" who finally saves and sustains. Rilke's God, the God on Whom he would depend, should finally prove Himself all-capable from *His* depth of depths:

> *known to me in his lifting from the earth*
> *tree-like, fragrant,*
> *drifting past my lowered face, gentle*
> *in his ascent.*

(An astonishing intimation this, arising from the utmost depths of Rilke's whole life, of the Orphic power he will only fully come into many, many years hence.)

In the meantime, Rilke acknowledges that, "[l]ike an old man" who must watch his "son", i.e., God, leave him to assume his own "throne", he has "stayed behind/failing to follow" (RANS 103). He is unable to understand quite what he is to make of the newer developments in his life or what can be created out of them:

> *understanding*
> *too little of the newer things to which*
> *the ungainsayable will of his* [the son's] *seed pulls him.*

However, the God of Rilke's new life knows what to make of these developments, and He is already journeying, with many resources, towards the place where all continues in ease:

> *Often I tremble at your ease of mind,*
> *sailing from me in foreign ships—*

In contrast with this God Who has gone before, to where all is or will be newly resolved, Rilke finds himself hanging back, wishing his God were still the One Whom he had formerly created with in "The Book of Monastic Life", all the more so as he fears that in his present experience of dispersal he may have lost his link to God completely:

> *Often I wish you back with me, into*
> *the dark mine that once nourished you.*
> *Often I fear you may no longer be,*

as I diffuse into the wastes of time.
(RANS 103)

Rilke here tries to help himself forward by actively imagining precisely how and why one would wish to leave behind what has grown old:

Don't we go,
as you have gone from me, grim-faced
from his empty hands and his helplessness?
(RANS 105)

With this deliberate effort of understanding, Rilke would impel himself beyond his present state of separation, but his additional leap from here is bewildering as it builds on the very poem to Lou by which he had once conveyed his absolute devotion to her, in the days before "Monastic Life". This love-poem to her, as we have seen, Lou had said was worthy to be spoken rather of Rilke's God, and she had proposed he include the poem in his *opus* to God. It had not found its way into "Monastic Life", but Rilke interpolates it here, the poem that begins

Put out my eyes: I see you still the same;
deaden my ears: I cannot help but hear you;
(RANS 107)

Thus does Rilke fall back on this form of expression of the *old* as a way of catapulting himself towards the new. He would claim, quite after the fact, that he still "sees" and "hears" his God but on the basis of this old poem, which will have us wondering what God this can be. Is not Rilke here, in spite of his ingenious manoeuvre, or indeed just because he is reduced to it, still caught up in a chimera of the old, still at the mercy of his former life? It was only *in* that life that he had found that God. However, as it happens, by means of this bewildering move Rilke does manage to polevault into an impressive *imagination* of the new relationship to God that he must now find. He has managed, in this artificial way, to work himself up to it. He is ready, he says, to offer his soul to the new God, just as the biblical Ruth, herself widowed yet faithful to the future, once offered herself to her mother-in-law's kinsman, Boaz. From the marriage between Boaz and Ruth, David, the future King of Israel, is born. In "Monastic Life" Rilke had, in his relationship to his God, already identified himself with David (RANS 59); here he desperately seeks the new David in a new communion of his soul with his God such as the widowed Ruth once sought with Boaz. So faithfully committed—"heaping you sheaf on sheaf" (RANS 109), Rilke will thus succeed in forging the (spiritual-poetic) line that will, soon he hopes, bring him to his new God, the God in Whom Rilke's new fate reposes.

"And you inherit" he goes on to proclaim, in a projection like David's own projection of the new Zion. In Rilke's God everything of this world, both past and future, reposes; thus Rilke can look forward to his immediate emotional predicament finding resolution in due course:

> *And you inherit the green*
> *of gardens over and gone, the silent blue*
> *of fallen heavens ...*

> (RANS 111)

All is collected from this world to be received by this God: "days of dew", "summers", "springs" "autumns", "winters", "all sound". And all "image makers" do the same: poets, painters, sculptors; "also all who love gather for you", and if not immediately then in time, "[f]or you", says Rilke, *"receive* the copiousness of things" (RANS 113). And in a throwback to the kind of recovery he once made in the days of his deep depression, when he still managed to re-affirm, in spite of remaining in despair, his view that "prayer":

> *breaks off and falls and falls*
> *until God stretches out beneath it*
> *like a rolling meadowland ...*

> (SN, *Diaries*, 170)

here, too, in the midst of his ongoing bewilderment Rilke maintains his ultimate faith that indeed

> *falls our abounding*
> *fullness into the valleys of your land*
> *when things and thoughts brim and spill over.*

> (RANS 113)

Bewildering indeed is Rilke's complex position in "The Book of Pilgrimage", for, in spite of his hopeful imagination of a new inheritance that he would like to think awaits him, the only thing Rilke can realistically manage for now is a relationship to his God as he has known Him. There is thus, at this point, a return to much of the basic content and even the manner of "The Book of Monastic Life". Rilke's newly understood God offers him potentially a much-needed resolution of his ongoing experience of alienation, but Rilke cannot at present reach to this new God. In the meantime, he can at least continue to re-affirm his God as he has known Him in the face of all that conspires against belief in Him: it is roughly along these lines that "Pilgrimage" proceeds from here, in fact all the way to its end, for twice the length of the poems that, contrastingly, look ahead to resolution. A certain continuity of theme with "Monastic Life" is thus maintained, if at the price of some disjunction in Rilke's immediate situation. He himself is aware that he does not know "what will follow" (RANS 115), but in the meantime he remains the defender of his God. In contrast with this position—maintained by him along with those who at least suffer from their alienated condition in a right way—are the many more who give evidence of "lives into which none have climbed", deliberately or ignorantly walking "paths" that "lead/to the arsenal of things unlived". This is the case, even though, dynamically contradicting this, "*all life is lived*" by God (RANS 117). Human beings err in this respect, unlike the things of nature. A measure of our sudden removal from the idiom of the first set of poems in this new "Book" is the fact that Rilke's God, Who has been projected as a "son" and a "heir", is now cast as an "old man", a universal blacksmith Who never ceases at *His* work even when human beings allow themselves their time of détente and escape:

> *When the mill stands, and the saw runs down,*
> *and the workers slow, steeped in drink,*
> *then we can hear your hammer-strike*
> *in all the bells of the city.*

The image of church "bells" ringing returns us to the idiom of "The Book of Monastic Life", and to the understanding that Rilke is here writing from such inspiration as he cannot deny. The "hours" that are chimed by these "bells" are the moments in which the sounds out of which his *opus* to God is being created rise up from within him irresistibly. Such sounding from within is still taking him over: it continues to speak to him of a God Who speaks "to those who bear the burden" (RANS 119), but his disciple has a certain way to go:

> *From watching things, he has to learn,*
> *child-like, how he may start again,*
>
> ....
>
> *but this disciple knows what his lesson must be:*
> *One thing he must know: **how to fall,***
> *and rest, patient, in gravity—*
>
> (RANS 123)[100]

This view serves as a significant counter-measure to the tendency Rilke had shown recently to hopeless despair, as he no doubt must have remarked to himself when writing these lines. But in context his focus is rather on the tendency in human beings generally to prefer other circumstances than those supportive of that natural living by which one learns to understand God's ways. Rilke is here recovering the sense of where his God is naturally to be found. Thus is this God a God of "familiar circumstance" (RANS 123), by which Rilke means reigning through a course of natural life that is closely bound to the rhythms of the "earth" (RANS 121).

The overwhelming pattern among human beings is rather to do and to go where one wills irrespective of the "laws of creation" (RANS 121), and from a lust for "liberty" that in fact only leads to "blank space" (RANS 123). At the other extreme there is the tendency to insist on "lock"-ing oneself entirely "outside" God's creation in "little zones" of comfort and security that only breed *in*security and a desperate loneliness. This is a God Who otherwise has no regard for showing Himself miraculously to please a heathen instinct (RANS 119), *or* for the elaborate theology of the Christian, who would vainly seek to prove God's existence and His qualities through "disputation". Rilke will, contrastingly, "ripen" (RANS 121) as he is naturally meant to ripen: "my *own* maturing / ripens your reign"[101]. In the meantime he will count himself among those who wish to know "*how to fall*" (RANS 123) as things fall in nature: in contrast with one who would "[pretend to think] that wings / flew him faster than birds fly." It is as if by this point Rilke had subtly manoeuvred himself *back* into fully believing again his moralizing thoughts of old, as if he had never left off writing "The Book of Monastic Life", and as if no further attention were being given to the insidious repercussions of the tragedy of his life after the writing of "Monastic Life". Yet had he not been changed and newly challenged by this tragedy, and did he not now have to find, with what was still only the prospect of a resolution of that tragedy, quite another, new way of reaching a God Who had, in the meantime, gone before him? Rilke's difficulties remained: this the early poems in "Pilgrimage" elaborately argue, and yet all this seems suddenly to have been disowned, indeed repressed by Rilke by this later point in the sequence.

"Submissive you want us" (RANS 125), Rilke next declares: it is as if his God had never left him or he had never left his God:

> *bent over your track*
> *as if the years bowed our back.*
> ....
> *To us you're new and good and near*
> *And marvellous ...*

Thus does Rilke now take himself back to the Russia of his ideal imagination: to that place in his mind known to him in the best of times with Lou, of which one could say that everywhere and at all times there was nothing but the quest for God. That is how Rilke continued to see Russia: as a "[l]andscape ... abandoned to the greater heavens" and a people in a condition of universal pilgrimage, seeking God even if it meant leaving the comfort of their isolated hamlet on the vast plains and risking death on their pilgrimage (RANS 127). And if one generation might not venture on this pilgrimage the next would. Russia is a place that is about leaving the security of home and the well-known day-world for the world of "night" (RANS 129) of this God, about cultivating the "folly" that is wisdom.

It is in this Russia that one finds monks who give themselves up to this God so completely as to deny themselves any vestige of a link to the life of the world, going so far as to literally build "underground" to bring themselves as near as possible to the point of death so that they might "come closest of us all to eternity" (RANS 131). Here we find those for whom the outside world "exists no more" (RANS 133), because for them there is only this God. And it is from this place that God's future is forecasted: these monks live their lives so drastically today only so that one day this God may "fill" these "vessels" made "indestructible" with His own "life's blood" (RANS 131). Paradoxically, it is out of the efforts of such monks that there will arise a new world made at last so real with this God there will by then be "no churches", only "houses open and hospitable" and

> *a sense of sacrifice illimitable*
> *in you, in me, and in all our dealing.*
> *No fruitless searching for what lies beyond,*
> *rather a wish not to devalue Death,*
> *learning to serve and practise things of the earth*
> *so we may feel familiar in his hands.*
>   (RANS 137)

Pilgrimages in the actual Russia of Rilke's own day point forward to a time when stepping out of houses to encounter this God on the road will be an immediate and a universal experience (RANS 139). Rilke claims, what's more, to have "seen" this future world in his mind:

> *But I have seen them wandering in train,*
> ....
> *so great their passage and the plains they follow.*

Clearly, some of Rilke's most deeply cherished ideals were being brought into focus in these poems, not least the idea of living natural-ly with death, and with and for the things of the earth through which Rilke's God moves: ideas we have come across before. Nevertheless, such a frankly utopian projection, in which Rilke continues to im-merse right through to the end of "The Book of Pilgrimage", awakens inevitably the thought that here he was escaping from his own present predicament and from himself. Rilke's new experience of alienation, which had already gone very far, had radically, and bafflingly for now, altered the terms of his relationship to his God. But it seems very possible that he knew that he was escaping; some lines from one of the poems suggest as much:

> *So would I seek you, taking alms*
> *reluctantly given on foreign thresholds,*
> *and if confused by many paths*
> *look for companions among the old*
>   (RANS 141)

A failure of spiritual life and a general confusion of values in the parts where he presently lives that are "foreign" to a culture such as Russia's—and here one must include his own confusion—all this has driven Rilke back to Russia's "old", or traditional, ways. He reserves enough of the old impulse to seek God, even from where he is, to be able to *re*-join for the moment those in Russia who "were indescribably close to me" precisely because of their traditional commitment to God even through their oppression. These include "ancient, shrunken men... /... in dreams", "the blind", "women walking exhaustedly ... pregnant". Rilke had, very simply, gone back to traditional Russia in his mind, certain that the great world lurking in it, with God at its centre, would be recovered: "The world will find the mould of its old might" (RANS 137); God Himself, he says, will recover His greatness: "You too, God, will be great. Greater than anyone / now living among us can describe" (RANS 139). Something of the desperation in Rilke's mental manoeuvre back to Russia is conveyed in the untransformed baldness of this last declaration as well as in the unembarrassed over-reaching wish that "if only I were many pilgrims" (RANS 141) so he could make more of an impression on others. Or was it rather to convince himself, that the line of thought he was pursuing here was not a happy dream only? Two poems later (RANS 145) he has *become* these many pilgrims whom he imagines on one of those chaotic, depressed, yet purposeful traditional pilgrimages with which he especially identifies Russia. The epileptic fit of one of these pilgrims, which is very minutely described, is pictured as, simply, another form of shamanistic ecstatic vision (147) from which the epileptic re-emerges feeling fresh and newly ready for prayer (149).

Rilke's strategic "return" to this Russia can be easily explained as a repressed wish come back to overwhelm him, for through all the trials of his life from the end of his time at Worpswede onward the idea of re-visiting Russia, of returning, that is, to the place where he had once broken through and flourished imaginatively before his trials accrued, remained his constant hope, and here he was belatedly satisfying this hope, filling a need for himself as it were, before going on or being forced to go on. We have made ourselves familiar with the many instances of repressed life in Rilke, and the perverse course of the latter part of "The Book of Pilgrimage" is yet another expression of this. He could hardly be blamed for it. The disjunction between the present challenges of Rilke's new life and his ideal past had never been so great, and the basically regressive direction of "Pilgrimage" graphically reflects this.[102] Already *The Book of Hours*, as a ringing testimony to an unshakeable commitment to God as Rilke had once shared this with Lou, had become a thing of the past. But it remained a work that Rilke felt he had to see through and fill out as he had meant it to be. He would fill out his *opus* even if it meant reverting to a mode of thought and a manner he had outgrown, so that his execution of it was bound to degenerate, as it does in the latter part of "Pilgrimage", into a form of imitation. Execution of this sort was something that came too easily to him, and he could have carried on with it indefinitely, as he would remark himself towards the end of his career, by which time he had, of course, greatly extended his range as a poet.[103]

In the third-to-last poem of "The Book of Pilgrimage", Rilke returns in a deliberate way to the metaphor of "summer" as if to bring unity to his structural presentation, having spoken of "summer" in the very first poem of this sequence. But in this 32nd poem of the sequence summer is a different thing: it concerns "preparedness", in the sense that one has made oneself fully ready and disposed towards the otherworld. "Summer" in the first poem refers rather to "a happy time" such as the one he had known with his Worpswede associations, which had then to give way to a new period of tragic living. The divergence in content reflects, in fact, a fundamental division in Rilke's sequence, which he had *tried* to smooth over, as we have seen by a bewildering shift back to old ways (as in "Put out my eyes" etc— see p.127). Some additional trick of perspective may be what Rilke was again attempting here, in speaking of a "summer" associated with both sections, but it is rather the *difference* between one section and the other that is highlighted, and by no means in the way of a progression. At the end of this sequence, Rilke is carrying on with the contrast between authentic seekers after otherworldly vision and those who allow themselves to drift meaninglessly in worldly time. This contrast, at a certain point in the sequence (in the 11th poem) Rilke had made into his principal theme, displacing the issue of alienation sounded in the sequence's first part. A comparative dearth of content shows especially at this later point, as if Rilke had reached the limits of what he could present on the basis of the Russian model of faithful living. The simple point is made: God is now implored not to take offense with those who continue to use the word "mine" when speaking of many things, for these pilgrims in life, in contrast with the worldly, know better than to pretend to possession when it comes to God (RANS 153, 155). The sequence then ends with a poem in which Rilke's latent personal desperation suddenly manifests dramatically: he projects himself as a tree sucking at God from the air, his hands, bloodied from digging for his God, having transformed in the meantime into branches: decidedly the ghastly projection of a stubbornly insistent wish:

> *And with them I shall suck you from the air,*
> *as though, following an impatient gesture,*
> *you had fragmented there, and now drifted*
> *downwards, world of crumbling dust falling*
> *from stars to the earth, softly*
> *as rain that falls in spring.*

(RANS 155)

The fulfilment is all *in* the wish, as that final reference to softly falling rain suggests, for Rilke's God of old had in the meantime indeed "fragmented" and turned into "crumbling dust falling". God Himself had moved on.

***

Rilke would have far more success with his impulse to fall back on Russia as a life-ideal and a recourse for righting[104] himself in "The Book of Poverty and Death". With this additional new segment Rilke was coming back to *The Book of Hours* for yet a third time, a full year and a half beyond "The Book of Pilgrimage". By then his circumstances had greatly changed again. He had just taken flight from Paris where he had had those many dreadful experiences that we have seen him describe in his letters to Lou when he first approaches her again. In this new segment to his poem, however, Rilke does not invoke the personal dimension to these experiences so openly. Such discretion about himself here contrasts with the forceful way he brings his personal experiences forward in the first part of "The Book of Pilgrimage". As a consequence of this reserve, in "The Book of

Poverty and Death" Rilke can be more consistently and genuinely in denial for the moment. His personal experiences, both at the time of "The Book of Pilgrimage" and the time of "The Book of Poverty and Death", pointed to the need for forms of resolution in his relation to his God that lay in the far future. The reality of alienation had, in fact, taken over, but in the meantime it was still possible for him to revert to the God he had known as *one* measuring-stick for dealing with what had become new challenges to his imagination. This was a different course from the impulse simply to revert to this God only as He was to Rilke before his experience of alienation, as in "The Book of Pilgrimage". The ideal of living fruitfully with the ways of earthly nature or of God's creation as He gave this to us, an ideal that included also accepting death in a natural way, continued to have a bearing on the forms the resolution of human tragedy would take. Moreover, to the problem that concerned him now, the still more horrible degree of alienation of city life, which Paris had especially impressed upon him, Rilke could naturally oppose his experience of Russia as a contrasting standard of truthful living (however oppressed Russian social culture may have been in fact). This was one way in which one would expect Rilke to respond to the alienation he had witnessed in Paris, which had indeed descended to the most unnatural forms of subsistent life. There was spiritual poverty in this sort, and another spiritual poverty that was an awakening to God, and Rilke would, given his background, naturally wish to re-affirm the latter in the face of the former as the true nature of poverty. At the same time Rilke could call on his God for yet another form of ideal hope that his experience of Paris had impressed upon him as a need: the standard of the "One" (RANS 169) who would have to come to set the world right also about the real nature of our relationship to death.

One of the horrible impressions Rilke's Paris experience made on him was of a population that had descended so deeply into alienation no death of any meaningfulness could come to them. Blighted destinies were being dragged out to the point where life had already become an extended death:

> *There the white-bloomed lead their pale existence*
> *And die aghast at their burdens' universe.*
>
> (RANS 163)

> *And deathbeds stand there in the gloom; soon*
> *and imperceptibly they come to want them;*
> *and die their dragging death in chains...*
>
> (RANS 161)

The death they already know in this predestined form becomes the one they seek:

> *forlornly*
> *they mill round outside hospitals, anxious*
> *and waiting shakily for late admittance.*
>
> *And death is there.*
>
> (RANS 163)

It was a social scene that had brought home to Rilke the need to learn the one great lesson of *how* to die:

> *O Lord, give each of us our own death:*
> *... born of each life,*
> *our own desire, our purpose ...*

A proper death, the poet argues, is the consummation of a life:

> *For we are only rind of fruit, and leaf.*
> *The great death, which each of us contains,*
> *is that fruit round which the world turns.*
>
> *Into it is given all the warmth*
> *of hearts*
>
> (RANS 165)

In contrast with this death, any death known to this alienated population could only be some form of final sterility: "hanging in them like a fruit/unripening, and green" (RANS 163). Yet Rilke is made aware that to a greater or lesser extent we all fail to die a proper death: "For we have all/less than entirely died" (RANS 167).

At this point Rilke suddenly gives expression to his own pessimism, which we have come to know well, speaking again the way he had in his *Diaries* when he himself was overcome with despair about his life. Rilke's way of expressing himself in what follows will evoke to an English reader the drastic pessimism of Shakespeare and his Jacobean contemporaries. Significantly Rilke returns here also to

that central mother-metaphor on which, at various points, all of his
destiny seemed to hinge:

> *Surely we have whored with eternity*
> *and when we come to childbed bring forth*
> *only the stillborn foetus of our death:*
> *embryo, bent, full of misery,*
> *trying to cover with its mere hands*
> *(as though in fear of the fearful) eyes unformed*
> *still; and on its bulged forehead stands*
> *dread of its destiny unmet, unsuffered—*
> *so die we all, like just so many whores,*
> *in labour pains, and from caesareans.*
>
> (RANS 167)

The expression at the last descends to the very level of endlessly bitter
hopelessness that Rilke had, for a time, experienced, himself. It is
the very malaise he had known in that dark transitional period lived
out with Lou between his return from Worpswede and his eventual
engagement to Clara. Yet it is of additional significance that when his
malaise comes to meet him as a *social* phenomenon, shared by many
others who have taken the experience to real depths, Rilke should
react in offense, turning his thoughts to the idea of the One who must
come to right this self-blighting disposition in human nature, and who
is to teach us the way once again to God's creation:

> *Send us the One*
> *who guides into our hands the precious skill*
>
> (RANS 167)

> *Create One who is glorious, Lord, and great;*
> *build into his being creation's seat;*
>
> ....
>
> *And give one night for mankind to receive*
> *what never yet trod deep in us—one night*
> *in which all things start to bloom ...*
>
> (RANS 169)

Over a few poems the One Who is to come is very powerfully
invoked, as is also Rilke's role in relation to Him. He is the first manifestation of the Rilkean Hero, of whom Rilke would go on to make

so much in the rest of his work, from the time of his early engagement with the Elegies onwards (that is to say, from the time of his momentous Duino experience, in 1912). In "The Book of Poverty" this Hero is no immediate Savior, rather an expression of that future God Who, precisely as the God Who is to be "completed", will only one day bring resolution to the tragedy of human living. There is a strong structural affinity to the God invoked in the first part of "Pilgrimage" Who has gone ahead to create the resolution needed to make up for Rilke's present inability to overcome himself.[105] In the meantime, as the One Who is created by Rilke's God, Rilke's Hero is a Christ-like figure but, consistent with Rilke's bias on this score, He is not the Christ of tradition:

> *But do not fulfil, O powerful provider,*
> *dreams of the woman who was to bear God*
> (RANS 171)

This Salvator Mundi is not about living our way into another life in a world beyond our own, but about properly living into our lives and into our deaths here:

> *but raise, real to us, our own death's bearer,*
> *and lead us, passing us through the hands of those*
> *who tread his path with him, to where he is.*

Rilke's Hero, as One who will once again bring in for mankind God's natural creation, is He who will manage to delve fully into the soul's creative resources as given from childhood—the very ideal Rilke had set for himself from the time of his encounter with Rodin as we have seen, and which in his own youth Rilke himself had failed:

> *Ensure he can re-learn his childhood, touch*
> *subconsciousness and the wonderful, re-hear*
> *in the lavish darkness of a saga cycle*
> *the intimations of his young years.*
> (RANS 169)

Rilke additionally sees himself as the "mouthpiece" (RANS 171) for this Hero; like another David dancing about the Ark, he is the one who would dance around this Hero and who would sing of Him:

And round this holy Ark make me your dancer,
player, baptist; make me the new Messianic
mouthpiece of the inheritance.

     I'll blossom into playing
my harp ...

Thus does Rilke consciously return to the "inheritance" he had projected for himself in the first part of "The Book of Pilgrimage" (see
p.128), and to some extent he has for a moment really come into that
"inheritance" here. He has reached at least some *degree* of resolution
of his personal predicament. He also appears to have *consciously* had
the sense of playing two roles in relation to his own and the world's
difficulties, of having two voices: one "to prepare/him who is waiting
in the distances", the other "simply as beatitude,/vision, and angel
of my solitudes". They are to be the "two voices" Rilke will bring to
bear on what he characterizes as "the wrath of time" (RANS 173).
Whether he conveys the sense of "beatitude" in the rest of his last
two Books is a moot point. Perhaps this is more a reference to the
sounding of the hours of his poetic inspiration as he was being driv-
en to write these poems, but the result is not quite beatitude, more
like a devoted faith to his past experience in Russia as *one* available
frame of reference for measuring the challenges of the time, though
one become anachronistic. The recourse to Russia is more successfully applied in "The Book of Poverty" than it is in "The Book of
Pilgrimage", but it too remains backward-looking. At least in "The
Book of Poverty" Rilke finds a way of convincing us that it was still
of some value to continue to have recourse to the Russian experience,
as a point of reference while awaiting the fuller coming in of Rilke's
Hero. Rilke himself was in transition, more disturbed than ever, in
fact, judging from the letters he wrote Lou within two months of
completing "Poverty", but he had won his way to some real hope
and, out of the prospect of that hope, was ready to accept working
from what resources he had in facing the new challenges—"if", as he
resigns himself, and speaking to his God, "into towns and fears you
wish to strew me".

  Imagining his way to his Hero, Rilke has at least found a way
out of the despair he expresses in the poems that open the sequence,
as to whether he can find a proper relation to a deeper experience of

alienation: his "potent angst before over-swollen cities / in which you have stood me, buried to the chin" (RANS 157). Rilke at that point imagined himself "affecting" his God "with my entire crying", feeling that he himself had turned to stone from the stony ways of Paris. He had been thrust into a very dark reality, without as yet having found any proper recourse, aware no doubt that here was an experience that the appeal to Russia could not quite counterbalance:

> *Everything is proximity*
> *and proximity has turned to stone.*
>
> *And I am no expert in the lore of pain—*
> *this great thickness of dark diminishes me;*
>
> *...*
> *........................and I*
> *affecting you with my entire crying.*

However, Rilke could feel supported now by his deeper hope in his Hero, a hope he had really begun to tap into in himself, the germ of which at least he had, for the moment, found. With this deeper hope in reserve, he could at the same time allow himself to carry on on the basis of those "hours" of inspiration that continued to sound in him unstoppably. Possessed of this double consciousness, Rilke could thus at least affirm himself with a fresh sense of the integrity of his purposes. Sorting himself out in this way, Rilke follows through with the rest of "Poverty and Death" with a considerable ease and even mastery, in comparison with the desperately anxious, one-dimensional expression we find in the second part of "The Book of Pilgrimage". It was an advance on the disjunctive split we have observed in "Pilgrimage" that Rilke had yet let stand. Now he was ready to pronounce on the scene he had taken flight from:

> *Great cities are untruth: faithless and false*
> *to child and animal, to night, day;*
>
> *...*
> *Nothing of the wide and real*
>
> *...*
> *happens in them.*
>
> (RANS 173)

What follows in the rest of The Book of Poverty" is a straightforward, if powerful, condemnation of modern cities and especially
of those city dwellers who, going along with the unnatural currents
of city life, become "subservient to cult and craze" (RANS 193). Such
dwellers engender in turn, by their own success at survival, a population of the marginalized who are not spared by them and who consequently are made "hesitant and vulnerable ... susceptible/and given
over to a hundred torments" (RANS 163). But these deprived others
are not, Rilke, insists,

> *poor, but rather the unrich,*
> *adrift without will of their own or world;*
> *marked out with the scars of ultimate fears,*
> *disfigured ...*
>
> *They gather to them all the dust of the cities,*
> *and all the waste of streets clings to their hands:*

(RANS 179)

They are to be distinguished, in fact, from the authentic poor, which
they could be making themselves into; only, they have allowed themselves to be dragged into the material degradation that has subjected
them.[106] Here is where Rilke's experience of the authentic poor in
Russia turns out to be relevant and especially valuable for measuring
differences. *These* poor have stopped short at surrendering to degradation, continuing to serve God in their poverty. They are, in contrast
with the "unrich", especially to be honoured and protected as a class
of religious-minded people, and they become from here the main
focus of Rilke's sequence over many pages. Yet, having carefully distinguished the class of the "unrich" from the class of the authentic
"poor", Rilke ends by breaking through the distinction, treating the
"unrich" (momentarily) as but another degraded version or degree of
the "poor", being those "poor" *in potentia* and in this kind especially
in need of God's protection. Rilke was surely thinking of his own
potential role in this picture where he entreats God:

> *If there by any mouth for **their** protection*
> *free it; stir it to the responsible.*

(RANS 193)

How confident, however, could he be about his role in *this* regard? Certainly he ends his sequence very strongly, by invoking, with great awe, the grand figure of St. Francis, the classic model and patron saint of poverty in the West, of whom Rilke says:

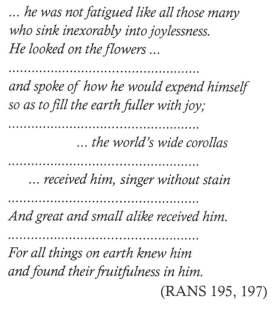

... he was not fatigued like all those many
who sink inexorably into joylessness.
He looked on the flowers ...

....

and spoke of how he would expend himself
so as to fill the earth fuller with joy;

....

... the world's wide corollas

....

... received him, singer without stain

....

And great and small alike received him.

....

For all things on earth knew him
and found their fruitfulness in him.

(RANS 195, 197)

This resounding invocation of St. Francis's achievement puts us in mind of Rilke's other, main Hero in this sequence who likewise represents the ideal of living by the standard of God's creation. However, St. Francis, as the classic model of a religious consciousness based in poverty, and as a 'saving' singer, will strike us, in the context of Rilke's presentation, as a somewhat obvious note to end on, and also not quite fitting. He is presented as a Savior of the poor, but of the "unrich"? He is, what is more, a figure from the West, while much of this sequence, not to mention *The Book of Hours* as a whole, had focused, almost perversely, on Russia in the East, raising yet another issue about the structural integrity of Rilke's *opus*. In the end West and East meet in the *Book of Hours* in less than fully certain terms (the reader is referred further to Rilke's predominantly Western attitudes in "The Book of Monastic Life" as illustrated above). However that may be, the appalling challenge to his imagination that Rilke faced in the "unrich" of Paris remained, and the sequence in the end barely addresses the problem of redress as far as they are concerned. There is one hint of the need for a spokesperson with God on behalf of their sufferings: a "mouth" stirred, as he puts it, "to the responsible", but Rilke would have much trouble thinking of himself in this desired role, if only because he dreaded the thought of knowing too well what these "unrich" exposed about a tendency to depression in himself. We know this from the letters Rilke wrote to Lou two months later, but also from his diatribes against Paris when he was still trapped in the city.[107] "The Book of Poverty and Death" had in the meantime served well as a necessary ballast, to keep him afloat while he began his long dealings with new forms of disturbance to his mind and soul that he had personally witnessed and shared in when in Paris. Russia had served as a momentary salve; the thought of extending what he had gained from his Russian experience as far as he could, in spite of the new circumstances, which had raised challenges more difficult than any even he had known—this may well be what had kept him together over this dark interim period, as he struggled privately with the actual terms of his personal experience, such as this had become.

In the meantime, *The Book of Hours* represented Rilke's past, an august past that continued to sound in him irrepressibly and that could not be denied, but it was the past all the same. To this past— which had become a monistically religious past—Rilke had indeed been more than faithful, even if his God had in the meantime long since moved on, very much to Rilke's dismay. It is when one looks back on *The Book of Hours* from the perspective of Rilke's changing experience, over the long period it took him to write it, that one appreciates to what extent this work was imposed on Rilke from the past. This did not make it any less a potent symbol, in fact all the more so, and not only for Rilke but also for Lou, especially when they eventually met in person, four years after separating, to share the accomplishment between them.[108] This work represented as much as could be celebrated of their shared past, and it certainly meant much to them both; one must think it had all the more meaning for them for being stained by the marks of repression and the inevitable reaction, on both sides, which this repression had generated. One imagines a scene of much pathos, of regret and forgiveness without a doubt, even if nothing would appear to have been explicitly said about this at the time. Things had very much changed by then, yet both seemed ready to accommodate this change. The Rilke whom Lou was meeting now was a man and a poet who knew his mind with an utmost degree of clarity; as we have seen (on pp.28-31), he knew himself better than Lou did, who would indeed quickly learn her own new position in relation to him. Rilke had, in fact, become his own guide, but he had also been marked by his destiny, a destiny that, at a certain depth, could only be shared with Lou. It was *their* shared destiny: the disposition to despair and to know despair, which he had brought to their relationship, that awful disposition which Lou, by her way of dealing with him, ironically *kept* him in, was now his to bear for good. He had been condemned to it, but he was also building a way for dealing with it. His return to Lou was a very essential part of that way. She would know, better than anyone else could, what disposition of mind and soul he could at any time fall into, this having now become the main challenge of his life, as a man and a poet. Every so often she would be needed to salve the wound, and she herself was only ready to serve in that role, making up in this way for her own part in it. It was also her way of dealing with the wound in herself, created by a full separation from Rilke that she had never really wanted.

A very unique destiny grew out of this for both of them. Between them they had opened up a sphere of the world that hardly anyone else would dare look into or take on but that Rilke would take on, would have to take on, to the great peril of his mind and soul, and his body. A certain depth of darkness he would have to descend into, but with the best hopes of clarity of mind that he and Lou, together, would help to maintain in him. This was to be chiefly his way—the way, as one might put it, through *Malte*. But in the meantime his resources of mind and soul would also have to be built up as far as they could; his progress as a poet who was destined to reach out in every direction would have to be satisfied, and he knew, had always known, better than Lou, all that he had to give expression to in himself in order to achieve this progress. It would have to be a progress not only in sounds (and their "hours") but also in images— thus the many poems he had been writing, especially since his stay at Worpswede with Clara and with Paula, and that had much to do with his development as a poet working with images. Here was a project that Lou might at one time have sabotaged, taking exception to what seemed to her the lesser culture out of which it originated. Rilke's stubborn commitment to the dictates of his own poetic conscience had prevailed against this position.

The Book of Images was the eventual, very fine result. Already three years before his reunion with Lou, Rilke had put out its first slim edition, and within a year of this reunion would put out a second extended edition, making it at last a fair–sized volume and the equal of *The Book of Hours*. Already, too, Rilke had been thinking more and more of a poetry of things, to fill out the range of his poetic capabilities further, this from the time of his close association with Rodin. The result of that thinking lay farther in the future, two years beyond the second edition of *The Book of Images*, but the progress Rilke would make also in this sphere was no less inexorable. It led in time to the magnificent two volumes of *New Poems*, to which Rilke might easily have given, and perhaps ought to have given—to highlight more clearly the overall project he had laid down for himself—the title *The Book of Things*. Finally, I have hinted at the psychological background to Rilke's development that made the later visitation at Duino, which runs directly counter to how Rilke was evolving up to that moment, itself inevitable, since Rilke had from the time of the aftermath of his experience in Florence become a divided being, oriented, by his destiny, in one direction when he was only too well made for another.

III

Rilke's Defeated Hopes After Florence

The main factors that made separation between Lou and Rilke inevitable included their great difference in age and the fact that Rilke was so young at the time they met, these combining with the fact that he was destined, when still relatively young, to become as great a poet and a thinker as Lou was a fiction writer and a philosophical thinker. The evidence of an exceptionally precocious mind in Rilke is there from the beginning, and it manifests most clearly for the first time in the Diary he wrote while visiting Florence in the spring of 1898. It was Lou's idea that he should begin to think of extending his education with a first-hand experience especially of Florence. The plan was for Lou to meet up with him there after a visit she had to make to her family in Russia. The remarkable enthusiasm of Rilke's entries in the first half of this Diary have much to do with the fact that he was suddenly exposed to the wonders of quattrocento Florence first-hand while on his own and with the reservation of knowing excitedly, too, that Lou would be joining him there. They would be more alone than they had ever been, more alone even than they had been when they set up in Wolfrathausen not long after first meeting and becoming lovers.

The first sections of the Diary are brim-full with Rilke's growing sense of self-identity, which he traces to a primordial feeling of "longing" that he now feels he shares with the great artists of the early Renaissance. As Rilke would have it, this was nothing other than, "the longing for oneself" that, unconsciously, reaches to God (SN, *Diaries*, 20). No other extraneous factor is admitted into this primordial "longing", which is presented as *identical with an immediate experience of historical progression and historical fulfilment*. It is impossible to say to what extent this and other declarations of first principles in this Diary stem from discussions with Lou when, anticipating this trip, they initiated their study of the early Renaissance together back in Berlin. One way or the other, Rilke has in this Diary clearly made such principles his own personal possession. The "longing" he would champion could, to be sure, be explained away as an expression of the pre-Raphaelite fashion of his time, but he himself insists that it is more than about such fashion: "It is not chance and whim and fashion that leads us to those who precede Raphael" (SN, *Diaries*, 38). There is a deeper *historical* continuity to trace in this case that makes the artists of his day potentially the legitimate "heirs" of that former time, however *not* with the static purpose of consolidating the experience of that time in a purely nostalgic way, or from a general historical "weariness", the actual significance of which Rilke also explains; on the contrary, he says:

> *you must forget your weariness: you inherited it from those who at the edge of the quattrocento perceived: summer is trying to break through, and we can only blossom ... and from those who felt: we are being kept from ripening into summer ...*
>
> (SN, *Diaries*, 40)

Rilke's Florence Diary abounds with the most remarkable insights about the limits of that former time and especially the unique perfection that was attained within those limits, which could not be repeated. Of the artists and indeed the people generally of this time, Rilke says:

> *They feel a plenitude of eternities, and because they nowhere venture all the way to the borders, they nowhere find barriers ...*
>
> (SN, *Diaries*, 37)

> *There is a chaste coolness in their Madonnas and the austere strength of young trees in their Saints ... the gestures of their figures are ... full of a trembling expectation ... consecrated by longing ...*
>
> *That was spring ... and ... it is left precisely for our era to begin the summer of this far-off and festive spring, and slowly unfold toward heavy fruit ...*
>
> (SN, *Diaries*, 36-37)

Inevitably, there grew out of the limits of that former time, in spite of the kind of perfection that was known to it, precisely the *consciousness* of limits and the impulse to evolve beyond those limits, but necessarily without avail. Rilke concentrates on the late Raphael[109], as well as Michelangelo:

> *Those in the Renaissance also received a budding strength that strove so rapidly toward summer: Michelangelo grew, Raphael stood in bloom. But the fruit never came ... They would have soon lived everything in a single breath out to the end. But the loving order slowed their tempestuous advance ...*
>
> (SN, *Diaries*, 40)

The distortions that followed in Michelangelo were an especially intense case:

> *Michelangelo ...* **that** *was someone with the strength for summer. But ... the season would still be only an immeasurable spring ... His Madonnas deny their springtime. They feign, to be sure, the happiness of a completely earthly fulfilment. One could almost believe them ... But this lie makes them hard and unfeminine, and they get beyond virginity and maternalness with one violent shove, to arrive at a kind of defiant heroism ...*
>
> (SN, *Diaries*, 62)

The progression from spring into summer in Rilke's own time would not, however, be as simple as one might suppose. For Rilke, progression would require, first, a genuine and full identification with the spirit of that former time (such as he was himself conveying in this Diary). This was in itself already a challenge: "You must *love* them", he says—"Can you still do that?", for "[t]hat", he says, "is the test" (SN, *Diaries*, 40). The main problem lay in overcoming a natural inclination to grasp that time only in one's conscious judgment, which would have to be denied: "You shall not know them and categorize them and judge them as is your wont". The progression from a mere theoretical idea to an actual historical identification with what has flowed out of that time is what Rilke experienced very early on this trip:

> *Then one day before Botticelli's* **Magnificat** *I forgot for once about my judgment and the judgment of the others. That's when it happened. I looked into a struggle and had the sensation of a victory. And my joy was like no other ...*
>
> (SN, *Diaries*, 20)

"*Their* longings" he adds, in celebration of his own victory at this moment, "live on in *us*", "[s]ince", as he puts it farther along, speaking of himself at least, "we now *grasp* that innermost beauty again" (SN, *Diaries*, 37)[110]. But "can our love", he asks further, "enable it to ripen further?" Even the young Rilke was under no illusion as to where things had come to historically: "We have lived through centuries since then ... We have grown older not only in years, but also in goals." In the meantime: "Spring's pale endlessness we have invented as a lie": and it would be necessary to abandon a decadent survival of a decidedly past experience. Also, as he points out, "you must forget your weariness", an experience which he depicts as an unfortunate symptom of living cluelessly in the shadow of that former time.

As we have seen (on p.53), for Rilke it came down to two additional things: acknowledging, as the artists of the Quattrocento did not have to, since they had not yet come into a consciousness of historical "barriers", first that "We must be human", and that "we know ourselves in a cramped finality". Second that "We need eternity, for it alone provides our gestures room." The resolving term, weaving hopefully between these forbidding poles, and without which there could be no progression from one to the other (and so the indispensable, magic-making term) is signalled where Rilke insists that "You must have your longing over you" (SN, *Diaries*, 38). It is that "longing for oneself" that Rilke finally makes into his all-in-all, that longing in oneself that ultimately reaches out to "God". None of this was a mere aesthetic project for him but the actual tenor and promise of his fundamental experience at this time: the fundament, he was certain, of his life-experience to come. We need to note at the same time that this was quite another direction from the one he was to take in his later commitment to the God of Russia, as we have seen. The early "longing" was rather in the Catholic and Western line of development, involving a deeper view of the prospect of Christian wholeness, one which could only be realized ultimately through first-hand experience of Christ's Redemption. Such "longing" was bound up, for Rilke, initially with a singularly wholistic view of his experience that included the prospect of a free life of shared personal and artistic development with Lou.[111] However, just as Rilke was proclaiming the momentous destiny which seemed reserved for him and for his time, there appeared, one morning, in the courtyard where he was staying a monk of the Black Brotherhood of Ultimate Mercy. He had come to collect alms from those in the villa within, and remaining in the courtyard as he did for some time, this figure looked to Rilke "like Death himself". Eventually a young boy appeared, to offer the Brother the alms he was waiting for, but in the meantime the scene had transformed—into a vision that played itself out in Rilke's mind. Suddenly he imagined that Death had come for "a white young girl" who was not yet ready to die. The girl has sent word through the boy that she herself "can't come yet" though she has already sent her heart: "I am truly tired, truly. I can't love anymore, take it. But let me gaze a while longer ... Only gaze a while longer" (SN, *Diaries*, 44-45). This was, indeed, a strangely premonitory and symbolic development for, very soon after, Rilke received a letter from Lou that had an effect on him very much like a death. It is impossible to say what Lou's letter contained exactly, but rather momentously he deduced from it the possible end of their relationship:

> *Suddenly it is so dark around me. I don't know where I am. I only feel that I must sit among strangers and travel one day and then another and yet a third in order to be with You at last—in order perhaps: to bid farewell to You.*
>
> (SN, *Diaries*, 46-47)

Certainly among the disclosures of this letter was the communication that Lou would not after all be joining him in Italy as originally planned, which would have been disappointing enough. But some more serious setback to their relationship must be inferred. Here we can only guess what this may have been, but it is possible that Rilke was, naturally, anticipating that their relationship would evolve further from what it had been: that they would become in Florence at last their own couple in spite of Lou's marriage, whereas the new plans, a temporary stay in the distant Baltic resort of Zoppot, actually included the visit of her husband to Zoppot at some point. Perhaps what so shocked Rilke was the inference that there was to be no independent future for them, or why would he be thinking of something so drastic as bidding farewell to Lou? In the meantime a stay in remote Zoppot struck him as fearfully "mundane", especially after the intense visionary import of his time in Italy. Yet, in spite of the turmoil in him, Rilke would come to accept the new plans, feeling that there were more than enough treasures gathered from his trip to share with Lou to allow them to transcend the limitations of their situation:

Why should I fear a mundane beach in East Prussia. For two whole months I have been scooping beauty with blissful hands; I have enough of it to tower up treasures before You and me so that we will be invisible to whomever else will be there too.

(SN, *Diaries*, 47)

Looking back, the defeated young girl who suddenly materializes in Rilke's vision begins to look very strangely like a real portent. If we take the young girl as representing how the relationship between Rilke and Lou would have appeared to him after receiving her letter, one draws the picture of a potential for love that has already died, such that all that remains is the memory of it, to gaze on, before departing from the world.

How true was this, in some sense, of Rilke's relationship to Lou, in the shock of the moment of hearing from her in her letter? Rilke himself seems to have seen something premonitory in the vision he had had, for it was soon after the letter, while still in Italy, that he began the first draft of *The White Princess*. The play would not take final shape for over another year, but in it we find the very import of Rilke's vision in the courtyard artistically transcribed, in metamorphic form as it were. In this play the White Princess awaits a lover whom she excitedly anticipates after eleven years of an unconsummated marriage, to a husband who has also been violent with her (Lou's marriage to Andreas was itself eleven years old and also unconsummated, and he had certainly been violent, though it is not so clear if towards her[112]). The Princess is to let her lover know that all is safe for him to come to her, by waving a flag. But a plague, in the meantime, intervenes, marshalling in the appearance into her principality of the Black Brotherhood, who show up to help with the sick and the dead. And just as the lover is passing through, they come into the Princess's presence, so that she is unable to signal to her lover at that moment. The lover passes by, Tristan-like, and all comes to an end thus...

In the meantime, Rilke would courageously take up his experience in Italy again in the several remaining days before he was to leave to join Lou. He starts up slowly but is soon immersed again in his many insights into the great early Renaissance painters. It is in this later section that he also brings his vision of the prophetic import of Botticelli's work, his Madonnas, the Primavera, and the Venus, to full climactic expression (SN, *Diaries*, 54-55). What Rilke had come into by way of a vision of artistic history arising from his understanding of that former time had become an irrepressible part of him, in spite of the intense personal disappointment he had just experienced. In fact, the revelation he had broken through to had changed him, and what remains, in spite of his difficult past and his recent disappointment, is his sense of the certainty of his historical vision, which had secured him, once and for all, in his own identity:

> *I know: not everything will remain a hymn in me, as in these days; darknesses and confusions will come. But deep within me I have a small garden surrounded by solemn festiveness and no fear will ever reach down that far again.*
>
> (SN, *Diaries*, 65)

Engaged in a conversation one evening over the view of historical destiny he was propounding, it strikes him how truly changed and confident he has become, and his immediate thought is to bring this new spirit of confidence to Lou, as the very strength she embodied and would wish for in him ("How I have admired that in You, my love: this carefree trust in all things, this kindness impervious to fear"—SN, *Diaries*, 38):

> *I wanted so—quickly, quickly—to come to You, for I am aware of something inside me that You don't know about yet, a new great brightness ...*
>
> *Something is sounding from deep within me that through these pages, through my tender songs, and through all my plans of future deeds wants to reach people ...*
>
> *I want to turn them* ['my words'] *to freeing people from the strange fear out of which I came.*
>
> (SN, *Diaries*, 63)

What had freed him from his fear was the certainty of his having tapped into a whole view of where humankind was headed in its history, and of what his role in this might be.

What a shock he would receive, then, when, on presenting himself with his Diary to Lou at their reunion a few days later, she should meet him in his newly found identity with merely an indifferent attention and only more of the same forbearing "kindness" as before. We have only *his* piercingly despairing account of what happened at this reunion, recorded at the end of his Diary, but what happened is clear enough: Lou failed to see the full import of the revelation Rilke had had, and that he really *was* changed inwardly. It is easy to see how she would have failed (like many a critic and biographer in our time) to read through to the deep structural unity of Rilke's account of himself in the Diary, in order to note that he now indeed embodied a whole new dimension of creative spirit in himself. It is easy to see why readers of the Diary would miss out on its deeper structural aspects, since early on into the Diary, and for quite a large part of it (see SN, *Diaries*, 25-33), Rilke is predictably diverted by the well-worn theme of the "crowd" or the "public" and *its* unknowing, debased forms of relationship both to art generally and to God. The contemptible philistinism of the public is invariably contrasted with the superior judgment and experience of the "creative individual" (27) who himself is living out the real issues at hand. As so often with this contrast, the weight of the emphasis falls on a tiring repetition of the usual platitudes about the absurd basis of public taste and judgment. It is not an original contribution; it is a mere rehearsal of what no doubt he and Lou would have discussed in finer tones between themselves. This rather self-indulgent display is long enough, however, to set the tone for the reader and to throw him/her off the scent in the case of the rest. Added to this alienating feature, for Lou, were, of course, the dark impressions Rilke recorded in response to the letter he had received from her that appeared to him to forecast the end of their relationship.[113]

Lou's failure to read Rilke properly is easily set down also to her own preoccupations at this time.[114] She was much engaged by her own work of fiction-writing, which had recently gathered steam. She had also her own studies, was preparing essays, and otherwise had her mind elsewhere than on any artistic fulfilment in terms of 'springtime' Italy. Her spirit was turning, rather, to Russian things whereto she was aiming to lead Rilke. We know how artistically fruitful the Russian trip in the spring of 1899 would be for him; one wonders, nevertheless, how their life together would have unfolded if Rilke's newly discovered identity after Florence had been duly and positively recognized by Lou. There is even more to consider if we take up what I have claimed may well have been his expectation that he and Lou would now be blossoming into their own couple and pursuing their independent life together. What if Lou *had* been given to the prospect of such a life, and, even if not, what if she had at least opened herself to what had been newly created in Rilke, such that his own development in his terms had been integrated into the common life they had going? This 'alternative' life, which never transpired but which very well *could* have, is an additional way of measuring the depth or extent of his despair on this occasion and indeed for the rest of his life. At the end of his Diary, in what has been rightly described as a "jarringly saddened—and powerfully written—coda" to all that precedes (see SN, *Diaries*, xi), Rilke gives a full, highly pained account of the depth of disappointment and frustration he went through at this time. At the beginning of this 'coda', written clearly after Lou had read the Diary, he notes that "much fear and poverty lie between back then and now" (SN, *Diaries*, 74). The strangely incongruous disproportion between his deep experience and Lou's casual reception of it, her inattention and insensitivity, are what compelled these strong words. It is true that in this account he acknowledges, in hindsight, that Lou did become "free and festive through the confidence in this book", but her reception of it, which was soon couched in an "endeavor to give him courage and to raise up his spirits", had hardly done justice to him. There had been something unfair and untruthful, something self-absorbed and condescending about the forbearing kindness of Lou's role at their reunion. This reunion had been, in fact, *dis*-couraging in the extreme.

It is clear that Rilke broke down badly in these circumstances, and he was immediately returned to the same abased role, as heretofore, of debtor to Lou's patient tolerance of his youthful insecurity. What intensified this imbroglio was the fact that Rilke would appear to have broken down instantaneously, without any discussion of the impasse between them. It appears that he fell back into that typical behaviour of complaint and dissatisfaction that had, every so often, burdened their relationship in their first year together. Here was that very tendency to breakdown Rilke felt confident he had broken out of on the basis of his self-transforming experience in Italy. No wonder he was plummeted into fearfulness—the breakdown was brought on by the rebuff, which Rilke experienced as an act of appropriation on Lou's part. As he puts it, despairingly:

> *Invariably I said to myself: "I can give You nothing, nothing at all; my gold turns to coal when I hand it to You, and I become poor in the process."*
>
> (SN, *Diaries*, 75-76)

Addressing this situation more closely, Rilke describes himself as

> *tormented by the fear: that now You, with the riches I had brought you and that You so quickly raised and made your own possession, could begin presenting **me** with gifts ... I was beginning to accept as alms of Your untiring goodness what **I** had fetched in blessed victories ... becoming so pitiful and wretched as this happened that I threw away or lost the last of my own wealth and in my desperation felt only the vague imperative to flee the environs of this goodness that was humiliating me.*[115]

To Rilke's impulse to leave the scene, Lou could only reply distantly and immovably:

> *Your estranged voice put to me the iron question: "What will you do?"*

Again, we can only wonder what alternative form their creative life together might have taken if Lou had opened herself more to Rilke's own particular line of development, if only she had made room for him, or given him any chance to show that he really had found his own identity. It is very likely that his tendency to fearfulness, which had held him in thrall until then, would have been left behind, and he and Lou from that point might have begun to assume precisely what he had projected as their joint future, hers and his: "I wanted You to be more than ever my *future*" (SN, *Diaries*, 76)[116]. As it is, Rilke was too young in relation to Lou; he still felt too subordinate to Lou's powerful personality, and so was unable to stand by his newly found identity, and collapsed. It is the great mystery of Rilke's life that he would, in fact, never again be able to draw away from the fearfulness that, from hereon in, would so encumber his life and his creativity—and also so paradoxically feed it. He had come into this fearfulness in childhood, when he was abused and withdrew into a sometimes unreal isolation on account of this, but it is clear that this fearfulness Lou herself helped to propagate. She offered him relief and many various outlets from the fearfulness, but she also kept him in it. No wonder, then, that summarizing his feelings about her after his Italian experience, Rilke could say about Lou:

> *I hated You like something too **great**.*
>
> (SN, *Diaries*, 75)

Many quite rightful expectations, rightful when seen from Rilke's point of view and the point of view of the import of their love, were stymied, Lou belonging to another sphere, with her own accomplished life to tend to, and representing another way constitutive of her own time in which she was already immovably established.[117] What their much troubled fate at this time would also appear to demonstrate is the irreconcilability of two grand artistic lives where differently destined roles are at stake. Ironically, very early in his Diary and before the accumulation of setbacks, Rilke had anticipated as much, though he could also, uniquely inspired by their relationship, hold out a grander ideal:

> *But two who are solitary are a great danger to each other. Neither shall place his hand on the other's art. For if he takes from one who is greater, he will lose himself ... but of the other's culture the artist may gladly and gratefully partake. In this way each may urge the other toward higher humanity and therefore toward purer art.*
>
> (SN, *Diaries*, 21-22)[118]

Where, then, did Rilke's experience of self-identity and his hopeful projection of a fully shared future life with Lou go?—underground, into his unconscious, where it was repressed and became a source of resentment and rivalry with Lou. There is an open admission of rivalry with her in the great coda:

> *I wanted this time to be the rich one, the giver, the host, the master ... I didn't want to feel Your consolation, I wanted to feel the power inside me to console You ...*
>
> (SN, *Diaries*, 75-76)

In the portion of the Diary that precedes the debacle, Rilke reveals not a rivalry with Lou but simply a natural pride and wonderment that he has suddenly come into his own, his first thought about this being to wish to eagerly share this new event in his life with his Beloved ("I wanted so—quickly, quickly—to come to You"). A richer life, he naturally supposes, will be theirs from the mingling of their shared consciousness of each other's visions, since he too now had "the faith for happiness and the confidence for fulfilment." After the debacle, however, all is sent down into Rilke's unconscious: the wonderment, the pride, the eagerness, the resentment; and the shame of his breakdown and regression to fitful complaining at this time would finally cement the repression. All would return, however, to play havoc with them, especially on their second trip to Russia in the summer of 1900, when their relationship reaches a final breaking-point. In order to continue with Lou he had had to deny his own artistic impulses, but he would not, in fact, be able to—could not—deny them forever, nor should he ever have had to.[119]

In the meantime, the process for him was one of adaptation and orientation back to Lou. Faced with "the iron question": 'What will you *do*?', Rilke responded by finally re-submitting to the relationship they already had going, which was primarily centred in Lou and *her* vision for them and for him. At bottom Rilke's life could only be linked to Lou's in spite of what would have to be the displacement of his own identity for now. There is something pathetic about his formal re-submission to Lou at this point—pathetic in the sense that calls forth a pained pity in us when one considers that this was a man of twenty-two who had grandly come of age. His re-submission to Lou was like that of a child that, because it remains un-free in its relationship to its Mother, must recover its wish for happiness by bowing to Her in spite of Her unfairness:

> *Your strings are rich; and however far I may go—**You are always there before me**. My struggles have in Your case long become victories, and therefore I am sometimes so very small in Your presence; but my new victories are Yours also, and I may present them to you.*

It was a classic case of a return to the Good and Terrible Mother.

The life Rilke was ready to submit to with Lou at this point included, among other things, resuming his subordinate position in the Andreas household where he also had his chores to do (this in return for Lou's cooking!) Soon the kitchen in this household would become a regular place of work for them both (since Lou's husband required the study for himself); this was especially the case when they began their Russian studies together, looking ahead to a planned trip to Russia in the spring of 1899 (their first time).[120] Over the next year, through the winter of 1898-1899, Rilke would give himself to various studies on art history as well as other isolated artistic projects, of minor significance in terms of his main artistic development (continued work on *The White Princess* being an exception to this basically functional state of affairs).[121] He had thrown himself back into work, which included also a fair amount of reviewing for newspapers and journals, in spite of his professed "loathing for journalism"[122]. One significant breakthrough at this time was his essay "On Art" in which he returns to his thoughts in the Florence Diary with a power comparable to the one he had expressed then. His revelation about a fundamental progression in history that is especially served by the artist who knows once again comes to full expression. And it is not a mere coincidence that once again it is a characteristic impulse of Novalis that finds some reflection here: Novalis in his *Hymns* also celebrates the knowing artist (prototypically characterized by him as a "singer") who traverses the centuries and is likewise bringing a future apotheosis closer to realization:

> *From a far shore, came a singer, born under the clear sky of Hellas, to Palestine ... Filled with joy, the singer went on* [over time] *to Indostan, his heart intoxicated with the sweetest love, and poured it out in fiery songs under the tender sky, so that a thousand hearts bowed to him ...*
> (MacDonald, 47, 49)[123]

This artist/singer who originates in a time before Christ has re-appeared centuries later as "the brother" whom Novalis is addressing in his own time:

> *I want to conduct you to a brother who will talk with you so that your hearts rejoice ... [t]his brother* [who] *is the heartbeat of the new age ...*
> (Stoljar, 148-149)[124]

Rilke puts it in this way:

> *Therefore is he who makes it* ['Art'] *into his life-view the Artist,*
> *the man of ultimate ends, who goes through the centuries, with*
> *no past behind him ... For the Creator, God is the last and deepest*
> *fulfilment ... the Artist smiles and says: "He will be" ... works*
> *and builds upon this God ... adds to him a power and a name ...*
> *so that God will be finally completed ...*[125]

Rilke's main line of work and studies over this time, however, consisted in the lengthy, strenuous cultural preparation that was required for the upcoming trip to Russia that Lou had planned for them. This project was all that was needed to help complete Rilke's adaptation, and he appeared to be committed to it[126]. He was, in time, of course to gain immensely from it: his first trip to Russia was decisive in making him for the first time into a major artist, with the production at last, two months after this trip, of "The Book of Monastic Life". We must understand that this work emerged after long immersion in his Russian adventure, and a submissive collaboration with Lou is what had made it possible. However, whether this work is *so much* a product of collaboration with Lou as many have supposed is quite another matter. Certainly it represented also a new and great victory for Rilke himself, a first breakthrough in the way *he* saw the process of fulfilling his artistic mission. It is, as we have seen, as much a work after his own notions of "God-completion" and the fulfilment of an historical "longing" as it is a work that builds on Lou's notion of subjective "God-creating".[127] With this work, Rilke had managed an extraordinary act of reconciliation, or at least of rapprochement, with Lou in spite of the personal setback he had experienced one year before. This was a work that embodied at once what she was, and what he had learned from her, and also what he was and had learned for himself. It finally harmonized the situation and settled the unconscious conflict between them, having made proper room also for him. However, in spite of coming through with "The Book of Monastic Life", or rather just because of this, the situation between himself and Lou would fall apart again—initiating this time a series of events that would decisively lead to separation.

The precarious state of balance Rilke had achieved would be upset when, on their second stay in Russia, Lou again took time somewhat secretly for herself—leaving him at some point altogether in the dark about her purposes.[128] In the meantime Rilke was, once again, struggling with his work; it had stalled seriously, in significant part also because tensions had re-surfaced between himself and Lou from the same causes: her preoccupation with her own affairs undertaken at his expense. In the meantime, he had also acquired the power to think well of himself, in spite of the present dry spell, for he was, after all, the creator of "The Book of Monastic Life": he had come into his own identity, and the scales had tipped in his unconscious rivalry with Lou. The question of his new search for a poetic form appropriate to his religious mission, which raised an issue beyond what Lou could address, became his way of at last affirming himself as his own person with his own mission. In reality, by insisting on this issue he was giving expression to his despair that Lou could ever provide him with that more thoughtful collaborative association he naturally expected of them as their own couple (cf. the end part of n.55). When referred to these more complex, actual developments, the official account Lou gives of the impasse created between them in her Memoirs (see above pp.13-15) reads, in fact, as a slanted version of what took place, inevitable perhaps in the context of a summarial account, but otherwise a partial view more favorable to herself than was the case.[129] The fact is that she had not been there for Rilke, and because of his now more aggressively assumed identity the situation had reached a point where he could express his resentment of her more challengingly. This took the form of saying, more or less, that in the completeness of his devotion to her he was guilty of a kind of depravity—only he did not say this in so many words. What he complained about, this time *mimicking* his usual behavior, was that in the completeness of his devotion to his God he was guilty of depravity. He was pretending to despise himself for his own great work, seeming to negate it. Faced with this clearly escalating situation, Lou would not be able to support the pressure on her, and this time she began to withdraw decisively.

Separation was, in any case, actually what Rilke, deep down, also wanted for himself, for he would simply have had, in time, to fulfil his poetic mission in the full confidence of who he was, without inhibition and however challenged he might be as for his deeper anxieties, left to rely on himself without Lou. For Rilke had to accept that he would be facing that fundamental fearfulness in himself that had now become, irreversibly, an established aspect of his self-experience. His life with Lou had not, in the end, spared him what he had very much hoped he might be spared.

APPENDIX I
from *The Way of Novalis* p.116ff

... and now we hear of this "son of the first maid and mother, the eternal fruit of mysterious embrace" (MacDonald, 46).

These last terms link up directly with the main focus of Novalis's vision: the revelation of the Mother through the mediation of his beloved [dead] Sophie. Embedded in his vision of *them* is the *further* vision of the Christ-Child in the arms of the Mother, as the Virgin Mary embodies Her historically: his "heavenly heart unfolded ... to a flower-like chalice of almighty love ... resting on the bliss-boding bosom of the sweetly solemn mother." All becomes focused now *in* this Christ-Child Who is at the centre of all that has become possible for Novalis, Himself the "fruit" of that "embrace" that has so occupied Novalis as the essential working of Nature's higher influence in us. The Source of that influence is here identified in *His* original historical role when He gave Himself up to Death and at last "in everlasting life death found its goal" (MacDonald, 48), since which time "thousands have, out of pangs and tortures, followed thee" (MacDonald, 49). Displaced though he was from this original scene, in his own latter-day experience Novalis might yet be counted among those who have been witness to His resurrection from death:

> *they see thee rise again, and themselves with thee; behold thee weep with soft fervour on the blessed bosom of thy mother, walk in thoughtful communion with thy friends, uttering words plucked from the tree of life*

Christ's action, as expressed at this time, one might say lived again in Novalis's own experience, which now saw *him* in his struggle with death "weeping" with Christ on "the blessed bosom of the Mother", "walking in thoughtful communion with his friends, uttering words plucked from the tree of life". Beyond this point, the resurrected Christ is described as "hastening" back "to his father's arms" but "bearing ... youthful Humanity" with Him, a sign that the revelations of the higher world are now open to us. In the meantime, a mysterious "singer" is said to have appeared at the time of Christ's intervention as a witness to it, and he is described proclaiming Christ's story to the far ends of the earth. This singer has been seen as an embodiment of the poetic genius of the Greeks[130], representing "the whole body of poetry which, having its origin in Greek antiquity, then embraced the imagery and the mythology of Christianity, to bring religious understanding to the world"[131]. If this is so, as I believe it is, he has made himself present again to Novalis in *his* time, as evidenced in the two sections of *Christendom and Europe* that suddenly grow ecstatic with intimations of "a new history, a new humanity" (Stoljar, 147) now in the making.

In *Christendom* Novalis speaks inspiredly of what has now become spiritually and culturally possible clearly on the basis of the revelation *he* has had and is having. His focus turned back to the Day world, he sees the prospect of a new religious order for Europe, beyond sectarian commitments. It will arise from a new inspirational revelation, and *along with* innumerable other members of a new church, Novalis sees *himself* in the role of the Mother embracing the Christ, having *incorporated* Her inspiration:

> *All these things are still only hints, disjointed and rough, but to the historical eye they betray a universal individuality, a new history, a new humanity, the sweetest embrace of a surprised, young church and a loving God, and the ardent conception of a new messiah in all its thousands members at once.*
>
> *Who does not feel the sweet shame of being with child?*
>
> (Stoljar, 147)

This Messiah Who is to be born is the re-appearance of Christ in Novalis's own time, and He is to be known along the way Novalis has travelled:

> *consumed as bread and wine, embraced like a beloved woman, breathed as air, heard as word and song, and with heavenly delight, amid the sharpest pangs of love, taken up in the form*

*of death into the innermost part of the body whose turbulence
ceases at last.*

(Stoljar, 148)

Working out of His own transcendent sphere in association with the
Mother, this Messiah reveals Himself further through the higher mystery of social communion (the lesson Novalis had learned while at
Teplitz). One's beloved has in the meantime merged into the way the
new Messiah reveals Himself in these terms, also through the word
and song by which nature's air is transformed and He is proclaimed,
as Novalis himself was in the process of doing. This higher life lies,
what's more, in a necessary intrinsic relation to death, for only by
the identification of life with death is the perfection of our destiny
assured until such time as we will merge more deeply with Christ *in*
death.

All the terms of Novalis's long and involved progress in vision
are enumerated here, and it is with a sense of all that has come
together in his own experience that Novalis invites the reader of
Christendom to give themselves to the same vision:

> *So come then you too...brush the gray net aside and gaze with
> young love at the wondrous splendor of nature, history and hu-
> manity*

In the forging of this new time, the "singer" of the *Hymns*, as "brother", has *his* crucial role:

> *I want to conduct you to a brother who will talk with you so that
> your hearts rejoice and you gird your beloved, expired sensation
> with a new body...*

In what became numbered as the fourth of his *Spiritual Songs*, Novalis
makes reference to "Whom I saw" (MacDonald, 96) in the moment
of his vision at [Sophie's] grave, which in context leaves no doubt
that this was the Christ "Who for us did die", but He Himself is
accompanied by another who would appear to *be* this same "friend or
brother". In *Christendom* Novalis announces that:

> *This brother is the heartbeat of the new age*

(Stoljar, 148, 149)

Of him it is said that

He has made a new veil for the Holy Virgin.

This new veil is none other than the new "song" of creation that this "brother" would inspire in Novalis's time. This brother's inspiration would extend beyond a "singing" that is merely its own activity to a new "musical" organization of the whole creation (a "music of numbers") inclusive of the "spiritual physics" Novalis hoped to see developed as a "science of the whole". Of this "Virgin" Herself, Who has re-appeared in Novalis's time in the form of his vision, it is said that "her lips open only to sing", "singing" having here become a "trope" for all expressions of the new creation:

For me her singing is nothing but the ceremonial call to a new foundation-gathering, the mighty beating of the wings of an angelic herald who is passing.

This "angelic herald", who is associated with the Virgin's singing, would appear himself to be that same singer or friend from antiquity become brother who has passed through Christian history before, transformed at the time by the new event of Christ's coming.[132]

In the rest of *Christendom*, Novalis had intended to provide a summary of how Christianity had fared over the centuries since Christ's coming. His ecstatic announcement of a new Christianity for his time emerges out of a closely considered view of all the tragic twists-and-turns in that long history before his time…

APPENDIX II

Breakdown of my revised version of the sequence of poems in "The Book of Monastic Life"

A.

Rilke's Sequence

(RANS 33-41)

Poem 29
"Those were the days of Michelangelo"

Poem 30
"The bough of the tree that is God"

Poem 31
"In those days they loved her too, the Maid"

Poem 32
"Yet as though the heavy-fruited garlands"

Poem 33
"And so one man above all portrayed her"

Poem 34
"With a bough so unlike the other"

Poem 35
"I cannot think that little figure Death"

B.
My Revised Sequence

Poem 30 become Poem 1
(Prologue)
"The bough of the tree that is God"

Poem 31 become Poem 2
(Prologue)
"In those days they loved her too, the Maid"

Poem 32 become Poem 3
(Prologue)
"Yet as though the heavy-fruited garlands"

Poem 33 become Poem 4
(Prologue)
"And so one man above all portrayed her"

Poem 34 become Poem 5
(Prologue)
"With a bough so unlike the other"

Poem 1 become Poem 6
"Bright with metallic strike, the hour/tilts
and touches me"

Poem 29 become Poem 34
"Those were the days of Michelangelo"

Poem 35
"I cannot think that little figure Death"

Endnotes

1. At the time of their separation in February 1901, Lou insisted that all correspondence between them be destroyed. Rilke kept his part of the bargain, but his Diary was not part of that understanding. Hence the critical account of her that survives. In the same way Lou's famous "Last Appeal" to Rilke at the time of their separation survives because it was sent to him after they had come to an understanding. Lou on her side kept the bargain only in part, clearly selecting what she wished to survive.

2. For Lou's psychoanalyzing of Rilke, see MCHL and von der Lippe, as well as Leavy.

3. See John Middleton Murry. *Son of Woman: The Story of D.H. Lawrence.* New York: Jonathan Cape and Harrison Smith, 1931, 366.

4. There is a remarkable record of such praying, all the more remarkable because Lou though physically absent at that moment is still intensely present to Rilke, in the Florence Diary. See SN, *Diaries*, 42.

5. This is Breon Mitchell's translation of the poem (see MCHL 86) as presented by Lou in her *Memoirs*. Rilke would place this poem in "The Book of Pilgrimage", the second part of *The Book of Hours*.

6. Another possibility of shared life with Lou, never to be realized, hung over Rilke's later disturbed episodes. Much follows from the undoing by Lou of his personal hopes after his trip to Florence, one year into their relationship. More on this in Part 3 of this Volume.

7. See his letter of October 18th, 1900 to Paula Becker (GRN 46): "Do you understand that it is an infidelity if I behave as though I had found hearth and home already fully realized elsewhere?" Here Rilke was privileging Berlin and the connections there that allowed him freer access to his Russian studies, but without any doubt a required proximity to Lou was at the centre of these thoughts. More

on this in the Worpswede section of Part 2.

8. See SN, *Rilke*, 44ff.

9. Reprinted in SN, *Rilke*, 39.

10. A complex title, untranslatable from the German: literally, "last shout" or "last calling out". The tradition has been to translate the German as "Last Appeal". See SN, *Rilke*, 365.

11. See SN, *Rilke*, xv. There is a significant tailing off of her own published work from the time of their separation, and Lou began to suffer from mysterious heart-ailments that continued for years after.

12. Emphasis mine.

13. Words written to Otto Modersohn, one of the Worpswede group, who by then had become Paula Becker's husband.

14. Words addressed to Clara.

15. A prototype of this experience is the one Rilke had in childhood when he found himself trapped and suffocating in a costume, frantically calling for help while everyone around thought it was a joke. Rilke narrates this experience in *The Notebooks of Malte Laurids Brigge*. See Hulse, 67-70. In this episode Rilke was almost literally possessed by the Spirit of the costume: "I lost all sense of myself. I simply ceased to exist. For a second I felt an indescribable, poignant and futile longing for myself, and then He was the only one who remained: there was nothing but Him ... I sank to the floor and how they went on laughing, supposing this was part of the game" (70).

16. Until now, Lou had only written Rilke in response to his first long letter about the more recent anxieties that had prompted him to reach out to her again.

17. See SN, *Rilke*, 48.

18. See SN, *Rilke*, 176, where Rilke wonders if he had, with this work, finally "gone all the way out into the current that will sweep me away and plunge me over the edge".

19. Contrast Rilke's attitude to the same prospect early on in his relationship with Lou when in Florence, when everything appeared to be free-sailing: "the artist's way must be this ... to build step after step, until at last he can gaze into himself ... calmly and clearly as into a landscape. After this return home into himself, deed after deed will

be a leisurely joy; his life will be a creation and he will have no further need for the things that are outside ... he places outside himself all things that are small and transitory: his lone sufferings, his vague longings, his fearful dreams ..." (SN, *Diaries*, 18).

20. See Edward Snow, in his "Introduction" to *Rilke*, ix.

21. These developments, of course, pointed both ways, for Lou had her own work to see to, based on her own way of conceiving and approaching life, being also well-advanced in the program of her work. Lou was also showing a new-found wisdom in leaving Rilke to his experience and allowing it all to happen for him. There is a new respect for the way Rilke's experience was unfolding here, in contrast with her early attitudes towards him when they were still together. More on these attitudes in Part 2 and Part 3 of this Volume.

22. Here I have in mind the sudden power over his poetic production that the extraordinary visitation at Duino exerted, which may be seen as a further attempt to take control of himself from a deeper level.

23. GRN 80. For the poem, see *The Book of Images*, tr. Edward Snow (New York: Farrar, Straus & Giroux, 1991), 121.

24. Wordsworth suggests himself here, who did succeed in the effort to trace the course of his development as a poet from childhood—in his *Prelude*, subtitled *The Growth of a Poet's Mind*.

25. Rilke puts the matter to himself in this way: "Might this handcraft lie in language itself, in a better acquaintance with its inner life and will ... might it be in some specific study, in the more exact knowledge of one area ... a certain well-inherited and well-augmented culture [?]" (SN, *Rilke*, 78).

26. For the relevant material supporting my presentation in this paragraph, see SN, *Rilke*, 101, 111. See also von der Lippe, 56, and Hulse, xvii.

27. See SN, *Rilke*, 110.

28. See von der Lippe, 59.

29. All these are Lou's terms, in von der Lippe, 57-59.

30. This was "wandering" in the literal sense, including a trip of several months that took him as far as Cairo, among other places he visited at this time.

31. All of this pursued in dismay of the complexity of his motives as well as continued fear of relapse, and consequently without too much further self-analysis. Cf. SN, *Rilke*, 88: "I scarcely dare question the steps in my "progress" for fear of discovering ... that they keep returning to that one notorious disconsolate place from which I have already started out so often."

32. I elaborate on these entries at what has seemed the most fitting place in my argument, paradoxically late in this Volume, below, in n.119.

33. This letter is alluded to by Rilke (in these terms) in the letter of his that followed it: see SN, *Rilke*, 31. Lou returns to this letter, from her point of view, in her *Memoirs* (MCHL 90) written a few years after Rilke's death. More on this episode below.

34. This from the time of Rilke's trip to Florence and its disastrous aftermath, one year into their relationship. He had been unable to get Lou to participate to his satisfaction in his enthusiasm over the extraordinary discoveries he had made about art and about himself while in Florence. More on this in Part 3.

35. See MCHL 91.

36. As already remarked (in n.11) Lou's continued need for Rilke was expressed through her mysterious heart illnesses which began with their separation and continued even after they re-connected as correspondents. See SN, *Diaries*, 278.

37. The other, early on, is the voice of the young Abel, which does have its place in the sequence: see RANS 11.

38. More on this in Part 3.

39. Besides what is presented in this section, this Diary is studied at length in Part 3.

40. Rilke in his Diary (SN, *Diaries*, 55) sees it, along with Botticelli, as a case of his Madonna feeling "too helpless and primitive to echo back somehow the depth of the confession ... [W]hen she tries to give freely from it, she cannot lift a trace of its fullness out of her soul." "She remains poor ... and solitary ... And for all that ... il-lumined through and through." See, e.g., Botticelli's Madonna of the Pomegranate.

41. In the details of this account (as given in the last four sentences, back to "In this regard"), there is a strange premonition of the intensely charged situation out of which the first and second of Rilke's Elegies will emerge. There is also the underlying link to Novalis, on which much more throughout the pages of this book. See, to begin, pp.56-57 in this Volume.

42. Stoljar, 149.

43. How symbolically expressive if Lou was, as some are adamant in believing, pregnant with Rilke's child during the time of his stay in Florence. In this account, Lou aborted this child; at the same time, Rilke's vision of a new age for the West was aborted, and himself returned to Lou's will after Florence.

44. Stoljar, 147.

45. By "his later work" I mean everything from the time the first Elegies were written at Duino in 1912. It is of no small significance in this connection that, at the very time he was plunged, quite suddenly, into the composition of his first Elegy, Rilke was working on the poems that became part of *The Life of the Virgin Mary*: see Annemarie S. Kidder, tr., *Pictures of God,* Livonia, MI: First Page Publications, 2005, p.28ff. In one of these poems, "The Birth of Mary", we find the following lines: speaking of angels who "have struggled/not to erupt in praises, like one might erupt in tears", the poet says "they knew that tonight would be born/the mother, who'd soon bear the son" (28). In "The Presentation", on considering the depth of Mary's purpose and what commitment to it would impose on one as renunciation, the poet alludes to "what shapes your identity and/what would be most difficult to remove/without tearing gashes in you" (28). I believe these lines have an intrinsic bearing on those from the First Elegy: "Isn't it time that we lovingly/freed ourselves from the beloved and, quivering, endured[?]" (Stephen Mitchell, 333). As I note in these pages, these last lines address what would have been required of Rilke in the course of his life to see himself through into his own proper "Novalis-vision": namely, the full decision to give Lou up, however much of a torment that would have been for him. This was the great paradox of Rilke's life. Antecedent to the experience of Christ's Redemption for Novalis was his renunciation of the life he had anticipated with Sophie. This he does by finally fully accepting

her death. Likewise would Rilke have had at some point to renounce the life that he had, from the first, anticipated with Lou. More on these dialectical developments in the rest of this book.

46. It seems all to the point that after his Florentine vision was squashed, Rilke should, during his sad time at Zoppot, resume work on his *Visions of Christ*, an early collection that he had left aside for well over a year, in which, sharing Lou's vision, he expresses his severe doubts about the efficacy, and even the reality, of Christ's Redemption. One must speak of a personal contradiction in Rilke at this time rather than a positive return to the sanctioning of his former view. There could be no greater contrast than between Rilke's depiction of Christ's inefficacy in the *Visions* and Novalis's presentation of Christ triumphing in His Redemption in *Hymns to the Night*, the very event Rilke had otherwise seen as the one after which Botticelli (and himself) inwardly yearned. For Novalis's account of his experience, see Appendix I.

47. Most spectacularly in Rilke's third Elegy. See Stephen Mitchell, 345.

48. Italics mine.

49. Novalis transcends this condition by giving up his earthly love, something Rilke was finally unable to do. See n.45, also n.68.

50. Cf. Donne (see *John Donne: Selected Poetry*. Ed. John Carey. Oxford: Oxford University Press, 1996): "Thou hast made me, and shall thy work decay?/Repair me now" (205); "rise and for thine own work fight" (200); "Restore thine image" (209).

51. Cf. Shakespeare (see *William Shakespeare: The Sonnets and Narrative Poems*. New York: Alfred A. Knopf, 1992): "This thou perceiv'st, which makes thy love more strong,/To love that well which thou must leave ere long" (39). In the end, Rilke speaks both with more confidence than the hysterically desperate Donne and less pathos than the tender-minded Shakespeare. Shakespeare was, of course, capable of his own near-absolute degree of proud will: "Not marble, nor the gilded monuments/Of princes, shall outlive this pow'rful rhyme" (30).

52. In "Monastic Life" there are references to the Sobor in two poems, to the czars in a third, to "another land" (i.e., Russia) in the

last poem from our Prologue, and otherwise only a general sense of the difference in artistic approaches to painting that separates the "Russian" narrator from his "brothers to the South" who practised their art back in the time of the Italian Renaissance. There is also the Ancient brought forward in the second-to-last poem, though Rilke does not invoke the Russian source of this figure. All told, specific references in only 5 poems on 67.

53. See Graff, 151: "In the last analysis the Russian aspects in Rilke's work are not there in so far as they are Russian but in so far as they are Rilkean ... [I]n him Western patterns and yearnings competed with Eastern, Slavic ones". See, also, 91: "Russia and the West were the two princes who found themselves at war with each other because they started out to woo the same maiden" (i.e., Lou).

54. Faust awakes at the beginning of the Second Part of Goethe's *Faust*.

55. In this remarkable capacity for fluidic expression of his God, Rilke may indeed be said to have introduced something new to the West, thus justifying his dramatic recourse to a transposed cultural setting, which does serve to highlight a new import and scope to his representation of God in these poems. In this tendency Rilke does go beyond the more decidedly Western intellectual approach that very strongly defines the voices, e.g., of both Donne and Shakespeare, whom I have cited, or even in modern times someone like Robert Graves, who comes after Rilke and would also claim fluidity. To a great extent even in Graves the invocation of his Goddess depends on a straightforward poetic assertion of baldly intellectual force, hints of which kind of direct claim we will note here and there in our translation of "Monastic Life":

> *Only my longing reaches to your chin*
> *and stands high as the tallest angel, pale,*
> *unredeemed, alien*

(RANS 31)

> *For you are not the Angel-hosted*
> *serried round by rich excess.*

(RANS 43)

You lived just briefly guested in that gold:
... only to answer pleadings of the day

(RANS 33)

Not before nightfall shall we let you be,
watching your coming contours dawning late.

(RANS 31)

One has but to read the quoted lines from Rilke as if Graves were addressing his Goddess, and one would have the basic ground-tone of Graves's poetry (see *The Modern Debacle*, Lincoln NE, 2007, for my main study of Graves).

The last seven poems of "Monastic Life" especially allow us to sample the peculiar blend of Western intellectual will and self-effacing fluidic form that characterizes Rilke's poetic emergence at this time. Clearly, the artist's historical task of completing God, as Rilke saw it, had shifted from its original Novalisian arc of development, dating back to Rilke's Florentine days, to something more nondescript, eclectic and unwieldy: a combination of Western willfulness and Eastern open-endedness that, for all its potency, was leading Rilke into a hinterland of continual, indefinite creation—not exactly a prospect constituted for reaching "completion". No wonder the issue of poetic form would re-emerge for Rilke during his second trip to Russia (see above p.12). Nothing had transpired along these lines of production for almost a year since "Monastic Life" was written. In the meantime, Rilke was feeling de-stabilized because of Lou's unaccounted absence from him. Their life of association was being neglected by her and himself ignored. This is in spite of the fact that they had made the trip to Russia without Lou's husband in their entourage and the moment seemed especially propitious for their collaborative life.

56. See Polikoff, 79ff, for the best treatment of Lou's themes.

57. So, Hendry, 40. Freedman (130) sees it as a case of Rilke being disinclined to get into a rivalry with Otto Modersohn, to whom Paula was secretly engaged. At the same time, Freedman (133) makes much of Rilke coming away with "empty hands", Rilke's own image from the poem he wrote that offers Paula his blessing when the engagement was made public. The no-nonsense Leppmann (126) sees Rilke's relationship to Paula quite differently: "If Rilke was on the

verge of falling in love ... Paula's engagement to Modersohn put a stop to that."

58. Again, Hendry, 39. Polikoff (205) concurs with this view: "In all likelihood, it was Rilke's discovery of Paula's secret engagement that precipitated his drastically sudden departure from Worpswede". It was Heinrich Petzet who first made the suggestion: Polikoff (717) cites Eric Torgersen citing Petzet. Freedman (130, 133) proceeds as though the engagement was already known to Rilke when he was still at Worpswede. Paula herself assumed as much (see Prater, 74).

59. Prater, 71: "The personalities of Clara and Paula remained for him curiously intermingled."

60. SN, *Diaries*, 222.

61. The concept of "things" emerges in several poems from "Monastic Life" (see RANS 3, 27, 33, 55, 81, 83). Characteristic of Rilke's approach to the value of things in this period are the following lines: "All things that go to make you I would unassumingly name"(81); "I find your trace in all these things" (27). We find an especially elaborate new sense of the value of things in the Schmargendorf Diary in the segment that follows the production of "Monastic Life": see n.119.

62. Can we imagine Rilke coming into anything more or greater as an experience than what he had already been through with the Worpswede group by this time? His experience with the group had reached conclusion. What more would he have gained from continuing at Worpswede than he had already? There would have been simply more of the same.

63. Very strangely, Freedman (132) takes the "everyday" here to mean "an ordinary everyday existence." See pp.95-96 for more on this.

64. See Prater, 74.

65. Cf. Freedman, 133: "Lou seems to have sounded some outraged reminder of his duties, calling him back to reality and away from those unending delicate entanglements that threatened to ensnare him." Also (139): "Lou believed she had to rescue him". See also Prater, 73.

66. See n.1.

67. Snow (*Diaries*, 235) misdates the entry, which should read

Monday November 12, 1900 (if one refers to the calendar for that year).

68. Here, we might say, is the great turning-point in Rilke's life, for if, in these inherited circumstances, he had been able to fully and finally give Lou up, Rilke would have been set on the very path that Novalis had travelled when *he* gave up on his attachment to earthly happiness. "I loved the earth so much", Novalis had said, rebelling so bitterly at first against his fate, before he finally plunged into a full acceptance of it. Rilke was likewise facing this issue, years before he would describe it so memorably: "Isn't it time that we lovingly/ freed ourselves from the beloved and, quivering, endured [?]" Perhaps only Lou's death could have moved Rilke to make the choice that was required of him, just as Sophie's death had imposed the choice on Novalis. As it is, Rilke would never be able to give Lou up, and consequently he remained stuck in a certain way of experiencing separation that is a more alienated way. It is the way *he* seemed meant for, as if he was called to fill out the situation he otherwise shares with Novalis—called, that is, to bring out an outstanding dimension to the problem raised by the demands of self-transcendence (as I will argue in these pages). That Rilke remained, at the same time, called to the way Novalis went is what the visitation at Duino would communicate to him even if he was for the most part unconscious of this (as shown in Volume 2). The depth of torment that was created in Rilke by this appalling contradiction can only be guessed at. It is Rilke's attachment to the idea of the happiness he had been denied that, paradoxically, kept him bound to this contradiction. And who can blame him? Happiness, in earthly terms such as had been promised him, remains one of our most deep-set ideals and is not so easily renounced. That is perhaps what the powers that be may have wished, through Rilke, to see explored further, until such time as we can bring ourselves to renunciation.

69. See Prater, 75. Like others, Prater takes this "illness" at face value, officiously going along with Lou's account of it. As I show in this Volume, the situation was far more complex than this: Lou was, in fact, responsible for the continuance of this "illness".

70. See, for example, the following lines from "The Guardian Angel", which take us back to Rilke's youth:

> *You have often snatched me out of dark rest*
> *When sleep seemed like a grave to me*
> *And like getting lost and fleeing,—*

(from *The Book of Images*, tr., Edward Snow. New York: Farrar, Straus and Giroux, 1994, p.33).

Kidder, *Pictures of God* (86), translates as follows:

> *You often tore me out of darkest nights,*
> *When sleep appeared like lying in a grave*
> *and being lost and running from it all—*

71. A reader of later modern English poetry will not fail to note of the sentiment expressed in this material the similarity with Ted Hughes's address to the dead Sylvia Plath in *Birthday Letters*. Plath's own idiosyncratic forms of expression seem anticipated here, and one wonders if she knew this poem.

72. "[I]nto the light", as opposed to "into the night", continues to point, pathetically, to Rilke's unrealized hopes.

73. To a reader of modern English literature, the rhythms of this prose in the first part will suggest Virginia Woolf, for example in *Mrs. Dalloway*; the content in the second part, of course, moves somewhat beyond Woolf. See also, for the Woolf rhythms, the second block quote on p.76.

74. At military school, Rilke continued to take abuse from the other children—for the sake of Christ, following the instruction of his mother.

75. The rhythms of the sentiment in this and the following excerpt suggest the utopian direction in Shakespeare, e.g., Lear's speech to Cordelia ("Let's away to prison") or Gonzago's vision of an ideal life, applied in this case to society as a whole, in *The Tempest*.

76. Two lines mark the transition from the first to the second part of the poem: "If I really need say: what I shall/call my life will always be" (269).

77. See Freedman, 136-137: "It was an intensely personal play for both Lou and Rainer—for different reasons. As early as 1897, their first months together ... Lou had written a novella ... [*A Case of Death*]

... Its plot was extraordinarily similar ... [A]t the time she wrote it Lou herself examined her own creative urge in the light of the unformed surrogate son, Rainer ... [N]either Lou nor Rainer could have been unaware of the parallels."

78. The theme of the first, the Florence Diary, is festiveness, and dis-illusionment. The theme of the second, the Schmargendorf Diary, is recovery. The theme of the Worpswede Diary is tragic accept-ance. The Schmargendorf Diary was begun in the wake of the dis-aster after Florence. The first part of Rilke's Worpswede experience is also recorded in the Schmargendorf Diary. The beginning of the Worpswede Diary coincides with Rilke's feeling that he felt at last at home in Worpswede. It is a little less than halfway into this Diary that Rilke returns to Berlin to contend with the consequences of another disaster, to the end of 1900.

79. Freedman, 137.

80. Freedman, 138.

81. Freedman, 137.

82. Freedman, 138.

83. Prater, 74.

84. The rationalizing is in relation to Paula and says much about the nature of their relationship; the excitability may well have come from another source: very likely Rilke's knowledge of his own engagement prospects with Clara (Paula being at this time herself engaged to Otto Modersohn). Rilke and Clara would become engaged less than a month after Rilke's letter to Paula. This letter does not give evidence of a romantic love between himself and Paula or anything like a basis for conjugal love but displays rather the affection of a greatly admir-ing friend, one who revered the life of his friend, which he had come to know so well (as he says himself). In the meantime the mystery of the gaze Rilke and Paula shared in the barouche-episode is explained: this had to do with what Rilke describes in his letter as "the certainty with which you loved life ... without becoming confused by it" (54). He goes on to indicate that "now [after reading Paula's diary] I have felt intuitively the rising shaft of that certainty with whose quiet, eye-dark blossom I was acquainted".

85. Freedman, 139.

86. Prater, 75.

87. Freedman, 139.

88. Prater, 76.

89. Freedman, 140.

90. See Prater, 76.

91. Prater, 77.

92. Prater, 78, who also quotes Rilke's own poem:

> *fair dark lute, granted to me*
> *that I may test my mastery:*
> *Life itself I'll play upon you!*

93. Prater, 81.

94. See Freedman, 145-147.

95. Prater, 83.

96. Prater, 83.

97. Prater, 83. Emphasis, in this case, mine.

98. The irony of this section of the poem is extensive yet masterfully sustained:

> *Is nothing audible but me?*
> *Or are there other voices crying?*
> *Is that a storm? I am one too,*
> *those tossing forests mine.*
>
> *Is there a song, if sick and short,*
> *turning your ear away from me?*
>
> *I am a song; hear mine ...*

Rilke *knows* that he is not alone, and that there *are* others, but that it is his own song that cries out to be heard since the song of others ("short and sick") cannot be quite so intent as his own. *He* will take up, with a greater resolve, the general care. They are words spoken in some desperation, in a condition significantly removed from the self-impelled confidence of the author of "Monastic Life".

99. Italics mine.

100. Emphasis Rilke's own.

101. My emphasis.

102. The disjunction between past and present at this point was extreme; it is to force "The Book of Pilgrimage" into a phantasmal unity to say that "the poems' religious mission is infused with the poet's secular anxiety" (Freedman, 148). "[R]eligious mission" and "secular anxiety" were, at this moment in Rilke's poetic career, years away from finding any proper relationship to each other, and they would, in fact, never quite "fuse", as shown in the rest of this book.

103. Graff (153) cites Ruth Movius in *Rainer Maria Rilkes Stundenbuch*: "he is quoted as having admitted later to Franz Werfel that he considered his *Book of Hours* formless, a mere inspiration. "I could have continued to write poems in that way indefinitely, without beginning or end" (Movius, 14-15), and to Hans Carossa he is reported to have said words to the same effect (Movius, 249)."

104. At this time it could only be a matter of "righting", not "saving" himself.

105. Contrasting with Rilke's conception of Him in "The Book of Poverty", by the time of Duino Rilke's Hero has turned into a highly ambiguous figure, one who is not so straightforwardly God-serving, especially when seen in relation to the Angel-figure to whom he is by then being directly referred. The prospect of a higher resolution of human alienation had turned into a progressively more and more conflicted experience for Rilke, even if and perhaps just because his Hero had grown much in the power of self-command. In the Elegies Rilke's Hero is set over and against this Angel even more emphatically as the representative of our distinctively human experience in this world as this continues to conflict with the Angel's forbidding otherworldly mission. See once again my view of this development in the Duino situation as formulated in n.68; it is fully presented in Volume 2 of this book.

106. The crucial point to note about Rilke's argument in this Book; otherwise everything is read awry, as Ralph Freedman for one has done. It is to stretch identities spectacularly, not to mention to force a unity on the sequence that does not exist, to speak of the circumstances of the indigents in the slums of Paris as "inversions yet confirmations of the saintly state which St. Francis encompassed" (189). These indigents suggest the authentic poor only by a violent yanking

or *transposition* of circumstances such as Rilke achieves in the sequence's key poem. Only if one thinks the condition of the indigents *further*, to some extreme point where they would be returned to the natural conditions of the "earth", as by a filmic metamorphosis of scene, can one see them as *potentially* the authentic poor:

> **if your earth found itself in extremis**
> *she'd thread these poorest on a rosary*
> *and wear them as a talisman.*
>
> *For* **they** ['they' projected into that state] *are purer than the flawless stone*
>
> ....
>
> *... needing* **one thing***:*
>
> *to be allowed the poverty they own.*
>
> (RANS 179)

Such perspectivism, very deliberately introduced into this material, is precisely what allows Rilke to bring the authentic poor of Russia onto the scene who, contrastingly, *have* retained (even in their own cities) a natural relationship to the earth. A shift to the natural landscape of Russia is what Rilke seeks from the outset of the sequence, at the first mention of degrading conditions in the city—"Send me into your empty lands/through which the broad winds drive,/whose grand monasteries are clothes/wrapped round under-lived lives./There I would accompany pilgrims" (RANS 159), and the later perspectival manoeuvre, from inauthentic to authentic, is what at last permits Rilke the shift to Russia he is looking for. The subject of the sequence from here are the poor of Russia; it is *their* condition of authentic (an idealized) poverty that Rilke goes on to celebrate, offering *them* to the attention of his God for protection. The two classes of people, the "unrich" and the "poor", are very clearly distinguished. Rilke, in other words, was *retreating* from the slum scenes of Paris to recover the sense of authentic poverty he had experienced when in Russia— this in order to take any sane measure of what he was now dealing with in Paris. Rilke was, for the moment, going back, not yet ready to take on.

107. See Freedman, 177.

108. The full manuscript had been in Lou's possession for two years

by then; it would not be published till six months after their reunion.

109. There is Raphael's *Transfiguration*, for example, though Rilke does not cite or comment on any specific paintings by Raphael.

110. Italics here mine. "Beauty" Rilke has already conceived in these pages as the "involuntary", and so self-referring, "gesture" in which the artistic personality "distills itself" (SN, *Diaries*, 14): what is distilled from the artistic personality that has, in other words, genuinely longed for itself.

111. Whether the way through to an experience of Christ's Redemption would ever have been possible in a shared life with Lou, as Rilke hoped for, remains to be debated. As it turned out, such an experience could only have been possible, given the circumstances of his life as he inherited them, if Rilke had proceeded to what was well-nigh impossible for him: namely, the essential renunciation of the idea of any life with Lou *especially* as he was so identified with it. See in this respect, also, n.68. Perhaps the most startling irony of all in the context of their remarkably involuted story was the habit Rilke and Lou had over many years of exchanging the Easter greetings that were typical of the Russia of their day—"Christ is risen!", "startling" since both pretended to deny the efficacy of Christ's Redemption.

112. Hendry (26) makes the relevant connections: "Lou had been married for eleven years and her husband was certainly violent."

113. Not long after recovering from Lou's letter, Rilke records his rich moments of conversational intimacy with a Russian woman who was also holidaying in Italy at this time. Would this not also have put Lou off when reading this Diary? It is well beyond these sections that Rilke reaches the climax of what he has to say about Botticelli and Michelangelo, among others. Otherwise the Diary as a whole is conceived as a unified presentation. Thus Rilke is careful to round out his account with appropriate and illuminating commentary on virtually all of the arts, including, towards the end, sculpture and portraiture, and, finally, sepulchral art with the inevitable focus on death and what especially distinguished Renaissance attitudes about it. The effect of so many commentaries on Renaissance art in the last part of the nineteenth century may have inured readers to the subject to the point where the special distinction of Rilke's eloquent comments will be missed.

114. Those preoccupations may go much farther than we have documentation for. Thus some have speculated, (speculation that Prater (46n.) himself vigorously discounts) that, without his knowing, Lou was pregnant by Rilke at this time, and that she had used Rilke's time away in Italy, among other things, to arrange for an abortion. If this was true, a profound irony attaches to Rilke's rhapsodic elaborations in his Diary at this time on "maternalness" as the highest creative ideal for his time. Prater (47-48) tells us (without offering documentation) that Rilke's trip to Italy was planned by Lou with the deliberate intention of putting some significant distance between them, so she could proceed to tell him, when he returned, that they could no longer be lovers. I very much doubt that she did so; there is nothing in the coda to his Florence Diary that implies any such cause for his deep disappointment on his return which was rather about other things: her strange indifference to his Florence discoveries, e.g. There is even less likelihood that saying they could no longer be lovers formed the content of her disturbing letter to him while he was in Florence: it is not likely that Rilke would have bounced back from such a shocking communication with the enthusiasm he resumes about his Florence experience not long after.

115. First bold Rilke's, second bold mine.

116. Italics mine. The emphasis in this statement is on the word "future".

117. Lou can be said to have belonged, unlike Rilke, more to the nineteenth century than the twentieth, not least in respect of her characteristic modes of thought and expression (which have been said to tend to overdensity and obscurantism, when in fact this is simply another level of logical thinking, characteristic of her time, that is quite penetrable with application). Especially does Lou belong to the nineteenth century in her assumption of an immoveable position of self-right and authority that could lead to an acceptance of "iron necessity" despite the intense feelings that also clearly existed between her and Rilke. (She had, of course, also made a *practice* of denial and self-denial over the years, especially with men.) It is Rilke (more so than Freud) who would initiate Lou into the twentieth century and its more open-ended ways of relating, however much these could open one to menacing anxieties and insecurities, and even confusion.

118. Many somewhat terrible ironies arise from the Diary, in hindsight, that contrast dramatically with Rilke's projected life-hope for Lou and himself. Thus, he really had thought himself suddenly free of his former fearfulness: "When I think that I myself was once one of those who look on life with suspicion and mistrust its power." (SN, *Diaries*, 49) Instead, Rilke was returned, by a form of sleight-of-hand enacted through Lou's appropriation of his experience, to a position that (pathetically) compares with those Gothic elements he had so superiorly described that survive on many Renaissance sepulchres: "the frightened little turrets ... suddenly lack proof of the heavens they were meant to proclaim, and they stand in adolescent embarrassment before the mature, compassionate forgiving of these marble-clear earthly thoughts." (73-74)

119. Precisely to what degree Rilke gave himself to his own ideas of his artistic needs over this time may be gleaned especially from those entries in the Schmargendorf Diary that Rilke made in the period immediately following "Monastic Life", his first major breakthrough. It is these needs that he could no longer deny by the following summer, over six months later, on the second trip to Russia. The ground-tone of these entries is represented in the words "I begin" (SN, *Diaries*, 88); "Why am I suddenly writing so much? Because once again: I begin" (90). Rilke at this point saw himself as inevitably and incontrovertibly growing into his own life, irrespective of his ongoing association with Lou for the moment. He acknowledges having had similar beginnings before: "I have already begun a thousand lives this way" (88), but this beginning expresses more:

> *All the same, I am perhaps already in the process of having begun my life: the life one doesn't let go of until one has completed it ... Once you have led up to a certain point it **will complete itself** at any cost ... so why be afraid?*
>
> (88, emphasis mine)

The entries in this period afford, in fact, a remarkable glimpse into the soul of a young poet who is suddenly in deep intimacy with himself ("Now I am alone with my strength"—118): Rilke was acting out that "longing for oneself that reaches to God" that was especially characteristic of him. He is in the midst of "silences that let me dive/so deeply" (113), and he wishes to be revealed as "the hand of someone/doing wondrous things with me" (112); "I'm so deep now/in the dark realm of the ground" (113). Also, those who primarily associate Rilke's idea of "things-in-themselves" with his later period under Rodin's tutelage will be piqued to learn that an intense new focus relating to "things" has already begun to manifest here, over several pages (122-126). This new focus on "things" coincides with a shift from his former "dreaming" to a new sense of the responsibility of "gazing" (136-138); "things" clamor for the gaze of the poet especially, who will see to it that they reveal the life that has been hidden in them, for the "things" already "hold/what someone put into their hands" (122), and, also, from one's own point of view, "[e]ach thing is only a space, a possibility, and it is up to me to fill it perfectly or poorly" (123). It is a matter, especially for the poet, of giving form to things: "Since all of me trembles to give form" (112)/"You must construct an image for each feeling" (121), anticipating with this last statement the purpose of *The Book of Images*.

Rilke reminds himself that such an achievement can only come from a profound commitment to creation; this he describes as a matter of remaining pure and available for the Other Who creates in one, especially at night with its special link to the unknown. Such availability requires a choice of solitude and, especially, the power of remaining detached from the world's many temptations which beset one especially at night: for otherwise, he says, "How will you usher into *this* night/That one person, the very One" (119) who should be "your *first* guest". In yet another poem from these pages, just when we thought Rilke might be invoking Lou, we realize that all is happening in Rilke's own world: her "You" has now given way to his "Night" (127). And solitude in this Night is very deeply envisioned: it is a case of going far in solitude:

> But you must go out beyond the desert, farther, always in the same direction. Only he who does that will know what lies on the other side of solitude ... (132)

Any proper "teaching", moreover, can only come directly from that farther space, and it is in any case a matter of knowing how to bear the knowledge that originates from there: "For voices are only worth anything/When silences accompany them" (134). Even so, with a characteristic sense of the limits of what can be realized, even a sage, this poet says, can only know so much about his own time (134). So many of Rilke's later tendencies, the ones by which we principally identify him in his fame, are already in evidence here, a full year and more before his actual separation from Lou.

120.   Prater (49) comments on Rilke's adaptation to Lou's demands without irony and even patronizingly, as if these demands were what, as a mere apprentice, he should submit to: "Lou was able now to school him in the ways that suited her". Astonishingly, Leppmann (100) passes over the conflict after Florence altogether! Freedman (86-87) for his part presents his own glossed-over version of the impasse, seeing only Rilke's regression in it.

121.   Leppmann (102) speaks of Rilke's work of basic self-analysis from this time as stemming from a "sunless non-Italian realm" (there is at least that much reference to Florence in his account).

122.   See Leppmann (102); the biographical accounts, almost to a man (Leppmann is the one exception) depict Rilke at this time as simply carrying on blithely and journeymanly with his work. Polikoff (91) speaks simply of his "continued journalling" during another long period of "close commerce" between Rilke and Lou, and Freedman (87) very simply that Rilke "set to work with renewed energy". Prater (50) quotes a letter from Rilke to Helene Voronin, the Russian woman in whose company he spent some time on his Florence trip, in which Rilke says that "much promise from his stay in Italy had been fulfilled". If so, this could only have been in the deeper recesses of Rilke's psyche: his attitude to Voronin had always been intended to impress her with his gallant optimism (see, e.g., the Florence Diary, 63). Prater seems to think that Rilke's collection, *In Celebration of Myself*, which he was at work on around this time, constitutes (!) the fulfilment Rilke speaks of.

123.   Cf. Rilke's Ancient in "Monastic Life", (RANS 91, 93): "Only, his songs are lost to him, / those he no longer begins; / from thousands of ears like pools / drunk up by time ... / And yet ... each song I heard / I saved and hid for him ..."

124.   "Singer", "brother", "angelic herald" (see p.56 of this Volume), all point in Novalis to the same figure. On this matter see my book, *The Way of Novalis*, p.182n.20. See also Appendix I in the present Volume, pp.165-166.

125. This translation by Polikoff, 91-92. Cf. the first block quote above, on p.117, from a Diary entry written over one year later.

126. Prater (49) quotes Rilke as saying to his mother that, in this respect, it was "an important time of hard work".

127. See Polikoff, 79-90, for the best treatment of this theme.

128. Freedman (118-119), as in most accounts of critical moments in their life, officiously follows Lou's version of events (in MCHL 90). Cf. Prater who, speaking of their last period together when in Russia this second time and what happened after July 26th, says: "this was effectively the end of their journey together, for Lou was to go on to Rongas in Finland ... leaving Rainer alone for nearly a month until the time came for their return to Berlin" (66). Prater notes in this connection Rilke's "desolation over Lou's absence. She left him without news for a week or so, and he felt 'inexpressibly uneasy' at the sudden gap" (66—GRN, 37, translates Rilke's phrase as "namelessly dismaying"). Prater's remarks begin to bring out how *Rilke* experienced this latest expression of Lou's wilful independence from him, in spite of which Prater likewise adopts Lou's version of Rilke's reaction: "This troubled her all the more now that the journey of rediscovery of her homeland had given her new strength and zest to go forward with the life she had chosen, whereas he, after the same experience, appeared 'shaken to the depths'" (67). But here, in fact, is yet another instance of Lou thinking only of herself—just the sort of tendency that Rilke desperately knew was undermining their relationship, for how could Rilke have been having quite "the same experience"? a significantly egocentric point of view, which shows that Lou left no room for what Rilke would have been experiencing. I have brought out the two other known instances (after Florence and after Worpswede) of the same dismissive behavior in Lou. We have only some notion of what such behavior signified for Rilke in this instance, from the letter he wrote after the "ugly" one he sent Lou in desperation about her silence ("ugly" being Rilke's own descriptive term—see SN, *Rilke*, 31). Among other aspects of the event alluded to in the second letter was Lou's "unexpected and swift farewell" (31) at the time she departed, pointing to something already disturbingly unexplained about her decision to depart. In the "ugly" letter, which has not survived, we can imagine Rilke breaking down with Lou as he had after Florence and

would again, it seems more quietly though no less desperately, after Worpswede. The second letter narrates another instance of Rilke's shamefaced return to the Mother after the incident, as after Florence (see above, p.158).

129.   There is a similar slanting of the facts in her earlier critical memoir that is exclusively on Rilke, composed three years after his death (see von der Lippe). Simple convenience may have been the cause in the case of some of the misleading narration. Thus Rilke's period of intimate association with Rodin, which took place in two segments, from 1902-1906, is drastically conflated by Lou, his second stay with Rodin from 1905-1906 being treated (von der Lippe, 50 bottom) as if it formed part of his first stay, from 1902-1903. More to the point, the strong divergence of opinions between Rilke and Lou at the time, as to the relationship between life and art, is entirely glossed over. At one point (44, bottom; see also, 50), Rilke's point of view on this question is presented as if Lou had never taken exception to it. At another point (54, top), Lou directly ascribes to Rilke her own point of view at the time, when he was kindly letting her have her own take on his difficulties, scrupulously maintaining his own understanding of his situation. All this concerns the differences in point of view I have elaborated on above: p.28 *passim.*

130.   See Charles Passage, tr., '*Hymns to the Night' and Other Selected Writings* (New York: The Liberal Arts Press, 1960) p.xii.

131.   See Margaret Stoljar, *Athenaeum: A Critical Commentary.* Bern/Frankfurt: Herbert Lang and Company, 1973, 139.

132.   This last statement should be referred back to Stoljar's account (in *Athenaeum*) of the singer-figure in *Hymns*, in whom she sees "the whole body of poetry which, having its origin in Greek antiquity, then embraced the imagery and the mythology of Christianity, to bring religious understanding to the world" (139). See, further, *The Way of Novalis*, p.182 n.20.

Additional Comment

Please note that on p.98 it was not possible, given the drift of my exposition at that point, to remark on the sad irony of the blessing Rilke pronounced on Paula at her engagement (cf. "the kind of blessing that would keep her fully safe through the "storm" of life"). Paula would die from complications attending on the birth of her only child only seven years later, at the very young age of thirty-one. Paula died in 1907. Rilke published "Requiem for a Friend" in 1909.

ADDITIONAL WORKS CITED

Freedman, Ralph. *Life of a Poet: Rainer Maria Rilke*. Evanston, IL: Northwestern University Press, 1998.

Graff, W. L. *Rainer Maria Rilke: Creative Anguish of a Modern Poet*. Princeton: Princeton University Press, 1956.

Hendry, J. F. *The Sacred Threshold: A Life of Rainer Maria Rilke*. Manchester: Carcanet Press, 1983.

Hulse, Michael. Tr. Rainer Maria Rilke. *The Notebooks of Malte Laurids Brigge*. London: Penguin Books, 2009.

Leavy, Stanley A. Tr. Lou Andreas-Salomé. *The Freud Journal*. Ed. Mary-Kay Wilmers. London: Quartet Books, 1987.

Leppmann, Wolfgang. *Rilke: A Life*. New York: Fromm International Publishing Company, 1984. Orig. pub. 1981.

MacDonald, George. Tr. *Novalis: Hymns to the Night and Spiritual Songs*. Maidstone, Kent: Crescent Moon Publishing. Ed. Carol Appleby, 2010.

Mitchell, Stephen. *Ahead of All Parting: The Selected Poetry and Prose of Rainer Maria Rilke*. New York: Random House, 1995.

O'Meara, John. *The Way of Novalis: An Exposition on the Process of His Achievement*. Ottawa: HcP Ottawa, 2014.

Polikoff, Daniel Joseph. *In the Image of Orpheus: Rilke, A Soul History*. Wilmette, IL: Chiron Publications, 2011.

Prater, Donald. *A Ringing Glass: The Life of Rainer Maria Rilke*. Oxford: Clarendon Press, 1994. Orig.pub. 1986.

Stoljar, Margaret Mahony. Ed. *Novalis: Philosophical Writings*. Albany, NY: State University of New York Press, 1997.

von der Lippe, Angela. Tr. Lou Andreas-Salomé. *You Alone Are Real: Remembering Rainer Maria Rilke*. Rochester, NY: Boa Editions, 2003.

BREAKDOWN OF CHAPTERS

Volume 2

Measuring Limits
(The Duino Moment)
(1905-1914)

Contents

Main References

Freedman, Ralph, *Life of a Poet: Rainer Maria Rilke*. Evanston, IL: Northwestern University, 1991.

Greene 1

Greene, Jane Bannard and M.D. Herter Norton, ed. and tr., *Letters of Rainer Maria Rilke 1892-1910*. New York: Norton, 1969.

Greene 2

Greene, Jane Bannard and M.D. Herter Norton, ed. and tr., *Letters of Rainer Maria Rilke 1910-1926*. New York: Norton, 1969.

Hulse, Michael, tr., *The Notebooks of Malte Laurids Brigge*. London: Penguin, 2009.

Mitchell, Stephen, ed., and tr., *Ahead of All Parting: The Selected Poetry and Prose of Rainer Maria Rilke*. New York: Random House, Modern Library Edition, 1995.

Prater, Donald, *The Ringing Glass: The Life of Rainer Maria Rilke*. Oxford: Oxford University Press, 1986.

Snow, Edward, ed. and tr., *The Book of Images*. New York: Farrar, Straus, and Giroux, 1991.

Snow, Edward, ed. and tr., *Diaries of a Young Poet*. New York: Norton, 1998.

Snow, Edward, ed. and tr., *New Poems*. New York: Farrar, Straus, and Giroux, 2001.

Snow, Edward, ed. and tr., *Rilke and Andreas Salome: A Love Story in Letters*. New York: Norton, 2008.

Wydenbruck, Nora, ed. and tr., *The Letters of Rainer Maria Rilke and Princess Marie von Thurn und Taxis*. London: Hogarth Press, 1958.

Lead-In

There is no doubt that the extraordinary reunion with Lou at Pentecost in 1905, after four years of pained separation, lent fresh wings to Rilke's creative life, this reunion reconciling him as it did to a profound negative direction in himself that might well have taken him over irreversibly. The uplift Rilke clearly received from this merciful reconciliation did not, however, take the form we might suppose. The negative life had been displaced or momentarily distanced from him, but it was far from having been resolved. The power of this displacement cannot be overemphasized; it would serve Rilke's creative life for a full three years, during which time Rilke would be free to escape. But the negative life would return.

It is easy to see that in spite of experiencing a deep joy at being with each other again, the meeting between Rilke and Lou would have been in many ways "a precarious reunion"[1]. Each had been through so much, and there could hardly have been enough time to address all that had worked to undermine their relationship, even supposing that they wished to go over the past.[2] Rilke's negative life was in itself a whole world, only fragments of which could be gone into[3]; that life could not, as it were, be fully taken by the horns, if only because there was no longer any solution to it: the harm had been done, and it was a matter of living and dealing with it in the depths. There was now, on the other hand, a fresh resolve in Rilke to see his work through as he knew it had to be, freed as he was now from Lou's former hold on his initiative, and much was brewing in him. There was the prospect of an expanded version of the *Book of Images* most of which had been written by then, anticipation of the *New Poems* some of which had already been written and more poems already conceived, and *Malte*. He would be free to give himself to these projects now also without any of the effects of the former conflict with Lou; on this front he was now at peace: the sanctity of their shared life in the past had been saved. In spite of the suffering they had caused each other, they had come through in faithfulness to each other, and Lou, he was now sure, would be there to help right the boat whenever it might begin to take water, if he should have need of her. Paradoxically, because of her assured continued presence in his life, richly confirmed for them at this meeting, that need became, in fact, less and less as time went on. What, in the meantime, had Rilke brought to Lou? Peace: assuagement for the 'heart'-ailment that had now become a more or less permanent feature of her matrix of life, which on her side would never quite heal, just as on Rilke's side he, in spite of his determined effort to escape it, would continue to be menaced by the negative life he had inherited from their relationship.

That Rilke did not now need Lou as he had formerly, or as much as we might think, is evidenced by the fact that when they met again one month later, as visitors to a mutual friend, Rilke decided to leave his company early, after only a few days. The point has been duly registered: "At the very moment when Lou had finally relented, when his effort of two years to be revived by her had been crowned with success, he absconded"[4]. It was a typical instance of life's dramatic reversals: just when reconciliation with Lou had seemed the most pressing concern of his life, Rilke's attention was immediately diverted to his mounting good fortune in literary affairs, which was now sweeping him away. This impressive transitional moment, marking Rilke's movement from one major phase of his life to another, has been well summarized:

> *Although Lou would continue to be his close friend and confessor, for the moment the reality of her presence—her philosophy, her psychology, her novels, and her academic and journalistic connections—was no longer crucial to him. Another world, a world of great wealth and distinguished titles, of ancient castles and heraldic symbols, opened its doors to him ... a world of mysterious splendor ...*[5]

This was the social side to the success from which Rilke was beginning to profit as a poet and author who was now on the rise. Success on this front was the welcome perquisite[6] of an artistic achievement that did not even include as yet *The Book of Hours* (which would not be published until the end of that year), or the *New Poems* (the two volumes of which were two and three years away), or, for that matter, the impressive, extended version of *The Book of Images* (which would not come out until late 1906). In respect both of Rilke's life and his work, the next three and a half years (from July 1905 to December 1908) would be, in fact, the most straightforward of all. For the first time Rilke was almost completely free to be himself, at peace now because no longer weighed down by the residual elements of his former struggle with Lou, and it is on the basis of this freed-up condition that he proceeded to fully *make* himself—in such terms as he had reached to date. All doors seemed to be opening at this time. He would find himself suddenly financially better supported, his work having already begun to bring in regular advances, while much of the financial strain of seeing to his family (to Clara and to Ruth) was alleviated also by generous invitations and stays at the homes of wealthy admirers and patrons of his work.

There was to begin with the admiring patronage of the Countess Schwerin who offered Rilke her home as a social-cultural resort[7]; then came the sudden recognition of his accomplishments offered to him by Rodin who now made him his personal secretary; then, towards the end of this year (1905), publication of a few longer poems two of which Rilke had written as far back as 1903 in Viareggio (poems that were to make their way into the first part of his *New Poems*, and indeed to crown that work[8]) bringing the further recognition and support of such literary luminaries as Hugo von Hofmannsthal. By then Rilke had already given one lecture tour, and a still bigger series of lectures would take place in the late spring of 1906. There were also significant setbacks over this time, but nothing that would derail Rilke from his artistic mission. His secretarial task with Rodin very greatly reduced time for his own work, but he still managed to begin to put the finishing touches to the extended version of *The Book of Images*; also over that winter a number of other poems would be written to add to the growing body that would form the first part of the *New Poems*. In the midst of Rilke's lecture tour in late spring, his father suddenly died, but neither this emotional event nor his curt dismissal by Rodin in May (on cooked-up grounds that Rilke had overstepped bounds in handling Rodin's correspondence) kept Rilke from considerably adding to the *New Poems*, both in the late spring and the summer of that year.[9]

Rilke was now well on his way in his new life and with his new work, and when in the following winter he learned from Clara of Lou's sudden strange patronizing of him, because of his insistence on maintaining his course at the expense of attention given to his wife and child, it merely struck him as contradictory of Lou who had herself always made a prime virtue of artistic independence.[10] No doubt Lou's judgment must have cooled somewhat the recent excitement he had shared with her, but Rilke would never allow himself, after Florence, to openly criticize her. (After their meeting in the spring of 1905, correspondence between them had been, somewhat strangely, minimal, and it would taper off more dramatically still between 1906 and 1909.[11]) Rilke was fully determined to see his artistic mission through, and the winter in Capri and summer in Paris in 1907 would bring in more work on the *New Poems* which were made ready for publication by August. The book would not go to print until December, and in the meantime there had been the sudden, disturbing, tragically wasteful death of Paula Becker in childbirth. Yet even this event could not stop Rilke in his course. He would have another winter of much correspondence and artistic reflection in Capri, before yet another full summer of work brought the "Other Part" of *New Poems* to completion. This volume came out in late November 1908. Earlier that month, on approaching the date of the first anniversary of Paula's death, Rilke could still easily give himself to his *Requiem* to her, which he wrote in a matter of but a few days, despite the trauma of his underlying grief. But this long period of Rilke's artistic facility would come to an end. The unfinished, still highly fragmented *Malte* material, to which he had devoted himself in very brief, abortive periods over this period, now loomed oppressively before him. There was nothing more to divert him from it, and that ghost of negativity which had plagued Rilke for so long, and which he had managed so forcefully to keep down since his reunion with Lou, now returned, and in that hopelessly vengeful way that only what has long been repressed will return...

I

The Book of Images and the Free Quest*

Meanwhile Rilke had accomplished much. Towards the end of 1906, the extended version of *The Book of Images* came out, his first major publication after *The Book of Hours* which had appeared almost exactly one year before. Their appearance one upon the other was, from a certain point of view, symbolically appropriate. For *The Book of Hours* could, in a certain sense, be said to be the book Rilke wrote *for Lou*, Lou having, as early as 1898, virtually dictated to him that his direction should be towards (her) Russia. Even the later parts of *Hours*, written as far along as two years after their separation in 1901, continue to show Rilke's chronic dependence on that former time with Lou, which was not easily shaken off. Contrastingly, *The Book of Images* is the book Rilke wrote *for himself*, containing as it does most of the work of this time conceived independently of Lou, although this was not in that direction of his own he was so determined to take, back in 1898 after his Florence experience. As we have seen, he had been utterly stymied in that direction, referred at that point with an iron will to Lou, and as for himself was from that time writing only what he could in the shadow of Lou's control over his development. Apart from only a few poems written later[12], the largest section of *The Book of Images* covers this period of Rilke's continued subjection to Lou, from just after writing the first part of *The Book of Hours* through the first year after their separation. Among these poems are a very good number lifted directly from his Diaries, though in many cases re-worked. In these, as we have seen, Rilke was coming to terms with the

*All references to Edward Snow, tr., *The Book of Images*. New York: Farrar, Straus, and Giroux, 1991.

depths of a despair that had been brought on after Worpswede once again by Lou's patronizing indifference to his own artistic impulses and drives. Within three months of writing those poems, Rilke and Lou would officially separate.

By 1906, Rilke was in the position to fit these poems into a broader, more universal pattern that transcended his personal case. There was the advantage, by then, of associating the earlier poems with a fair number of new poems that extended the range of his artistic vision and show him concerned with reaching out to progressively wider spheres of life. The result, as Rilke put it himself, was "in content a new and highly characteristic unity, a truly new book and I may say, without making too high a claim, one that is justified"[13], surprised as he was by the book's "simple, serious, convincing effect"[14]. The point needs emphasizing since this volume has had a fairly cool reception in critical tradition[15], in comparison, say, with *The Book of Hours* and especially *The New Poems*. Unlike these latter volumes, *The Book of Images* has been seen merely as a catchall, with no apparent overall design except for its proliferating variety of artistic forms. It is misleading, however, to speak of this volume as "almost studied in its variousness"[16], since with the exception of the last poems written for it, every other poem would seem to have been conceived and produced, quite independently, in the specific mood of a particular moment, with no thought of any long-term design, variety included. It is all the more significant that these "various" poems should, over time, have fallen into a significantly unified design of their own, which will have something to do with how a poet will be said to have been finding himself. It is equally misleading to speak of "the volume's scattered, hybrid quality"[17], for, as we shall see, a fairly straightforward and significant design does reveal itself, though this would not have been any deliberately conscious one, which Rilke would have set out to fulfil from the outset.

If all we had received from Rilke in the period to 1908 were *The Book of Hours* and the *New Poems*, we would have been left with the sense of a significant gap in our understanding of his artistic identity, not to mention the sense of a patently hyperconscious poetic career. Apart from these two volumes being almost obsessively one-way affairs—all of the poems in each volume falling into the same conscious design, whether towards "God" (*Hours*) or towards "objectivity"

(*Poems*)—we should not have had any sense of how this poet himself had fared over those years, if only by way of a foil. Comparison does not merely advantage *The Book of Hours* and *New Poems*; it also advantages *The Book of Images*, which has what one might describe as "the free quest" for its design, just as honorifically—within the limits, that is, of living under Lou's shadow. That design has been astutely linked to "a ripening in silence"[18] that is distinctive of much of Rilke's production in this volume. Besides possessing this unique characteristic among Rilke's works, the volume deftly outlines what a poet's progress would consist of if one honestly went back to the beginnings, and proceeded inevitably from there outwards into the world, as far as one would get, over a certain period of one's development. Rilke had an especially strong sense of momentously, if slowly, shaping his creative identity with every work he was putting out at every stage of his production, even from very early on.[19] It is too often overlooked that, to get to the point where a poet has begun to dazzle the world, he has had to take himself, like any developing organism, inevitably through early stages of growth that constitute the ground on which he finally lifts himself up, and which he need hardly be ashamed of.[20]

"The First Book, Part One"

Thus, in "The First Book, Part One" we have for theme The Poet's Coming Out, with the inevitable sense of being "called", as a poet, into the world. We may choose to dismiss the first series of poems, to "Girls II", as the stuff of the juvenile's dreams, were it not for the already remarkable fluency and sureness of rhythmical development these poems bear witness to. Besides, why should we not give attention to the fresh energies of the youthful poet (and to their primal sources, in an ideal reckoning[21]) as the poet quietly and tenderly comes forward to assume his chosen role? This initial series of poems in any case serves as a form of preface and has fundamentally a generic metaphorical significance, advertising the volume's main theme, which is, precisely, that of the quest. Just how seriously engaged this poet is can be deduced from the sharp contrast with this initial series of poems suddenly achieved with "The Song of the Statue" and "Madness", which follow. In the former poem he is already setting his chisel to the hardest stone, considering where he stands in his own mortality in comparison with the life he will be giving to his art. Of what use is this art, which pleads to come alive, if the artist himself cannot be saved? The compassionate impulse to redeem matter remains, for all that, overpowering and irresistible in the poet. In the latter poem, already the poet is taking on that strange realm of dereliction (which was uncannily to absorb Rilke to disturbing lengths later*), where abandonment ("A no one's child") and destitution ("all poor and bare") give way to compensating delusions of grandeur ("from such a child a princess"). What is striking about this presentation is the poet's readiness to hear this beggar's story out, for the value it has for itself, compassionately and without judgment, and even as a form of triumph.

Then follows a series of poems on the theme of emotional dispossession focused on an elusive beloved ("Woman in Love", "The Bride", "The Silence"). Highlighted here is the extent to which one can become enslaved by passion where the object of love is conceived in terms of physical possession. From such humble beginnings Rilke will go on to fashion, in the poems of his maturity, his powerful myth of the lover whose faithfulness to love is fulfilled only in the renunciation of the physical relationship. There is the meta-physical primacy in the meantime of the self that antedates emotional love ("Woman in Love"[22]), emphasis also on the extent of that self's power to relate immediately to the universe in every other particular except in the case of the absent lover ("The Silence"), the struggle with absence being a measure of the constraints placed upon oneself by the expectation of physical presence in love.[23] In the extreme terms of the drama in "The Bride", failure of the lover to appear leads to a plunge into madness.[24] Rilke's implicit perspective in these poems does not, on the other hand, preclude an intense sympathy for the victims of such love. He is, however, from the outset (already in "Entrance", the volume's first poem) oriented towards a "far-off" that is driving him beyond love of this kind; the "free quest" in early Rilke already assumes this form. Thus, though they will so naturally inspire poetic "images" as if made for such a world, 'girls' cannot, in spite of this, constitute an end in themselves, and the poet, to see his quest through, must remain "alone in his garden". The next poem, "Music", continues with

---

*In Paris, and in *Malte*.

the idea of resistance to emotional enslavement, which here takes the form of an unrestrained absorption in artistic creation. One thereby loses that freedom of soul by which one gives oneself to the "deep(er) delights" to which one is called by God.

Virtually all of the poems in "The First Book, Part One" were written over the course of the year that followed Rilke's writing of the first part of *The Book of Hours* (only one poem was written in the same period or just before[25]). Over this dilatory time (between "The Book of Monastic Life" and the next trip to Russia in the summer of 1900), Rilke continued in the same vein of devotion to his God that we find in *Hours*. His God re-appears as an explicit theme in the poems that immediately follow "Music": in "The Angels" and "The Guardian Angel". It is the same God Who is depicted "leafing through the pages/in the dark book of the beginning" in the former of these poems, while in the latter the poet calls on his Guardian Angel to "at last name Him/from whose seventh and last day/shards of glory can still be found". The idiom of these poems is still very much that of *The Book of Hours*, which is here (in *The Book of Images*) embedded in a broader, if still only adumbratory, view of the poet's development. "Darkness" is the element by which one knows Rilke's God: it is the element of God's power and the source of His Creation ("The Angels"); it is likewise the element of the poet's inner darkness in which he will occasionally feel helplessly plunged until he is helped out by his Guardian Angel, of whom the poet now asks that he *name* this God as if for greater support.[26] In a certain sense Rilke has his God without religion. To his developing sequence Rilke now adds poems that might have come straight out of his *Visions of Christ* most of which he had already written before he met Lou. "Martyrs" and "The Saint" in *Images* share with the finally unpublished *Visions* the same withering scepticism about religion. These are very complex poems inasmuch as the poet shows a deep sympathy for both martyrs and saint, but only because, as he insists, they have sacrificed themselves to no purpose.

It was indeed Rilke's insistent view, belying his deeper development which he had in the meantime renounced (we shall return to this theme from my Volume 1 in due course), that Christ's attempt at the Redemption of the human race had failed or somehow gotten stuck. It follows from this that the fate of martyrs would be likewise ineffective and, indeed, meaningless. Rilke's sympathy for martyrs lies all in this direction. In "Martyrs" the poet focuses on two sisters one of whom was beheaded and the other stoned. The sisters linger in their sleep of death in some ghostly world where they struggle to bring relief to each other's wounds, the one pleading with the other to hold her arms around her neck more tightly, while this other seeks to hide her crushed brow in the folds of her sister's gown. Then in a form of surrealistic take, the poet imagines the two sisters suddenly returned to life after their martyrdom, without "glory" and "to no one's consternation". They are returned to the world's unassuming activity simply as it is, and "*as if* to Easter, but with no wreath". The position Rilke assumes with respect to the religious realities is, precisely, all in that "as if": it is but a simulacrum of Redemption in which one participates as for the religious observances that mark that moment in the religious calendar. Rilke's general sceptical point of view on religion at one time, as expressed, for example, in the *Visions of Christ*, is in dramatic evidence again here.

In the poem that immediately follows, "The Saint", the same sceptical view of religion is highlighted. In the context of the unslaked thirst of an entire nation/race, a girl, herself "thirstless", is sent out to release water from stones. She finds she is unable to do so, until her thoughts turn to a boy of whom it is said that he is the only one who is genuinely suffering. At which point, a young willow bends down to the girl, itself "thirsting like a wild beast", the effect of which on this "saint" is that "now she went blossoming over her blood,/and her blood went rushing deep beneath her". The poem ends there: there is no further reference to the "parched nation" that sent her out in the first place. It is not difficult to see that here is a contrast between a society that is so given to its abstraction from life it finds itself utterly without joy, romance, desire, etc. (i.e., thirsting), and a young woman who, in her own free, if at first naïve, innocence (which her society takes for guiltlessness), at the thought of "a sick boy" comes of age, in this way coming fully into life herself. In keeping with Rilke's point of view both in *The Book of Images* and *The Book of Hours*, this poem is not intended as an endorsement of sexual freedom. Rather does this woman go "blossoming *over* her blood", this blood "rushing deep *beneath* her". Underlying this presentation is Rilke's view, as I have expressed it in Volume 1, that "in the natural forces of the blood" lies "something deeper that links one spiritually to God"[27], or as Rilke's narrator-monk puts it in "The Book of Monastic Life":

> ... *there are night-alley rumours* **sourced in God**
> *That run unquenchably in your dark blood.*[28]

Here is an ideal attitude towards life that would build on the basis of the full force of natural impulse, as opposed to abstracting oneself from it, an attitude we may suppose Rilke wished for himself. Somewhat too insistently perhaps, he embodies this attitude in his monk. Like others who would feel the force of passion rushing through them, "my blood", the monk boasts, "rushes on, full of its murmurings", going on to add, however, "but in my *substance* I am pure longing"[29]. This is, in any case, as far as Rilke goes in "The First Book, Part One" of *Images* with what we may describe as adult vision. We are, for now, only to go that far. That Rilke was bent, in the meantime, on offering primarily the outline of a *biographical* development, going back to one's youth, is what explains the reversion in his next poem to a stage of life that takes us suddenly back to early childhood.

Another level of contrast is, in this way, created, which is the level that principally concerns Rilke here. There has been, on the one hand, a movement forward into adulthood that goes only so far in its ideological considerations (bearing on love and religion), and now (in "Childhood") a movement back that would measure this advance against the comparatively weak-minded and unsuspecting claims of childhood. The contrast is startling, but not absolute: Rilke supposes a capacity in the child, from the midst of his weariness with the constraints of school, to project himself into a future life, "to look far off into it all" when, it is supposed, "terror" might one day alternate with "trust", in a world where men, women, and children might be also "different and bright". In the meantime, it is the child's experience of his own alienated "solitude" (1.3), in the midst of these constraints, that gives rise to his dark intuition:

> *O sadness without reason; O dream, O dread,*
> *O depth without ground.*
>
> *O ever more escaping grasp of things,*

The dreadful depth, and indeed abysmal complication, of life's paradoxes, including those highlighted in Rilke's views on religion, await the maturing man as it does the growing boy. In keeping with his emphasis in this segment, Rilke next offers the additional vignette, drawn "From a Childhood", in which a boy sits alone in a room in the wondrous darkness of his dreamy solitude (echoing in this "darkening" Rilke's previous focus in his work on the connection to God). He is interrupted in this dreaming by his mother who suddenly appears in the room, intent on playing the piano for them, as is her wont. The mother still belongs to the boy's dream initially, when she first breaks into the room, but very soon an anxious consciousness of the impending event comes over them both. There is a powerfully oppressive ambiguity to the mother's playing: the boy is "caught" up by it, but the effort of playing turns out to be "fearfully", even dismally, labored ("as if it trudged through deep snowdrifts"). Again that which awaits the child, in the stark adult world that will require such labor, is pictured as ominous and dreadful, especially as this world conflicts with the rich depths of childhood's primal dream. And as if the primal impulse would now wreak its revenge on this stark world that lies in store for it, in "The Boy" a great fantasy is now indulged, in which a boy imagines himself coming down on the world, like a horrible warrior of old, precisely out of that contrasting "dark" world of freed imagination ("a black solitude/through which we race like a rapid dream") in which this boy (the poet himself) presently lies...

Pursuing yet another form of contrast, Rilke shifts the emphasis again in "The Confirmed" from the steep grandeur of childhood's dark imaginings to the picture now of a group of recently confirmed children lingering in the aftermath of that sacramental celebration. There is the sense, attributed to them by the poet, of another life looming that will be quite different from the sanctified life the children are experiencing at this moment, but there is in any case the present interim to give oneself to, in which nothing of that future life yet shows:

and what comes now will be something changed.

So let it come! Does not now the interim begin,
the wait for the next striking of the hour?

The poet himself chooses to indulge in this experience of the celebration, lingering, as the children are, in the deep sensual satisfaction of that moment: "a church cool inside like silk", their "white veils" seeming to "hold hidden flowers", and even "with the wind" comes "a distant flowering" from the "gardens outside at the city's edge":

> *It was as if things wreathed themselves,*
> *they stood* [so] *brightly—infinitely light and calm …*

However, there is now yet another stark disjunction of terms as the volume shifts, in the next and final poem in Part One, suddenly back to life's austere demands. Rather dramatically, the focus shifts now to that drastic moment when, after the Last Supper, Christ leaves his disciples, to re-assume his "deep action". There is "panic" and "terror" among the disciples as "the old solitude comes over him". Much is made of this (for Rilke) all-encompassing virtue of solitude from which alone comes the power of creative action, and without which there can be no strength to face up to what the world holds in store by way of existential challenge. We have seen that there are limits, in Rilke's view, to what can be claimed of Christ's effort of Redemption, but it is his power of solitary engagement that is nevertheless taken up by the poet, this power being needed "everywhere" and in all things. It is this power that forms the basis of this poet's concept of his own life-mission, separating *him* drastically from all the usual social attachments in which others remain caught up and by which they are, indeed, enslaved. In this way does the poet set up to explore himself without inhibition, as he does in the volume's next Part, where he has begun to sound the depths of his potential for a more comprehensive imagination of the world.

"The First Book, Part Two"

On the one hand, this poet already senses the depths of "happy strengths" in himself, as announced in "Initial", the first poem to the Second Part; on the other hand, these "strengths" realize themselves in a world so oppressed they can only manifest themselves as "tears", albeit "tears" that are made to "dance" through the music of the poet's creation. The poet sees his purpose as associated with "sing"-

ing others "to sleep", with being "the one in the house/who knew",
at one point "hold"-ing them "gently", at another "let[ting]" them
"go/when something stirs in the dark" (re: "To Say Before Going to
Sleep"). As we have seen, darkness for Rilke constitutes that depth of
imaginative soul-life that connects us to God and that can be either
confounding in its inscrutable challenges (and so, requiring support)
or alternately satisfying (in which case the soul of the one in sleep
should be allowed to run free). Among the masses of human beings
again, who are merely "surface-dwelling" ("Pont du Caroussel") and
who occupy a "wavering world/all heaped up at random" ("Human
Beings at Night"), the poet stands apart, "force[d]" by *these* "from fear
to sing" ("The Neighbor"). The poet is not alone, however: a dere-
lict blind man, who, "ever unchanging", stands apart (in his begging)
"on the bridge" (the "Pont du Caroussel"), will also be a centre from
which the universe can work its influences, such a man being additionally, in another guise, also a "dark entrance to the underworld".
Both extremes of the universe open themselves up to us in him as they
will also in the devoted poet...

What the poet holds in himself as a world of unbounded imaginative potential is the "great homeland" in which his thoughts,
feelings, and words roam about like "wild animals" ("The Solitary").
These, he is made to feel, must be kept in check "out of shame", such
is the confining prejudice with which he is confronted in the outside
world. The metaphor of "wild animals" prepares us, of course, for
the next poem ("The Ashanti") where a set of wild animals are literally presented at a zoo, "unrelated" in *their* confinement "to the antics
of the new/alien things which they don't understand", themselves
"with their fierce instincts all alone". The immense force of what the
poet must himself contain and keep in check in his own alienation is
thereby evoked. This poet works in the universal, being without a hereditary line and working beyond any lineage in a literal sense ("The
Last of His Line"). What *he* has to bestow as heritage falls away into
a stream of time ("a wave") that is not so easily grasped or perceived.
Yet suddenly (see "Apprehension") his song, which until now has
seemed "meaningless" to a jaded social world (cf. "the faded forest"),
can seem at least to him, and to those who are truly listening, crucial.
That song gathers to itself the greater universal world beyond, with
a message as if to say that some form of transformation and rebirth

will come out of any moment in which one is truly ready, creatively, to give oneself up to that world ("to die" into it). This is to account for the poet's vertical, inward life; on the horizontal outer plane, of nature, all things seem for a long time now to have deceased (see "Lament"); there is even an intimation of some final end: "I heard something fearful being said"; "a clock/just struck". Yet, according to the poet, the influence of one star at least has lasted; it shows its influence in the form of the life of that inner world the poet will bring to bear on a new future. In the course of the poet's deliberate meditations, "solitude" has, in the meantime, been made into a fully sustaining force: coming upon the poet especially by night, by day also it now "flows with the river"; that is to say, it now finds its own sure place in the day's ongoing events (re: "Solitude").

This depth in the poet's faith, in the last analysis, comes from the assurance of his connection to his God. Virtually all of the poems collected in this Second Part were written in the period that immediately followed "The Book of Monastic Life" when Rilke's connection to his God was still a direct one. This was before the strenuous circumstances of his life began their long subversive action against that connection, starting with Rilke's drawn-out, progressive estrangement from Lou, which dates from as early as a full year-and-a-half before their separation, coming to a head especially with his introduction to Paris, as we have seen. Significantly, many of the poems collected from that period, when placed in the present sequence, do not show at all the depth of personal distress and indeed despair associated with them when they first appeared in the Diaries from which they were taken, e.g. "The Last of His Line", "Lament", "Apprehension". These stated poems were written at the time of Rilke's catastrophic return to Lou after Worpswede.[30] Other poems, "Progress" (originally entitled "Prayer") and "Presentiment", were written in the days of greatly renewed promise when Rilke was still at Worpswede. Yet in *The Book of Images* these poems come after the three just mentioned. In the present sequence Rilke's actual biography is thus reversed and re-written in an insistently positive direction, the negative being considerably dampened. Rilke's actual biography is thus belied by the simple, progressive vision offered in this sequence. The poet is here intent on producing the picture of a steady, forward-moving growth such as he might have wished for himself and perhaps even believed of himself, the ghost of his negative life having been banished from view—at least for the time being. He was once again (he had done the same when applying himself to the second and third parts of *The Book of Hours*[31]) returning to his former faith in the God he had come to serve from the time of his first visit to Russia, notwithstanding the great deepening in negative experience he had known in the meantime that he could see represented a direct countermeasure to this God. Indeed the whole of the rest of this Second Part is rooted in this faith in God, in spite of a few hints, e.g., in the "End of Autumn", of a world calculated to oppose it. Some of the poems that follow in this Second Part might have come, in fact, straight out of "The Book of Monastic Life", notably "Autumn Day", and "Autumn" as well as the last poem of this Second Part, "Strophes".

"Autumn Day", which follows on "Solitude", begins with the line "Lord: it is time. The summer was immense". The poem is in the very idiom of "Monastic Life": "Command the last fruits to be full/.../urge them on to completion", and we find here even the same, almost arrogant self-confidence: "Who has no house now, will never build one". It is true that in "Memory" the anticipation for the New Year of all one could wish for—"the stupendous,/the awakening of stones,/depths turned toward you"—all this is countered, on the other side, by the thought that over the past year only so much was finally possible, steeped as the poet is in the equally insistent relativeness of his struggle: "And then all at once you know: that was it/.../there stands before you/the fear and prayer and shape/of a vanished year". Also, in "End of Autumn", the poet continues to be confronted with the intractable alienness of the outer universe (things on that plane are for a long time now deceased): "the solemn, ponderous/relentlessly denying sky"; in "Autumn", the poem that follows, the poet focuses on how "the heavy earth falls/from all the stars into aloneness". Human beings are no less involved in this process of universal decay: "We are all falling. This hand is falling." *And yet* all this decaying creation, we can be sure, lies in the hands of God: "And yet there is One who holds this falling."

In the very midst of the process of decay, the poet can already divine a mysterious *other* life reflected, for example, in the fact that this process of decay (which repeats itself from year to year) is a strangely long one (even in autumn), and that, equally strangely, he can see very far into this process: "down all avenues", and "[a]lmost to the distant oceans" ("End of Autumn"). It is the assurance that his God is fiercely present deep within even this process that gives this poet his power to bring "whatever wanders lost in things/…/ toward the light". This light is invoked by the "dancing tone" of the poet's creation and through this creation is imagined falling into "the old/abysses endlessly". In this way does the poet come to mediate between the wondrous "vastness" of the universe and "the darkening land" that preludes "the murmuring darkness" of nightfall in the midst of which the poet can, among other things, hear "the weeping of women" and feel "the grudge of whole generations". "On the Edge of Night" is the poem from which these last many phrases are taken. Of all the poems that comprise this First Book, it is, along with "Prayer", the poem that follows it, unquestionably the most imaginatively resonant and far-reaching. The two poems represent the climax of Rilke's expression of his faith in this volume as a whole. The former of these poems was written in January of 1900 when Rilke was still basking in the great achievement of faith of "The Book of Monastic Life". "Prayer" was written in December of 1900 two months after leaving Worpswede when Rilke was beginning to sense some renewal of his faith after the catastrophic return to Lou. This poem is likewise set at Night where "things" are imagined "raised up/ into One Darkness's One Stillness". As much as the poet takes up the "light", he returns to the view that he will also commit to the depths of the "darkness" in which his saving God also lies (a "darkness" that has become still more foreboding to Rilke by then). To these two poems Rilke now adds two others of likewise renewed promise written when in Worpswede, Rilke having by then recovered from the most recent conflict with Lou during their summer in Russia—the poems "Progress" and "Presentiment". In the former of these poems Rilke boasts of being able, once again, to reach up to the heights as well as down to the depths, while in the latter he boasts himself ready to confront on his own, out of the depths of his inner self, "the great storm" of life that he sees himself destined to take on and positively wishes will come on, that he may prove himself with his God once again…

Clearly with this sequence of four poems Rilke was drawing on the best moments before and after his various periods of intense suffering from his relationship with Lou. As we have seen, in this suffering Rilke had, in the most disturbed way, eventually lost sight of his God (nor would he be able ever to recover Him in the precise form in which he had known Him until then).[32] The whole of his anguish on his return from Worpswede is explained by the fact (as I have argued) that just when he was on the verge of working his way back to God after the setback in Russia, on returning to Lou the whole of his inspiration that way was crushed. With *The Book of Images* Rilke was in the position to *re-write* his life such that he appears here as the one he would have wished to be and could have developed into, had it not been for the repeated subversion of his aims. He was in the position to do so, of course, because he was free to shape *The Book of Images* as he saw fit on aesthetic grounds, but it is the disjunction that results, when one refers this re-construction of himself to the actual condition of his life both in the past and also at this time, that especially impresses in a broader view of Rilke's development. *The Book of Images* abstracts only a certain aspect of Rilke, wrenches this ossified identity, as it were, from the way the poet was actually making himself in the depths, even if Rilke did not know this, or did not wish to know this at this time. In 1906 when he put *Images* together, he very possibly thought that he could give himself again the identity he was fashioning here, that he had (especially after the reconciliation with Lou) at last come free of all that former negativity in himself by which he had felt so threatened. *The Book of Hours* had just come out; *The Book of Images* was presenting the same case of faithfulness to his God. As for the negative life, that lay in the shadows; it was to be addressed directly in *Malte* (on which Rilke was already working, though the book was at this point in a condition of deep formlessness). Very possibly by then Rilke thought he would now fully manage the negative material that would be addressed in *Malte* with the same power of artistic detachment he felt he had now attained. Such detachment would only heighten, in fact, with his further application to the *New Poems* which builds so self-consciously on such detachment as a matter of principle. I have already indicated (in Volume 1) that more likely, however, Rilke knew, in the depths, that the negative life continued to challenge him as it always had, and that he was, over the period of *Images* and *New Poems* both, knowingly escaping, satisfied with thinking that with those projects the darker demons could be counterbalanced and held in check. In the meantime, he was offering with *Images* a model of how a poet could be seen developing on the basis of faith in such a God as Rilke proclaims is a ubiquitous Presence and an ever-reliable Support.

My other main point in this chapter concerns the reputation in which *The Book of Images* is held: it has, quite misleadingly, been generally slighted in relation to *The Book of Hours* and the *New Poems*. If I have entered in some depth into the detail of these poems, especially in Part Two of this First Book, it has been to bring out a very fine and rather unique coherence to *The Book of Images*. The volume has, in fact, a complete coherence, both structurally and thematically, in comparison, e.g., with *The Book of Hours* which I have shown (in Volume 1) is in a number of ways structurally flawed, perhaps even seriously so. Even the *New Poems* cannot be said to possess the complete coherence, structural and thematic, that we find in *Images*. The *New Poems* may aim at consistently displaying the one structural notion of a purely objective presentation of its material, but one would be hard-pressed to speak of any thematic coherence to its presentation otherwise, in spite of the suave, even seamless, shifting that takes place from one section to the next in terms of quite a variety of thematic material. On the one hand, there is the often quite abstract if powerful rhetorical emotion of *The Book of Hours* putting great demands on the comprehension of the reader, also extensively, the sequences running on to great length without any specific section breaks. On the other hand, there is the somewhat dire pretension in the *New Poems* to a purely objective presentation of material divorced from all subjective impressions, 'dire' because fully successful in fact in only a very limited number of cases (as we shall see). *The Book of Images* lies, happily, somewhere in between, in what is contrastingly a more fully accommodating middle ground…

In the poems from this collection there is, first, a distinct (smaller or broader) visual focus for each subject, and sometimes also for each theme (thus "images", first, in this sense), then, out of the midst of this distinct focus, what has been wonderfully described as "traces, invisible connections, imaginings, remembrances, intimations of things lost or unrealized, waiting to be recalled or brought (back) to life"[33], ("images" also in this richly permutating sense). Most obvious is the case of "Storm" (towards the end of "The First Book, Part Two") where, when one looks at this poem on its own, a literal storm in nature is altogether the focus. However, the poet has in the meantime set this poem in the immediate context of "Presentiment", where he blazons forth his readiness to take the measure of the storm of life in the world. A literal presentation thus transforms into one that is now personally metaphorical and symbolic. A more subtle case is where evening, as in "Evening in Skåne" and "Evening", (to go on with this sequence) becomes the focus for seemingly remote ruminations respectively on the "miraculous structure" of sky, "moved within itself and upheld by itself", and *our* contrasting, troublesome involvement in life's dualism, as "the lands divide from you,/one going heavenward, one that falls". Such sophisticated subtleties of imaginative development abound in this, "The First Book, Part Two" of *Images*, ultimately with God and the challenging extent of His creation the prime focus. All comes, in the end, to a focus in Him: "weeps for [Him]", "walks toward [Him]", "looks at [Him]" (see "Solemn Hour"), and yet such is the poet's deliberate sensitivity, it can still rankle with him, in a way that sets off yet another new challenge, that "many" can still be "speaking evil of [H]im"—as in "Strophes", which is significantly the note on which this Second Part ends.*

I have spoken of *The Book of Images* in relation to the idea of "the free quest", which undoubtedly it is in comparison with *The Book of Hours* and *New Poems* where the poet greatly confines himself respectively to the idea of "God" and of "objectivity". Comparatively more by way of content is made possible by the concept of "the free quest"—in short the whole world of experience in which we have our being (and really settle our fate), somewhere in between "God" and "objectivity". There are, at the same time, significant limits to Rilke's idea of the free quest in this volume, as we have seen, inasmuch as this quest rears itself on what is a deliberately, if not an artificially, *aesthetic* choice which has Rilke re-writing his life as he actually experienced it and continued to experience it in the depths—this life that would, indeed, return to haunt and to hound him, for a long while seemingly without issue or end, as we shall see.

---

*Compare the more troubled, ambiguous form "Solemn Hour" takes in Rilke's diary (at that time an untitled poem), reflecting the deep contradictions in his life at the time. See my commentary on this material on p.88.

"The Second Book, Part One"

Despite its radically different poetic idiom, Part Two of the First Book of *The Book of Images*, as we have seen, shares a great deal with *The Book of Hours* in its quite insistent focus on God. If Part One may be titled "The Poet's Coming Out", Part Two could have as title "The Self and God". The main subject of Part One is "Time", the main subject of Part Two "Metaphysics"—all this to the extent, of course, that Rilke could grasp these things by the time he was twenty-five, by which time almost all of these poems were written. *The Book of Images* is, indeed, principally a volume about a young poet making his way, and he now spreads his wings still farther. In Part One of The Second Book, the subject, which could also serve as title, is "History"—though, again, history only as Rilke could conceive of this by the time he was twenty-five. It is a radically telescoped history and entirely post-Christian, although Christ Himself is given no great value or even very much acknowledged here. That history begins with the Annunciation and is followed by the visit of the Magi; from here, with only one other poem intervening, we are then precipitated forthwith towards the Last Judgment, in a poem of great, almost insupportable gravity. It is only after being drawn into this wildly foreshortened perspective on history as given in religious tradition that we then get the poet's two forays into history proper, with the poems on Charles of Sweden and on the Tsars, from which more specific cultural-historical points are drawn.

The radically sceptical account Rilke gives of Christ and of the Christian religion in his early *Visions of Christ* continues to show its influence in his first four poems here. Scepticism in these terms is at the same time counterbalanced by hope in the figure of the Mother, Mary. In "The Annunciation", Rilke's Gabriel, the (arch-) Angel who appears to Mary to announce the imminent birth, manifests from an otherworldly region made all the more obscure by the fact that he has forgotten what errand he is on (at first he blames his forgetfulness on the confusion that his coming into space has created). In fact, what knowledge of his purpose does come to him is derived in the end almost entirely from the effect Mary herself makes on him, in whom he can sense some portent about to take place. (Himself and all the other angels have in the meantime grown afraid as with some intimation of this "something" about to happen.) Gabriel has simply been drawn towards Mary as the epicentre of the imminent event: "You are a great, high shining gate,/and you will open soon./ *You*, my song's most celebrated ear,/now I feel .../And so I came that way." The vagueness of the impending event reflects on the fact that it is finally Mary who is not only its creator but, in creating it, up to a point the event itself: herself or what she is in herself is the event. The value Rilke attaches to Mary in this respect, in contrast with his altogether indifferent treatment of the Christ-child, is typical of his religious views in this period (to October 1900), although the attention given to Mary may have a provenance other than in what underlies the ethos of the *Visions of Christ* and may be unconsciously drawing on Rilke's Florence experience. (I will return to this issue in a moment.) In "The Three Holy Kings" Mary remains the central focus of attention, the "dawning" over which she presides being set in turn (in addition to being set against the obscurity of the other-world) against the "confusion" of the non-Christian and pre-Christian world. There is the danger that what Mary is about to give birth to will be appropriated by that earlier world to its own over-extended, chaotic, and errant ends. Mary is thus counseled to turn her attention away from that world and to her own purposes, the problem of relation to that other world being thus put off for now. It is the problem of Mary's being "Everywhere" in what she stands for, in contrast with that other world's tendency to be forever "On the Way". An openness to the universal to be found "Everywhere", because centred in Mary, is opposed to the wilful directedness of the Kings who, "On The Way", would appropriate all experience only in their perversely chaotic fashion (and who in this respect are far from holy). A strange lightness of tone otherwise characterizes Rilke's presentation, which is to be credited, it would seem, to the certainty of Mary's own calming power and influence over these events. Mary, and the figure of the mother and of woman more generally, play, as we shall see, the most significant role perhaps in Rilke's idea of the final configuration of history, certainly as presented in this section of his work.

In the meantime, the spirit of the Christian religion in *its* repressive effects is a major sphere of negative reality for Rilke, as in the case of the Carthusian monk who is the subject of the next poem, "In the Certosa". In a scenario symbolically typical of Rilke, this monk is associated with an abusive father, and a mother who, once "a glass, all delicate and clear," has been abused ("smashed") by him. "[I]n an hour of wild distress", to expiate his horrid life, the father consigns his very young son to the monastery, and the unhappy monk now lives caught in the entanglements of vows that have cut him off entirely from his natural desires. This monk's "stifled strengths" contrast sharply with those "happy strengths" that in an earlier section of this volume had absorbed Rilke as the promise of a lifetime's work in freedom as a poet (see "Initial" from "The First Book, Part Two"). This monk is kept constantly at the mercy of "the force/that rolls impatiently through the dark," without any other outlet for his desires than the garden that he "devoutly" tends with the purpose of reaping from it the mere "image" of desires or "strengths" thus horribly "stifled": "Who will set [this garden] free?" asks the poet. The darkness of God, which in *The Book of Hours* Rilke celebrated as the bedrock of his poetic afflatus, takes the form here of a "force" the monk has not been able to properly assimilate, unlike Rilke's prototypic monk in *Hours*, because this monk has not been left free to work with it but has rather had to repress it.

After we are given this sorry picture of a sterile religious culture, tenuously linked back to the symbolic situation of the father and the mother, we are then precipitated, quite wildly, towards "The Last Judgment", the volume's next poem and by far the most impressive poem this volume has offered us to date. Here it is, contrastingly, Rilke's monk from *Hours* who is speaking! Back in September of 1900 (by which point this poem had been written), Rilke was still very much caught up in that intense relationship to his God that he had so strenuously given himself to in the first part of *Hours*, "The Book of Monastic Life". Not only in its content or the attitude conveyed but in its very voice, "The Last Judgment" might well have appeared in the last section of "Monastic Life", where such final realities are considered at some length, were it not that the poem is far too concentrated in gravity, and too dark even for that solemn context. The event of the Judgment is dramatized here in such detail, for example in the case of those who will be called to judgment, as will even suggest Michelangelo's terrible painting on the subject. There is the fanciful thought that God might yet, as a last favor of creation, send his Son down (along with Mary Magdalene) to relieve those called to judgment, but the counter-view is as soon expressed that those called would much rather not be brought back to hope and life. As opposed to having to support that extreme effort of conversion from their settled condition, those called would rather choose to die again and forever: the prospect of such a last option from God would only be seen as "the last hate".

This is a population that has determined that their single course of life in the direction of hopelessness, free at last of all moral contention, is, very simply, the easier choice. Rather than have to struggle greatly in order to be saved, their choice is to be at last related, by a simplifying arrangement, to the final anger of God, which they have called down upon themselves by their perverse lives. All creation will have come to an end by then, and Rilke the poet, in the character of the monk, asks how God could bear this end or the Judgment that would bring in this end. God is suspected of having, in the meantime, absconded, from shame or fear of what his creation has come to. The poet would appeal to God to at least put off the last reckoning for some time: "O, set yourself against the wheeling of all days", and he sees himself as, in fact, heroically capable of helping this effort ("*[w]e will stem the great wheel*"). Another solution may, in the meantime, come forth connected with the poet's conception of a saving hero who, Orpheus-like, will have the strength to "descend" into those many "dark deaths" the creation has witnessed, in order to "extract" from them "the meaning, the desire, and the soul":

> *one who, engaged with all his heart*
> *and yet serene, swims through all things,*
> *the powers' nonchalant consumer,*
> *who plays himself on all strings ...*

It is rather he who may in the end manage to help right the creation and bring all those who have succumbed to its perverse direction back to the path of hope that his example of a consummating serenity, impervious to despair, will lay open again. In this role, Rilke's Orpheus takes over the function that had been traditionally assigned to Christ.

The prospect of such a "Last Judgment" and its forbidding challenge to hopefulness is thus set alongside Rilke's ongoing commitment to a view of how the influence of the Mother, as classically embodied in Mary, also casts its embalming light upon the historical scene. It is an archetypal opposition of terms for Rilke, deeply related to the horrible conflict he underwent over the two years prior to the production of "The Last Judgment", in which, as we have seen (in Volume 1), his spiritual fate was being determined. In the light of events from that period (duly covered in that Volume), it does not seem far-fetched to suggest that "The Last Judgment" bears the imprint of Lou's repression of Rilke at this time, over and against which was set the serene, finally "festive", vision of historical evolution associated with the figure of the Mother, which Rilke's solitary Florence experience had opened up for him, though it was almost as soon to be stymied by Lou. In the rest of this "Second Book, Part One", Rilke continues to focus on his beneficent vision of how human history does (or at least ought to) resolve itself in the depths of its antithetical progression, if only we could penetrate to the determining value of this beneficent vision. This would be in the face of the terrible view of universal hopelessness and Judgment that Rilke also insists on continuing to bring forward here.

In the meantime, the shift at this point, once again suddenly, from the dark, nebulous depths of "The Last Judgment" to the historical clarity and simplicity of the life and fate of "Charles the Twelfth of Sweden" is itself more than startling. This latter poem must in turn be appreciated in another broad context: over the next few poems, yet another dimension to Rilke's vision of historical evolution will emerge from which the poem on the Swedish King assumes its specific meaning. In "The Tsars", a poem written under the influence of Rilke's Russian trips, one finds the germ of an idea of the meaning of civilization which sheds light on the significance of a life such as that of Charles. In the first two parts of "The Tsars", the legendary medieval figure of Ilya Muromets is presented as a great founder of civilization: he is seen as grappling mightily with primal forces of chaotic disorder which he and his companions are finally able to outlast. In this way does a fully proper centring power emerge that, channeling these forces rightfully, forms the basis of a civilization that can be said to be authentically creative, a civilization lying (ideally) beyond "fear and hardship":

> *Those were supremely strong ones, who stayed there,*
> *not worn down by that immensity*

that out of throats as out of craters broke;
*they **lasted**, and aging bit by bit,*
they grasped the dread that Aprils held,
and their peaceable hands took many
and led them through fear and hardship
to days when they, more resilient,
built their walls around the city founders.

The ultimate strength these founders demonstrate (as expressed in the poem's second part) depends paradoxically on a power of deep waiting (patience) and a maturing, or power of ripening in the spirit (as presented in the first part), that depends on such waiting; these combined forms of power are what give these founders of civilization their seemingly easy capacity to forge a reality out of an abysmally intractable world: *in this sense* "[t]he real is like the miraculous". Such a power of deep waiting is what Rilke sought to develop in himself, sensing how from it would come in time his own capacity to forge a new world out of the distinctive poetry he saw himself creating, this creation being an expression of the idea of civilization he is already formulating here. Rilke sensed this possibility of a complete creation for himself as early as the period of his Russian trips, and it is almost as if his own daemon were speaking to him here by way of an oracular exhortation, the kind of communication that one suspects could even have manifested to Rilke in his dreams:

For they shall stride who for long hours sat
in their being's deep twilight.

Here is a clue as to another ground on which Rilke saw history unfolding, besides on the terms in which he saw his all-powerful if errant God proceeding. The latter has left such a great portion of humanity at the mercy of His final judgment. We shall return to the deep conflict and tension between these competing views of history in short order, as well as to the role that Mary and the figure of the Mother also figures in this concatenation of developing perspectives on the potential meaning of human destiny…

The third part of "The Tsars" is an indication of how fully in tune Rilke could be with the structural implications of his poetic thought, even when getting back to his material a good number of years later, since this poem was written as far along as six years later, in 1906, the year in which *The Book of Images* was to appear in its second, expanded form. It is the only part of this poem (there are three other parts) that was not written back in 1900. With this new poem Rilke had found a way of bridging the first two parts with the last three. The poem dramatizes the mad reign of Ivan the Terrible in the 16th century, filling out a crucial link between the opening section on the legendary achievements of Ilya and the last three parts where the seemingly effete but religiously inspired reign of Ivan's son, Feodor, is considered. Ivan the Terrible in his madness serves as an illustration precisely of how the "fear" that Ilya had so strenuously overcome in the depths of his psychic nature can return to plague our humanity:

> *nothing but the fear …*
> *nothing but the daily fear of everything,*
> *which hounds him …*
> *   … he no longer knows:*
> *Who is the holder? Who the held?*

The life of Charles the Twelfth of Sweden stands for its part on the extreme other side of the violent historical situation Rilke fills out in this "Second Book, First Part". Charles's life represents an example of a civilization become so ingrown the horrible glamor of war for war's sake is everything. The threat to Ivan the Terrible comes from within: it is as if he were fated to kill (he was to kill even his most beloved son) because he is unable to "question", or detach himself from, the chaotic aspect of the dark energies that overwhelm him, which bring on his fear (re: "fear/… which hounds him/… on past dark unquestioned/perhaps already guilty hands"). With Charles darkness confronts him, rather, from without, in the form of the horrible ethos of war from which, yet, "wild delights" will suddenly re-emerge:

> *The darkness steamed, stifling,*
> *what darkened was not time,—*
> *and everything was turning gray,*
> *but suddenly a new log fell,*
> *and once again the flames fanned out*
> *and raged for wild delights.*
> *They all attacked …*

Darkness, Rilke's typical term, sends us back to the deep problematic aspect of God's creation from which, on his own level, the Carthusian monk of "In The Certosa" also suffers. As we have seen, this monk is unable to free himself sufficiently to be able to channel the natural energies with which that creation challenges us towards spiritual ends, with the result that a deep repression sets in. Otherwise, as in "The Last Judgment", we are made aware of a vast horde of human souls who give themselves to this darkness wantonly and despairingly, fatalistically bent on the primrose path to the everlasting bonfire.

As we have noted (to a great extent also in Volume 1), Rilke sees himself, as poet, as one favored to parley with this God, first for more time (Rilke was still quite young). Perhaps as in "The Last Judgment", as Rilke believes, a hero will emerge ("Perhaps you can still raise one from us") who will manage to bring hope and salvation to the human species (this Hero who, for Rilke, is not Christ, and who has already been invoked in some depth in "The Book of Monastic Life"—see Volume 1 of this study)[34]. For now, at least a direction in new hope, the prospect of a "dawning", has been offered through the figure of Mother Mary and woman generally—this being the other main aspect of Rilke's presentation in this section of his Book. There is also Rilke's highly valued idea of a practice of deep waiting conducive to a proper centring in one's experience of the world (and for which an extension of time is needed). In "The Son", the poem he placed between "Charles the Twelfth" and "The Tsars", Rilke explicitly presents such centring practice as the ground of historical authenticity:

> *and afraid and hollow are those times*
> *when behind their vanities*
> *no force presides that is at rest.*

Rilke presents this practice in the form of the Son's vision, which he experiences in association with his mother and with all those who were (and are) ready to give themselves to this vision (cf. the "we" of the poem's address in the last part). It is the same vision that motivates Ilya and his companions who, before they undertake their great civilizing mission, as we have seen "for long hours sat/in their being's deep twilight". Significantly, Ilya himself is presented as "the son" who "came, immense, from being wakened". It is typical of Rilke's deep structural sense of his unfolding work that the Son's vision of centring practice should belong to a section of the poem that was written as a later addition to the poem's first part, as if to provide a bridge between "Charles the Twelfth" and "The Tsars", and to expound further on a key perception in this section of *Images*.

A versatile poem, "The Son" also provides a central analogue for the profound tensions that prevail between, on the one hand, a degenerating civilization and its disturbing discontents and, on the other, that deep inner world of spiritualizing power that goes into creating and re-creating authenticity in its midst. The poem associates the disturbed condition of civilization with the poem's banished king who is the Son's father, while the other world of spiritualizing tendencies is associated with his mother. The father is described listening to his son's curious inquiries into a civilization, which the son has yet to know, "with darkened/brow for nights on end". In keeping with Rilke's essential account, the father endures the world's darkness in its untransformed condition: "My father was an aggrieved one/who knew little rest." The mother, contrastingly, communes with the darkness that has become for her a source of free transformation:

> *she, left all in white,*
> *before vague shapes of evening*
> *walked through dark gardens.*
>
> *wandered all white through the green,*
> *and felt for stirrings of that wind*
> *before the evening glow.*

It remains for the son along with her (and all other able souls) to tap into the still greater world of the "meadows" that lie beyond this embattled family scene, in which "a dark humming still runs—/(there are many voices and yet no choir)".

In the fifth part of "The Tsars", Feodor, the seemingly effete son of Ivan the Terrible, grasps suddenly that all the more successful efforts of previous Tsars to bring an authentic civilization into being took their inspiration in fact proleptically from what he has come to embody in himself:

> *And he grasps suddenly who they were*
> *and that they often, to give their darkness sense,*
> *dived down into his own depths*

and used him, the gentlest of the anointed,
greatly and devoutly in their deeds
long before his own life came.

. . . .

He was the strength for their exuberance,
the golden ground against which their broad lives
Mysteriously appeared to darken.

All the more to the point of the structure of Rilke's vision in this Book, Feodor himself takes his inspiration from Mother Mary and, also significantly, only in her condition of promise, the birth of her son having still to take place. Feodor gives himself in utter reverence to "the royal lady/who will be overflowing with that son", as conveyed in the holy icon of Her before which this Tsar kneels:

The Tsar kneels before it, speaks:

'did You not feel how we thronged into You,
with all feelings, longings, and forebodings:
we wait for Your loving countenance
that has vanished from us; vanished where?'

She herself had yet to manifest fully (also in Rilke's life), and there is the momentary anguished thought that she may even have vanished from us, just as Rilke's God may appear to have absconded. In spite of this despairing thought, however, and perhaps because of it, this Tsar "broods and broods" until finally he passes on into this Mary, joining her triumphantly in death "(In order [at last] to meet her countenance)".

In the last two poems of "The Second Book Part One" Rilke's subject now shifts from political history to a broader social scene, as in "Those of the House of Colonna". Focus here is on the portraits of these now dead men, who in their day exercised considerable political power and influence. In these paintings they are portrayed in all their social pride of "that great confidence/that everything *is* and *counts*". Not so fancifully, the poet then contrasts the unwavering realism of these men that has made them look so stiff in their portraits with how it must have been for them in their boyhood when all was poetic enthrallment, by fountain and garden, for example—the poet returning us in this way to a running theme in "The First Book, Part

One". Over this scene in boyhood presided the unassuming influence of Mother Mary a painting of whom at the Nativity scene hung at an altar in a solitary side aisle of a church they would have worshiped at. Her influence, so the poet imagines, would have been felt all the more for being noticeably unobtrusive, exercised from the wings, so to speak, of their existence. To their adult insistence on "everything that is and counts", Rilke has already opposed, in the poem that precedes, "The Singer Sings Before a Child of Princes", the "life" that in terms of political realism, "never existed", namely that potential, ideal promise of life that the child-bearing Mary archetypally embodies and is otherwise brought to a focus in this "child of princes" (this poem being an astonishing tribute to Rilke's dear friend, Paula Becker). This "child" (or ideal soul of the adult Paula) is imagined as the central meaning, the be-all and end-all of all social existence, which is associated here with a world of "princes":

> *and thus trivial things and hard took place*
> *only to give you for this daily living*
> *a thousand great similes and likenesses*
> *by which you prodigiously may grow.*

It is a measure of this child's power over the darkness also of historical creation, which the poet would tap into:

> *In the dark poet each thing silently*
> *repeats itself: a star, a house, a forest.*
> *And many things that he would celebrate*
> *stand all around your moving form.*

> *Past upon past has been planted in you,*
> *in order out of you, like a garden, to rise.*

In this way is the poet in the position at all times to *re-create* history and indeed all historical happenings, confirming, with an utmost confidence that is all the more bewildering in light of the ominous dire aspects of "The Last Judgment", Rilke's ongoing faith that a Hero might yet be found who will indeed manage to "descend" even "down into all deaths" to finally extract from these "the meaning, the desire, and the soul" of all human existence—thus to turn all to good, Rilke's secret hope as a poet being, in the depths, no less than all of this...

"The Second Book, Part Two"

It is the great contradiction of Rilke's life at the time of the writing of the poems sampled in *Images*, that, on the one hand, he should be given to such a complete hope in the face of all that, on the other hand, already very much disturbs him and seeks to drag him down ultimately without hope. Perhaps only our knowledge of this complex meta-drama from his life at the time will accommodate the very radical shift that now takes place as we move from the end of "The Second Book, Part One" to the beginning of "The Second Book, Part Two", with the poem "Fragments of Lost Days". In "The Second Book, Part One", "The Last Judgment", through its very bleak content, does cast a long shadow over the rest of that section's group of poems. Even so, it is not so clear that what this section finally leaves us with is not rather the more hopeful side of Rilke's vision. The sudden shift back to the highly depressive "Fragments" may thus seem (once again) more than startling. Perhaps some will feel that the shift *is* aesthetically harmonized with what comes before, but I doubt this is the case. Others will say that these are the poems Rilke had left to display and that they form at least a whole in their own section. They do indeed form a whole there and a magnificent one at that, but a fundamental disjunction remains as we shift from the insistent hope of the previous section very suddenly to the hopelessness of this.

The shift is otherwise not unfitting inasmuch as it re-enacts Rilke's own experience in the period when these poems were written, which was in its own way paradigmatic. That was in Rilke's post-Worpswede experience which, as we saw in Volume 1, plummetted him suddenly from a great hope, with respect to the work he saw himself doing on behalf of his God—so enriched as this had been by his recent experience at Worpswede—to the great despair of Lou's fundamental indifference to his designs and her continued repression of his purposes on his return to Berlin, without her knowing quite what effect she was having. It is significant that the poems that open this next section of *Images* should have been written somewhat farther along on his return to Berlin than those poems from the previous section that had begun to outline hope (November rather than October of 1900); by that point, his growing estrangement from Lou had begun to look to him more and more decisive. In deferring to a re-enactment of the pattern of his life at that time, Rilke was (perhaps intentionally?) reversing the approach he takes in "The First Book, Part Two". There the idea of hope for the emerging poet inverts the actual process of his life experience in this period more generally, the poems of renewed hope which Rilke had written when still at Worpswede overriding in that section poems he was to write later during the post-Worpswede debacle.[35]

We have already covered the main poems outlining hopelessness in this new section ("The Second Book, Part Two") in Volume 1 of this book (pp.93 and 99): "Fragments from Lost Days" and "About Fountains". The hopelessness here is of a quite different order from that of "The Last Judgment". There the hopelessness is thought of others but not of the poet himself. In "Fragments" the hopelessness has, also, an altogether different context belonging to a world without reference to God, being thus experienced at a deeper level, since here no recourse remains. Here is the glimpse of a world where no God has any chance of ruling; rather, what rules is a "huge and incensed" Power "that … stalks" and "would strangle each one of the sick". A violent storm in Nature serves the poet as an expression of this Power: the world presents itself as a habitation of the sick who marvel at the brilliance that re-appears in Nature after the work such a storm will do, but without their taking stock of the actual nature of this Power that has swept through and by which alone Nature is re-created. At the same time, these sick marvel at the brilliance of Nature without any perceptible alteration in their own depressed state ("They see only the bright majesty"). The poet for his part has become intensely aware that behind such a storm lies a Power that is its own principle of destruction, separate from God, affecting human life disastrously at every level. The poet has lived into the sphere of this Power and knows: we have traced the origin of this world of feeling pain to Lou's driving him back into a debilitated condition he had borne with from the time of his youth and that he otherwise felt hopeful he had transcended. Rilke's reversion to this experience at this point in the *Book of Images* has a shocking effect also in the volume's present poetic biographical terms, though this effect is immediately alleviated by the series of nine small snapshot poems that follow, which Rilke wrote as many as six years after the rest of the poems that are found in this section (in 1906).

This series of poems, with the group title "The Voices", is marked by that deliberately impersonal, somewhat bloodless, "objective" treatment characteristic of Rilke's work on the *New Poems* which was well-begun by that point. This interposed series, one can see, offers some aesthetic relief from the intensely personal nature of the account in "Fragments". They have for a theme "the destitute", bringing into sharp if somewhat abstract focus the life-conditions respectively of beggar, blind man, drunkard, suicide, widow, idiot, orphan girl, dwarf, and leper. The characterization of each typifies, without evoking any individual who is subjected in this way. We marvel at the technique perhaps more than at the content. Yet these poems have the function of offering the reader some distance from the more depressive realities of life that have just been invoked. In the meantime, another startling shift has taken place, for now God is once again brought back into the picture, this God who sounds very much like the old God of "The Book of Poverty" pressed once again into new service (see my Volume 1, p.136ff). Other human beings may treat the destitute as "things" they pass by,

> *But God himself comes and stays a long time*
> *whenever these maimed ones bother him.*

Three years after "The Book of Poverty", this God, grown somewhat effete, could still preside for Rilke over the experience of extreme dispossession of these many types. Contrastingly, in "About Fountains", the poem that follows and itself written three years before "Poverty", Rilke is re-presenting this God when in His greater potency, when Rilke was more intensely, indeed directly, related to Him, namely the God of "The Book of Monastic Life". That great poem was only a little more than a year old when "Fountains" was composed. Rilke was specifically invoking the extraordinary experience of that great poem where he talks of "heavens" that "reach hands/toward many things and into this commotion", this being the very power Rilke had ascribed to his God in those former days.

The emotional structure of "Fountains" is immediately grasped when one refers the poem's details to the whole pattern of Rilke's life up to that point. Thus the "fantastic dreaming" of his Florence days to the late spring of 1898: this had brought on "tears" when this "dreaming" was squelched by Lou's overbearing indifference to his poetic designs on his return to her in Berlin. The tears were forgotten when Rilke managed to re-create himself in the light of his Russian God-experience of 1899 as conveyed in "Monastic Life". Something of his own more personal poetic spirit, experienced separately from his association with Lou, also came to his aid as consolation to him over that period: the same poetic spirit that would find renewed outlet during his time away from Lou in Worspwede. And now, at the time of the writing of "Fountains", separated from Worpswede and again subjected to Lou's repression of his poetic purposes, he is "remind[ed] of all that happened" in that former time of "tears" and is "again" "seeing" the "waters" that weigh everything "downwards". At this point in this section of *Images* Rilke conveys the sense of being (or at least having been) in some part of himself buoyed up in his depressive experience. There is at least that degree of positive suggestion to "Fountains", as compared with the unalleviated pessimism of "Fragments". This latter poem sent us reeling into the depths; the poet then offered some indication of recovery, re-invoking his God in one degree and another, so as to provide the necessary ballast again. We were dragged down very suddenly, but along with the poet are again set right. The various shifts in this segment of "The Second Book, Part Two" serve to enact a large range of contradictory levels of experience in Rilke's life. Whether, in one's aesthetic encounter with this segment, the reader can absorb these shifts smoothly seems to me doubtful, but in any case the poet is now (more or less) set up to resume the more balanced, intentionally optimistic, approach he has taken in the rest of his volume. In the meantime, it chastens us to see how, in the midst of the (admittedly conditional) exuberance of his "free quest" on which he otherwise seems bent, the poet should again bring himself face-to-face with what his life has actually been about.

Both "The Man Reading" and "The Man Watching", the poems which come next, were written in the period beyond Rilke's full break from Lou, when he was more or less comfortably settled into his married life with Clara. "Reading" presents a rather special case in Rilke's life, a poem of intense momentary peace and reconciliation with the world, in which something of the ethos of his Worpswede experience, where he had met Clara, breaks through. After a long afternoon of rain, everything is restoring itself: "over the overfull/glittering gardens the skies are vast/.../what's dispersed

collects into a few groups/darkly, on long paths, people wander ..."
This was his experience now, under the same skies, in the neighboring
Westerwede, where he and Clara had taken up residence. Speculating
as ever on his relationship to the world, the poet typically recapitu-
lates the different stages of his engagement with it. There is a first
stage of *vision* which we may associate symbolically with the period
of "The Book of Monastic Life": "There outside *exists*, what here
inside I *live*/and here and there the whole of things is boundless."
This is followed by a second stage of *experience* representative of his
time in Worpswede: "save that I weave myself still more with it/when
my gaze shapes itself to objects/and to the grave simplicity of masses." And now, in this third stage in Westerwede, when entertaining
renewed hopefulness, he envisions a still greater possibility as "the
earth grows out beyond itself" and "seems to encompass the entire
night sky", so that even "the first star is like the last house". The poet
believes himself to be on the verge of a still greater reality: a poetic
reunion with the world such as would extend to the universe itself,
the universe to be brought thus within the compass of the human
imagination—such being the bold forecast of this poet already at the
age of twenty-five. In the meantime, in "Watching" we are returned
to the experience of a storm and its deep-life symbolism for Rilke. We
see that the poet has been through an evolution, from "Presentiment"
through "Fragments" to "The Man Watching": from an expression
of readiness for what is to come to him as the "storm" of his life during a period of recovery when at Worpswede (having been through
a deep estrangement from Lou over the summer before), through the
dire sense of the storm as a power of destruction, on his return to Lou
after Worpswede, before which his life then seemed as nothing, finally to a renewed power of encounter, drawing on a refreshed strength
when at Westerwede, in which the stormy aspect of life now appears
as an occasion for being, rightly, taken over, for only then can one
say that one will have come fully to terms with an experience of the
world. The Power that underlies this stormy aspect of our lives Rilke
now characterizes as a wrestling Angel whose purpose *is* to overcome
us, so that we may emerge from the experience "erect and justified/
and great out of that hard hand".

What the poet offers in this respect is a perspective only, viewed
from without, of "the one watching"; likewise in the case of "the one

reading" we are offered a perspective on wholeness that is viewed from without, the perspective of one who is similarly set at a distance from what he is contemplating, who is only suddenly distracted from his studies. The full experience still lies beyond the poet's grasp in his present young condition. But the terms of the engagement *are* grasped. Any thought of approaching the wholeness envisioned in "Reading" would necessitate coming to terms with the hard force of nature and of fate that is addressed in "Watching". The poet's "growth" will depend on it: an experience of wholeness with respect to the world must entail allowing oneself, through a form of Nietzschean submission, at some point to be "defeated" by this hard force: "His growth is: to be the deeply defeated/by ever greater things." Not "to be deeply defeated" but "to be *the* deeply defeated": given his identity thereby. At the risk of a relative infelicity of terms, this section of the volume might be said to have as theme "Ever Greater Things", or, to bring the description into line more felicitously with the rest: "Nature and Fate" (**see** the titles bestowed upon the rest on p.215). It is a striking feature of Rilke's presentation that the stormy aspect of one's destiny and one's experience of a storm in nature should be directly associated: the same Power underlies the two; the experience of a violent storm in nature will awaken our sense of our *life*'s storminess, which makes the shift to "After a Stormy Night", the next poem, altogether of a piece ("After" is here given the sense of "Along the Lines Of"). This may not be the strongest poem in the volume (it has been described as "effete"[36]), but it is a serviceable one: on "Nights like these" (as the refrain and opening line of each poem in this series goes) prisoners are set free into nature again; the dying recover a remembered life; the dead almost seem to come alive; society is thrown back upon itself in confusion from fear; the life of the living dead is accentuated; the ailing momentarily recover health. Everything that is both actual and possible is brought to full definition, as if life were being stretched out and coming to terms with itself, however dismal the general fate may be. Proper stock is at least being taken of the world, which is a poet's vocation, whatever else the reader is to make of it all, beyond a noting of all these diverse contexts and facts of human experience.

This final section of *Images* then ends with two poems we have looked at in some depth in Volume 1; they incorporate once again the very dark period Rilke experienced on his return to Berlin after

Worpswede: "A Blind Woman" and "Requiem". The personal application of these poems to Rilke's life, which I have already noted, does not show very much here, except for the fact that the poet *has* thrown a shade of personal implication over this section as a whole with the poems that initiate it in the case of "Fragments" and "About Tears". When we look at *Images* more fully in its own right, however, "A Blind Woman" and "Requiem" serve to fill out Rilke's basic presentation by extending the range of the poet's consciousness to include more dramatic instances of personal tragedy where hope still shows through. In "A Blind Woman", a hopeful spirit shows itself again in a woman suddenly struck blind; in "Requiem", a great honoring gesture is extended to a woman who, though young in life, has gone to meet death—the former a fictional case, the latter the recent actual death of Clara's friend, Gretel. A measure of the unbounded task the poet has set himself is conveyed especially in "Requiem" where his imagination takes him deep into the ongoing life of that woman's corpse, as if he was free to offer consolation and hope even in that dimension of the woman's experience, redeeming death in this strangely out-of-the-way area of life's phenomenal developments.* That treatment points in the end to the recognition, registered in the volume's "Closing Piece", that "Death is great". Death is seen as a most forbidding reality with which one inevitably closes, though it does not *have* to lie beyond what the poet can imagine and take on...

---

*See Volume 1, p.102ff, for a full reading of this poem.

II

From *New Poems* to *Malte*
and the Dark Ascent

By June of 1906, when Rilke was working on "The Voices", the
last poem to be written for the expanded version of *Images*, he had
already composed as many as thirty of the poems that were to find
their way into his next major collection of poetry, the first volume of
New Poems. Only a few months after the expanded version of *Images*
came out in December of 1906, the first volume of *New Poems* was
virtually complete, and it was to be published in December of 1907.
By then Rilke was thirty-two. *The Book of Hours*, *The Book of Images*,
and the first volume of *New Poems*, all came out over a span of but
two years. I have called attention to the comprehensive "program"
of work these volumes constituted for Rilke more or less consciously
when taken together. They represented excursions respectively into
the world of sounds, images, and things, thus laying the basis for a
comprehensive formation in poetic sensibility. However, *New Poems*
was, additionally, a real parting of the ways. Both *Hours* and *Images*
belong decidedly to the period of what we may call the Lou-event: except only for "The Voices" (which ironically was Lou's favorite piece
in *Images*), everything else Rilke was offering with these two volumes
was conceived during the period when Lou's decisive influence on
Rilke was at its height.

This was a very significantly repressive influence, as we have
seen: it sets things back for him also in the case of *The Book of Hours*,
to the extent that in that poem's second and third parts, written respectively one and two years beyond his separation from Lou, in 1901
and 1903, Rilke reverts to the consolation of a God become by then
effete. In His once real stature, as conveyed in the poem's first part,
God marked that former time when Rilke and Lou had reached at

least a conciliatory form of creative agreement about his work. This God Lou had otherwise imposed upon Rilke by insisting that, in the development of his poetic vision, he go her Russian rather than his Florentine way. (This is to simplify a highly complex situation that we have covered in some depth in Volume 1.) In this poem's second and third parts, Rilke was reverting to this now somewhat displaced God because he was even by then, settled though he was in his married life with Clara, still at the mercy of the effects of Lou's repression of him. With *The Book of Images*, Rilke was returning to the material he had written largely for himself, almost clandestinely, still during his difficult time with Lou (poems written between 1899-1901 for the most part). We have seen how he sought through this volume to invert the process of his experience during that time of great turmoil, as if trying to restore himself in the hope of his own purposes. There was much wishful thinking in this effort, but the more neutrally aesthetic context of this volume, separated as it was from the actual process of his personal experience in that former time, allowed Rilke to re-fashion himself as the artist of the free quest which he had always seen himself as being or wished to be. At least by then, by 1906, he had freed himself sufficiently to be pursuing poetic projects of his own devising. The *New Poems* represent a still more significant advance in this direction.

A New Conceptual Strength

That as many as thirty of the poems from this volume were composed by June of 1906 (a few go back to a date as early as March of 1903) is an indication that Rilke was already set on his own path even during the first few years after his separation from Lou. His reconciliatory meeting with her in the spring of 1905 had set him on his own path still more freely and firmly: finally he had come to terms with Lou, even if he was still far from coming to terms with himself or with the lingering consequences of her repression of him. Still, all this he was managing to put away for now, as if it were behind him. He would manage this, more or less, for almost four years, until January of 1909. His meeting with Rodin in the fall of 1902 had been a great turning point. When Rodin suddenly displaced Lou in Rilke's life as his prime associate and mentor, Rilke was more or less set free, for the first time since he had given up his Florentine project (even if, indeed for the rest of his life, he remained far from fully free).

There was additionally the violent shock of Rilke's encounter with Paris more generally. Rodin and Paris had combined, the one by his masterfully superior artistic genius, the other by its scenes of appalling degradation, to force upon Rilke and to inspire in him, almost as a matter of survival, a new form of strength for dealing with reality. This new conceptual strength is clearly reflected in Rilke's letters to Lou between 1903 and 1905 (as I showed in Volume 1), and it was the kind of strength that would find more and more expression in his *New Poems* as he was going along. In these new developments, there would be finally too much of conceptual strength perhaps, as Rilke begins to settle, at some point, a little too comfortably into a purely formalistic poetry. He was thereby risking stasis and repetitiveness. In comparison, there is the more open-ended force of those deeper inspirational rhythms that had especially determined the progression of his poetic vision up to that point, and that will finally account for his uniquely comprehensive achievement in the long run. We have a measure of this obsessive direction towards formalism in this period in the fact that as we get deeper into the *New Poems*, especially the second volume entitled 'The Other Part', Rilke settles almost consistently into verse that is favoring strictly the quatrain and the sonnet form, as compared with the many other freer verse forms that come before and after *New Poems* that are more immediately expressive of his comprehensive direction in inspirational vision (the *Sonnets to Orpheus* being the great anomaly in this development of his poetic craft, as we shall see in due course).

Continuity with Previous 'Old' Work

*[For purposes of clarity and economy from hereon in, I will refer to the first part of *New Poems* simply as 'New Poems', and the second part as 'The Other Part'—in this case as named by Rilke.]

At least four to five years of further maturation separate the first long series of poems in 'New Poems' (to "The Panther") from, for the very largest part, the poems that Rilke had brought forth in *The Book of Images*. Another, more assured, depth is at once felt in this new production, even though the volume's initial themes carry over directly from those Rilke had been pursuing in that earlier period (they had remained his charactcristic themes). He had always felt badly entangled in his social experience, but there were also the bad entanglements that followed from the love-relationship as well as from artistic obsession. The theme of bad entanglement, which already sounded randomly in *Hours* and *Images*, comes more fully into its own here, especially in this first part of the *New Poems*. This theme extends through "Abishag" (and even "David Sings" where the entanglement is in relation to the untranscendable determinations of the life-cycle) as well as "The Song of the Women to the Poet". This theme is eventually cut into by Rilke's typical expressions in anti-religion *via* Biblical and Christian subjects, the characteristic concern of the bitterly sceptical author of the *Visions of Christ*: thus "Joshua's Council", "Prodigal Son", "The Olive Garden" (in the latter two of which the theme of "tangledness" recurs, in the case of "Olive Garden" in relation to corruptible "dustiness"). Then there is the figure focused on in "Buddha": "He who forgets what our life teaches/and abides in the wisdom we're denied"*, another expression of Rilke's sceptical critique. The really new poems in this collection, in respect of subject and theme, begin, in fact, with "L'Ange du Méridien", which introduces a section (through to and including "The Prisoner") expressive of a new realism in Rilke's focus, imposed upon him by his experience of Paris, sometimes in the company of Rodin. Until at last we reach the first of the famous, so-called "thing-poems", of which it is the classically cited case, namely "The Panther", which was composed in fact as far back as 1902, the year Rilke first arrived in Paris (in the fall).

At the time 'The Other Part' of *New Poems* was being put together, Rilke wrote his publisher to explain that, while he was working out the sequence of poems for this second volume, it struck him that "the course [was] almost parallel" to the first.[37] Thus both volumes begin with Apollo poems and subsequently shift through classical subjects, then the religious subjects based on Biblical and Christian material, then a short section of realistic focus stemming from Rilke's experience of Paris, thence to thing-poems: "The Panther" in the first volume, "Snake-Charming" and "Black Cat" in the second ("The

---

*All references to Edward Snow, tr., *New Poems*. Farrar, Straus, Giroux, 2001.

Panther" appearing as the 22nd poem, "Snake-Charming" as the 26th). There are significant differences, however, just in respect of theme, and these already go a long way to distinguish the basic approaches in these two volumes. The main theme of the opening section of the first volume, which is dedicated to classical subjects, is "Entanglement". The basic point of "Early Apollo" is that there is a higher value in the potentiality of poems and of experience than in the actual realization of these, the latter development (actualization) involving one, invariably, in a form of degeneration from the inspiriting life ("petals loosened") and, to this degree, subjection. While Apollo's head has not yet imposed itself on the scene of creation, to dictate an over-extension of faculties (it is merely "the *shadow* of his gaze" that intrudes here), one is left free to revel in the greater "splendor" of one's motivating inspirations. Though the poet acknowledges that his "Love Song" has its own enticements and satisfactions, his additional and perhaps prime concern lies with remaining free of these so as to continue in a relationship also to "other things", "lost things" that themselves demand a redemptive attention. The tendency of the "love song" is to entangle one to the point of continual distraction with every "stirring" of its own depths.

The "you" addressed in "Sacrifice" is one who, also in respect of the dangers of the love-song, would free the poet from his "old life". There is an implied association, across these first poems, between this "old life" and the "rule" of Alcaeus to whom Sappho (in "Sappho to Alcaeus") must complain: "under your rule our sweet/maidenhood would miserably perish". Women in this picture take the lead by virtue of a form of love and life that wishes itself free of the entanglements of the love-passion that binds women to men, or the poet to his "love-song" alone. Women especially, and here the poet would follow their lead, have the possibility, in their inherent power of love, of being "launched … far" ("Eranna to Sappho"), precisely towards "other things" beyond the love-passion, "distant and given over" to an unbounded life. Over and against the normally prescribed life for women, a life among "domestic things", Sappho would "pass" Eranna "on like the grave/to Life" ("Sappho to Eranna"). It is a matter, among other things, of "keep[-ing]" one's "soul" ("Love Song") and rising (in "Song of the Women to the Poet") above the direction "blood and darkness" take towards entangled passion (the poet is thus admonished to give himself up to another level of "craving"). This is what gives the young girl who has died in her unspoiled youth her power in the poet's memorial tribute to her in "Funeral Monument to a Young Girl": she has been able to lie in "that god's/"blood" into which we are naturally born, not having capitulated to the material entanglements of passion with which that "blood" also threatens us.

Such language reminds us of Rilke's puristic perspectives on passion in *The Book of Hours*, perspectives that are carried over into *The Book of Images* (as we have seen). Whatever later developments in the *New Poems* may reflect by way of a "greater depth", to draw on Rilke's own description of the achievement[38], both in respect of conceptual strength and formal coherence, Rilke is in this first volume carrying on in the same modes of thought to which he had been given for some time. We find at least that amount of continuity with previous "old" work, before Rilke's creative impulse takes him on to ground that is also thematically "new". This link back to old work at the level of poetic vision, such as marks the opening sequence of 'New Poems', brings a greater dimensionality to that volume, in fact, than what the opening sequence of 'The Other Part' will have to show for itself. The impression of engaged vision in the opening sequence of the first volume is also, in comparison with its counterpart in the second volume, consistent: thus we find the same imaginative application, in this first volume, across such very different contexts as those presented in "Eastern Aubade" and "David Sings Before Saul".

In "Aubade" the lovers would press themselves "against each other", like "flower petals around the stamen", before, that is, those "petals, loosened[,] .../will drift down", as "Early Apollo" puts it. The lovers would save themselves against the threat of that "unrestrained" element in life that would subject them, on the one hand, to the "dark, uncharted" ways of animal passion at "night", and on the other, to the impingements of the same old social life, "what outside is slowly dawning", by "day". So with David and Saul, on an existential level that parallels the love life. From the pattern of their own lives the youthful David draws for the aging Saul the moral that "heaviness becomes spirit"—or so it should or one would wish. But Saul's life is recreated by David's song: in this way do "[g]irls [still] flower, still ripe for you". The moments of fulfilled passionate love David would also wish to "bring back": "And how lovely, weakened by your prowess,/O how lovely all those bodies were." Only, to be able to do that, David's song would have somehow to accommodate and to transform, in its own element of etherealness, "those dark moans of pleasure" that underlay "bodies" made so "lovely", and this David's song cannot do. Despair follows from this, but all hope is not lost: "days ... are approaching" when it will be possible to rise above passion by transmuting it into "spirit", when all the "heaviness" of passion's "dark" entanglements will have been transcended: song will then have gotten the better at last of the life. By that point in (perhaps only far) time, passion will have been channelled *into* spirit, as the effect of song, but until then, it must be a matter of song and life "cleaving to each other" ("cleaving" having the formal literary sense here of "sticking close to"). It is as if in that anguished tension of reference to each other, paralleling the effort of the lovers in "Aubade" to press themselves "against each other", passion will in time find a way to overcome itself. What is old and aging as a way of life ("heaviness") will by that point have transmuted (into "spirit") through the continuous influence and effect of a song youthful and new.

In "Abishag" David appears by himself, by then an old king: his life is over, his own "pleasures" no longer felt, and in the evening he muses on his own "tangled life .../abandoned like an ill-famed coast" while the youthful girl, Abishag, lies upon him to warm his chilled body. He has been himself over the course of his life a victim of his own "depths". In the Biblical story the ancient king does not possess the virgin; if Rilke was adhering to this account, then the remarkable picture is given of a deep unconsolable tension between an aging king who once capitulated to passion and a youthful virgin who remains unspoilt and is kept free from spoiling by passion. "David Sings Before Saul" offers more hope about this tension. However, it is not so clear that Rilke has not in "Abishag" divagated from the Biblical account to paint the picture of the king capitulating to his passion one last time: "He hearkened like a hound/and sought himself in his last blood." That would make the ending of Rilke's poem more pessimistic, dramatizing a final hopeless capitulation. It is just as possible, however, that Rilke *was* adhering to the Biblical account and that he presents his king as finally giving himself up to his lifelessness, his "last blood" in that sense, and so declining or refusing passion. In this case, the final vision would redound more to the honor of the king, but it would not offer much more by way of consolation.

Parallelism and Complementarity: The Two Parts of *New Poems* Compared

In spite of the parallel created by the poems on classical subjects in the opening sequence of 'The Other Part', we find there no comparable effect of unified vision. The parallel was clearly willed by Rilke. Thus focus in "Archaic Torso of Apollo", as in the poem that begins the sequence in 'New Poems', is likewise on the head as an outstanding factor. In "Early Apollo", as we saw, the head has not yet exerted its degenerative influence on the process of creation by over-extending the creative drive and diverting this from its original impulse. In "Torso", contrastingly, the head has already done its work but without continuing to interfere in the process: "procreation thrive[s]" without any accompanying debilitation; all is an order that coheres just because the head (the abstractive faculty) has withdrawn or absented itself, having accomplished its properly subordinated work of influence, which is, nevertheless, no less crucial; without this, the body of creation would be an empty cipher. As it is, this body of creation is endowed with a perfectly ordered life that has the effect of exhorting one to "change your life". Sounding of this moral sends us back to the main theme of the opening sequence of 'New Poems' in a way that is perhaps too obviously deliberate; the moral is merely grafted onto the effect of a creative order that impresses primarily in its own right. "Cretan Artemis", the next poem, likewise relates back to the opening sequence of 'New Poems', by virtue of its focus on the goddess as one who, "all-knowing", is "fixed on the farthest point" of unbounded experience (free of the same old life), beyond the turmoil of the "screamings-out" (in childbirth) that will "only sometimes" be heard from the earthly human realm (Artemis being the goddess associated with childbirth). So very splendid though she is in her free life—"shape[d]" by the "[s]mooth headwind", the goddess jars us in her indifference to the human plight and already marks a turning-point in Rilke's focus, which is here more earth-bound. Hence his approach to the classical story of Leda and the swan which follows: the god, suddenly startled by the beauty of the swan into which he has entered, becomes especially enraptured by it in the moment of the penetration of Leda and consummation: "with what delight!—he .../became truly swan." The sexual act, which in the first volume had come in for so much censure, is here being delighted in, indeed somewhat rudely celebrated.

Sympathy for an earth-bound love is now the emphasis—also, in "Lament for Antinoüs". Mourning the sudden death of the youthful Antinoüs, the Emperor Hadrian rebels against the thought that his favorite boy has been transformed or deified by death. Hadrian rather insists on continuing to see Antinoüs as he was to him in earthly life, and also in death simply as he is ("Why can't he just be someone dead"). Confronted by this check to his earth-bound love, Rilke's Hadrian raises the challenge: "Who then can love? Who has the strength?"[39] Another perspective on love is thus entertained that is more typical of Western *angst* than the spiritually-directed imperatives governing Rilke's expression in the opening sequence of 'New Poems'. Impressive as the earth-bound perspective is, it yet does not represent the essential thrust of the opening sequence of 'The Other Part'. "Lament for Antinoüs" is immediately followed by "The Death of the Beloved" where the perspective is reversed. In "Antinous" Hadrian's lament is that he "cannot get close to" his dead favorite; for the man in "Death", contrastingly, separation from his beloved who has died leads to an opposite experience: "the dead became to him so intimate." An opposite kind of death has occurred, the woman "not ripped away from him" but "gently loosened", and if the man "refuse[s] to listen" to the exhortations of his companions it is likewise in an opposite way: contradicting his companions, he insists on transposing the centre of his being to the otherworld ("name[s] that land/the goodly placed"). Contrastingly, Hadrian refuses to listen to his company's exhortations to seek consolation in the deification of his lover among the stars. The effect of these two poems, lying side by side, is clearly complementary. "Leda" and "Cretan Artemis" are also complementary, the complementary basis of reality appearing as the actual subject of "The Island of the Sirens" where the sea is depicted on the one hand as "the raging/and the fury" and on the other hand as offering a sirenic "song that no one can resist". This effect of complementarity extends to that point in the opening sequence where "Adam" and "Eve" are given, though nowhere in fact beyond this.

Contrasting with the presence of a *unified vision* running through the opening sequence of 'New Poems', *complementarity*, then, is the main thrust of the effect, or the basic principle, of the opening sequence of 'The Other Part'. Apart from this, each poem in this second volume is presented as a world of its own, distinct, separate, in-drawn, each subject of each poem a world unto itself. Not only in the opening sequence but throughout, 'The Other Part' works on behalf of multiplicity; contrastingly, not only in the opening sequence but throughout the whole at least of its first half, 'New Poems' works on behalf of unity. Right through to "The Grown-Up" in 'New Poems' we find the poet working in each poem out of the same tragic tension, between an old life characterized by bad entanglement and the prospect of a free expression of vital and affective energies such as Rilke had been struggling to co-opt from the time of his unhappy subordination to Lou. This is the case as far along as the poems of realism in this first part, as, for example, in "The Capital" where "anguish", "anger", and the "worry" into which these are neurotically resolved appear in tragic tension with what the capital is accomplishing as an expression of free spirit: "driving everything/*up* that [otherwise in the untranscendable life] with darkness always falls" (we are speaking here, of course of the "capital" as an architectural item). Farther along, the "Roman Sarcophagi" offers an image of the possibility that "rage and hate" and the "confusion" that "abide in us" may yet see an "eternal water channeled into them". So are "our hours" and "our lives" enigmatically met by the immoveable "smile" of "L'Ange du Méridien"; so is our life of "chance", through the conscious "destining" of work on the Cathedral in the poem of that title, or the image of "our [recalcitrant] blood" in "The Rose Window" through the power of our "gaz[-ing]" on the window, met by the possibility of being drawn to "God". There is the "boredom" that continues to display itself on the corpse in "Morgue", the "stone" wall of "The Prisoner", the "small life" of "A Woman's Fate", the "heaviness" of "The Swan" etc., in each case countered by the idea of potential freedom from such unhappy constraints ("Saint Sebastian" is the only poem in this whole group that offers a *triumphing* image, that of "great will" in the face of "the destroyers"). Even in the Biblical and Christian sections, the same tragic tension is depicted, as we have seen in the case of "Abishag" and "David Sings Before Saul", also in "The Olive Garden", and even in "The Departure of the Prodigal Son". Contrastingly, where the opening section of 'The Other Part' shifts into *its* Biblical-Christian context, the governing impulse is simply the parallel with the 'New Poems' as in "A Prophet" and Jeremiah", which are somewhat too obviously intended to echo "Joshua's Council". The shift here is simply once again to anti-religion, more specifically to the same old protest against dictation by an angry God and the overrunning of the human will generally, the latter theme opening the possibility of incorporation also of the sybil's plight in "A Sybil". There is otherwise no other structural principle that would link these poems either to those that precede them in the classical section or the poems with a Christian import that follow, as in "The Last Judgment" and "Crucifixion", which themselves continue almost reflexively in the old spirit of Rilke's *Visions of Christ*.

The Plunge into Multiplicity

One significant feature that marks *New Poems* as a whole from the rest of Rilke's work is reflected initially in the shift to "Going Blind" in the first volume. From this point in the volume, we plunge with Rilke, from an effort that is taking place on behalf of unity (all of those poems are travailling along the same lines) suddenly into sheer multiplicity. In 'The Other Part' we are plunged into multiplicity from the start, apart from the further narrowly localized perspectives of complementarity and parallelism that we have noted of its opening sequence (to "Adam" and "Eve", which also form a complement between them). Each of the subjects from "Going Blind" onwards is very deliberately bestowed its own free-standing space (if not "free-standing integrity" or "presence", which in both respects is only the case, in fact, in a few instances*). Each subject profits from Rilke's complete focus without any further reference to the other subjects around it or even to very much in the rest. This long run of poems (from "Going Blind" in the first volume right through the second volume) is interrupted only by a short masterful sequence in quite another vein towards the end of the first volume (beginning

---

*In the first case, Snow's terms from *New Poems* p.169, in the second case my term.

with "Tombs of the Hetaerae") and another, also in another vein and likewise masterful, towards the end of the second volume (beginning with "The Solitary"), outstanding sequences whose unique import we will consider below.

In a letter to his publisher written when 'The Other Part' was virtually completed, Rilke spoke of his production of the *New Poems* as a matter of progress in "the ever more objective mastering of reality, out of which, entirely of its own accord, the wider significance and clearer validity of all things emerges"[40]. At this stage, objectivity implies multiplicity, i.e., an indefinite extension in space where all manner of subjects are met, all of which in the hands of the poet may be turned into "things made", which is to say given their own respective forms of "volume and contour"[41]. This intention, however, has the consequence of separating each subject one from the other, with the effect at some point of suggesting that Rilke was merely taking on this subject and that; at times it will even appear as if he were merely exercising himself as a poet (in the view of this reader, in poems like "The Square", Roman Fountain", and "The Carousel"). No universe can come of this narrowly particularizing approach, and in any case no mind can reach out to "all things". This approach can only train the poet at best to penetrate the "thing-ness" of subjects in space, subjects that can never become full objects in any case, for it is always a matter of the interpenetration of the subject and the poet's consciousness. By concentrating his attention on each subject to the full extent he intended, Rilke could achieve a certain degree of the consolidation of his faculties but only by giving up, in the meantime, all inspirational directedness that would begin to relate one subject to another and thus create a universe.

Consolidation in this volume reaches a climax in what have been famously called Rilke's "thing-poems" with which *New Poems* has been mistakenly identified, for there are in fact far fewer such poems in these volumes than we are led to believe. There are "The Panther", "Spanish Dancer", "Black Cat", "The Flamingos", and possibly "The Lute" (and only possibly again "The Snake-Charmer"). The reader may yet wonder where we are left when we have finally had the experience of these "things"? We are no further along than the space in which they have been conjured; after all is done, we step out of this space, however intense our experience has been, back to wherever we were or are, without any progress emerging from it. These "thing-poems" have been especially identified with what makes *New Poems* new, but, in fact, such poems have an incidental, not a dominant, presence in these two volumes, which feature a good many other particularities of poetic creation that are not so easily brought under the one rubric of what makes the volumes new.

Much has been made, also, of yet another distinguishing feature: what appears to come across in the poems from these volumes as a fulfilment of that "art of living surfaces" with which Rilke especially associated the sculptural achievements of Rodin. Rilke's concern with accomplishing the same, as we have seen, goes back some ways, as many as three to four years back in fact (see, once again, Volume 1). However, once again, only in a very few instances does Rilke in *New Poems* reach to something like the very special achievement of Rodin along these lines. There is, indeed, a wealth of "living surfaces" in these poems, among which we often find a very subtle "interanimation of object and consciousness"[42] as it has been put, or, as one might also put it, of "subject and consciousness" ("subject" in the sense of matter or theme). However, nowhere do we find among these poems that informing depth of existential *angst* that in Rodin is also everywhere in his surfaces—nowhere except perhaps in "Portrait" and in "Pavilion". Rilke's subjects in these volumes are brought into greater and greater "objective" focus as we go along, but at the same time more and more without that typical *angst* of his own that had until then always been an essential part of *his* artistic engagement. The dissipation of *angst* in these poems will be counted by some as a strength (a sacrifice of "subjectivity" to "objectivity"), but such a strength may also be a loss; it leads more and more to what has been described as a certain "hardness" in these poems that has been seen as "near-pathological": "Rilke sometimes seems to be courting distance for its own sake, even trying to expunge feeling itself."[43]

Certainly there could be no future in this direction, only stasis and repetition in the present. The future for Rilke lies elsewhere in these volumes. It is carried by what are the really "new" themes of female desire and inwardness[44], both of which ironically give the lie to, or at least finally move beyond, his momentary modernist obsession with outward "things". We have already looked at the theme of female desire as an end in itself among the first poems of 'New

Poems'*, but it is especially in the masterful poems that complete this volume that the theme of female independence attains to a form of greatness, most notably in "Orpheus. Eurydice. Hermes" and in "Alcestis". This theme would constitute a cornerstone of Rilke's poetic thought to the very end of his life, and would form the basis of his best view of love's possibilities, which Rilke's women especially embody.**

With "Eurydice" and "Alcestis" we are returned to Rilke's focus on the revolt against entanglement, in this case marriage. The dead Eurydice has lost all sense of the value of being connected to Orpheus, is entirely absorbed in the completeness of her own condition in death, and when returned to the underworld has not had any awareness that anything has been happening beyond the condition she is in: "She was within herself .../filled with her great death .../ in a new virginity/and untouchable .../so weaned/from marriage." The poem was written in Capri in the winter of 1904, a few months after Rilke got in touch with Lou again after a silence of two years. Separation from Lou would appear to have inspired in Rilke the thought of the power of being a woman reserves for herself that puts her beyond any link with men. Even the poet who has otherwise been magically transformed by separation, so that, Orpheus-like, he obtains a power to re-create the world in all its living power—"that .../ from lament a world arose, in which/everything had life again: forest and valley/and road and village ..." etc.—even he is left standing and empty-handed. Reference to Eurydice as "the blond wife" will invariably invoke also Paula Becker whom Rilke had always referred to as "the blond painter" while in Worpswede and for whom he wrote "The Singer Sings Before a Child of Princes" ("[y]ou blond child of princes"). It would seem that Paula especially represented for Rilke the kind of woman who sensed she was a principle unto herself; he

---

*In a letter to Clara dated September 4, 1908, Rilke speaks in connection with Sappho of a "sensualité d'âme") (**Greene 1**, 335).

In a letter to Clara dated September 3, 1908, Rilke describes this as a matter of "the will of the woman out beyond satisfaction" (Greene 1, 332). Earlier in this same letter he speaks of "women who do not want to hold on to the man". A further refinement (to be encountered in Rilke's later work as a major theme) celebrates the power of women to "transcend the need for [their] love to be returned" (Prater** 161).

saw her in this respect as something like the focus of all existence, as we have seen. That could only make later developments in Paula's life all the more shocking. "Alcestis" was written in 1907, only a little time after the news that Paula had, perversely, capitulated to her husband's entreaties, returning to him after a period of separation in which her creative powers had been burgeoning. Here we have the picture of a woman (become again) "frail and sad in the pale wedding dress", who says of herself: "no one's life is over/the way mine is …/ the bed that waits there inside/belongs to the underworld." Over and against the figure of Orpheus in "Eurydice" we find here the figure of a husband who "stumble]s] drunkenly" towards Alcestis after she has chosen to die as proxy for him—unlike Eurydice, she is a victim forever.

"The Birth of Venus", which immediately follows, though written at the time of "Eurydice", restores the picture of a triumphant womanhood, although even this triumph is menaced by the dolphin that is finally thrown up from the sea after Venus, "[d]ead, red and open", a symbol of the potential spiritual death that threatens woman in her sexuality. "Tombs of the Hetaerae", itself composed in the same period as the latter two mentioned poems, would seem to contradict or at least counterbalance Rilke's critical view of the sexual situation between men and women. There is not a more sexually explicit poem in Rilke's oeuvre before this: it is a poem that unabashedly celebrates the natural power of sexuality, and in no uncertain terms, but only because the courtesans of this poem embody their sexuality in a way that absorbs all men into the purity of their own given life-force, as a riverbed will carry all manner of waters poured into it: "And they *were* riverbeds …/Then they filled with smooth clear water/across the whole breadth of their wide-course." "Tombs of the Hetaerae", in its very generous(!) vision of sexuality, opposes itself to "The Birth of Venus", which it thereby complements; so too are "Eurydice" and "Alcestis" complementary, thus preparing the ground for the complementarity that characterizes the opening sequence of 'The Other Part", all four poems serving in this respect as a masterful structural transition-device for linking the two parts of *New Poems*.

Inward Resolve as Creative Goal

Standing apart from these four poems at the end of 'New Poems' is "The Bowl of Roses". This poem expands on the theme of inwardness beyond even the power of women to embody this in themselves. Inwardness has become with this poem a universal principle of nature that sets the standard for all human aspiration. It is another of Rilke's great life-themes: humankind is, in the end, referred to nature, though only where the latter embodies purity of existence, as in the essence of these roses whose principal virtue lies in their "self-containing" power—where "self-containing" implies having "transform"-ed "the world outside/.../into a handful of inwardness". As a result of this process, these roses are "wholly filled/ with that utmost of being and bending,/ of offering up, beyond power to give, of *presence*". Contrasting with the great *centrifugal* force of female apartness and desire, which is its own ideal, we have, thus, also the great *centripetal* force of nature: both directions give the lie finally to the obsessive focus on outward "things" with which many would primarily associate Rilke's efforts in these two volumes.

In relation to these "things", Rilke is in any case only really seeking, in the end, to prove his own creative prowess, the moral of that effort being captured in "The Mountain", a poem that appears towards the end of the second volume. Like the Japanese painter Hokusai, whose work Rilke is considering here, he too finds himself, among the "things" of his poems, "exhausting each image in its instant,/from shape mounting onto shape/indifferent and distant and opinionless—,/... all-knowing". And yet this is not everything. Over and against this inevitably momentary focus, designed in any case merely to exercise and to further develop conceptual strength, is the direction in a greater universality which would finally settle what for us must be the pre-eminent question and issue: namely, human destiny itself, both in its desire and in its being. Here it is "The Apple Orchard" (also given towards the end) that functions as exemplary expression: the focus here is on an experience of the "green" of the Orchard (which is no discrete "thing"), and it is especially what follows from this that matters: the further visionary power of the thoughts this "green" will have inspired:

> *... so that now*
>
> *from feeling and remembrance,*
> *from new hope and half-forgotten rejoicing,*
> *all still mixed with inner darkness,*
> *we could scatter it in thoughts before us*

This almost reads like Rilke's statement of future intention, taking us back at the same time to what had always been his prime focus: the "darkness" within that can work either to overwhelm us with its destructive energies, or else save us by bringing us to a greater resolve to work our way out of it upwards towards the light—pointing forwards, through the "dark ascent" of *Malte*. Here is the ideal upon which Rilke would found the whole of his life-quest, as upon the grass under the apple-trees: "serving, full of patience[;] reckoning/ how that which exceeds all measure must yet be gathered in and given up."

Rilke is, in this moment, profoundly clear as to how this ideal realizes itself and on what basis it unfolds: it does so "when one willingly, throughout a long life,/wills that single thing and grows and holds one's peace". This is the "single thing" of "new hope" that human destiny will resolve itself, in the form of such "thoughts" as the poet can scatter "before us", like the apple trees in their "hundred days of labor". One has learned to "hold one's peace", much as Rilke's Buddha does, who has himself been through a long evolution in Rilke's mind over the course of these two volumes. Initially (in the first "Buddha" poem) he is a figure who seems almost offensively inhuman, "[h]e who forgets what our life teaches/and abides in the wisdom we're denied". From here he develops (in the second "Buddha" poem) into one who is created through a process by which "things were melted down", having found the power thereby of "touching space the way it does itself" (by now he has become a devotional image or a thing)—until at last (in "Buddha in Glory", the last poem from these volumes) this Buddha manifests as himself, as the "[c]enter of all centers" to whom "nothing any longer clings". To what extent, we will ask, had Rilke in the production of his *New Poems* put *himself* through this arduous process of self-containing strength, and how inwardly ready can we say had he made himself for the further action of self-confrontation that continued to loom large before him in the guise of *Malte,* from which he could, in fact, only momentarily free himself?*

"Requiem"

In early November of 1908, two months after completing *New Poems* and sometime before its publication, Rilke sat down to compose his famous "Requiem" for Paula Becker. It would have been very strange indeed if he had not at some point addressed her death in this or any other similar form, and it must have been on his mind to do so the whole time since Paula had died a year before. His mind would thus have already been focused on this task, which he seems to have put off until *New Poems* was quite done. As such this task extended the respite from *Malte* that had come his way by the time he had begun to put the expanded version of *The Book of Images* together. From the evidence of "Requiem", Rilke would appear initially to have taken Paula's death in stride, at least in this sense, that, while it would no doubt have been personally shocking and painful to him, it was but another form of a contradicting reality that challenges us to come to terms with it on behalf of our life which continues. "Darkly" is Rilke's typical word for forces and powers that threaten to overwhelm us in our chosen crusade on behalf of life but that, properly transformed, finally serve to advance our lives:

> *That we were frightened when you died ... no; rather:*
> *that your stern death broke upon us, darkly,*
>
> ....

---

*That Rilke would appear to have been brought to this precise focus at this time is corroborated by his statements to Rosa Schobloch in a letter dated September 24, about one month after final touches were put to *New Poems*. Here Rilke speaks of "the situation confronting the artist" which has to do with "going into himself" and "round[ing] out his inmost world ... [in order] to set on a par with itself the whole external universe, all of it, even to the stars" (Greene 1, 339—Cf., also, from *The Book of Images*, "The Man Watching" discussed above, pp.230-231). An essential part of this whole process would involve Rilke's readiness to come to terms with Malte, who would require of him an "acquiescence in his going under", as expressed in a letter to Clara earlier that month (Greene 1, 337).

this concerns us: setting it all in order
is the task we have continually before us. *

Eventually, however, Paula's death struck him as its own peculiar generic case on which some quite new things would have to be said, although it takes time for an understanding in these terms to dawn on Rilke. In fact, the poem suggests that a proper understanding of Paula's death in these terms is only coming upon him in the very moment of writing this poem (although the inspiration for it, we can assume, must have already come upon Rilke perhaps even long before he actually sat down to write it).

Initially, Paula's death would appear to have struck Rilke as a form of progression for her, as if she had already accomplished all that she had to transform by way of things in this world: "you who have achieved/more transformation than any other woman." There did not, at that level, appear, then, to be anything unduly tragic about her death. Rilke held Paula in such high regard, as for her own person, he saw her as acting by nature "out of kindness, out of your great abundance ... /... so secure, so self-contained", already blessed, so it seemed to him, with a disposition that was most favorable for living life out fully, whatever life might bring, including her premature death. It is how he expected her to be in death also, since only in death, as he sees it, are the things of this world, by the power of our creative transformation of them, given real existence (until then, "nothing yet exists"). However, he finds with time that Paula has not progressed beyond the world, that something of her has stuck and remained behind, pleading with him as if over some "discontent" that has yet to be addressed. What then dawns upon Rilke and now has him suddenly lamenting with her is that her own share in this experience of the creative life was, towards the end, in a disturbingly real way undone, and only now is Rilke coming into a full sense of the tragedy of that undoing.

The poem's commemoration of Paula's death becomes in this way the occasion for elucidating what Rilke felt was—especially as his own Paula was made a victim of this—one of the most signifi-

---

*All quotations in the case of this poem from **Stephen Mitchell**, ed., and tr., *Ahead of All Parting: The Selected Poetry and Prose of Rainer Maria Rilke*, New York: Random House, Modern Library Edition, 1995.

cant and indeed lethal forms of opposition to the spiritual-creative life, especially where women who have become their own creators are concerned. Rilke's thoughts on this issue, which had the value of an original theory at the time, are well-known and indeed famous. In short, life-forces that are profoundly given over to the spiritual-creative life cannot be suddenly wrenched from out of this sphere and violently withdrawn into the physical, the body and its will. Paula, the woman-artist who had freed herself, experienced just that when she gave herself back (especially because of her deep resistance to this fate otherwise) to daily life with her husband and thereafter too soon to childbirth. These expansive creative forces turn lethal when suddenly forced into the narrow circuit of such a life. One of the most moving passages in Rilke's poem enacts the process by which Paula pretended to take control of this dire shift in her life:

> *And you thought,*
> *because you had grown used to other measures,*
> *that this would be for just a little while ...*
> *... bending*
> *the abundant strengths of your abundant future*
> *out of their course, into the new child-seed*
> *that once again was fate ...*
>
> *When it was done you wished to be rewarded ...*
> *But you yourself knew ...*
> *... inside was mere deception ...*
>
> *And so you died as women used to die ...*
> *... who try to close*
> *themselves again but can't, because that ancient*
> *darkness which they have also given birth to*
> *returns for them, thrusts its way in, and enters*

"That ancient darkness" takes us again to the heart of Rilke's vision of our experience in this world, which in yet another way, has here overcome Paula. Coming into his understanding at last of Paula's fate, Rilke is then moved to his deepest expression of lament in this poem, which is nothing less than an extreme outcry spoken in tragic protest against the shattering effects of such a fate:

> *Can you hear me?*

> *I would like to fling my voice out like a cloth*
> *over the fragments of your death, and keep*
> *pulling at it until it is torn to pieces,*
> *and all my words would have to walk around*
> *shivering, in the tatters of that voice …*

In addition to what Rilke describes of this tragically sad death in his poem, we have a letter from him written some seven months later that enters more prosaically into the process that lay behind it.[45] From this letter it is clear that Rilke had had for some time a presentiment of the workings of this process, which in Paula's death was openly demonstrated. "This tangled suffering of spurious love", as he formulates it in his poem, extends to the many ways in which society as a whole thrusts itself on the creative will, obstructing what he describes as "the freedom of a love" by dragging us back into conventionally enforced roles and models of living. Pre-eminently it showed itself where (especially married) men imposed themselves upon women in a manner intended to serve themselves in their daily lives. Rilke was already emphatically into his crusade against entanglement, as we have seen, in the production of his *New Poems*; it is expressed, for example, in the disturbed focus on "tangledness" in "The Departure of the Prodigal Son". Society's exploitation of guilt, grounded on the inculcated idea of how by choosing freedom one "hurt[s]" others, is at the forefront of the presentation there. The possibility of Rilke's being taken over by this process himself, even as a man, he sensed had always been there, as he implies in his letter:

> *This destiny I sensed long ago, but I actually experienced it only*
> *when it grazed me personally and stood so big and close before me*
> *that I couldn't close my eyes because of it.*

In a reversed fate Rilke had more or less successfully disentangled himself from any possible menace to his creative freedom from his own marriage; Paula in her marriage had not been so fortunate, or consistent. Even so, one could continue to suffer from the great web of entanglements one would have endured from youth, as Rilke himself knew too well. These would have shaped one down to one's biological nature, and in this deeply instilled form could return to oppress one. This had long been Rilke's own experience, which (as we have seen, in Volume 1), he had not been able to transcend with

Lou, even though for a while he saw the prospect of doing so with her. To a great extent *Malte* loomed as a possibility of coming to terms at last with all that had menaced Rilke in this respect, by way of the darker social and psychological forces with which life could confront one. He was attempting to raise himself above all that oppression by facing it head on, and he was finding, when he came back to this project immediately after *New Poems*, that in conceptual strength and in inward resolve, as well as through his growing mastery of prose technique[46], he was having significant success. This is how he was feeling about *Malte* right into the New Year, 1909, a couple of months beyond writing the "Requiem". In relation to Malte, the character, Rilke speaks of "a joyous and difficult obligation to be there day after day entirely for his memory"[47], and of "such singular joy and progress as my present work has been affording me all these last weeks"[48]. However six months later, in that letter that goes again into what his "Requiem" had been about, Rilke complains that he has been for some time now in ill-health; it had been the case, as he remarks, "almost simultaneously with the [new] year … a period of exhaustion, of sickliness, finally of sickness"[49].

It is remarkable that, almost as soon as Rilke was expressing his seemingly untrammelled joy over work on *Malte* to which he had now turned full-time, he should have fallen into such a debilitated condition: "a complicated interaction of physical and spiritual depressions"[50] as he otherwise describes it at this time. Such a transformation will appear remarkable only to those who do not know that Rilke had been struggling with the menace of such a condition ever since he could remember. It is because he could build on first-hand knowledge of comparable processes in himself that he had been able so trenchantly to fathom what Paula's fate dramatized of the tragically treacherous relations obtaining between the spiritual and the physical, however much one would wish to be in control of these processes. Rilke's fears for himself concerning these relations remained, as his "Requiem" itself bears witness. The poem ends with his appeal to Paula to help *him* in his own struggle:

> *hear me; help me. We can so easily*
> *slip back from what we have struggled in vain to attain,*
> *abruptly, into a life we never wanted …*

> *... Anyone who has lifted*
> *his blood into a years-long work may find*
> *that he can't sustain it, the force of gravity*
> *is irresistible, and it* [the blood] *falls back, worthless.*
> *For somewhere there is an ancient enmity*
> *between our daily life and the great work.*
> *Help me, in saying it, to understand it.*

Rilke's anxiety about himself was real, in spite of the fact that, over the few months after the *New Poems* was completed, he continued to enjoy that seemingly unbridled sense of his creative power that had freed him, from the time he was reconciled to Lou, momentarily from deep conflicts in himself of which we have learned much. To some, the phase of the production of *Images* and of *New Poems* seemed like a diversionary excursion from Rilke's more personally committed writing as displayed, for example, in the *Book of Hours*. One of Rilke's correspondents complained as much.[51] To this Rilke insisted that his latest production was, no less than *Hours* had been, the expression of an artistic development that was inevitable, on which he was sternly bent, from "extreme necessity"[52]. In any case, an exclusive focus on the material of *Malte*—now that the latest phase of his creative project was over—was bringing Rilke face to face again, almost as he wished, insistently, with those deep conflicts in himself about which he could not feel so sure and which were bound to engage him more personally. It was simply a matter of time before he would find himself overwhelmed once again by those negative forces from his life's experience that had so often before affected him both psychologically and biologically, which the *Malte* material now reflected back to him almost directly.

How fully had that conceptual strength and inward resolve that he had worked at so strenuously, in conjunction with the production of his *New Poems*, prepared Rilke for the deeply problematic task he had now set himself? In the same letter in which he alludes to his most recent period of affliction since the new year began ("sickliness, sickness" etc.), in this letter in which he comes to his own defense as for the "same great need" to develop his art through all that he has undertaken to write to that point, Rilke provides us with a revealing account of his most basic perception in pursuing his artistic work,

than which perhaps there is nothing more essential to our understanding of him in this period,

> *... art flings itself upon all things (all things without exception) ...*

And these "things" should include also those from "the sphere of the
terrible":

> *In the sphere of the terrible there can exist nothing so renunciatory*
> *and negative that the multiple action of artistic mastery would*
> *not leave it behind with a great, positive surplus, as something*
> *that affirms existence, wants to be: an angel.*[53]

We shall see how far into the future this incisive perception of his
own purposes, in fact, extends. At this point, afflicted though he
had been for months, Rilke can still manage to continue to insist on
his far-reaching and ambitious artistic project, which was already
underway. He would never cease to do so, in spite of the fact that
his affliction grew and grew over a long period of years beyond this
point, as we shall see. Already by the point we have reached, his had
been a long case history of engagement with the terrible; however,
he was bringing to this now a whole new depth of artistic mastery
based in a conceptual strength that had itself been deepening with the
years. Even so, Rilke's purpose in *The Notebooks*, as expressed through
Malte, targets a form of power over the terrible that was, to say the
least, more than ambitious, especially when one considers the state of
mind Rilke was in over a large part of the period during which that
book was written.

The Return of *Malte*

To a great extent, the first part of *The Notebooks of Malte Laurids
Brigge* (to section 23) recreates Rilke's own experience from the time
he first set foot in Paris in the fall of 1902. As far back as 1903, in
his letters to Lou Salomé, as we have seen, Rilke had already gone
in some depth into his disturbing experience while in Paris, though
hardly to the extent of spilling over in such complete, and even lurid,
detail as in this novel. Creating a fictional medium for his narrations,
in the figure of Malte, is what allowed Rilke to raise the sluices so
to speak, although anyone familiar with his life up to this point will

gather straightaway the almost purely autobiographical import of many of the dark accounts that are there recorded. Accounts like these must have been familiar to Lou from their time together in the years that led up to their separation, especially the accounts that are set in childhood. Fevers that laid open a paranormal world of objects assuming a horrifying life of their own were certainly among the experiences touching on his past that Rilke would have shared with Lou. However, Malte narrates the still more frightening development of the resurgence of such experiences in his present, fully conscious, adult life; he is twenty-eight at this time, precisely the age Rilke was when he was writing some of these sections in 1904.* Something along the lines of these narrated episodes was certainly his own experience, even literally so, and they would have informed his somewhat desperate disclosure that he was on the verge of his "worst hour" when he wrote Lou for support after two years of estrangement from each other (back in 1903). Here is Malte speaking:

> it was there again for the first time in many, many years—that big thing that had instilled a first profound terror into me when as a child I lay sick with a fever ... it was growing from within me ... like a second head ... a big dead animal that had once been my hand ... or my arm. And my blood was flowing through me, and through it, as if through one and the same body ... [S]o things from my childhood that were lost are lying here and there on my blanket, seeming new again. All my long-lost fears are back.
>
> (Hulse 40-41)**

Rilke's return to *Malte* was bringing him back to all of this. He had been working at his novel piecemeal for more than four years at least when he came back to it full-time in the fall of 1908. At first there was great confidence on returning to it, but, very suddenly it would

---

*Rilke turned twenty-nine only in December of that year.

**It is a matter of speculation whether Lou would have experienced in Rilke states of mind precisely such as these, among the various episodes accusingly attributed to him by her, during their four years of life together. What is clear (it is a matter that I establish at great length in Volume 1) is that Rilke was destined for a further reckoning with this condition from the time Lou began to repress in him the form of personal and poetic development he seemed otherwise made for and that would have released him (and had already begun to release him) from his former dispositions.

seem, Rilke slipped back into the deep problematic syndrome of the experiences out of which it was being fashioned. It is impossible to think that he fell back *directly* into the condition of mind and body to which his letters to Lou in 1903 bear witness, and out of which his conception of *Malte* originates (if at first vaguely and uncertainly.) Five full years had intervened during which Rilke had gained enormously in conceptual strength and personal assurance (especially after his reconciliation with Lou), not to mention also inward resolve. Something about where he stood in relation to *Malte* by late 1908/ early 1909 is reflected in the structure of the work itself, which falls into two parts. The first part, which corresponds roughly to the first notebook (*Malte* consists of two such notebooks), is marked off by the death of the Chamberlain Brigge's wife (the Chamberlain's own death having taken place *after* her own, even though his is among the first things narrated in *Malte*). It is in this first part that Rilke presents Malte's oppressive dealings with *his* paranormal experiences, so closely related as these are to an uncontrollable "capillary action" (54, 48) of the blood, and to fevers and screaming in his childhood the echoes of which experiences Malte is re-living in adulthood (41). Much of Malte's life in this regard can be said to express something of what Rilke was himself re-living especially during the years 1902-1904. In the second part of *Malte* (in the second notebook), there is no narration of this aspect of Malte's life; in this part we move on to a broader view of human disturbance, as reflected both in past history and in Rilke's present, that has taken some distance from Malte's own experiences. This is a development in a broader tragic sense of life more indicative of what Rilke's experience must have been on returning to *Malte* by late 1908/early 1909. This is not to say that this tragic sense of life was not accompanied by distressing physical symptoms in Rilke that may have been connected to earlier conditions he had known, but the evidence of the novel points to a more evolved experience including new, if still highly uncertain, signs also of a positive direction into which the tragedy of the human scene might be channelled.

Not that Rilke did not find himself in some disturbing way re-living his own difficult past when returned to the material of *Malte*. After the extensive aesthetic raptures of work on *New Poems*, in which he had been free to move masterfully among things, turning from this discrete subject to that, to have now to make sense of, and to give form to, the sprawling, seemingless limitless life of Malte: this must have seemed, at a certain point, more than disconcerting, distressing. It would appear that at first Rilke felt himself equal to the task, speaking of the "difficulty" but also of the "sweetness" of his renewed undertaking—the "sweetness" of it pointing to the success he was having with the "massive" prose he was working out in formulating his subject, which he said was intended to be "enduring"[54]. But here was a problem of content as well as of form: how to assimilate the paranormal and the full depth of a new modern alienation he himself had known into a greater and finally positive understanding of the course of human destiny? Knowing that the subject in this case bore intensely upon his own experiences, as he had known them even until recently, a certain personal bitterness and dismay were bound to enter into the process of his work, serving to weaken and undermine him. All the more so as the stakes were so high: to make sense of it all, and to give form to it, not just for himself but for his time. Central to the exposition in the novel's first part is Rilke's elaboration of a new concept of "the terrible" for his time, one which incorporates both an experience of paranormality and a distinctively new modern alienation, the menace coming both from without and from within. In this respect, Rilke was operating with the (Nietzsche-like) sense of filling a void that had yet to be filled in the history of human life and thought: Malte's entirely new condition of modern "nothingness", to which he has been reduced, has begun to speak:

> *[i]s it possible, it thinks, that we have neither seen nor perceived nor said anything real or of any importance yet ... Is it possible that despite our inventions and progress, despite our culture, religion, and knowledge of the world, we have remained on the surface of life? ... Is it possible that we have the past all wrong?*
>
> (Hulse 15)

We must remember that Rilke was writing this sometime between 1903 and 1905, which makes him a very early pioneer in the account of a new modern nothingness, anticipating Sartre, for example, by as many as thirty years.

In Malte's experience of a new modern world, there has been a breakdown from nature as well as from super-nature. The story of the Brigges, Malte's paternal line, covers the one term (nature), while the story of the Brahes, Malte's maternal line, covers the other (super-nature). At one time death was distinctive in the case of each person ("they bore their death within them like the stone within a fruit"—7), and at the same time death was an entirely natural experience. This is so even in the case of the Chamberlain Brigge, Malte's grandfather, despite the horrible noise of his manner of death which imposes itself mercilessly on everyone across his estate.[55] This is marvellously con-veyed in the scene in which the Chamberlain is brought forth into "the room in which [his] sainted mother ha[d] passed away", and which no one else but he had been permitted to enter since. The excitement that spills over into the room from all and everything that follow the Chamberlain as he is carried in, and that have at last been allowed into this room (including all the dogs), overbears the scene of death and turns it into a perfectly natural occurrence, notwithstanding the horrible unease in which the Chamberlain lies (on the floor in the middle of the room).[56] Contrasting with this outstanding yet still nat-ural scene of a distinctive death are the pathetically stretched out lives of "the dying" in Malte's own time, who, in untold new numbers, are content to be dying before they have begun to do any living, as well as the "banal" forms of the so-called "deaths" of these modern souls:

> *Who cares about a well-made death these days? ... the wish for a death of one's own is becoming ever more infrequent. Before long it will be as uncommon as a life of one's own. Dear God, it is all there waiting for us; along we come and find a life ready to wear on the rail, and all we have to do is put it on ... You die as you happen to die ... In the old days, people knew (or perhaps had an intuition) that they bore their death within them like a stone within a fruit.*

(Hulse 6-7)

Here is the distinctively new world of modern alienation, the world not of the poor but of the wretched "unrich" as Rilke had de-scribed them as early as the "Book of Poverty and Death" (which he wrote just after his first season in Paris, in the spring of 1903). Among this class of people we find, on the city streets, also a new species of "untouchables" (26) engrossed in the most unreal forms of pseu-do-esoteric behavior, as if they were beckoning Malte into another unspecified and also unlocalized world:

What on earth did that old woman want of me? ... I sensed that it was a signal, a sign for the initiated, a sign the untouchables recognize; I felt intuitively that she was prompting me to go somewhere or do something. And the strangest thing of all was that I could not shake off the feeling that there was some kind of agreement between us, that the signal was part of an assignation ...

(Hulse 26-27)

Malte finds himself (silently) addressed by these "untouchables" as if it was already agreed that he was one of them and understood them. It is the same with one such person especially, whom one day Malte suddenly finds sitting in his place at his own regular table in a restaurant. This man is the model of one who, very strangely, without any overt action that would proclaim him in this way, "was now making his withdrawal from everything" (34). Malte feels that he fully understands that man because he feels he is himself withdrawing from everything. It is not long after this episode that Malte puts himself in the hands of doctors. At a hospital where he is waiting to be seen, he is suddenly overtaken by a paranormal vision of that "big thing", appearing like "a second head" and then "a big dead animal", which we have noted above. The background to this psychologically more dramatic level of experience is the breakdown from supernature that is the other side of Rilke's complex thematic presentation in this first part of his novel.

In the process of his withdrawal Malte has begun to "see" things. On the maternal side of his family, there has been, in fact, a history of supernatural "sightings", of which the most dramatic had involved the regular apparition, in the midst of everyone, of one of Malte's aunts (Christine), who was actually "seen" by everyone: in this case, an objective supernatural event! Another, less fully objectified "sighting" concerns the more recently dead figure of another of Malte's aunts (Ingeborg): her presence is intensely sensed in her dog that continues to behave as if this aunt were still making her usual appearance among the family, throwing itself at her ghost in mid-air. There is an implied *association* in Rilke's narrative between "objective" sightings of this sort from the past and the radically displaced, psychologically unhinged form of "seeing" things to which Malte is now subject, as an atavistic survival of mediumistic powers.

It is in the context of such powers on this same side of the family that the story of the Comte de Saint-Germain is recounted (significantly, in the second, more positive part of the novel). Malte's maternal grandfather had, as a child, looked directly into Saint-Germain's preternaturally capable "eyes", which are said to have been able to invoke even absent things as if they were present ("those eyes could have *looked* Venice right into this room"—97). This Saint-Germain is also said to have been able to read, without recourse to books, in his own "blood" the events and stories of the past (98). In comparison, Malte in his time can only throw *his* "blood" (40), which has been reduced to a purely physiological phenomemon, into the appallingly distorted form of that unrecognizable "big thing" that, like a dead animal, would take his blood up into its own shapeless gargantuan outer sphere: "And my blood was flowing through me, and through it, as if through one and the same body." The modern world is, indeed, seen to be a deterioration from a former time when nature and supernature still held together as fully recognized and fully shaped realities in their own right and were fully lived into with faculties equally designed to support them as realities.

Needless to say, there looms for Malte through these several uncanny experiences, which pull at him from one side and the other, the real possibility of schizophrenia, which might take either of two forms. Colluding with the deep withdrawal symptoms of the man in the restaurant, Malte sees the same experience taking form in himself ("something ... is starting to withdraw me and part me from everything"—34), and he is plunged into the fear of his own impending "transformation":

> *a day will come when my hand will be far away from me, and when I command it to write, the words it writes will be ones I do not intend. The time of that other interpretation will come ... this time it is I who shall be written. I am the impression that will be transformed.*
>
> (Hulse 34-35)

In this case, schizophrenia would take the form of an extinction or cessation of consciousness—there would be some form of mental "translation" in these terms—as Malte is finally taken over *from within*.[57] But there are also his episodes from childhood which, in his intensely alienating circumstances, he is suddenly re-living in young adulthood. In this sphere, schizophrenia would take the form of an uncontrolled exacerbation of consciousness identical with madness; in this case, Malte is threatened with the prospect of being violently given over to what is taking possession of him *from without*:

> *it was there again for the first time in many, many years—that big thing that had instilled a first profound terror into me when as a child I lay sick with a fever … it was growing from within me … like a second head … a big dead animal that had once been my hand … or my arm. And my blood was flowing through me, and through it, as if through one and the same body …*
>
> (Hulse 40-41)

Malte is threatened, in relative degrees, from both sides, but it is the latter menace that appears especially to characterize his situation. And it is principally in those terms that he (and Rilke through him) now introduces his concept of the influence of "the terrible" in the world at large.

Suddenly, additionally, we are asked to think (48) that the outer world (the world without) continues to bear in itself as living forces all the remnants of the world's terrible events from the past—"all the torments and horrors suffered … possessed of a tenacious permanence"—and that these forces, moreover, hold sway as a network of effects and influences into which one can be "sucked up", losing all control over oneself. One's inner space would seem to offer a refuge from the sway of these forces, for one would think that "it is impossible for anything of any great size to abide in those cramped confines", but

> *outside, outside there is no end of it; and when it rises out there, it fills up inside you as well … in the capillaries, sucked as if up a tube …*
>
> *Your heart is driving you, out of yourself, your heart is after you, and you are almost beside yourself, and you can't get back.*
>
> (Hulse 48-49)

The immediate application is to Malte, but Rilke was himself familiar with the experience, or something very similar to it. And it is this reality of "the terrible" in human experience, the understanding and assimilation of it, if possible, into a greater whole, that Rilke had by now made into his principal personal and artistic concern. Baudelaire and Flaubert are seen as forbears in this undertaking: of Baudelaire it is said that "[i]t was his task to see, in these matters that were terrible but only seemingly repellent, the abiding essence of being that lies below all that is" (49)[58]; from Flaubert we learn of the crux of the matter: "whether a man can bring himself to lie down beside a leper."

We are taken back further in time to the case of Beethoven, and then settle on someone who among these figures is the closest to Rilke in time—Ibsen. Of Beethoven it is said that "from out of you there came the new arising of all that had fallen in us" (50). Here the focus is on what is fallen in *us*, and not as yet on what is fallen in the world at large: "if only you could have mantled the whole world, not merely us!" It is only in Malte's imagination that Beethoven is conceived as playing the music he has composed as if the greater world in *its* terrible aspect also might be transformed. On this purely imagined level Beethoven "would have poured forth ... giving back to the universe what only the universe can endure". Even Beethoven fell short in this respect. Ibsen's case is the inverse of Beethoven's; unlike anyone before, Ibsen had been in the process of engaging the "terrible [new] beasts" who move almost imperceptibly inside us: he is the one who had been "deep inside, deeper within than anyone had ever been" (53). Malte (Rilke) sees Ibsen's "work" as engaging him in a pursuit of "equivalents for what [he] had seen inside" (54), "bound of necessity to transform that capillary action ... into the most persuasive gestures"—"persuasive" in the sense that they might serve to clarify the reality of such processes, and so bring them within the reach of human understanding and control.[59]

Clearly Beethoven and Ibsen stand at opposite ends of a process of experience that had yet to manifest in the still more terribly fluid and indeterminate form that Malte (Rilke) was contending with. In this case the outer world has now loosened to menace us with a network of elusive "shadow"-influences before which our inner life has become powerless, as if it were about to be possessed and drawn up into them. Malte's experience of the world anticipates in this respect the one that would come to be known over twenty-five years later by Hemingway and by Sartre, both of whom recognize in the indiscriminate reality of "nothingness" an actively nefarious power of influence in the world.[60] In this more distinctively modern phase of "the terrible", the outer world has grown *its own* nefarious life: as Malte puts it, "[t]he existence of the terrible [is] in every particle of the air [;] ... [y]ou breathe it in" (48), and human beings, also in their inner nature which struggles to hold on to itself, find themselves on the verge of being taken up into the terrible in this new guise. Even abandoned buildings, especially in their interiors, continue to exude the influences of the lives that have been lived in them in an unnaturally extended, decomposed form, mostly in their more sordid aspects, and modern human beings are now subject also to these degenerate influences in their environment:

> *And from these walls ... there issued the air of those lives ... There they all hung, the midday mealtimes and the illnesses and the breath exhaled and the smoke of years and the sweat of armpits that makes clothing heavy and the flat reek of mouths and the clammy odour of perspiring feet. There they hung, the acrid tang of urine and the smell of burning soot and the steamy greyness of potatoes ... The sweet lingering smell of neglected infants ... the stuffiness of pubescent boys' beds. And a good deal more was admixed ... there was a lot more besides of unknown origin.*
>
> (Hulse 31)

The experience of the terrible, and of the endurance that would have to be drawn on to meet it, has grown out much further than in the time of Rilke's forbears, or at least it has accrued a whole set of new aspects, and here is the basis on which Malte can claim that "we have neither seen nor perceived nor said anything real or of any importance yet"[61] (15). The terrible had grown a whole new set of terms, and an account of a greater synthesis of experience, incorporating a new extension of the terrible, was consequently in order. In the entry that precedes his new idea of the terrible, Malte summarizes the symbolic value of the situation of the Panthéon, which, along with its patron Ste. Geneviève, looks out over the whole city of Paris. Thus, "[t]he saint watches over the sleeping city" (46-47)—and this makes Malte weep. He weeps over the fallen city not from any superior sense of righteousness about it, but from a profound, debilitating sympathy with humankind, which can still manage to sleep in spite of its desperate condition; he is in dismay about how to cope with the challenges to it of a terrible existence. Significantly, Malte has given in to the city's "temptations" (47), by which he means that he has embraced the influence of its terrible existence, if only because this also is a reality with which humankind must contend. Admitting this reality has, what's more, imposed a new sense of life on him, as he says: "[u]nder these influences, I have formed an altogether different conception of everything under the sun.[62]"

To what extent was this for Rilke also "an altogether different conception of everything?" Rilke was almost literally in this state of mind already not too far beyond his arrival in Paris in the fall of 1902; it is clearly indicated in the mood of his letters written to Lou after 1903. He had, it is true, hinted at a similar experience as early as the "Book of Pilgrimage", composed in the fall of 1901, where he considers the case of those whose "paths" have led "to the arsenal of things unlived".* Such "unlived" existence Rilke had at this point contrasted with the fact that in God "all life is lived". Up to this point he continued to refer "everything" to his God. Even in his most direly pessimistic conditions of mind on his return to Berlin to Lou after Worpswede in late 1900, Rilke saw this as an extreme case of "God-forsakenness", still with reference to God, even though such conditions of mind were seen as themselves not presided over by his God.** It was a simple step from there to a view of human alienation that would deny God, though Rilke does not take that step. Nor does he take that step even in *Malte*. However, by the time he was writing the above passages from *Malte*, well into his own experience of Paris, his view of the terrible would appear to have evolved into something more elaborate: he would appear to have settled into a position which saw him taking sides more forcefully with an oppressed and depressed humanity to the point where he now stands deliberately short of God.

Someways into the second part of *Malte*, this position has consolidated. Malte has been considering the fantastic forms of the revolt of instinct that characterized a former time, with reference to paintings such as those by Hieronymous Bosch[63]: "those wondrous pictures in which things intended for limited and regular uses stretch out and attempt each other, lascivious, inquisitive, quivering with the

---

*See my discussion of this on p.129.
**See above, p.114.

casual lewdness of dissipation" (Hulse 118). In the midst of this lurid scene we find the opposing figure of the saint who is himself greatly tested by it:

> *And the saint writhes and flinches ... concedes that these things are possible ... already his senses are forming a precipitate in the clear solution of his soul.*[64] *Already his prayer is losing its leaves and rises from his mouth like a dead tree ... The lash of his scourge is ... weak ... His sex is once again in one place alone ...*
>
> (Hulse 118-119)

Although Malte had thought such former trials obsolete, he confesses that he never doubted their authenticity. Now, however, he thinks such trials came from the pretension of "over-hasty zealots who wanted to get straight to God from the very start, whatever the cost" (119). Significantly, and signalling a further evolution in Rilke's thought, Malte concludes that there can be no such direct route to God for a modern humanity:

> *We no longer feel equal to these trials. We sense that He is too difficult for us, that we must postpone Him so that we may slowly accomplish the long work that separates us from Him.*
>
> (Hulse 119)

This new, somewhat rebellious view *vis-à-vis* the pursuit of God represents Malte, but it is very likely that by this point Rilke himself had assumed it or, at least, was very close to doing so. Certainly, it is a view that eventually very much determines the course of his imaginative life. This is to judge by the still more elaborate forms of expression of this basic view that Rilke gives voice to, in his own person, in the *Elegies* (the first segments of which were some three years away). We have made ourselves familiar with Rilke's idea (including the many difficulties he faced in relation to it) of the need to find a way to organize his whole life around the creative work he felt bound to accomplish, and now we hear more emphatically of "the" work that is to be done, which may be described as a matter of reconciling God to our existence, with all its terrors and fears, with the emphasis now falling on "our existence" rather than on God Himself (a dramatic inversion of the vision that had initially impelled Rilke in the *Book of Hours*). This is what Malte may be understood to mean when he says "I have formed an altogether different conception of everything under the sun". How, as it were, to gather everything up, including what is terrible, into a greater synthesis of human experience in relation to God but without the abortive impulse to reject *any* aspect of that experience, which only *appears* to our judgment to be perverse, at least where human beings are clearly seen to be suffering from it? This is what, in Rilke's view, has become the work of the creative "solitary" like himself, who, in modern life, has acquired the functions formerly reserved for the "saint":

> *Now, however, I know that that work is just as fraught as saint-liness, that these tribulations beset anyone who is solitary for the sake of the work, just as they beset God's solitaries in their caves and bare shelters, in bygone times.*
>
>   (Hulse 119)

Sometime before Malte comes to this conclusion, he has brought the question of our terrible existence down to an effect of "fear", such existence constituting a "force" that "engenders" fear (107), and he stops to consider that that "force" is precisely what is "*ours* ... all our own", to be distinguished from what God might have ordained for us when He created "heaven". This "force" is precisely what is distinctively ours to contend with and to come to know, and is therefore not to be rejected but rather embraced, in knowledge. And yet: "do we not know the least about what is most our own?"—we do not know, precisely from our impulse to reject this "force" (apart from the fact that, for now, we feel that this "force" is "too powerful for us"). Hence the direction of Malte's (cosmological) thoughts: "At times I reflect on how heaven came into being, *and death*: we put away what was most precious to us, because there was so much that had to be dealt with first ..."

It is the figure of the blind news-vendor, brought forward in the novel's second half (133ff), who is held up as a model of the deepest form of endurance possible to us in our distinctively modern circumstances: "[t]he absoluteness of his misery, mitigated by no wariness, and no role-playing whatsoever, was beyond the power of my imagination" (134-135). Rilke sees in this figure, by a supreme paradox, the proof that God exists: "This, then, is to Your liking; this is what pleases You. If only we could learn above all else to endure and not to judge." Rilke's text, in the second half of this novel, is very specially marked by summarial forms of expression of this characteristic vision, as in the statement:

> *If only we could learn above all else to endure and not to judge.*
>
> (Hulse 135)

Here is another of these summarial forms of expression:

> *We have never seen anything longer lasting than wretchedness.*
>
> (Hulse 137)

This latter position now serves to introduce a longish section in which Rilke ventures further into the historical record, to a specific period of time in the late Middle Ages (that period being, along with the early Renaissance, a favored trove for Rilke's historical insights). Malte's sudden passion for books at one time is what narratively motivates the attention now given to history, the implication being that books depicting past events serve as a source of insight into the present human condition, as worthy as any real experience we may actually be having in our lives.

Focusing at this point specifically on the lives of Charles 6th of France and Pope John Paul the 22nd, the banished pope at Avignon whose death the other papal faction sought, Rilke directs our attention to "that weighty, massive era of desperation" (145) when men knew themselves subject to an existence in which all "drank from the same cup" and "mounted the same horse", caught in a common universal struggle which invariably offered them "one thing *and* its opposite" (147). The success that was sought could only implicate them in the defeat by ambush that awaited them in turn, as fortunes passed back and forth mercilessly: "Who in those times was unaware that the worst was inevitable?" (146) Such an existence Rilke sees as an emblem of that "common distress" that continues into our modern present, though we do everything to avoid acknowledging it:

> *We are forever watering down our understanding, stretching it to go round, instead of wailing at the wall of our common distress, behind which that which passeth understanding would have time to gather its forces.*
>
> (Hulse 150)

Nothing, in Rilke's view, is finally possible unless we are ready to confront this distress that is rooted in our existence as our very own. This we shall do in order to break through at last into a proper fulfilment, an existence that by this process alone will have become fully real. In the midst of this distress one can also find madness, or the random subjection to it, such as was experienced by Charles 6th, whose strength at last was that he could endure and survive those moments. Out of his emblematic condition Rilke weaves the image of what all humanity finally faces, what he calls "that great anguished profane passion" inclusive of even the most terrible and subversive human experiences. Pathetically, in comparison with the fully lived out reality of the past, in the modern present, according to Rilke, "we do not know our part" (148); we are "without action", living in craven "fear of the very worst" (151) that might manifest in the way of distress. Over and against this, on the other hand, was the example of the great heroic actor of Rilke's time, the contemporary Duse (150ff), whom Rilke makes into the finest representative of a proper human engagement in his time: such distress is all that would concern *her*, though no playwright has been able to offer her a proper action to perform in, or a proper part to play.

It is, at the same time, no less part of our modern predicament that someone like Rilke himself cannot fully take on the challenge of the times, but must find himself rather languishing in some impotence, overrun by the common distress, though he knows better than to think that he has any choice but to continue to confront all this and seek to integrate it into some greater, finally fully real synthesis of life. In another of those startling summarial expressions of his characteristic vision, Rilke admits not just of himself but of all his equally committed contemporaries:

> But we, who have embarked on the quest for God, **we can never accomplish an ending.** We keep postponing what our own nature prompts us to, needing more time.
>
> (Hulse 152-153)

We never seem to be able to work our way through the distress. The position and sentiment expressed here are perhaps the most far-reaching of all that has been articulated by Rilke hitherto as for the direction his poetic thought and experience are taking. This position and sentiment he will carry over with still greater insistence and depth into his work on the *Elegies*. At this point in *Malte*, Rilke refers his account back to his concept of "the night"; this concept by now has passed through yet another depth, more immersed than ever in all the ways in which humankind has been subverted, and has subverted and subverts itself. *This* is our experience, to be dealt with first just because it is *our* experience, though it is also the case that we do *not* deal with it, and *that too* will be accommodated. However, this will mean our also passing through the "illness" through which alone we shall be made well again—"behind which that which passeth understanding would have time to gather its forces". It is not a matter of determining how much time will be required for success in this, for we are, in fact, already involved in God through this process:

> *What is one year to us? What are all the years? Even before we have embarked upon God, we are praying to Him; let us go through this night. And then illness. And then love.*
>
> (Hulse 152-153)

How we pass on to love is then communicated through Rilke's "recluse in his night" (153ff), who is nothing but Rilke's "solitary" captured in the process of doing "the work". On the one hand, this mysteriously capable figure "grasps the dynamic significance of that early unity that was in the world" in "ancient times" (154); on the other, beyond those "times", moving towards the present, lies "the sadness of all that could not yet be subdued". Especially does he fathom how "[a]round all that has been perfected there is the unachieved" (155). Only one extreme possibility seems left: for the powerful "woman in love" to take everything up in herself, because "all the ecstasies and despairs which are the full, sole span of the ages [crowd] towards the deeds of her heart, to be lived". How she lives them is the point, for what she "laments" is "not some one man who had left her to lie alone, but rather that other, no longer possible, who might be [have been] equal to her love". In this way is she "ready to offer the whole of love to the very end". Love, that is to say, is carried in itself, in defiance of the violent contradictions both in the world and in us that, for now at least, can only ever lead us back to themselves. This deep seemingly impassable gulf between general pathology, on the one hand, and free love in this kind, on the other, summarizes a great part of the *Malte*-scene. But how more generally to endure and how to find a lasting love in relation to all that has to be endured turn out to be Rilke's more far-reaching concerns. For him it is not possible to pursue the work of love in that kind without in the first place resisting the oppressive trials of "that terrible position of being loved" (165), of which we have already heard in some measure in *New Poems*: "Oh those nights of desolation, when the gifts that had flowed from him were returned to him in pieces, heavy with transience" (163-164). Rilke had found himself (to the great dismay of the women in his life) quite capable of such resistance. But there was then the far more oppressive task: how to endure separation from the beloved, for as he will put it in his first Elegy: "[i]sn't it time that we lovingly/freed ourselves from the beloved[?]": on this front, Rilke would not find his way so easily...

In his monumental re-writing of the story of the Prodigal Son, with which Rilke ends his novel, yet another form of account of his developing vision is given. The hard life this Prodigal Son has inherited, by renouncing forms of love that would only have debased him, hard inasmuch as his life has placed him, as a consequence of his resistance, in a most vulnerable relationship to the world's oppression—even that hard life cannot compare to the appalling humiliations he would have suffered had he submitted to the usual yoke of love: "[e]ven during the times when poverty was alarming him with new hardships daily ... horrified by the filth in which he had been abandoned ... even then ... his greatest horror was that his love might have been returned" (164). In the meantime he has learned to "love existing", apprehending at the same time, as we have seen, "the great remoteness of God", and he has also found or heard a "language" by which (battling impatience and his own beggarly youthfulness for now) he may continue to live and shape his and our experience. Such are the contours of that distinctive area of experience in the world within which Rilke would proceed: "[h]e was learning to love ... shown how unthinking and unworthy all the love he had thought he had given had been" (165). And yet, he "wanted to leave nothing out", and thus does the Prodigal Son (amazingly, because he has every reason to turn his back on them) return to his roots, as far back as to the especially difficult conditions of his childhood, "to take up all of that once more" (166), in order, that is, to re-write his life, in this way to re-live it "genuinely". Imagining what an ideal development from childhood would be for the aspiring artist had been for some time one of the principal revisionary tasks Rilke had conferred upon himself, and this just because *his* had been so *un*-ideal a childhood.* Thus shall we find Rilke at every turn putting the maximum pressure on himself to reach out to the whole spectrum of forms of experience in the world that have dispossessed, and continue to dispossess, us of ourselves, for as long as we shall have our own existence separated from God. Rilke's project constituted no less complete or wholistic an undertaking than this, hopelessly vulnerable though he had made himself, and subjected as he now was, in this process of aiming to reach so far...

Surviving *Malte*

All this, we can say, was Rilke's very own experience, although, of course, right through the novel all continues to communicate itself through the fictional character of Malte. Standard literary convention would lead us to suppose that Malte's thoughts, being the thoughts of a fictional character, are not necessarily Rilke's thoughts and that they should not be taken as representing him. However, many have remarked on the fact that Malte is a rather barely disguised (pseudo-fictional) mask for Rilke himself, and it is too easy to see that in many parts Rilke is indeed speaking on his own behalf, giving voice to what are clearly his own views. Especially is this so in the case of the views expressed by Malte, in the second part of the novel, on the supreme value of the powerful love of women that transcends time, which one might suppose lie strictly beyond Malte to conceive, to the extent that he is his own character. It is not clear just how much time elapses in the course of Malte's notebook jottings, whether a matter of weeks or months perhaps, but the impression is of a continuous production over roughly the same period of time in which Malte records the episodes of his present "illness", which makes the more unbelievable the sudden transition to thoughts of transfiguration in love brought forward in the novel's second part. Rilke's relationship to Malte is more than highly involved, and beyond what we would generally consider novelistic. Rilke was ready at least to *listen* to the

---

*As indicated above, on p.33.

view, as expressed by his wife, Clara, which would regard Malte as "an individual", to the point of "motivat[ing] his existence from away back"[65], but it is in quite another sense that Rilke speaks of him as a "figure ... quite detached from me" with "existence and personality".[66] We have a measure of what this imports where Rilke pronounces himself many months after the completion of the novel: "It makes me shudder a little when I think of all the violence I exercised in *Malte Laurids,* how, *with him,* in consequential despair, *I* reached beyond everything."[67]

"*With him,* in consequential despair, *I*" imports a great deal: nothing less, in fact, than an extreme *identification,* as with an alter ego with which Rilke had been for a very long time familiar, and of which he was desperately trying to free himself. The extreme challenge Rilke faced in thus seeking to free himself from himself is measured by the view he had also expressed, after completing the novel, that the figure of Malte "interested me the more intensely the more differentiated it became from myself".[68] One could speak in Rilke's case of a certain extreme degree of the polarization in himself of two identities, what we might clinically describe as a form of "schizophrenia", only this was the "schizophrenia" of the great artist of genius quite consciously bent on reconciling himself to the terrible in his own being. Rather than seek therapy in the form of the psychoanalysis that was recommended to him at this time (among others by Clara and her analyst Gebastell; Lou herself had begun to embrace this at-the-time, nascent science), Rilke had chosen to cure himself, for he alone could know what it was that was afflicting him from the depths, the solution to which would have to come from him, he says, if it was to be a lasting one:

> Only I myself, who know their cause and the basis of their confusion, am able to break up this complicated interaction of physical and spiritual depressions ... To endure and to have patience, to expect no help but the very great, almost miraculous: that has carried me along from childhood up; and so this time too, although the distress is lasting longer than usual, I would like not to move my nature along by shoves from the outside, but, as one of the last, to wait until it takes the decisive leap of itself: only then shall I know that it was my own strength and genuine, and not

borrowed or just a foreign ferment that bubbles up only to sink back again among cloudy sediment ...[69]

Rilke knew well enough that it had been necessary to return to Malte because only by taking himself through the disturbed psychic world known to this character would he be able to put both himself and the world right again: "I can only go through him" he says: "he stands in my way"[70]. Two months away from returning to his novel, Rilke indicated that he had been wrong to put off work on it over the previous year when he gave his attention to the "Other Part" of *New Poems*.[71] He seemed then to have suddenly grasped more clearly what Malte himself imported: "And all at once (and for the first time) I understand the destiny of Malte Laurids", namely that a certain "test surpassed him", that "he did not stand it in the actual"[72]. He compares Malte to Dostoevski's Raskolnikov who likewise was "left behind, exhausted by his deed"[73]. However we interpret the comparison with Raskolnikov, to the extent that Malte *is* Rilke, that is to say a substantial identity of his own, this account does not bode well for Rilke: it suggests that what would be required is a more-than-terrible effort on Rilke's part to overcome and to transcend a seemingly hopeless aspect in himself that Malte ineluctably embodies. At the time, Rilke put it as follows: Malte's failure consists in "not continuing to act at the moment when action ought just to have begun"[74]. Malte could not "stand" the "test" of the terrible, unlike, for example, Cézanne, another figure with whom Rilke compares him, who for his part did "forcefully w[i]n from himself the extreme possibility of love"[75] and so won his way through precisely by means of the "love that has endured". Malte, Rilke says, has the vision, partakes with Rilke in the vision, but he cannot himself bring the vision to realization ("in the actual"). He is rather a tragic testament to the fate of the one who "goes under"[76] and does not return. *A significant part of Rilke*, we thus infer, has gone under *and has not returned*. And thus does Rilke's most fundamental concern, with the seemingly unresolvable dynamic between pathology and love, find here its most forbidding expression: in the dark depths of his own person.

Rilke explains his vision of the fundamental human condition further: "Real work, an abundance of tasks, all begin only after this enduring."[77] This is the case for the artist also, as in every other vocation, and at some point it was Cézanne who, after Rodin, became Rilke's great model of the triumphing artist. Cézanne's life of dedicated, continual artistic work bore the impression in every moment of his successfully enduring that most extreme point in the human condition where the terrible in life is forever being overcome. Thus is Cézanne emblematically described as that "old man who has gone on ahead somewhere, far alone, only with children after him who throw stones".[78] This possibility of "a love that has endured" is inextricably linked for Rilke with "the work" that the genuinely great artist is called upon to do. While Rilke can certainly be said to have been slowly and surely ascending in his own commitment to "the work", a profoundly unresolved, and in this sense still unfaced, darkness in himself continues to clog his progress. However, this is only as he might wish it to be, for nothing "real" would finally be "possible", as he had said, if he could not somehow accommodate into his developing vision (salvifically, so to speak) also the common tragic fate of "going under" or what it must mean that some/many human beings, in their individual fates, have *not* been able to rise to the task of love. It is in this sublimely tragic sense that Rilke could foresee that not only the beautiful would be an angel, but "the terrible ... [also] an angel".[79] Rilke knew this, but he also did not want to know this. Naturally he wanted to think that with *Malte* he had finally accomplished his task of facing up to the deeper negative aspects in himself. In early spring of 1910, after sending in the last of the proofs of *Malte* to his publisher, Rilke describes this work as one that has duly served as an "underpinning" to the "fair" or more positive developments in vision to which he could now look forward:

> *Much will go on taking shape in me now, I think; for these journals are something like an underpinning, everything reaches farther up, has more space around it, as soon as one can rely on this new higher ground. Now everything can really begin for fair. Poor Malte starts so deeply in misery and, in a strict sense, reaches to eternal bliss; he is a heart that strikes a whole octave: after him almost all songs are possible.*[80]

However, if Malte "reaches to eternal bliss", as Rilke here fancifully suggests, this is only because Rilke is left behind to do the further "reaching". Malte himself fails, but Rilke has intervened beyond the failure (investing Malte with a further power of vision only by proxy), and Rilke remains to carry forward the vision that he (Malte) could not. The achievement of *Malte* was, as Rilke put it, that it had "led so far in all directions"[81], both in the negative and the positive: it had had its own inherent comprehensiveness and all-encompassing aspect, so typical of Rilke's engagement with his materials at every stage of his career. But it is significant that Rilke should add that *Malte* is "by no means anything complete" and that it is the mere "sketch of an existence and a shadow-network of forces": those forces would work on to completion, both in their positive and negative aspects. True, a few months later (in midsummer of 1910), Rilke was speaking of *Malte* as "the end of a period. One cannot simply go on writing, one has to begin again, right from the beginning".[82] Rilke's wish is that he could somehow free himself of work in this kind, corresponding to a "period", and find himself completely anew ("but only think of the youthfulness, the self-confidence, the joyfulness which that entails"). But this wishful view of his novel would seem to mask a deeper conflict the influence of which in himself, in a moment of breakdown a few weeks later, Rilke can no longer suppress or keep hidden: "Rilke suddenly began to talk about … the impossibility of writing anything else after *Malte*—of the uncanny feeling he had, as though his work were now terminated—he had said all that he had to say." [83]

This dramatic admission, confession one might say, was in that moment accompanied by a plunge into that very condition of soul in which Lou had so often found him and which his new patron and confidante, the Princess Marie von Thurn und Taxis, herself experienced: "that was the first time I experienced something of his terrible attacks of deepest melancholia and despondency, which would sometimes assume the most unexpected forms."[84] What was this "attack", experienced by the Princess at first hand, if not a resurgence in Rilke of that very condition of soul he had otherwise duly and so thoroughly engaged with over years in creating Malte: a full admission, in other words, that Malte had not passed beyond him, could not pass beyond him, and that what he hoped would be an end of him was, in fact, no end—to the point where nothing more by way of a new, or even an ongoing, creation—nothing more by way of a "real" progress—seemed possible again? It is in this context that we begin to fathom what Rilke says so revealingly about Malte only two weeks later: "how, with him, in consequential despair, I reached *beyond everything*, so to say even beyond death, so that everything became impossible, even to die."[85] Malte's influence over Rilke extended that far: the reaches of his *via negativa* would seem to have had no conceivable limit.

Such hopeless limitlessness is a consequence, Rilke believes, of the *form* of despair it was based on: it is a matter, as he says, of where he was left after an extreme *artistic* effort of realization: "[i]t makes me shudder a little when I think of all the violence I exercised in *Malte Laurids*." Rilke is now of the view that art itself is to blame for the extent to which he has "gone under" with Malte, as if his art had turned violently from Nature in this respect—great, creating Nature. To this Nature Rilke would thus now return as to a source that must hold for him the prospect of some degree of release from despair, if not a new source of miraculously transforming power. He is now ruthless in his condemnation of that direction towards an exclusive practice of art that he had determined upon from the time he was describing that prospect to Lou as early as 1903, principally, at the time, from the influence of Rodin, though that of Cézanne would also add itself later. If Rilke has achieved his art, it has been, as he says, *"at the price of* concentrating on things—that was a kind of stubbornness, and I am afraid arrogance, too—dear Lord, and it must have been an immense covetousness". This was to be a great, if not the great, turning-point in Rilke's life and career as an artist and poet, involving an almost complete renunciation, no less, of his most recent extreme, puristic undertaking in the practice of art (misleadingly referred to as a commitment to "things", which, in fact, have quite another nature than what is attributed to them by art—or, for that matter, philosophy):

> *I believe nobody has ever experienced more clearly how fundamentally opposed art is to nature, it is the most passionate inversion of the world, the road back from the infinite.*
>
> *On that road the trusty things move towards us, now one can see their entire form, their face comes nearer, one perceives their movement in detail—yes, but who* **are** *we that we should be permitted this—to go in this direction against them all, to be always turning back and thus deceiving them* [the things] *by making them think we have already arrived at some goal and are at leisure to retrace our steps?*[86]

Things belong to great, creating Nature, first and foremost, and the artist will be left hopelessly stranded with them, perhaps even to the point of madness, to the extent that one pretends to shackle things to the violently extreme form in which they survive and perpetuate themselves in what is finally only a direction in art...

So now Rilke conceives of what he so desperately needs at this stage: the great distance that would have to be sought from his recent life as an artist. This he specifically conceives of in the form of an actual journey he would now take to some distant area of the world. This notion would not be realized, however, until another three full months had passed, in November of 1910. He had already had some premonition of the need for such a journey as far back as April, is already hinting at it to his new confidante, the Princess Marie, even then. Contrasting with the way he had presented himself to his publisher only two weeks before, full of the buoyant sense of new and greater accomplishments to come after *Malte*, to the Princess he confides that his task in Germany over recent weeks, which involved dictating the manuscript of *Malte* to his publisher and the tedious protracted proofreading that followed, has left him "unwell, perplexed, exhausted" **(Wydenbruck** 5). He had been saddled with this task for much longer than he could afford in view of the need he had for a great new distance from himself: "my inner tension had been directed to far more distant things, so to speak, expressions of a remote world, into which one has to translate oneself"—"more distant" yet than the Rome he was now visiting again, which seemed to him merely "synonymous" with his old life. His "plans", he says, "were rather great ones"; they had become "great, unfulfilled plans" (Wydenbruck 7) when he was then forced to return to Paris; here especially he became acutely aware that something else would have had to transpire: "[t]here must have been room inside me ready to be filled with memories of distant things." He would leave Paris in turn because "everything there had become so much at one with my own toilsome, painful days", and he is complaining again of the "so many humiliations ... imposed on me ... by my ailing body" (Wydenbruck 9).

This impasse disturbed him all the more as he continued to feel inwardly that so much more was being required of him, especially at this stage of his mission as an artist: "I had hoped to do so much— as usual, everything." Art had claimed too much of him, but he remained for all that an artist, with a need to find a new great distance from himself that would allow him to carry on as the greater artist he knew he had to become. The distance he sought was not just from the extreme form of artistic practice he had been giving himself to for years, but also from that part of himself that had trapped him more than ever as a result of the identification he had forged with Malte and all that he represented of the negative life. This was both Rilke's own negative life as well as the general negative life reflections of which were to be found almost anywhere in the world around him. Part of Rilke himself had gone under with Malte. Bewilderingly, in the deepest part of himself, this was, in fact, only as he had wished, for he was now committed to engaging with the terrible in life as never before and as much as any artist had been. But it remained the case that he must also find a way to rise above and beyond this terrible, with all that life itself could offer him also in respect of the positive, the beautiful; he would be meeting pathology with love—to formulate the essential dialectic with which he was now wrestling in the depths.

To realize this final, ultimately total venture, which he could only half-consciously conceive even now, some great new, encompassing space was needed that would allow him to accommodate and contain the great opposing forces that he was carrying in himself, beyond Malte's mere "vision" of how these forces might be resolved or reconciled with each other. For it was now a matter of realizing this venture "in the actual". In November 1910 Rilke at last set sail for a trip through Mediterranean Africa, and he was to stay away for as many as four months through late February 1911, by which point he is signalling his imminent return to Europe to the Princess. He claims to have found through this somewhat erratic trip at last the large psychological distance from himself he had so needed: his time away "comprised so much that was incredibly new, that I had longed for and probably really needed" (Wydenbruck 13). He feels separated from his former crippling constraints sufficiently to be able to say that "a world is piled up between then and now, a mountain of a world", and it has served in fact as "a watershed"—"and I shall have no other choice than to flow down, with every urge, in this new-found direction". This was at least what he hoped. Certainly a new and profound assurance underlies Rilke's communications with the

Princess henceforth, in spite of the many complaints he continues to voice about the difficulties in his immediate circumstances as well as his customary dilatoriness, as a result of which no work would be done for months to come. He owed this new assurance in part to his long trip abroad, but another large and perhaps the greater part of this assurance, in the midst of what was beginning to look again like a continued dry spell, had to do with the fact that Rilke knew that the Princess's residence at Duino was looming for him as a venue for the new work that he hoped would come. Duino Castle, perched high up on a coastal hill and with its vast views of the Adriatic sea, had all those characteristics of distance in the natural perspectives it offered that Rilke's struggling imagination was crying out for. At some point he knew he had this place in reserve for the future.

To return to an earlier time, it was in the week of the 20th of April 1910, not long after sending off his last corrected proofs of *Malte*, that Rilke visited Duino for the first time, and is recorded (by the Princess) as having said "over and over again": "'Now all is well, yes, all is well'" (Wydenbruck 6). For the moment, however, Rilke's struggles continued even while at Duino, his stay at which for this reason he cut short, and, after re-settling in Paris where he had hoped but again failed to recover from himself, he was more or less appealing to the Princess for some form of reprieve from his condition, anticipating an invitation from her to stay with her at her country estate in Lautschin (in the present-day Czech Republic). It was at Lautschin, in mid-August, that Rilke had his first breakdown before the Princess's horrified eyes. In spite of this, he would soon after speak of his time there as "a real watershed": his "work", he said, was "dormant, but deep down in life itself something is moving" (Wydenbruck 12). He already sensed then, even though still only deep down, some form of prospective breakthrough: he knew that in the Princess, in Lautschin and in Duino, he had at last found that so greatly needed shelter from his former world, and that on all of this he could rely when the time came for him to come through again. Apart from this, Rilke's journey to North Africa for four months, begun in November 1910, had brought that deeply needed distance from himself to a first stage and, with that, the assurance that a new direction had indeed been found. For this reason, he was more tolerant of the creative doldrums in which he continued to languish, again for some time, on his return to Europe. "Oh, these intervals" (Wydenbruck 16), he cries out, suddenly with a refreshing sort of humourous self-irony, and in the confidence that another period of creation lay beyond this latest "interval". Once again Lautschin would offer its own momentary experience of shelter, and before long he is again casting his thought on Duino as the place in which he will at last summon the truly new creative work that had made itself necessary. He is now all for solitude again and Nature: after Lautschin he feels "the real necessity to be very, very much alone" (20) and is soon linking this need with the vast views at Duino: "I do not want to speak, or to look up, except into the featureless, outspread void, the sea, the ocean—that will be right for me"—"[y]our letter, Princess, by putting the great solitary prospect of Duino before me, was exactly what I was in need of." (21) "As to my plans … they are entirely dependent on yours, and all converges on Duino" (23); "Duino is the cloud that will shelter me, away, away then, to live thus reft away—you feel, do you not, how needful this is to me?" (22)

Duino today

III
The Duino Moment

Anticipations

By the time Rilke was at last left alone with himself at Duino Castle, almost two months into his stay, in mid-December of 1911 (except, of course, for a few servants left behind in attendance), a whole set of profoundly conflicting and competing forces was swirling within him. These, not without great psychological strain and at a significant cost to his artistic identity, Rilke had been forced to leave to themselves, to sort out as best they might. He had been creatively idle for a full two years, not having produced any new work over this entire time and awaiting a decisive breakthrough the form of which he had no way of anticipating. Nor could he be sure that there would *be* a breakthrough; this was, also, always a real and potentially damning possibility (Rilke had for some time been grappling with the fact that, at the relatively advanced age of thirty-six, he might then be left with no vocation to speak of at all)—real, and yet perhaps also not so real, for this was, in fact, a period of intense expectation, marked by the, almost, certainty that something momentous would indeed be happening. In a letter written to Elsa Bruckmann (the Princess Cantacuzène) at this very time (mid-December), Rilke reviews his decision to settle at Duino, and his need for this, with a telling declaration:

> *I have long wanted to be here alone, strictly alone ... to live by my heart and by nothing else ... outside, the sea, outside, the Kartz, outside, the rain, perhaps tomorrow the storm—: now **must appear** what is within by way of counterweight to such great and fundamental things.*
>
> (**Greene 2**, 30)[87]

The day after Christmas, in a letter to an unidentified N.N., offering advice as to the poetic work of her young male friend, Rilke describes the task of the poet in terms that speak immediately to his own condition, even if he is here describing a requirement necessary for any poet from the outset of his career:

> *The development will always be this, that one makes one's language fuller, thicker, firmer (heavier), and of course there is sense in that only for one who is sure that **the cry too is growing** in him ceaselessly, irresistibly, so that later, under the pressure of countless atmospheres, it will issue evenly from every pore of the almost impenetrable medium ...*
>
> (Greene 2, 31)[88]

These words apply to the whole of Rilke's own career, and so to a great extent to what he saw also as his continued work in the future. One is especially startled here by the thought of the "cry" Rilke is himself harboring that would soon issue in the great opening of the First Elegy, as we shall see: "Who if I cried out" etc. Four days later, in a letter to Princess Marie, he returns to the thought, formerly expressed in relation to his prospects at Duino, that "all will be well" (Wydenbruck 28). He considers, in spite of the creative drought he has experienced over the last two years ("two whole years!"), that he knows he is on the right track now, where before he had been only pretending to precipitate himself into the future:

> *Some time ago I thought I was already on the way to better things, but it was only as it is when a broken bone heals together in the wrong way. Now I have broken all the bones anew, and so a perfectly sound anatomy is to be expected.*
>
> (Wydenbruck 28)

Once again, we feel that these words address what Rilke saw himself as creating looking ahead to the whole of his work in the future, but they have an application also to what he anticipated would at least begin to show as work again, even possibly in a momentous way, in his immediate situation at Duino. Rilke was readying himself for something significant to happen especially then, given, in one respect at least, the ideal nature of the setting at Duino for fresh creative work, for which he had been longing for some time.

The hopeful note that suddenly intensifies in Rilke in his letter of December 30th to Princess Marie is to a great extent also explained by the fact that he had just written Lou again two days earlier after a lengthy hiatus in their own correspondence. It is indeed remarkable that, filled as he was at this moment with such intense expectation, Rilke should draw Lou back into his situation, re-instating a correspondence between them that had grown silent over more than a year and that had indeed dwindled considerably (to but a handful of letters) after their second reunion in the spring of 1909. That had been more than two years back. Over this time Rilke had not even shared with Lou the fact that he had been on a major journey of four months through Africa. Why, then, was he drawing her back into his situation at just this moment? Clearly, we will say, if he was to break through in any way, he needed to bring himself together, to fully bring especially his disturbing thoughts about himself into conscious focus, and naturally, given his situation, this meant getting into *Malte* again: "there is a clue", he declares to Lou, "*Malte Laurids Brigge*". It meant getting again into the darker aspects of himself that Rilke had so often shared with Lou in the past, and that she alone could mirror back to him. This remained so, notwithstanding the close, and otherwise in its own way intimate association Rilke had since established with Princess Marie who had bestowed Duino on him in anticipation that fresh creative work would unfold there. There is no clearer explanation than the one Rilke now offers to Lou as to how he saw himself in relation to Malte, that most personal of situations that had grown so very problematic to him for more than three years now. His summary of it to Lou in this moment crystallizes all that we have been gathering from scattered comments he had been making to the Princess over the many months that preceded his present sojourn at Duino:

> yet no one but you, dear Lou, can make the distinction and judge whether and to what extent he resembles me. Whether he, who doubtless **is** in part created from my perils, is destroyed by them, in order to save me, as it were, from destruction, or whether with these journals I have finally gone all the way into that current that will sweep me away and plunge me over the edge.
>
> (**Snow, *Rilke*,** 176)

Breaking Through

This second way of seeing his situation *remained*, yet Rilke still hoped to find a way of coming free of the experience he had insisted on engaging by coming to terms with the dark complex in himself he had bodied forth in Malte. One way or the other, he was now a "damaged" soul as a result of the process ("damaged" is the way he puts it in a letter to Lou that follows on this one), as he himself notes:

> *but the other one, the one who was destroyed, he somehow used me up ... he appropriated everything with the intensity of his despair ...*
>
> (Snow, *Rilke*, 176)

"Everything", again, is the key word here (see above p.274). Whatever else Rilke was in the position to make of the negative dimensions of Malte's life, in an incontrovertibly determining sense that negativity had engaged Rilke in the essence of his own being, the part of him that was, in fact, already profoundly caught up in such negativity even before he undertook to write Malte. Writing Malte had only perpetuated that negativity for him, whatever hope he may have had otherwise of accomplishing through his imagination of the Malte-condition some necessary release from it for himself. In conceiving of a possible re-emergence for Rilke from hopelessness, we are thus bringing into focus the idea that for him hopelessness continues *alongside* the hope with which he is naturally also identified. His famous terms for this larger experience, that in writing Malte he was on the path of a "dark ascent", do not imply a re-emergence that would leave the "dark" behind as a condition that would be finally transcended, but the kind of re-emergence that will have also brought the "dark" along quite fully in its own right, for, in the full scope of its own ongoing influence in human life, it is no less a measure of reality, certainly as things stand and would continue to stand. The "investment", he says, was "*in* the loss" (176): "[i]t has been my ambition to invest my *entire* capital in a lost cause."[89] Whatever ideas Rilke might properly have of a full spiritual evolution beyond the terrible in the future, that terrible remained for now, and the more pressing question for Rilke was consequently how to continue in the venture of hope when hopelessness continues also as an incontrovertible aspect of human experience, as the more insistent case in fact.

More than a paradox, here was a contradiction Rilke would not, because he could not, let go of. How to carry forward both the hopelessness and the hope, as it were, in tandem, so as to discover through a seemingly impossible dialectic between them, which yet would have to give in time, that "remote and neglected part of heaven" that represents a deeper and more complete experience of heaven than we have so far been able to imagine, one that is to be finally truly an answer to the terrible because it will have thoroughly addressed it, through our having in very deed fully engaged with it. There was in all this the very real danger of "going under" himself, in a way that might engulf Rilke for good. He was watching Rodin himself collapsing before his eyes and overwhelmed by "life-sized life", which had left even that great artist scuttling about in old age "grotesque and ridiculous" because of the sense he had come into that his life was finally "utterly unachieved" despite the (very) grand record of his artistic output. "[A]nd what in all the world *is* this work", Rilke thus complains, "if one cannot learn and undergo everything in it?" (Snow, *Rilke*, 177) Such a view of what should be the final pre-eminence and thoroughness of art in embodying our full reality we should place in turn alongside the additional view we have seen Rilke beginning to embrace that "art", threatened as it was by "life-sized life", would have first to seek to co-opt "nature", if art is indeed to have the thoroughness that alone will finally justify it in our eyes.

***

Among the issues Rilke brought up to Lou at this time was what he describes as his "need" for people. "Often since [returning to] *Malte*" he has had the "longing" to "lodge [his] solitude with someone" and "to put it under that person's care" (Snow, *Rilke*, 177). Since completing *Malte* he has waited in vain, he says, on the hope that he would rise up the way his legendary hero of old, Ilya, had after *his* period of great trial: "In the very years when Ilya von Muram rose up, I sit down and wait and my heart knows no occupation" (see above, p.219). Rilke has had to face up to the fact that he has not come through in spite of preparing for his emergence over many years. He then expresses the wish to be with Lou again "sometime", if only this was possible for a week or so, to discuss what may be "the signs of a new illness", he says. What is significant in all this is the

somewhat shocking contrast between the way Rilke has been addressing the Princess Marie in his letters to her at this time and the way
he addresses Lou. In his letters to the former he is all intense, almost
ecstatic expectation; in his letters to the latter he is all negativity, the
depressive complainant he had always or so often been with Lou in
the past. At the same time, it is clear that Rilke is further inspirited by
his having reached out to Lou. In a letter written to the Princess two
days later and before he has heard back from Lou, he is allowing himself that (somewhat horrid) expression of hopefulness we have noted
of him, in which he speaks of having this time (which is to say in this
latest period of creative dispossession) properly broken all the bones
in himself, so that he feels that only something altogether sound can
come out of his situation now. He is more accepting of his fate than
ever; to the Princess, he says: "But, don't you agree, the utmost terror
has its place in the world and can take us a long way if we come to
terms with it?" (Wydenbruck 28) Lou's reply to his latest overture to
her may well have reached him when, one week later, Rilke speaks
more acceptingly than ever to the Princess of his place in the midst
of barren "thickets", out of which he has begun to focus more insistently on the "nightingales" that should be appearing to lodge there
(Wydenbruck 29). Four days beyond that, he has replied to Lou, and
with the Princess is in greater expectation than ever of the creative
influx he has been hoping for: "the divinely ordained solitude is really
beginning to work". He says that, in his letter to her, he is "writing
like a madman" but that his excuse is that "[t]he voice which is using
me is greater than I—I am only rustling like a tree moved by the wind,
and I must submit to it" (Wydenbruck 30). Something of great note
would appear to have been stirring in Rilke already at this time.

Lou's reply to Rilke's letter makes clear that she has returned
to the same discourse about his negative tendencies that they had always had between them, and that this episode looks just like all the
others that had preceded it: "You are right, it has probably always
been like this with me" (Snow, *Rilke*, 179), Rilke offers to say. But this
is also different, he explains: the "strongest" part of him he fears has
been "damaged", and the critical question thus arises how "despite
everything [to] move on?" (180) Among other things, we will ask how
it is that Rilke could be entering into such a discourse with Lou, a
discourse of unmitigated oppression, when his expectation of a fresh

breakthrough was, in fact, never higher than at this moment? It is easy to understand that, out of the depths of a fruitless solitude such as he had recently known, Rilke would inevitably be considering what form of relief he could count on as a matter of principle going on into the future, who or what there might be to take the edge off and to give him a sense of any possible life lived if he should no longer be writing—that is the ostensible import of his remarks. But Rilke was not at just this moment experiencing his solitude in this way; he was, rather intensely, anticipating a breakthrough, and another discourse must therefore be assumed to be taking shape in him at this moment, propelled by another, less obvious motive.

Expanding on the issue in his own reply to Lou, it turns out that Rilke is not, in fact, thinking of relief in the future so much as what he mystifyingly alludes to as "real influences" now. Such influences come from a radiant "presence" in certain "special people" who, without their even knowing it, would be naturally disposed to providing the circumstances that would allow for the wholesome human environment Rilke says he so desperately "needs" (181). He claims that the notion began to take shape as long before as when he was working on *New Poems*, and that he expected it to be supporting him when he finished up with *Malte*. It did not, and he is, consequently, making an effort to revive it here; he is deeply involved in connecting with it. He illustrates his notion by an experience he had while in Capri, an example that takes us back several years (180). It was a matter very simply or not so very simply of sitting out of doors on an evening with two women and a girl among whom there were no expectations of each other whatsoever: everyone there was very simply or not so simply, present to the others in the simplest activity (doing needlework, peeling and eating an apple). "There was no hint of destiny between us", Rilke points out. This deep moment Rilke sensed even then was giving him "strengths", the very "strengths" on which he believed he was able to rely "in [his] arduous solitude", both in that general period (roughly around the time of *New Poems*) and later (*Malte*).* Of "what was born" in that moment Rilke notes that

---

*From this account it would appear, then, that there was more to what Rilke needed than the self-involved "inward resolve" he was depending on as a consequence of the disciplined exercise of his functions as a poet when creating the *New Poems* (see above, p.248). He now sees himself differently: "In the very

name it has none, but I experienced from it something that was
almost like the mystic nourishment of the Eucharist; while it was
still there I knew that it was giving me strengths and later, in
my arduous solitude, I recognized these strengths among all the
others; it was strange: they were the ones that held out the longest.

(Snow, *Rilke*, 180)

On the basis of familiarity with such an experience, Rilke could envision the possibility of a level of human association with a foundation in a communicated "presence" that would be entirely strength-giving, without taking or needing to take. There are the "special people" who do this for the sick; Rilke maintains that there might also be a special people that could do the same for the healthy, so that it would be a matter here of going from health to greater health: "God knows how far" (Snow, *Rilke*, 181). This is to imagine beyond his own present case, however, for he is himself to be counted among the sick: "Do you understand that I imagine some presence that would make the things I have blown out of all proportion ordinary and harmless once more?" Rilke knows that it is his own special destiny to share in the experience of what it is to be among the sick, as *their* representative, and for some time to come yet. But here he is insisting on imagining a situation of communicated health that would have an effect towards ever greater and greater creativity. The further question comes through his account: "Can you imagine that there is a human being who can give this?" (180) There is no doubt that here Rilke was thinking of Lou herself; he cites her as the prime example of an incision of such "influences" in his life in "that one special year when, as things were not progressing at all, or better yet, not getting anywhere (for there *was* nothing there—), *you* came". In his previous letter to her, he had said of her that "your being was so truly the door ... into freedom" (178), and so he stands up, he says, against "the same doorpost on which so long ago we marked my growth", by writing her again now.

---

years when Ilya von Muram rose up, I sit down and wait and my heart knows no occupation" (Snow, *Rilke*, 177). A new, deeper, more broadly based resolve that lay beyond his own efforts with himself was the focus at this time, which Rilke was just now attempting to connect with. More on this below.

Return to the Repressed-of-old Self

What Rilke was doing in these two letters, in fact, was *going back to the time he shared with Lou before and up to the debacle after Florence* when a complete experience of the sort he is now laboring to re-envision was within his/their grasp. He is acutely aware that the situation he has in mind of complete, mutual support between two (or more) human beings must make itself of its own; it is conceived of as a "miraculous" (181) development for which there could be no preparation, and he is the more acutely aware of this necessary condition as it is what *was coming to fulfilment for him/them back in that time.* He still carries that sense of what was possible then within him, can on occasion live his way back into what was becoming of him then, latterly as in that special moment in Capri when he responded to the influences of the three women with "my own warmer and happier being" (181). It is a phrase *that takes us back*, to Rilke's experience and vision, when in Florence, of the full "happiness" that, it was too clear to him at the time, awaited them both, if only Lou had been ready or attuned and open to the boundless prospect it opened up then. In the letters he was now writing to Lou from Duino (perhaps the most extraordinary of any he had written or was to write), Rilke was doing nothing less than living his way back into his old, pre-lapsarian self, looking to draw on *this* for inspiration as the one and only element of his nature that was left to him that he felt could successfully and fully support him in his anticipated breakthrough in this moment.

In fact, in this moment, anticipated breakthrough and return to his repressed-of-old self were like hand and glove, or rather each was both hand and glove: it was the one process in two guises. There is, indeed, a deeply mysterious, full-scale synchronicity to this moment that defies logic, or any ordinary sense of reality.* Part and parcel

---

*Another strange synchronic development at this time concerns the sudden prominence of psychoanalysis in Rilke's correspondence not just with Lou but with Viktor von Gebsatell, a psychoanalyst who had been treating Clara, Rilke's wife. As we shall see, the sudden intrusion of psychoanalysis in Rilke's life at this time only serves to highlight the more the fact that he was bent on his own analysis of himself, his flirtation with the possibility of psychoanalytic treatment being just that: a substitute-discourse courteously conducted with his friends that masked the actual treatment he was pursuing with himself. See

of this old self, the self Rilke fully was when in Florence, was, as we have seen, that profound vision of creative evolution that was inspired into him through his first-hand encounter with the Madonna figure in early Renaissance painting (painting of the quattrocento)*. In *The Life of Mary*, the new work in which he suddenly found himself immersed when at Duino, before the *Elegies* ever emerged, Rilke was being returned to the very groundwork of this vision. He was without any thought of working on any such project while at Duino, when, out of the blue, his publisher wrote him about a proposal to return to a manuscript he had put together a decade before while in Worpswede (that second Florence). This manuscript, his publisher suggested, might serve as the basis for a poetic cycle on the Virgin Mary. This cycle would be illustrated by his former friend, the painter Vogeler; it was the latter who was, through Rilke's publisher, in fact reviving the enterprise in which he and Rilke had been involved in that long-ago time. Altogether hesitant about returning to this at first (Rilke's sights were at this moment set elsewhere), Rilke nevertheless succumbed on reviewing the pieces he had once written, for the most part re-configuring these so as to form a now more or less complete approach to the topic.

With that manoeuvre Rilke was suddenly and beyond himself re-immersing in his prophetic experience of old that had once centred in the Madonna. That experience had led him to proclaim the prospect of a new creation for his time that he anticipated would be all of his concern, a prospect that, as we have seen, has indisputable affinities with the prophetic historic-creative vision of Novalis.** This is how Rilke had put it when back in Florence:

> *We shall be like mothers ... let it be known: we shall be like mothers ... you must learn only to believe; you must become pious in a new sense ...*

Prater, 203-204: "there was increasing confidence in the efficacy of his own treatment ... of his non-productivity at least." Also: Freedman, 328: "If his determination to 'treat himself' through his art is seen in this way, his apparent 'game' with psychoanalysis can be viewed in a very serious dimension." All this is clear enough from his letters to Lou and to Gebsatell at this time.

*See Volume 1 of this study, p.50ff.

**See Volume 1 of the present work, pp.56-57, also pp.159-160.

*As pure as each loved one was in the Renaissance-spring: so holy shall each mother be in the summer **we** inaugurate ...*

(Snow, *Diaries*, 38-39)

Novalis had put it this way (in "Christendom and Europe"):

All these things are still only hints, disjointed and rough, but to the historical eye they betray a universal individuality, a new history, a new humanity ... Who does not feel the sweet shame of being with child? ...*

The veil is for the Virgin ... her indispensable instrument whose folds are the letters of her sweet Annunciation ... For me her singing is nothing but the ceremonious call to a new foundation gathering, a mighty beating of the wings of an angelic herald who is passing. They are the first birth-pangs, let everyone prepare for the birth! **

Rilke's sudden fresh immersion in the profound figural destiny associated with the Virgin Mother, as he had once lived this out so intensely for himself, would surely have contributed to his growing perception that something of moment was about to take place at Duino. Or rather all was of a piece and seemingly co-terminous (i.e., synchronic): the anticipated breakthrough, the strong backward-working drive to recover his old unrepressed self, the re-appearance from that earlier time of the Mother's great power of historical birthing, *along with* that key figural Angel who, from another world, was the one come to announce that whole new development, in the time of Mary as now in Rilke's own time—all was the confluence of one and the same event. Rilke must have been struck by the uncanny correspondence of his language in these Mary poems to the situation he was living out at present. His letters to the Princess at this time already show a tendency to live into this meta-drama that is reflected to him in his activities, and in which a creative breakthrough seemed to him to be boded, as where he speaks of "writing like a madman" and that his excuse is that "[t]he voice which is using me is greater than I," when referring to the words he has just put down in his letter to her offering

---

*See Margaret Mahoney Stoljar, ed., *Novalis: Philosophical Writings*. Albany, NY: State University of New York Press, 1997, 147.

**Stoljar 149.

advice on her family situation (Wydenbruck 30). Alluding again to these words in his next letter to the Princess, he paints it all as a case of having been "violently dictated to", as if he had been St. John on Patmos (Wydenbruck 31). Remarkably, these words do not refer to any production of the Elegies at this point, which were yet to appear; in fact, they simply acknowledge that he was in a rush against time to address his Princess's problems and to get his letter to the post-office before it closed! But clearly some other drama was brewing. As for the meta-drama as reflected in the Mary poems: in "The Birth of the Virgin Mary" we read of what the Angels knew: that "this night the mother will be born".* In "The Visitation" the poet remarks that "no one could go/beyond the power that she now experienced", and the Angels in "The Annunciation to the Shepherds" proclaim that "Now something new will be/from which the world will spread out in circles".

It was more than a matter of mere verbal intimations. Rilke was being imaginatively set back: that great creative birthing Mother of old, as experienced by him when in Florence, was now, once again, with the poet, She who seemed in Herself to forecast the era of a new creation to be fulfilled in his time, if not by Rilke himself then by another later. Moreover, in contrast with the Madonna in Botticelli, who for Rilke marked the sad imaginative limits of that former era, as we have seen (in Volume 1)—limits that Rilke hoped to transcend—the Mary of the *Life* has progressed further; She is now, finally, directly involved with Christ in an achievement of Redemption, if still hedged round with a lingering bafflement of His deed that does not deny continuing pain. This is precisely the shared achievement between the Mother and Christ that lay tragically beyond Botticelli, and that also came to be later denied by Rilke when he sets his mind again to his *Visions of Christ*, that moving work of the symbolic defeat of his imagination that he had returned to as a consequence of Lou's repression of his creative vision after Florence, and in which the effectiveness of the Redemption is almost ruthlessly denied. Here, in *The Life of Mary*, there is at least a movement back towards it, as in "The Virgin's Time of Ease with the Resurrected Christ".

---

*All references to *The Life of the Virgin Mary*, tr. Christine McNeill, Dublin: Dedalus Press, 2003.

Oh to her first. How inexpressible
the healing was between them.

And they began / ... /
the time of their utmost contact.

Christ's Redemption is, by the same token, no simple achievement, *or* a complete one, as the Virgin's admission after Her assumption into heaven imports:

I am his longest pain.

We may wonder to what extent Rilke was conscious of a restored poetic self in these precise terms, and to what extent he was in this moment actually once again given to this self, though I have often remarked, in this ongoing study, on Rilke's astonishing shrewdness, not always directly expressed, when it came to how things stood or were developing with him. That he was more or less consciously living back, in his letters to Lou of this moment, into his original, unrepressed self of old before the debacle with her, the self he had been when "warmer and happier" with her, seems to me incontestable. That was an expression of his own deliberate effort to return to his old self, to which was added the rather uncanny synchronic return to his former work on *The Life of Mary*.

Why, we may ask then, or how was it that he was thus returning? Very clearly he had reached complete impasse as for the course he had been on ever since those former glorious days. Nothing else whatever was coming through in those terms (i.e., after *The Book of Hours* through to *Malte*). Yet Rilke could sense, very powerfully even, some mysterious fresh development growing (some anticipated breakthrough) to which he found himself contributing precisely by reaching back to what he had been before the curtain of repression had fallen upon him that had hemmed him in and fated him to impasse. In this he was also being helped as if by a power outside him, returned in this moment to the profound figural symbol of the Mother with his resumed work on his *Life of Mary*. However, he could never have thus managed to reach back in any actual sense without first *undoing* the whole process of repression that had separated him from that self so long ago. He wanted to be as ready as possible for what seemed about to take place, which seemed to bode something of great moment, as if he was actually being called. This meant doing what he could to be as free as possible of his repressed condition, this condition which had now fully arrested him and which was directly associated with the subordinating power Lou had once so fatefully exercised over him, one would have thought irreversibly.

We are struck in this regard by the seemingly natural way in which at this point Rilke enters into this process of undoing himself, which is not without some significant disingenuousness. We note, with some unpleasantness, the peculiar strangeness of his continued obsequiousness with Lou in his letters to her in this moment, as if he had remained the very same person he had always been with her going back almost a full ten years. Not only had he grown, over the years, very much beyond this assumed persona with her, a great deal of the problematic element in his life was also in the present moment being worked out, one could even say had been worked out. One feels he was really coming to terms at last with that clogging darker side of himself that had brought him to complete impasse. He had become, in this moment, as clear about this as he had ever been. Thus his description of his share in the Malte-nature in his letter to Lou stands as a fuller or more complete account than what he had ever managed before. Yet this description comes, as it were, after the fact: he was not *at this moment* struggling with his illness, certainly not to the same extent that, as of old, he lets on with Lou. Here it is *a role that he is playing*; he is falling back into the same old game with her, re-enacting the part she had always expected him to assume with her. His complaining to her is both untrue and unreal, as where he states his fear that he is "never to be occupied again" or that he will be "left without a calling, superfluous" *just when* he sensed that a breakthrough was about to take place:

> *Can you understand that in the wake of this book* [i.e., *Malte*] *I have been left behind like a survivor, stranded high and dry in my inmost being, doing nothing, never to be occupied again?*
>
> (Snow, *Rilke*, 176)

> *How is it possible that now, ready and trained for expression, I am left in fact without a calling, superfluous?*
>
> (177)

Rilke may have had such feelings, even over an extended period of time, over the many months that preceded this moment, but he is not feeling this way now. He is in this moment, in fact, feeling more buoyant than he ever had perhaps since his Florence days, feeling himself on the verge of a profound breakthrough. But it is also true that part and parcel of this extraordinary disposition was his need to be acting things out with Lou again *in order to free himself* (to the extent that he could, for his purposes in this moment) *of his Lou-complex.* This *complex* of almost fawning subordination and subjection, as we have seen*, had been for all intents and purposes the efficient cause of his continued subjection to his own illness including its further expression most recently as the Malte-condition in himself. Malte is indeed Rilke's case, reinforced and finally established in him over time by Lou, and *breaking out from under this* was now the real need. Rilke needed to revive his original self, his self at Florence, over and against his assumed self, the one imposed upon him by Lou after Florence. That's if he *was* to break through, and he was determined to break through, sensing that it *would* happen now, and that he had to make it possible: there was no further development to be had along the path he had been on up to that point: *there* was pure impasse.

Breaking out from under *this complex* is the real need that underlies his writing to Lou in this moment, after a good many months of silence between them. This he had now to do to ensure that any breakthrough at this moment would turn out a fully genuine experience. How conscious was Rilke that this is what he was doing? I believe far more conscious than we would suppose. At every stage of progress through his life, Rilke, as we have seen, had an exceptionally acute consciousness of what his situation was. (Thus he knew that Lou was the efficient and, in the end, the decisive cause of his continued repression and his ongoing illness, even if he never let on with her that he knew, through all those years! This we have established in depth in Volume 1). Was there, in fact, *any* blindness in Rilke to anything that was happening in and around him? In his address to Lou in this moment she is what she had always been almost from the start: both the One who saved him and the One who obstructed his way (at once

---

*In Volume 1.

Muse and Covering Cherub*): "your being was so truly the door" (Snow, *Rilke*, 178), he says, and he is right, but by the same token she is the One who had then blocked the door and was blocking the door still. His need for people as he describes this to Lou here is, as a matter of course, made to seem like a need for her: "I wish I could be together with you sometime for a whole week" (178), but it could not be the case that he wished to be with her at this moment, especially as she is or has become to him. He is rather, as we have seen, going back to what she *was*, before the debacle, as a basis for understanding the kind of world he had once sought for himself that he still has intimations of now and would somehow desperately revive. He is, as we have seen, much buoyed up suddenly on talking with Lou again, but not so much for the reasons one first brings to mind, not just because Lou is there to support him (though this too is his need). It is because deeper down he needs her to be there *to re-live his complex—in order to break free of it* (to some extent, as I have said, for the complex was otherwise there to stay). One winces at how Rilke receives Lou's reply to his first letter. He is ready as ever to offer to entertain her own (customary) understanding of his situation to which he has played up ("You are right, it has probably always been this way with me"—179), but never more than in the following perhaps is the somewhat pitiable depth of his played-up obesiance made so obvious:

> *your good letter ... I can't tell you how warm and comforting it was. I am the single small ant that has lost its direction, but you see the anthill and assure me that it is undisturbed and that I will find my way back into it and make myself useful.*
>
> (Snow, *Rilke*, 179)

The drift of Rilke's experience in this moment is well known to psychology, and Jung is especially illuminating here, where he says, for example, that:

> ... *regression is not necessarily a retrograde step in the sense of a*

---

*To draw on terms from the poetic theory of Harold Bloom whose deliberations serve as an especially revealing account when one applies these to Rilke's situation. See *The Anxiety of Influence: A Theory of Poetry*, New York/Oxford: Oxford University Press, 1973, 2nd edition 1997. I make a further application of Bloom's theory below.

backwards development or degeneration, but rather [can represent] *a **necessary** phase of development.*[90]

*the process that at first sight looks like an alarming regression is rather a **reculer pour mieux sauter**, an amassing and integration of powers that will develop into a new order.*[91]

Sue Mehrtens[92] accounts further for this process, quoting from Jung:

... regarding the psyche as having some sort of goal or direction. What was it aiming at? A "reactivation and reorganization of [the] *contents" of the conscious mind."[a] Such a reorganization could include "a complete **orientation towards the inner world**,"[b] to provide a counter-balance for our usual focus on external things ...*

Jung also saw, in his work with patients, that regression can "carry [a person] *into a new time and a new dimension"[c] which would require the patient to make "considerable efforts at re-adaptation"[d] ...*

... regression ... "makes the creative fantasy inventive ..."[e], ... "stimulate[s] the creative imagination, which gradually opens up possible avenues for ... self-realization."[f] This can result in the patient attaining "a level of consciousness higher than before,"[g] so that "the whole personality undergoes a change for the better."[h]

In one of the most extraordinary moments in modern poetry, and a significant moment in its own way surely also in spiritual history, Rilke found himself suddenly drawn up into this "new order" of which Jung speaks that *will*, miraculously, emerge on the basis of a process of regression. Taking himself through such a process with Lou, while at the same time yearning for what he had been of old before the debacle, Rilke suddenly breaks in again upon that old self of which we have been speaking, which now re-asserts itself out of his psychic depths. A whole new creative impulse now emerges for him from beyond his present condition, as if from outer spiritual spaces, an overpowering impulse which we inevitably associate with the Angel-figure that has suddenly become, in his First Elegy, the central reference point of a new poetic breakthrough.

The First Elegy

We have the Princess Marie's account of the crucial moment:

*Later Rilke told me how that Elegy came to be written. He had no
idea of what was preparing itself within him ...*

*One morning he received an annoying business letter. He wanted
to deal with it as quickly as possible and found himself forced to
concentrate on figures and other prosaic matters. Outside a strong
Bora was blowing, but the sun shone and the sea was radiantly
blue, crested with silver. Rilke climbed down to the narrow path
which connects the bastions jutting out to the east and west at the
foot of the castle, from where the rocks fall down to the sea in a
sheer drop of 200 feet. The poet walked up and down this path,
entirely absorbed in thought and wondering how to answer the
letter. Then, suddenly, as he was pondering, he stopped dead: it
seemed to him that he heard a voice call through the roaring of
the wind: "Who, if I cried out, would hear me from the ranks
of the angels?" ... Taking out the note-book he always carried,
he wrote down these words and several more verses that formed
themselves without any conscious effort on his part ... Then he
went up to his room quite calmly, laid the note-book away and
dealt with the business letter. Yet by that same evening the entire First Elegy had been written down. Very soon afterwards the
Second, the "Angel" Elegy, was to follow.*

(Wydenbruck 33-34)[93]

This moment's experience, out of which the whole of his later poetic
production develops, became translated in Rilke's First Elegy with
reference to that forbidding symbolic figure of the Angel who suddenly looms very large in Rilke's poetic world. It is as if the words that
had been spoken to Rilke out of the *Bora*-wind at Duino had come
to him from just such an Angel and its greater world. This Angel
comes out of a world that Rilke had not consciously known until
this time. A number of uninspired efforts have been made to trace
the lineage of this Angel-figure back to Rilke's earlier representations
of Angels in his work, but the task has proved futile for this reason.
For *this* Angel is an utterly new experience for Rilke. It is none other
than that Angelic herald that, in developments paralleling the poetic

experience of Rilke's precursor, Novalis, would have naturally manifested to Rilke at a climactic point in that *other* progress he had been bent on, as we have seen, from the time Rilke came into his vision of the momentous future that awaited him as a poetic creator when everything came together for him in Florence.*

It is as if Rilke had been secretly, inwardly, always been moving in that other line of progress as his own deepest wish-fulfilment, in contradiction to the assumed poetic life he had been *compelled* to live as a consequence of Lou's acts of repression back in those former days, this life that he had continued to see through right up to the time of *Malte* when it had finally reached its limits. It is just as well that Rilke was visited from this other sphere at this time, for not only would he have gotten nowhere other from here as a poet, have not found his way through the impasse as he had come to know this, very likely he would have (to some degree at least) succumbed to that fateful condition he so disturbingly shared with Malte that was at the root of this impasse. By the same token, Rilke is already caught up in the depths of such a condition, including the view of the world this has imposed on him, so that when he *is* suddenly visited, it is out of those same depths that he necessarily responds. The words that come into his mind in this moment, which emerge spontaneously from those depths, are a direct despairing *inversion* of those Novalis had pronounced at a time when, deep into his own struggle to come through, he had given voice to his *faith*, on which his own very different future rested. Thus Novalis:

> *Without thee ... /*
> */ ... to whom had I poured out my pain?***
>
> *—to whom could I my care address?****

---

*These comments, and others that follow across the next few pages, take up from my presentation on this subject on pp.50-57 of Volume 1, especially pp.56-57. See also above pp.292-293. More allusions to the Novalis link will be found farther along in the present volume, and in Volume 3.

**See *Spiritual Songs*, tr. George MacDonald, Maidstone, Kent: Crescent Moon, 2010, 89.

***Care, concern, need. The second version of the latter line, from William Lindeman's translation of *Spiritual Songs,* Mercury Press, 1986. The former line and its sequel, in MacDonald, read fully as follows: "Without thee, what

And Rilke:

> *Who, if I cried out, would hear me among the angels'*
> *hierarchies?*
>
> *Ah, whom can we ever turn to*
> *in our need?* *

(Mitchell 331)

Rilke's lines take up and develop or (as one would say in the poetic theoretical language of today) "complete" the negative implications in other lines by Novalis:

> *Who, that had not a friend in heaven,*
> *Could to the end hold out on earth?***

—about which more below.

Novalis, moving along his own route, was in the final outcome led at last to his Angelic herald, the same power who has now visited Rilke here, and who provides suddenly the only impulse that could have driven Rilke through impasse. Novalis's support was his Christ and the Redemption He has brought, through whose power Novalis prevails in his own despair, eventually reaching a greater and greater vision of other worlds. Rilke too, in his Duino moment, had, momentarily at least, turned to his Christ as we have seen, with some restored sense likewise of the power of His Redemption, even if this is, more typically of Rilke's experience, only partly acknowledged and only partially lived out. Nevertheless it is enough to have brought Rilke momentarily again into tandem, as it were, with the prophetic import of Novalis's vision some version of which Rilke was once destined for. This import, arising from the depths of another world, has, in the form of the Angel, gratuitously and providentially come back to save Rilke here, to drive him on his way again, who had for some time quite fully lost his way. Rilke is here preternaturally absorbed back into the world of his old prophetic self, the world he had come

---

were life or being!/Without thee, what had I not grown?"

*All references to the *Duino Elegies* taken from Stephen Mitchell, tr., *Ahead of All Parting: The Selected Poetry and Prose of Rainer Maria Rilke*, New York: Random House, Modern Library Edition, 1995.

**Spiritual Songs*, 89.

into so briefly in a "happier" time, long enough for Novalis's Angelic herald to manifest to him for one decisive moment, breaking through into Rilke's world as the saving factor that will now be driving him onwards again.

Another way of formulating this extraordinary event would be to say that, in the shadowed footsteps of Novalis's achievement, the Mother has indeed given birth here, on the basis of Christ's Redemption, but to Rilke, at this advanced point in his assumed life, only for a moment, before *he* immediately brings to bear on this event all the despairing human concerns that, as we have seen, have been preoccupying him more and more and that he has otherwise been called to account for, implicitly in relation to that once-longed-for achievement. (This is the point to which we said we would come in Volume 1.) Thus Rilke immediately turns away from this visitation from another world:

> *Who, if I cried out, would hear me among the angels'*
> *hierarchies?*
> (Mitchell 331)

Rilke turns away from this otherworld that is yet the one that here sustains him, that has lifted him momentously out of his condition and given him the focus he has needed and been looking for to be able to understand the import and the meaning of *his* way. The continued thrust of his inherited (assumed) condition does not allow him to respond to the visitation other than on the basis of his by now highly developed experience of human despair, which he now consciously comes to see as lying in an implicit relation to the great vision of human hope such as was once expressed by Novalis.* Oriented out of what has become his commitment to the problem of human

---

*Rilke had been cut off from his original visionary self by what Bloom's theory denominates the "Covering Cherub" (*Op.cit.*, 35). In Rilke's case this Covering Cherub was a living person, namely Lou, who once acted and continued to act precisely as a "personified superego" (59) the effect of which on the poet is "a kind of separation anxiety" marked, among other things, by "the desperation of seeking to foretell dangers to the self" (59)—all of which characteristic ongoing symptoms we have noted of Rilke. Yet "strong poets" is Bloom's description for poets who manage to fight their way through such anxiety to assert themselves in the end as their own creators.

despair, with its challenge to hope, and carrying this despair inevitably into this moment, Rilke can now formulate precisely what the
greater challenge consists of that would reconcile the terrible realities
of human experience to prophetic vision. For now, it can only be a
matter of breaking down before the idea of any such possible reconciliation because the terror implicit in despair is as yet far from being
fully worked through and assimilated. Thus, invoking what has transformed into *his* newly created Angel, who, as a projected symbol, in
himself embodies this final reconciliation of terms, Rilke must for
now admit that

> *even if one of them pressed me*
> *suddenly against his heart; I would be consumed*
> *in that overwhelming existence. For beauty is nothing*
> *but the beginning of terror, which we still are just able to*
> *endure...*
> (Mitchell 331)

All the same, we note of the first Elegy that emerged suddenly a
whole new powerful idiom substantially quite different from anything
we had encountered in Rilke's poetry before. We are here given a
whole new level of language and of thought that one feels will have
something to do with the freshly injected, life-altering inspiration
Rilke has received in his Duino moment. Language and thought have
suddenly become more philosophical, more rooted in a typifying
generality as distinct from a more particular existentiality, as already
characterized in the poem's lead question: "whom can we ever turn
to/in our need." Three typical spheres are then named and rejected as
for any satisfying support they could offer for this all-essential "need":
angels, humans, animals. There are experiences *in the world itself* that
seem to offer a fairer chance of finding the necessary support, as if *it*
rather held the key to free us from our unhappy existence, experiences
to which the poet is saying we need to bring more of our attention and
a more acutely focused attention, this being almost anything that is
happening immediately around us and also from moment to moment.
It is as if we were being called by such things: "All this was mission"
(Mitchell 331), it could be some tree, a street, the wind, night, springtime, a violin.—"But could you accomplish it [this mission]?" (333)
So much, in the meantime, lies in the way of coming to terms with

the unhappy lot we have inherited as our own, which is the fate that has been distinctively ours. In the long run—so the poet conceives of it in these Elegies, though he has already been thinking this for some time—we shall have made something only more truly distinctive of ourselves. This shall be when we have successfully found a way of finally incorporating this fated unhappiness, so distinctively our own, into that greater happiness that "we", if "we" are to be finally completely human, must in the meantime be bringing into being, for only *such* a combined outcome would represent the truly new and finally "real" humanity that, historically, has escaped us thus far.

This, indeed, is the final basis and the ultimate purpose of that all-inclusive "need" that, deep down, we continue to suffer from whether we will or no. Rilke's visiting Angel has transformed in the face of this outstanding "need". He is no longer the beatifically creative Angelic herald of Novalis and of Rilke's former self, who has passed beyond the terror of our existence, rather a newly re-fashioned Angel who incorporates in himself both the beauty and the terror, without himself being in any way undermined by the terror that continues to undo *us*. He is a symbolic fulfilment of Rilke's altogether distinctive intention according to which, as we have seen, not only the beautiful but "the terrible would also be an angel". In the meantime this Angel out of its full experience bears "serenely" with Rilke in his confounded state, which is made all the more confounding because there is also no option of being "annihilated" (331) by it. It must all of it be borne; neither will comfort come from that Angel. Rilke is merely thrust back upon his terrible existence, to fend for himself; he will have to stifle his call for aid and, returned to his "need", deal alone with what he describes as his "dark sobbing" (331). At the same time, we note in Rilke's account here a strange new distance from the terrible, a hitherto unencountered tone that is less directly engaged by it. We have only to compare this tone with the depth of Rilke's involvement in the terrible during and beyond the writing of *Malte*. We remember, however, that Rilke had been seeking a special form of distance from his experience, if I may quote myself here, "some great new, encompassing space [that] was needed that would allow him to accommodate and contain the great opposing forces that he was carrying in himself", forces which had seemed to him to be linked too much, we will recall, to his effort in art. It is precisely from the midst of this newly-found encompassing space, in which he had been for months now seeking to lodge himself, that Rilke in this poem, in an entirely fresh venture, is involving both his reader and himself somewhere between the beauty and the terror of our existence, in what can only be described as an application in—compassion.

The shift in tone is marked by what was a dramatically new form of poetry at the time, poetry that strangely enough, incorporates into itself the distinctive, philosophising rhythms and the confidential voice of prose, without ceasing to be at the same time poetry. This somewhat tensed-up peculiar *rapprochement* of the two worlds, of prose and of poetry, goes some way to explaining the more universal appeal of this poetry as distinctively philosophical, in comparison with the very differently based lyrical and technically outstanding forms of poetry Rilke had written up to that time (which, of course, have had their own different levels of popularity). It is in this specially created context of philosophical confidentiality based *in* the poetic experience (which is its own rhythmic experience), a context designed, as it were, to bring us more fully along and to win us over the more completely, that Rilke proceeds to offer us his main lesson in this Elegy.* Initially, his focus is on "the solitary heart" (331); caught up in its "need", it seeks correspondence with the world around it; submerged in its vision of the terrible and the burden of *its* never-ceasing oppression, and so "not really at home" in the world—thrust back continually only on an "interpretation" (331) of it—this "solitary heart" can look for consolation in all the ways in which the world appears to be calling to it, as if the world knew that the answer to the heart's "need" lay in its own midst. Tree, street, wind, violin: the world of *Malte* still shows through here, but as if newly impregnated with a farther design in the midst of which "the solitary heart" might be putting itself together. It would be a matter ("simply"!) of freeing oneself of the fetters of a burdensome emptiness and *expanding past* it *into* this greater world, which is only waiting for us to live into it:

---

*The reader may wish to consider that, many years after Rilke's achievement here, W.B. Yeats and T.S. Eliot would likewise pursue a more pronounced philosophical confidentiality in their poetry (in their case in late age), and consequently gained for themselves a still greater audience for it, greatly extending their appeal.

> *Don't you know yet? Fling the emptiness out of your arms*
> *into the spaces we breathe: perhaps the birds*
> *will fill the expanded air with a more passionate flying.*
>   (Mitchell 331)

Not, however, that the world does not continue to show itself opaque in its meaning or disillusioning because of an undeciphered otherness in it, but it is at least always in attendance on us and is so without judgment: it "remains" to us, in one way and another constantly, in this larger suggestion, beyond opacity.—(The recognition of the world's potentially saving role points far ahead to the time when *The Sonnets to Orpheus* will emerge on the basis of a full reckoning with the world in the terms suggested here, a reckoning that would secretly engage Rilke, it would appear unconsciously, over many years.)— But the lesson (for now) is this: we are continually "distracted" from this "mission" by "expectation" (Mitchell 333), and so dispossess ourselves of our part in this great calling that is sounding from the midst of the world, distracted most especially by the thought of at last finding in this world our "beloved" whom we are always "longing" to find and by whom we are constantly being beguiled: "as if every event/announced a beloved."

We think we have at last found her, or are about to find her, or else are thrust back onto her whom we think is already found, though in fact it is rather that we cannot escape her, every new event of moment drawing the beloved into it when the event waits on us to take hold of it for itself. What takes this account beyond a stock notion of the tyrannizing power of love is the way Rilke leads into it. The mode of address ("Don't you know yet?"—331) is ambiguous: it is also, and indeed especially, he himself he is talking to, his own "solitary heart" ("my heart", as he addresses it more openly farther along in this poem). It is he himself who cannot escape the entrapment of his love: "Weren't you always/distracted by expectation[?]" (333) And so the main lesson turns in on himself also: "Isn't it time that we lovingly/freed ourselves from the beloved and, quivering, endured[?]" (333) He is in the process of exhorting us all (it is "we", and we are also the "you"), himself included while he is himself unable to fulfill the exhortation. It is a thrilling imagination of freedom the poet offers us, nevertheless, one filled with the tension of what it would mean to release ourselves at last from the tyrannizing bind of the love-relation-ship. That process would be bound to smart (hence "quivering"), but we would then find through our very love the power to make more of this love than we ever could while we continue to be bound:

> *Isn't it time that we lovingly*
> *freed ourselves from the beloved and, quivering, endured:*
> *as the arrow endures the bowstring's tension, so that*
> *gathered in the snap of release it can be more than*
> *itself*[?]

A greater and more encompassing truth should already have con-vinced us of the inevitability of this transcendent manoeuvre:

> *For there is no place where we can remain.*

—another special thought that Rilke will take up at great length and in great depth, in his next (the Second) Elegy, as we shall see. The poet also calls attention to the "huge strange thoughts" that continue to absorb our consciousness (also through the night) and that concern themselves with the whole issue of our existence. Such inevitable thoughts leave little room, he implies, for properly accommodating one's beloved also in one's consciousness and in this regard them-selves point to the need to pass beyond her. These "huge, strange thoughts" are the full range of "thoughts" that Rilke will be giving voice to as he moves along through the whole group of Elegies he will be writing over the next ten years...

The challenge, and task, of finally renouncing his beloved, as stated, is yet another dramatic manifestation of that underlying Novalis-voice in Rilke (which is also his own voice) that is suddenly haunting Rilke in this great self-defining moment. For Novalis was the one who, after a great struggle, did finally manage to renounce his beloved, aided, admittedly, by the fact that in his case Sophie had died; he was freed in one sense in spite of himself, though the more drastically challenged in that it had been a violent unwilled separa-tion. We imagine what Rilke would be expected to do and would have expected himself to do, to the end of seeing his original Novalis-vision through, back in the time when, just returned from Florence, he faced Lou's repressive indifference to the direction he knew he should take: instead of subordinating himself to Lou, he would at that point have "freed" himself of her, would have renounced his earthly love in order thereby to see through his otherworldly vision of the transcendent power we may have over our tragic fate, along the lines on which Novalis had moved. At that time Rilke had swerved from his Novalis-fate. Ten years later, so very deeply ensconced by then in the fate he opted for when he tied himself down to his love, he is now asking the fateful question: "Isn't it time that we lovingly/freed ourselves from the beloved, and, quivering, endured[?]"

As out of the *Bora* there came an otherworldly voice impelling him to re-create himself in the face of deadening impasse, so out of the "wind" as a general experience there comes the voice of those who died young who "murmur" to Rilke to "remove … the appearance/of injustice about their death" (335). We should see that these young have been freed from the problem of earthly attachments, have been in fact free of them all along, in contrast with ourselves who carry on only to be with time radically compromised in this respect. We must learn the lesson of these young, the poet offers, and begin that process of disentanglement from the earth that would free us from the tyrannizing bind in the way we love because of our attachments. We imagine along with these young dead what it means to be fully and finally detached from the earth, strangely difficult as such an imagination is for us:

> *Of course, it is strange to inhabit the earth no longer,*
> *to give up customs one barely had time to learn,*
> *not to see roses and other promising things*
> *in terms of a human future…*
> *Strange to no longer desire one's desires. Strange*
> *to see meanings that clung together once, floating away*
> *in every direction.*
>   (Mitchell 335)

One hears through this picture of a deep-set, inevitable balking before the task at hand Novalis's own words of resistance when he faced the task of having to give up his beloved. This was before he embarked on the excruciating process of disentangling himself from his attachment, long before he came through in otherworldly fashion to bring in a whole new prophetic order of creative life hitherto unknown:

... it is my fate that bewilders me ... So sudden a change is very painful—it is certain that I must forget my entire former existence.

I loved the earth so much—I had so much joy from all the dear little scenes that stood before me ...

Just as I previously lived in the present and in the hope of earthly happiness, so I must now more than ever live completely in the genuine future and with faith in God and immortality. It will be very hard for me to completely separate myself from this world that I have studied with so much love; the renunciation will lead to many frightful moments ...*

Novalis had spoken these words on the near side of his act of renunciation and subsequent otherworldly commitment; Rilke, for his part, is speaking his words on the far side of what was his failure to renounce many years before, so that the injunction to renounce now, insofar as it concerns him, will strike us as a far more abstract matter: a case of renouncing where there has been no renouncing, and will not be any, since Rilke clearly remained and would continue to remain attached—to Lou, and to what he had known with her at one time. (This he himself will recognize so movingly in the original version of the Tenth Elegy penned a year and half beyond the First Elegy, as we shall see.**) We note in this respect a certain abstractive distance in all that Rilke is proposing at this point as if it were all being entertained as an *ideal* injunction, one that he and all the rest of us are bound to continue to struggle with, even without any great hope

---

*See *The Birth of Novalis: Friedrich von Hardenberg's Journal of 1797, with Selected Letters and Documents*, tr. and ed., Bruce Donehower, Albany, NY: State University of New York Press, 2007, 73-74.

**In the last portion of this original version, Rilke's elegiac terms are unmistakable, taking us back to his original fall-out with Lou in the late summer of 1898, and to a repetition of this experience two years beyond that, as we have seen in Volume 1: "Far too much you belong to grief. If you *could* forget her .../you would call down .../one of the angels (those beings unmighty in grief)/who, as his face darkened, would try again and again/to describe the way you kept sobbing long ago for her" (Mitchell 403). This account conforms with the "dark sobbing" with which Rilke begins his sequence of Elegies. The long-ago "sobbing" has by now (over ten years later) grown much in stature, far beyond the experience Rilke knew originally.

of being able to fulfil it. We continue to be aggrieved by disappointed love, even if we *can* have a sincere wish, as Rilke does, to emulate the example of someone like Gaspara Stampa. She, in her turn, is held up as a model of what it can mean to renounce the beloved and to continue *in this way* to build on the free spirit of love without dread of frustration or being compromised by attachment, which in any case can never offer any sure basis in reality: "For there is no place where we can remain."

Rilke's ideas from his *Malte*-period are here undergoing an evolution, implicitly brought into a new relation and submitted to a new understanding, the consequence of the impact of the Duino moment. The idea of free love, as in the Gaspara story, and the idea of the freed life of those who died young, who have no attachments to the earth, are now being properly referred to the intermediary process of renunciation both ideas assume, which, clearly, is no easy matter for the rest of us. We ourselves, and this includes Rilke, resist renunciation, have not reached the point yet of embracing this process. It is as if *we* still needed both attachment and the tragedy that comes from living through the thwarting of attachment—whether by death, loss or disappointment—in order to grow in spirit, not having yet reached sufficient maturity to do without the repeated need to be undone: "we for whom grief is so often/the source of our spirit's growth—could we exist without *them* [i.e., "the great mysteries" of "earth's sorrows and joys"]?" (335) *We* retain a need for the tragic song that is spun out of our sorrow over the loved one who has been lost; that transforming harmony enraptures us, comforts us, and helps us further on our way (337). In the meantime an imagination of what actual renunciation entails is also greatly developed in Rilke's poem, in terms that put us in mind again of what Novalis himself successfully underwent as a process:

> *And being dead is hard work*
> *and full of retrieval before one can gradually feel*
> *a trace of eternity.*
>
> (Mitchell 335)

In time, through this process, we would reach a sphere where the living and the dead occupy one world between them, among whom angels move:

> *Angels (the say) don't know whether it is the living*
> *they are moving among, or the dead. The eternal torrent*
> *whirls all ages along in it, through both realms*
> *forever, and their voices are drowned out in its thunderous roar.*

This is, in the meantime, a powerful imagination, to say the least!

But this is Rilke projecting himself poetically, knowing perfectly well that he is *not* on the way to occupying such a sphere. On the contrary, at one time he swerved away from renunciation, and is now in the process of completing the pattern of life he opted for. This has brought him into deep areas of human alienation, which includes grief over separation from a beloved whom he cannot renounce. He is thus left in "need"; he must find a way of reconciling himself to the strain of the terrible existence that has come from his alienation; this he continues to endure, while imagining the possibility of being freed at last from such an existence. That old mythical idea of his continues to support him that speaks of a hero who will one day be "achieving his final birth" after his "downfall" (333). His immediate hope would seem to lie in what the world itself appears to be communicating of solidarity with him, beyond the pretenses and tyrannies of love, though this hopeful prospect is not pursued much further here. In *Malte* his focus had been on the tyranny of "being loved" in that form that has no regard for the free spirit of the soul who is being "loved", as in Rilke's recreation of the story of the Prodigal Son; in this First Elegy the focus is on the tyranny of continued attachment to the beloved even after inevitable disappointment.

Emotional love can, in any case, only bring painful disappointment, since

> *Nature, spent and exhausted, takes lovers back*
> *into herself, as if there were not enough strength*
> *to create them a second time.*
>
> (Mitchell 333)

The end of all is death, and yet we continue wilfully in such love; lovers continue to abound who are recklessly impassioned in their love, emotional and sexual. In this way they ensure their "downfall", having become in the meantime a "distraction" to themselves, and a "distraction" to others. Rilke knows that it is rather a matter of being entrusted with a "mission", which is to find a solution to the phenomenon of terrible existence in which humankind continues to languish by one ill-fated route or another. There is the self-defeating course of love in emotional and romantic terms as developed in the Elegy, and also, as we have seen, a social world in which the human spirit has been so profoundly defeated no love of any recognizable kind remains as an option for it, as this is conveyed in large parts of *Malte*.

There is then the abstract ideal of free love, "soaring, objectless love" (333) as illustrated by Gaspara and others: in the Elegy this ideal is implicitly associated with the somewhat unpromising process of a "singing" or "praising"of such love that is "never-attainable" (333); in *Malte* this love, associated with women, is otherwise succinctly described:

> *They hasten after the one they have lost, but with the very first steps that they take they already overtake him, and before them is only God.*
>
> (Hulse 151)

Rilke's relation to this last kind of love is somewhat convoluted, not being the love to which he is actually committed, whether he will or no, for under the whole great complex of swirling ideas to which he was giving himself, his attachment to Lou remained, in significantly earthly terms. There is no evidence in Rilke's life of his pursuing a Gaspara-type love in connection with anyone, for while Gaspara's love *is* finally objectless and can only have "God" as a distant goal, it begins as a complete, definitive love of someone, of a kind that Rilke himself never knew other than with Lou. If anything the Gaspara-love would have an application rather to the women whom Rilke himself abandoned or could not abide with, and as such would seem to serve as an elaborate form of compensation for the guilt he must have been feeling about this. On the other hand, there is also the equally serious problem of being overloved or possessed that informs Rilke's anguished re-writing of the story of the Prodigal Son, as we have seen above.

On yet another front, the transcendent power that Rilke is ready to extol in connection with those who died young has not been his poetic direction either. Rilke's poetry has given sign rather of tragic protest against cut-off youth, as in his two "Requiems," one dedicated to Clara's friend, Gretel, the other to Paula Becker. In his "Requiem" for Paula, his lament is on behalf of those who have been, very sadly and also maddeningly, diverted by the very pretense Rilke is seeking to expose in his Elegy, namely the pretense to attach and to be attached that a misled society is sold on and imposes upon one as if this were the first principle of living. Both the Gaspara-love and the transcendent young constitute for Rilke, in the end, merely abstractive supports: significantly real ideas inasmuch as Rilke pursues these with an impressive forcefulness (especially in the case of the Gaspara-type love, to which he returns at length in his letters at this time[94]) but nevertheless in the end merely ideas: they stand as forms of directive thought that would allow us to break loose somewhere in our spirit while we all continue to struggle with the multifarious forms of attachment that have us in their power. In this sense they serve essentially as forms of consolation.

Far more to the point of Rilke's experience is what he had described in *Malte* as the "love that has endured" and the "work" by which one continues to bolster oneself in "love" of that kind. In fact, the Elegy is nothing less than the comprehensive form Rilke had hit upon that allows him to pursue this "love" and this "work," theoretically, almost without limit. As such it allows him to make of himself, in the end, a poet of the whole scene. This includes his relationship to the process of renunciation he would at one time have wished to act on and that remains a constant other reference-point in the depths of his mind; his main reference-point is otherwise the many emotional thought-forms through which both he and all the rest of us continue to be attached to an earthly existence that we seem *unable* to renounce, with all the attendant ills that must also follow from this as a matter of course. It is this realistic dialectic that makes him precisely an *elegiac* poet rather than a romantic or a tragic one, let alone a Platonist (as in the Gaspara-line of thought); hence the utter suitability of the Elegy form Rilke was suddenly engaged in. There is, at the same time, another creative tension in these poems produced by the fact, which is paradoxically even celebrated, that such earthly entanglements as we suffer from have been and continue to be *our* experience; they seem to be what we are finally meant to accept, engage, and come to terms with on behalf of a fuller, more far-reaching resolution of terms that we may look forward to at some point in the distant future.

The Second Elegy

In Rilke's Second Elegy, which appears to have come through more than one week after the First Elegy, Rilke remains caught up in the theme of the futile attachment of lovers to their love. Even while insisting on the obvious impermanence of such love, he can see nevertheless how behind love pursued in this form lies the impulse to *find* permanence: "If only we too could discover a pure, contained/human place" (Mitchell 343). Still, in this Elegy Rilke brings his lovers face to face with the testimony of an ancient (Attic) art that insists on an attitude of "caution" in the expression of love because *it* is very much aware that "love" is inevitably associated with "departure" or loss, i.e., impermanence, which is why such "love" must be borne "gently" or "lightly" and not pursued beyond certain limits. Why, we will ask, would Rilke have concerned himself with this issue so much? It devolves on us, as a matter of final dignity, to break out from any and all self-defeating forms of life, also in the greatly misleading sphere of romantic "love". *Even so*, Rilke acknowledges that his lovers will be "astonished" to discover that it *is* finally about limits, since "our own heart always exceeds us" in any case, an undeniable fact that is not necessarily resolved by consciously seeking limits in love—or art. It is also that the "gods", by their own mysterious decree, will at any time "press down harder upon us", involve us suddenly in a deeper passion without our say, even where lightness in love has been cultivated: another measure this of the fact that "there is no place where we can remain". And that is our complaint, and why we inevitably lament.

The Third, Sixth, Tenth, and Ninth (beginnings)

What else will have conspired to keep us subjected, we seem to hear Rilke asking in the Third Elegy, which was at least begun while at Duino. There is the profoundly subverting power of dark passion in the "blood", which Rilke powerfully traces here to ancient, mythical origins:

> *Oh the dark Neptune inside our blood, with his appalling*
> *trident.*
> *Oh the dark wind from his breast out of that spiraled conch.*
>
> (Mitchell 345)

Rilke had often addressed the issue of the "blood" before, as we have seen, but almost always from the point of view of what should and must be simply resisted for the higher good of the genuinely creative spiritual life (as in *The Book of Hours*, and *The Book of Images*). In this Elegy the point of view is not so simple: the challenge of the "blood" from *its* profound depths turns out to be unalterably real and fundamental, and hardly to be resisted so easily. This abysmal influence of the "blood" for its part "remains", and this is over and against the power whence the inspiration of "love" springs ("the lover's desire for the face/of his beloved"), which Rilke traces to the "stars/... the pure constellations". No more will be said about this fundamental opposition until Rilke returned to this Elegy when in Paris in the autumn of 1913, over a year and a half later, as discussed below.

In the meantime, some of the first lines of the Sixth Elegy were also put down during Rilke's stay at Duino. These highlight yet another contrast: between our tendency in our love-passion to identify with its "blossoming" over and above its "fruit" (our tendency, that is, to give ourselves to passion especially for its own sake) and the exemplary life of the fig tree, which itself almost forgoes "blossoming" altogether:

> *Fig-tree, for such a long time I have found meaning*
> *in the way you almost completely omit your blossoms*
> *and urge your pure mystery, unproclaimed*
> *into the early ripening fruit ...*
>
> *But we still linger, alas,*
> *we, whose pride is in the blossoming ...*
>
> (Mitchell 365)

This contrast Rilke will take up again fully, fittingly while sojourning, some six months later, in the ancient town of Ronda (at the far tip of southern Spain). While still at Duino, he would also produce the first fifteen lines of the original Tenth Elegy as well as a scribble of other lines, the beginning of the Ninth.

His lines from the Tenth Elegy are an extraordinary statement of hope and acceptance of his greatly troubled lot, considering just how deeply submerged in it he was in this period of his life: there will come a time, Rilke greatly believes, when, "emerging at last from the violent insight" (401), he will be "singing out" his "jubilation and praise to assenting angels". At that time, Rilke speculates, it will seem to him that he ought to have cherished his moments of "anguish" more. We always project ourselves beyond the experience of our present pain, he notes, prematurely seeking its end, and thereby lose the opportunity to learn more about ourselves from the experience than we could otherwise, thus "squandering" ourselves. These ongoing experiences of trouble and pain are *also* "really/seasons of *us* .../... *our* inborn landscape", as much a part of who we are as our moments of happiness, and indeed quite as truly unique and special evidence of the "home" of our existence:

> *Though they are really*
> *seasons of **us**, **our** winter-*
> *enduring foliage, ponds, meadows, **our** inborn landscape,*
> *where birds and reed-dwelling creatures are at home.*
>
> (401)*

It is as our own "creatures" that we naturally inhabit this other seemingly more forbidding "landscape" of ours. Finally, to this whole production while at Duino Rilke would add one more challenging thought that begins the Ninth Elegy: "why then have to be human—and escaping from fate, keep longing for fate?" (383), why when "this interval of being can be spent serenely/in the form of a laurel"—if only it *could* to any extensive degree. Rilke's explorations of the issue of our strangely divided existence would continue...

This, however, is as much as Rilke could bring, while at Duino, of content to the potentially all-containing form that had been inspired into him in the case of the elegy. Even so this Duino moment would cast its shadow in time far forward. The First Elegy was composed on January 20th 1912, the Second sometime towards the end of January/early February, as were also the few lines set down for the Third Elegy and the Tenth, the very few lines of the Ninth appearing

---

*The additional emphasis here, in "us" and "our", is mine.

in early March. A full year later in early 1913, while in Ronda, Rilke continued with the Sixth Elegy, and in the autumn of that year, when back in Paris, he rounded out the Third, the Sixth, and the Tenth. The Fourth Elegy, which was not composed until late 1915, two full years after that, really belongs to a new phase of Rilke's poetic career that is only here foreshadowed and that does not come to full expression until some seven years beyond that time, when Rilke settled in at Muzot, in the winter of 1922, when the rest of the Elegies were written and the whole at last completed.*

***

Already by mid-to-late February of 1912, that great original impulse of the Duino moment (the impulse of his Original Other) is petering out, and Rilke is once again "complaining [to the Princess] about his restlessness and inability to concentrate" (Wydenbruck 37). By the 1st of March he is again writing Lou in that same dire mode of self-oppression and desperate need that had always accompanied the attacks he suffered in his "body" from the influence of an over-charged "blood". Unlike when he wrote Lou when on the verge of a breakthrough, the symptoms at this time are really and truly again dominating him, driving him as ever to generalize his life in these terms:

> *Many a day I look at all of created life with the fear that some pain may erupt in it and make it scream, so great is my dread of the abuse that the body in so many ways inflicts on the soul ...*

> *knowledge ... passes into my blood, mixes there with God knows what ...*
>
> (Snow, Rilke, 195)

> *as if a few drops of lemon-juice had gotten into my blood.*
>
> (197)

---

*Stephen Mitchell, somewhat predictably, dates the First Elegy sometime "between January 12 and January 16" (Mitchell 551). This looks like a judgment based on the somewhat frenzied language Rilke used when writing the Princess on the noted dates. Rilke's language in these letters can easily read as if it was referring to his having composed the Elegy, but it does not, as explained above (see p.294).

Two weeks later, there is more talk of the same, of his "malady", and its "evil" (197), and that, quite in spite of himself, he finds he is always "on the side of the tempter" (197). *His Malte-nature has taken him over again,* and he is once again ironically and sadly turning to Lou for comfort, she who had long ago brought this "malady" back upon him and kept him in it over all these years.* Only two months after his great moment at Duino, he is thrust back upon a mere "nostalgia" for what once was:

> *Sometimes I see myself as if on the path to a joy ... but as if I could no longer make it all the way there ... the joy suddenly scatters, dissolves before I can grasp it, and everything is reduced to the nostalgia of once having been capable of doing so ...*
>
> (197)

Once again, his thought is that it is Lou who could have helped, if only he had turned to her and she had been there after he had put all of himself into the writing of *Malte*:

> *Had I but written you then, the very moment **Malte** was completed ... things would never have arrived at that difficult stage which I had to go through last year which ... did some internal damage to my soul ... because it warped my spirit ...*
>
> (198)

Nevertheless, in spite of what he is saying here, it is not to Lou that Rilke turns to now. On the contrary he will once again stop writing her, not to contact her again for another nine months...

His crying need was now rather to get away again, to leave Duino, and he stops over in Venice to begin with. There his main experience stems from his sudden, unexpected meeting with Eleanora Duse. He describes her (to the Princess) as the one woman he had had an especially burning wish to meet.[95] He was to get more than he had bargained for. Everything went awry, and significantly because of that very problem of attachment in love, between herself and her woman lover, our hopeless entanglement in which Rilke had just been lamenting in his Elegies. Her own story at this time was, uncannily, a microcosm of the very situation Rilke had been rehearsing

---

*This being the whole demonstration of Volume 1 of this study.

in the Elegies: she was at this time, after three years away from the stage, unable to properly come through in her creative life (futilely conceiving a return to the stage); her love affair was failing, eventually falling apart—at which point the Duse left Venice. By an additionally sad irony Rilke found himself over an entire summer futilely trying to mediate in that love-affair in the hope that something might be salvaged for the Duse, to allow her to take up her career again.

Luckily another course was opened to Rilke in a later episode when back briefly in Duino where he took part in a number of séances (he might have been back in the world of the Brahes family as presented in *Malte*). At one of these séances some details were spoken by the ghost of an "Unknown Woman" that confirmed for Rilke the resolve he had already taken to travel down to Toledo, Spain where he planned to study the work of El Greco, for "spiritual renewal"[96]. About this plan, wishfully and somewhat pathetically, Rilke confided to his publisher: "perhaps I'm exaggerating but it seems to me that this journey could be as significant for my progress as that to Russia was once."[97] He was still feeding on the past, for the reason that, once again, he felt he did not belong to himself, and had not belonged since Russia when he was at least momentarily compensated for the sacrifice of his own vision. (He had stopped belonging to himself, in fact, for a good year before that.*) Another way to look at his distant journey to Spain, which in the end took him as far south as Ronda, is as an expression of the same impulse he had indulged when he set out for Arabia, before his long stop-over amidst the vast spaces of Duino almost a year later. He was looking to create for himself that sense of remote distance from his own preoccupations, on the basis of which he had finally come through when at Duino. Such necessary distance from himself might allow him to recover some of the power that had reached him, when at Duino, for dealing with the large issues he had been struggling with for some time: "the state of expectancy I'm still in since the last great effort may also be a factor in my desire to try this new direction, in which I suspect the most varied lines of my work will converge."[98]

The yield, even so, would not be so great as far as immediate work on the Elegies goes. Otherwise Rilke proves to be, as ever, a

---

*All of this detailed in Volume 1.

shrewd aesthetic commentator both on Toledo and on Ronda. From the "uplifting" landscapes of these cities he sensed at once that he was indeed "on the path to a wider participation in the ultimate realities" (Snow, *Rilke*, 201). Too soon, however, "discomforts" also "sprang up alongside" so that he was at last compelled to focus on whatever arrangement those landscapes might offer him of "a better distribution of my tormenting blood". He was again "failing" in his hope to find the grand influences that would offer him a change for the better. He did, in spite of this, have his moments. In "The Spanish Trilogy" (Mitchell 103) Rilke is once again, as of old, in a prayerful mood, imploring of himself that he might hold together in the face of the many influences from the world that continue to "pierce" him, as he puts it, rather than, as they should, "penetrate" him (Snow, *Rilke*, 201). In "Ariel" (Mitchell 109) he is once again contemplating his relationship to his art in its association with nature, wondering whether he has not already "let go" of it despite himself, and what a "consummate" (111) achievement it would be to make oneself free of it (as Shakespeare's Prospero finally does). In "The Almond Tree in Blossom" (101) Rilke continues to consider one of his reigning thoughts, which is if only "we" could learn, like the almond tree, how to "blossom" properly, without obsessing as we do with the expectation of permanence in our blossoming (thus dispossessing ourselves, among other things, of the power to face death properly). Otherwise at this time Rilke is still living very much in the past. To Lou, to whom he returns in his letters at this time, recalling how he had written her at just about the same time the previous year when at Duino, he laments that if only he could be in Schmargendorf again or in Gottingen where they had had their life together (Snow, *Rilke*, 203) and as when "The Book of Hours began": if only it had been so, he speculates, "who knows what could have been [further] achieved" (205) with the great inspiration that had come his way recently and "what was then delivered to my power". He is for the moment once again, in spite of what he had recently accomplished, which were yet but "fragments" (205), at the mercy of his continued dependency on Lou.

More of the Sixth Elegy

What he does manage to do, while in Ronda, is to continue with the 6th Elegy, though this will be all for now. Here he was returning to his old concept of the Hero who is possessed of the power to prevail over all those impediments to a positively creative human life that seem only ever to stymy the rest of us. He develops the concept here perhaps only for the first time with a relevant maturity, moving somewhat beyond his presentation of it hitherto as a largely mythical projection. In the succession of unfinished thoughts of which he had been delivered at the time of the Duino-impulse: in the First and the Second Elegy thoughts of renouncing the attachments of love; in the Third Elegy thoughts of the depths of lustful passion in the blood; and in the Tenth Elegy of a time when a higher unity will at last apprevail and all will be well again—the additional thought of a Hero who actually exists, who can already prevail by virtue of a power to move in a dimension that sends him past all temptations in love, fills in another gap. Some "few", Rilke claims, have managed to set the tone for actually resisting that "temptation to blossom" without regard to the "fruit" of love (Mitchell 365) of which he has been speaking already in this Elegy (begun at Duino). Such instances of the hero belong with those who have died young (who were a key focus in Rilke's First Elegy); both can embrace life in all the fullness of its "danger" (365), both lie beyond resistance to the life-and-death process, like the fig tree (the initial subject of this Elegy) and the almond tree, both of which had at this time fully captured the attention of Rilke's imagination as symbolizing this process. In contrast with us who "linger", "whose pride is in blossoming", heroes "plunge on ahead" (365):

> *He* [the hero] *lives in continual ascent,*
> *moving on into the ever-changed constellation*
> *of perpetual danger.*
>
> (Mitchell 365)

Who, we will ask, could live up to this forbidding ideal of living? We have seen (in Volume 1) that Rilke thought Rodin did for much of his life, perhaps also Cézanne. In any case, it was for Rilke more a matter of "hearing" the hero in them, who now comes through to him from the depths of mythical imagination in himself:

> *Few could find him there. But*
> *Fate, which is silent about us, suddenly grows inspired*
> *and sings him into the storm of his onrushing world.*
> *I hear no one like **him**. All at once I am pierced*
> *By his darkened voice, carried on the streaming air.*
>
> (365)

This is a mighty projection, especially in the last two lines. It is remarkable that in this burdensomely somber period of his life, feeling largely incapable himself Rilke should yet be able to imagine capability so powerfully: in contrast with himself—the ideal achiever. Imagining such a capable nature developing from as far back as childhood and supported by the right education for it—this had been another of those ambitious revisionary projects Rilke had been entertaining for some time, and this just because *his* had been so *un*-ideal a childhood. He returns to the idea yet again here:

> *Then how gladly I would hide from the longing to be once*
> *again*
> *oh a boy once again, with my life before me …*
> *… and reading of Samson*
> *how from his mother first nothing, then everything, was born.*
>
> (367)

If he would "hide" from this "longing", this is because his had *not* been such a childhood, whose so problematic consequences he has been contending with ever since, but also because his "longing" to have had it so has been so strong, his imagination of such an achiever being otherwise so strong.

Besides the usual troubling matters brought up to Lou by Rilke, just before this material was produced, was naturally the idea of meeting with her again: "if only we could see each other, dear Lou" (Snow, *Rilke*, 205). Lou's response to this renewed overture was inevitable, even calculating: "it should be possible for us to be together quietly and without any effort at all on invisible paths" (206), until, that is, such time as they would meet, as she surmised, over the course of the summer, a good many months away. In the meantime she offered him the very picture of himself that he knew only too well but which she was saying was the one that would have to define him as a writer, since he had been called as the one "who most deeply experiences all that defines the *essence* of being human", a "strange capacity" that "almost cruelly" he would have to exercise whether from bliss ("given over to all things") *or* horror ("mixed up with everything isolated or unclaimed"—206). Losing himself as he did to his ideal achiever after this account of his own troubled condition was but another instance of Rilke's heroic capacity for strong imagination achieved by abstraction from his actual condition.

Back in Paris by the spring at Lou's prompting (he had been considering going elsewhere after Spain, in spite of an apartment already reserved for him in Paris), Rilke was to write a few other poems which show him still much abstracted from the newly conferred task of the Elegies. In "The Heavens" he is much caught up once again in the pure inspirations of night and sky and stars, about which he says: "Let me put aside/every desire, every relationship/except this one" (Mitchell 115). Yet this hope so desperately adhered to is contravened significantly by Rilke's never-satisfied "longing" for his beloved, as in "Startle me, Music, with rhythmical fury!"

> *Why do you long for the hidden face of the distant beloved?—*
> ....
> *she in whose absence you are withering ...*
>
> (119)

He feels he should be filling the over-arching spaces of the world with the music of his craft, since only if he can do so, he speculates, will he make himself worthy of being restored to his beloved. But it is just because he was once deprived of his beloved (and continues to be deprived of her) and is unable to stop longing for her that he finds himself finally incapable of this music, even when invoking it so strongly as here. Even when desperately invoking this music, it is the absence of his beloved that finally claims his being. Needless to say, by now Lou had turned at once into the figure of the ideal Beloved of the past, who at one time was not so remote, and the figure of the ideal Beloved of the future, remote almost by definition.

Rilke's unchanged dependency on Lou is as clear here as ever (belying the vain hope expressed that he might yet be "startled" instead by "the fury" of his invoked craft), and it is as well for him that two months after writing this poem, in July of 1913, he found himself once again admitted to her company. She had been for ever so long the Prime Mover in his life-story, and she would have this effect yet again in this latest period of time. In mid-July they would spend two full weeks together, followed in September through October by another five weeks of active association. Then coming away from her again (which one biographer actually describes as a case of "becom[ing] irritated at having been with the same person for too long"[99]), towards the end of October he drifted back to Paris whence he wrote her to confirm all that had been brought into focus for him from their time together and the conversations they had shared. She had set him right again, he says, by confirming that he was still the same Rilke who would be producing again and continue to produce: "You have shown me that I am still somehow the same" (Snow, *Rilke*, 224). It is a less than complete confirmation (re: "somehow"), and the same he was, but in an opposite sense. As a consequence of his confidential time with her, he had been thrust back, as we shall see, upon all that had led him down to this point, back to *the terms by which he had been deprived of her*, and with this to the Third and the Tenth Elegy, which were taken up again at this time.

Back to the Third and the Tenth

In the Third Elegy he returns to the reality of the "blood" in himself and its oppressive "darkness", by which he had been defeated with Lou, and in the Tenth to "how" he lost her and "kept sobbing, long ago, for her", the two events being, of course, connected: in the Tenth, he adds: "if only I could forget" (Mitchell 403). His hope as expressed to Lou on returning to Paris *is* that he "can grow used to myself again in the good old sense: contented … my happiness, the happiness, long ago, of my most solitary hours" (Snow, *Rilke*, 225). This "happiness", he adds, he has since been inclined to project onto his experience with every woman he has met, knowing at the same time that it could not be found with any of them. This is the "happiness", to make the point again, that ought at one time really to have been possible for him, and that, in some depth of himself, he is still hopelessly looking for, at the expense of integration in the present:

I would be satisfied with everything if only it were wholly mine
again, without seeping out into longing.

(225)

Rilke would just have his "happiness" be, and not be approaching it from the outside as a pathetic "longing", these terms having, sadly, separated out from the time they were one experience when at Florence.* Rilke notes that long ago, when putting the *New Poems* together, he had seen what would be required of him: it is the thought that more and more will be taking him over as he proceeds with the Elegies: "To let all this slip past without/ desiring", to which he adds, however: "And I who did nothing *but* desire" (225), and who, moreover, will be left with the consequences of that desire, till all is finally worked out. In the meantime the stage had been set: "What's left to do is up to me and the Angel, if only we stick together, he and I, and you [Lou] from afar."

For one great, miraculous moment the Angel of Rilke's Original Other, as we have seen, had come through again, beyond all sense and reason. The effect of that visitation was to shock Rilke out of his impasse and drive him forth on his way again. This visiting Angel, as we have also seen, is at once altered by Rilke into the compound form that reflects to him what had in the meantime become the "bliss" and the "horror" of his own life, the "beauty" and the "terror", that has left him in dire "need"—the "need" in the end, of a resolution of these terms. It would be up to Rilke now to carry on on his own by building on the impulse the Angel's visitation had bestowed upon him. For her part Lou remained at once the confounding and the saving Third. There was still a very long way to go…

The Duino moment, as such, would end with further work on the Third and the (original) Tenth Elegy, marked by poetry that, for now, would be in a largely recapitulative mode, reflecting the terms of Rilke's life as they had shown themselves up to this time.** Taking up

---

*"Longing" and "happiness" being Rilke's key terms back then, as his Florence Diary testifies. See above p.51ff and p.147ff.

**Rilke would also return to the Sixth Elegy to which he would add a few more lines. Somewhat pathetically, these lines contrast sharply with the general downhearted tenor of his writing at this time; their focus is on "the hero" as one who is "lifted … up, beyond love" (Mitchell 367).

again with the Third Elegy, in late autumn 1913, Rilke was coming to terms with the oppressive darkness in himself perhaps as never before. He had no choice but to do so. It may have been Lou who was responsible for thrusting him back into this condition at a time when a shared and equal life of love between them would have lifted him at last from this darkness—she had been unable to share herself with him in this way, belying the love that was in fact theirs—but the harm had been done, and Rilke was left dealing with the consequences of it. Naturally, he would have to think that *he* was to blame for his darkness in the first place, for he was left with no choice but to deal with it, although that was far from being the only perspective or view he had of his predicament. He could not in any case give up a form of love between them that he knew had been forever established in him and that continued to have as much validity as the actual life he had inherited and had been compelled to assume. As we have seen, a whole other ontology and eschatology would have emerged from such a love that was shared at one time.

In the Third Elegy, once again an account with reference to a general "child" and a general male "lover" takes Rilke himself up into its compass. He is here accounting for himself, his own dark nature, known from the time *he* was a child. The account rehearses at some point the same material gone into in *Malte*, for example, where the poem highlights a child's relationship to a Mother who is blessed with the power to dispel the forces of darkness by which her child feels oppressed and haunted:

> *you made it harmless: and out of the refuge of your heart*
> *you mixed a more human space with his night-space.*
> *... set down the lamp, not in that darkness, but in*
> *your own nearer presence ...*
> *... [s]o powerful was your presence*
> (Mitchell 347)

This child's "fate" was in this way put off ("delayed for a while"), for his encounter with a "world that is alien" was inevitable. Even in its outerness the world bears an inner threat: it is a "night-space" that is also a "surging abyss", and in it "his restless future" also lies contained. We are familiar with these notions from *Malte*: this child

> *seemed protected ... But inside: who could ward off,*
> *who could divert, the floods of origin inside him?*
>
> (347)

This Mother's child is described as lulled to sleep: "sleeping,/ yes but dreaming." At this point, a still deeper dimension to this threatening world is brought to light by virtue of the poem's powerful mythologizing technique taken up again from the first lines of this poem written when at Duino. Drawing almost certainly from the directions of thought encountered in the developing psychoanalysis at this time, with its focus on dreaming and the unconscious world opened up to us in that sphere, the poet conceives of this child as already given over ("submitted") to an interior "wilderness" that is itself perversely "loved", and that takes him from its at first "primal forest", through "his own roots",

> *... down into more ancient blood, to ravines*
> *where Horror lay, still glutted with his fathers. And every*
> *Terror knew him ...*
> *Yes, Atrocity smiled ...*
>
> > *... How could he help*
> *loving what smiled at him?*
>
> (349)

In this deep sphere of our existence, the collective unconscious of psychoanalysis and the "common distress" of history, where violent madness figures largely, meet quite sensationally, as if we had here the historical view in *Malte* again but in miniature, encapsulated, referred further to an unconscious source in every one of "us" that was beginning to be better known in Rilke's time. In this collective unconscious, being born into it ("already while you [Mother] carried him inside you .../... dissolved in the water that makes the embryo weightless"), the child discovers, in spite of himself, that he loves *also* all these "seething multitudes" of human souls that he finds there

> *... the fathers lying in our depths*
> *like fallen mountains; also the dried-up river-beds*
> *of ancient mothers—; also the whole*
> *soundless landscape under the clouded or clear*
> *sky of its destiny ...*
>
> (349)

All of this, the poet explains in desperation, "preceded you", now addressing the "beloved" to this male figure. All of this, the poet knows, has been stirred in this male figure on his suddenly "desiring" her. Earlier in this Third Elegy, the poet has appealed to the beloved to take her lover into her "heart" where he might find "shelter", even though Rilke knows too well that her lover is, deep down, at a loss with the darkness in himself:

> *Call him ...*
> *but you can't quite call him away from those dark*
> *companions.*
> *Of course, he **wants** to escape, and he does; relieved, he nestles*
> *into your sheltering heart, takes hold, and begins himself.*
> *But did he ever begin himself, really?*
>
> (345)

In spite of the actual facts, as we have elaborated on them in this study, Rilke is now pursuing his account as if in the rupture between himself and Lou it is he who was essentially to blame. He pretends that all was lost to begin with, and that what Lou could have offered was a hope that could never have materialized in any event. He sees it here as a case of not grasping that he had never been possessed of the love shared with Lou in the first place. He was bound to lose her one way or the other, generalizing this as an incontrovertible fact of life in love: "that is how, always, you lost:/never as one who possesses" (Mitchell 403). And yet—and this is the main point—the poet also affirms: "Far too much you belong to grief. If you *could* forget her" (403); reference was made, in the part of the Tenth Elegy written out at Duino, of "my hidden weeping", a phrase that is now explained. The case still, for now, is that Rilke cannot forget. And it is because he cannot forget that, as he understood the matter, he would be finally unable to find happiness with any other woman. *In spite of which!* when the beautiful and gifted Magda von Hattenberg suddenly came into his life in early January of 1914, he could not help but throw himself headlong into what seemed to portend his one real chance of ever finding happiness with another woman, never to be known otherwise. He was hoping against hope, even though the outcome was more than predictable. When Rilke proceeded to recount his failure in this special case to Lou, "in a series of anguished letters"[100], Lou could not keep from weeping herself—"weeping" with the knowledge of his plight? his plight, and hers? For the moment, in a poem written just beyond the debacle with Magda, simply titled "Lament", sadly enough Rilke could only return to the still-commanding motif of his First Elegy:

> *Whom will you cry to, heart? More and more lonely,*
> *your path struggles on through incomprehensible*
> *mankind. All the more futile perhaps*
> *for keeping to its direction,*
> *keeping on toward the future,*
> *toward what has been lost.*
>
> (Mitchell 131)

> *You who never arrived*
> *in my arms, Beloved, who were lost*
> *from the start.*
>
> (125)

> *You, Beloved, who are all*
> *the gardens I have ever gazed at,*
> *longing.* *

---

*The last two quotations, from the poem "You who never arrived".

Endnotes

(Bibliographical references for the authors in bold
to be found under "Main References" above.)

1. **Freedman** 226. Cf. **Prater** 121: "She was far from well, and unable to get out very much, and he took long walks alone."

2. For some of this time Lou continued to be bed-ridden from the mysterious ailment that had come upon her on their separating four years earlier. I have already touched on this in Volume 1, on p.18 and p.47, including notes 11 and 36.

3. Thus Freedman 226: "Rainer's long wish list of problems to be discussed could not be fully exhausted."

4. Freedman 228.

5. Freedman 228. Freedman elsewhere describes it as "that titled society of the affluent and culturally engaged, whose castles were glittering citadels of artistic taste and intellectual exchange". (239)

6. Welcome because of the financial reprieve it offered him (as the invited guest to many); he was thereby able to hang on to what income he could manage himself to benefit also his family (wife and child).

7. Short-lived as this was at least in her company, since the Countess died very suddenly less than a year after Rilke's stay with her in July. However, her family and especially her sister continued to offer Rilke refuge and support through much of the next immediate period of his life.

8. These are his great narrative poems: they end the first part of *New Poems* with a bang: notably, "Orpheus, Eurydice, Hermes", "The Birth of Venus", and "The Tombs of the Hetaerae".

9. Rodin was overwhelmed with visitors and art dealers at this time, in some ill-temper that so many precious occasions for his own work

had been lost, even as Rilke was beginning to manifest more openly his own displeasure over the same constriction on his work occasioned by too much in the way of secretarial duties (see Prater 132-133).

10. Lou went so far as to propose to Clara that the police be called on Rilke for neglecting his financial duties towards her and their child, Ruth. However, the arrangement Rilke and Clara had made years before was that each living separately (and often in different cities) would be responsible for his/her income, while Ruth would be kept for the most part by Clara's parents in Oberland. Rilke would provide additionally for Clara and Ruth when his resources permitted. There were times, as at this specific time, when Rilke, battling impecuniousness, could not provide, and he could only then re-affirm his basic position: "his calling was that of an artist. His main obligation was 'work, only work'" (Freedman 263). Still, Lou's admonition to Clara to call the "police" would no doubt have "hurt" (263).

11. Various reasons may be proposed for the rare correspondence (which was, in fact, almost nill on Lou's side). Having re-established their presence in each other's lives, and at last found peace and thus a new sense of direction in each case, there may not have been any immediate need for much correspondence, but it is also that Rilke had in this present period no special need for calling on Lou for her voice in his affairs. At this point in time he knew his way better, as it happens, than she did (see Volume 1) and was, moreover, spared for now any immediate struggle with the ghost of negativity which, from the time of their first estrangement, had always been, and would recur as, perhaps the chief cause of communication, and the main challenging matter, between them.

12. "The Voices" (comprised, in fact, of ten short poems) was written in June of 1906, towards the end of his production for this volume, the Third part of "The Tsars" also written in that year, while a few, e.g., the "Pont du Caroussel" and "The Ashanti", originate from his Paris period begun in the fall of 1902.

13. Prater 141.

14. Freedman 262.

15. Being, also, "the least familiar of Rilke's major works". See Edward **Snow**, **tr.**, *The Book of Images*, ix.

16. Snow, *Images*, ix.

17. Snow, *Images*, ix.

18. Snow, *Images*, xii. See also my Volume 1 to this study, endnote 119.

19. He is aware of it all as an inevitable progression as early as the Florence Diary when he was but twenty-two; see **Snow, tr., *Diaries***, 78: "With each work that one raises out of oneself, one creates space for some new strength." All was in relation to that consummate achievement in later age which, without his consciously pretending to this, is yet what Rilke saw himself working towards: "And the last space, which comes after a long process, will bear everything within itself that is active and essential around us; for it will be the greatest space, filled with all strength."

20. Much might be learned that would be of aid to the aspiring artist if we were to bring more attention to these early years of development. In his book on Rodin, Rilke considers that unearthing the early biography of the ideally progressing artist should be one of the main projects of a more thorough art criticism that would lay the ground for stronger artistic creation generally from the outset. Rilke had an especially strong sense of this need just because his own early life had been so problematically ill-fitted to such progression.

21. See again n.19.

22. Consider the line: "back then, O how complete I was."

23. "The Bride" and "The Silence" could be read in quite the opposite way as addresses to God (as Groom and as Beloved) seen as a primary or ultimate reality if finally elusive, but I do not believe Rilke was writing in this vein here. In this period, the experience of God remained for Rilke its own experience and has quite another import. See my commentary on this in the next paragraph.

24. Re: "then I must pour myself out of my hands/into the gardens of/dark blue ..."

25. "The Guardian", as it happens.

26. Contrast the "darkness" into which the dispossessed lover despairingly casts herself in "The Bride". See p.202 and n.24.

27. Volume 1, p.58.

28. See Susan Ranson, tr., *Rainer Maria Rilke's "The Book of Hours."* Rochester, NY: Camden House, 2012, 45.

29. Ranson 47.

30. This we have seen in Volume 1. See p.93 passim.

31. See Volume 1, from p.123.

32. *Ibid.*

33. Snow, *Images*, xii.

34. See Volume 1, pp.138-139.

35. See above, p.209.

36. Snow, *Images*, xiv.

37. **Snow, *New Poems*, 170.**

38. Snow, *New Poems*, 170.

39. Here Rilke reverses the Hadrian story. See Snow, *New Poems*, 191. The historical Hadrian responded to the death, in fact, "with extravagant acts of mourning".

40. Snow, *New Poems*, 170.

41. Snow, *New Poems*, 4.

42. Snow, *New Poems*, 5.

43. Snow, *New Poems*, 178.

44. Snow, *New Poems*, 178.

45. See letter to Hugo Heller, June 12, 1909, in **Greene 1**, 345.

46. See the letter to Rodin, December 29, 1908, in Greene 1, 341: "to make prose rhythmic one must go deep into oneself"; also the letter to Anton Kippenberg, January 2, 1909, in Greene 1, 344: "I am training for myself a massive, enduring prose."

47. Letter to the Countess Lili Kanitz-Menar, January 2, 1909, in Greene 1, 342.

48. Letter to Anton Kippenberg, in Greene 1, 344.

49. Letter to Jacob Baron Uexküll, August 19, 1909, in Greene 1, 346.

50. Letter to Karl Von der Heydt, August 5, 1909, in Greene 1, 346.

51. Re: "a game", said of the *New Poems*, which seemed to this cor-

respondent comparatively limited by their "hard objectivity and un-feeling quality". Letter to Jacob Baron Uexküll, Greene 1, 348.

52. Letter to Jacob Baron Uexküll, August 19, 1909, in Greene 1, 347.

53. Letter to Jacob Baron Uexküll, August 19, 1909, in Greene 1, 347.

54. Letter to Anton Kippenberg, January 2, 1909, in Greene 1, 344.

55. See, e.g., George C. Schoolfield, "*Die Aufrzeichmungen des Malte Laurids Brigge*" from *A Companion to the Works of Rainer Maria Rilke*, ed., Erica A. Metzger and Michael M. Metzger, Rochester NY: Camden House, 2001, 161: "The restless, imperious death of the chamberlain is connected with his strength of will."

56. A scene that, in respect of this "horrible unease", otherwise invokes the main theme of the novel which focuses on the questioning of God and the terrible.

57. The episode with the man in the restaurant has been grossly misinterpreted in the criticism on Rilke. See, for example, Walter H. Sokel, "The Devolution of the Self in *The Notebooks of Malte Laurids Brigge*" in *Rilke: The Alchemy of Alienation*, ed. Frank Baron et al., The Regents Press of Kansas, 1980, 177, and 186-187. This man in the restaurant is not sitting there just about to die or already dead, as thought by Sokel and others: such a case would not be especially interesting in the context of Malte's experience since this is full of consideration of the cases of death, the dead, and the dying. This man is suffering, while still alive, from the extraordinary and extreme condition of self-withdrawal (a form of acute schizophrenia) that I am describing: "Yet he knew he was now making his withdrawal from everything: not only from humankind. One moment more and all of it would have lost its meaning ... While I do still offer resistance." (**Hulse** 34) The reference in this same section to the experience of "somebody dying" who "no longer recognizes anyone" is by way of clarifying the situation of the man *by analogy*. It is not the man's literal case.

58. There is a similar movement, in a rather different context, to find God's being behind the terrible, in *The Book of Hours*.

59. Not, of course, that Beethoven did not have an inner concern or Ibsen an outer concern, but this is not how Malte focuses in on them.

60. See, for example, respectively "A Clean, Well-Lighted Place" (1933) and *Nausea* (1938).

61. Are we to hear an ironic echo of St. Paul in these words?

62. An echo this of Ecclesiastes.

63. E.g., "The Temptation of St. Anthony." See Hulse 174, n.38.

64. Cf. "The existence of the terrible in every particle of the air. You breathe it in as part of something transparent; but within you it precipitates ..." (Hulse 48)

65. She is cited in a letter to Anton Kittenberg, on Good Friday (March 25th) 1910, in Greene 1, 360.

66. In a letter to the Countess Manon zu Solms-Laubach dated April 11th 1910, in Greene 1, 362.

67. In a letter to Princess Marie Von Thurn und Taxis, his new aristocratic patron and confidante whom he met after completing *Malte*, in **Wydenbruck** 12, italics mine.

68. In the same letter to the Countess Manon in Greene 1, 362.

69. In his letter to Karl von der Heydt, August 5th 1909, in Greene 1, 346.

70. Greene 1, 337. In this and the following eight references, in letters to Clara in the fall of 1907 and the fall of 1908.

71. Greene 1, 337.

72. Greene 1, 315.

73. Greene 1, 316.

74. Greene 1, 316.

75. Greene 1, 315.

76. Greene 1, 337. Cf. Nietzsche's Zarathustra?

77. Greene 1, 315.

78. Greene 1, 311.

79. See above p.256.

80. To Anton Kittenberg in the Good Friday letter 1910, in Greene 1, 361.

81. In a letter to the Countess Manon zu Solms-Laubach written

three weeks after the letter to his publisher, in Greene 1, 362.

82. In a letter to Princess Marie, his new aristocratic patron and confidante, in Wydenbruck 9.

83. Spoken by Princess Marie in her *Reminiscences*, first published in
1932. See Wydenbruck 10.

84. Also from the Princess's *Reminiscences*, in Wydenbruck 11.

85. In Wydenbruck 12. This and the next three main quotes from the
same letter to the Princess, dated 30 August 1910.

86. See n.84.

87. Emphasis mine.

88. Again, emphasis mine.

89. Emphasis mine.

90. See (1960) "The Structure and Dynamics of the Psyche," *CW* 8
¶69. Princeton: Princeton University Press.

91. See (1954) "The Practice of Psychotherapy," *CW* 16 ¶19, 2nd ed.,
Princeton: Princeton University Press.

92. See Sue Mehrtens, "Is All Lost If We Are Going Backwards?
Jung on Regression", The Jungian Center for the Spiritual Sciences,
Waterbury, Vermont: jungiancenter.org/lost-going-backwards-jung-
regression/

References for quotations are to the *Collected Works*, Princeton Univ.
Press, in sequence [a]_CW5 ¶631. [b] CW8 ¶67. [c] CW13 ¶332. [d]
CW5 ¶332. [e] CW13 ¶332. [f] Ibid. [g] Ibid. ¶313. [h] CW11 ¶159.

93. From the Princess's *Reminiscences*.

94. See **Greene 2,** 46, in a letter to Annette Kolb dated January 23,
1912.

95. Prater 212.

96. Freedman 349.

97. Prater 214.

98. Prater 214.

99. Freedman 371.

100. Freedman 377.

BREAKDOWN OF CHAPTERS

---

*All the poems from each Part are covered and discussed in sequence.

**The first five chapters present all poems from the two parts of *New Poems*. The subject of the "Requiem" is Paula Becker.

III.
The Duino Moment

Volume 3

Coming to Completion
(1914-1926)

Contents

Main References

Greene, Jane Bannard and M.D. Herter Norton, ed. and tr., *Letters of Rainer Maria Rilke 1910-1926*. New York: Norton, 1969.

Mitchell, Stephen, ed., and tr., *Ahead of All Parting: The Selected Poetry and Prose of Rainer Maria Rilke*. New York: Random House, Modern Library Edition, 1995.

Snow, Edward, ed. and tr., *Rilke and Andreas Salome: A Love Story in Letters*. New York: Norton, 2008.

Wydenbruck, Nora, ed. and tr., *The Letters of Rainer Maria Rilke and Princess Marie von Thurn und Taxis*. London: Hogarth Press, 1958.

I

The Long Road to Muzot

Back to Lou

Needless to say, the Magda fiasco had Rilke again turning to Lou for relief and support, as he had so many times before. The series of nine letters that went between them at this time, covering a period of approximately four weeks, from early June to early July 1914, bear witness to virtually the same dialogue they had had as far back as ten years earlier, when Rilke first contacted Lou again after their initial two-year separation. The present exchange begins with Rilke informing Lou of the recent breakdown of his relationship with Magda of which Lou was hearing for the first time.[1]

Rilke had come into a relationship with Magda only a few weeks after returning to the project of the Elegies begun when at Duino, having recently completed, in Paris, the Third Elegy and the Tenth, and added to the Sixth. It may well have seemed to him as if, with the prospect of a relationship with Magda, he was riding yet another fresh wave of support that was taking him more fully past the wretched condition he had known over the years to a sphere in which he could at last be the happy person he had for so long hoped to become. At the thought of this budding relationship, as he puts it to Lou: "a spontaneous liveliness welled up", and there came a "joyous streaming"; he felt as "someone inwardly turbid and muddled" now

---

1. **Magda von Hattingberg** was a pianist from Vienna who had written Rilke to say that she loved his *Stories of God* "as no one had yet done" (Ralph Freedman, *Life of a Poet: Rainer Maria Rilke*, Evanston, IL: Northwestern University, 1991, 373). A very intense correspondence was inaugurated between Rilke and herself from that point that eventually led to a close intimacy.

"become clear":

> *as if now finally an alternative ... had been found in a current*
> *of steady fatefulness ... even the past, whenever I talked of it ...*
> *enriched me, belonged to me—so that for the first time I seemed*
> *to become the owner of my life ... through a new truthfulness that*
> *flooded even my memories.*
>
> (Snow, *Rilke*, 238-239)

Rilke owed his most recent output in writing towards the end of 1913, one must think, to the renewed conversations he had had with Lou just a few months before, after a full year of waiting un-successfully to see more work on the Elegies produced. Now, with Magda, there seemed to be the further prospect of fully making his own life of love beyond his relationship with Lou. He was grasping at the possibility of freeing himself at last of the dark life-struggle that had engaged him for so long, which had continually left him without a full set of resources to depend on. Now, he anticipated, there would be a "steady fatefulness", which would come from a stable love-life and a proper life of his own. He wished to be less at the mercy of those dark stirrings in himself that continually upset him in his effort to find a proper space in which to see his way through life, in order to write most especially of all.

Fantastically, this was but to *dream* of being free of a life-struggle that could not be finally settled except in one way: by undoing time and returning to that condition when only one love-life could make a difference. It is his abiding love-life with Lou, otherwise forever dead and imprisoned in time, that made any other conceivable normal love-life finally impossible for Rilke to manage. *This* love continued to have its influence on him, and in a complex, roundabout way. Those symptoms of "illness", which were the direct consequence of unreciprocated love with Lou at one time, symptoms thrust back upon Rilke just when he thought himself free of them by virtue of this love, could not but re-assert themselves when he was faced with the alien demands of a new relationship. Their re-assertion would have to be seen, as they were seen by Magda, as a sign of Rilke's sad inability to love. However, the new relationship fails because it is predetermined to fail: Rilke's love was with Lou, and it could not be with anyone else. After the fiasco with Magda, Rilke's despair of his chronic condition, as expressed in his second letter to Lou, was again running deep:

> [W]ith heaviest heart I think of the future … [f]or I no longer doubt now that I am ill, and my illness has spread through much of me and even lurks now in what I used to call my work …
>
> (Snow, *Rilke*, 239)

One will wonder, of course, to what extent Rilke *understood* the underlying cause of his condition as I have described this over the many pages of this study. Given the depth of their acute capacity for understanding in each case, I believe that Rilke did "know", and that even Lou "knew", but they could not afford to know: they were in survival mode, the solution to Rilke's condition lying deep in the irrecoverable past, so that there could only be a question of dealing with the situation between them as it now presented itself. Lou *would* have to "weep" (241)/"cry" (242) about that situation, confronted as she was in this instance especially with the brute depth of Rilke's despair, but even so the greater part of the burden of survival lay with Rilke, and it is with *this* sense of the situation that Lou declares that in this instance Rilke is "completely to blame", not for failing the relationship with Magda so much as for entering into it in the first place, as well for the renewed bout of "illness" that was the inevitable consequence of Rilke's ill-managed designs. "[I]t *is* you", Lou insists, all the while as she maintains also that "it really *isn't* you" (242): the deep "grief" Rilke experienced over the episode she cites as evidence that he "could not" at the same time "be *less* guilty of those things". Lou had to "weep"/"cry" over his letter, she says, on observing how "[l]ife really does treat its most precious human beings in such ways" (241).

Given the depth of what Rilke otherwise "knows", this last declaration must have struck him as especially painful in its "unknowing" irony. For what Rilke "knows" is that from a certain point in his life, as we have seen, tragedy installed itself for good as a result of Lou's failure to treat him with the full worthiness he deserved, at a time when a love-life was meant for them that would have fully installed them as a couple. The irony deepens if one can believe, as I do, that Lou herself "knows" as much in her own depths. Given the hopelessness of their situation, however, she herself could only be making do with what remained between them that had to be worked out. At this conscious level, she *had* to make Rilke responsible for himself, whatever had happened, if only because only Rilke could find any final solution for his now permanently inherited dark condition such as would release them both at last from their tragedy, which was otherwise inevitable.

We note, especially, the extreme length to which Lou goes in making her point in her letter: "in *this* death you alone are completely to blame, have no excuse, no palliation..." (242). In her conscious self, Lou had become a stern task-master: at this point her role and purpose in Rilke's life could only consist in driving him on through his struggle with his condition with the expectation that he would prevail, notwithstanding the seeming impossibility to him of the challenge. And it is because *she* can already see the makings of victory over his condition, so she claims, that she must "cry differently" as she puts it: for unlike Rilke, she notes, *she* already sees the prospect of victory; she sees it in the very fact that he can have such an advanced consciousness of his condition, as evidenced in his uniquely strong articulation of it. Her argument takes us back to as many as ten years before, when this very same dialogue went between them: what she has in mind, in calling attention to the power of his articulation of his condition, is "exactly, exactly exactly *the old undiminished strength* [that Rilke yet reserves] that makes life out of death" (emphasis mine).

Yet could the mere articulation of his condition really bode so much? How easy for Lou to say so, Rilke must have felt, while the burden of proof rested entirely with him, and when ten years later nothing really decisive or very strong was there to show for all of Lou's certainty that he would triumph one day. And yet Lou "cries" also because she knows that Rilke does not see it as she sees it. She is aware that her own words, given his present condition, cannot mean to Rilke what she intends him to know by them, and that they must appear "inept, stupid, weightless". She has claimed, in spite of this, that nothing is lost, not even what he had experienced while writing his letters to Magda—that happiest sense of having "for the first time ... become the owner of [his] life". This experience is bound, she claims, to continue to shed its influence somewhere in him, since he has experienced it, even if this experience would seem to have tragically retreated from him for now.

"Turning-Point" and "Narcissus"

After her response to his two letters concerning Magda, Rilke would send Lou, about a week later, a new poem entitled "Turning Point" (also translated simply as "Turning"). Lou's further analysis of Rilke's condition on the basis of this poem, which includes her exegesis of the evidence in the poem of an advance in his vision despite his own very real sense of impasse, goes to show the almost extreme distance that separated Lou and Rilke in their approach to his present struggle. In short Lou was looking far ahead towards the end-goal of this struggle, to that eventual triumph in Rilke's life-experience that would be achieved through the uniquely empowering medium of his artistic method, while Rilke for his part was very clear that for now nothing of the sort was shining out to him. And this for good reason: it devolved upon him to settle, for himself and for them both, among other things the deep problem that had been created with Rilke's continued attachment to Lou in love. This attachment continued even long after her failure to reciprocate it in that former time when everything went a way other than the one Rilke had properly expected of them. To the extent that he *was* conscious of it, Rilke "knew" only too well, far more than Lou was ready to allow herself to think, not only that it was this love that stood in the way of his giving himself to anyone else, but that it bore a profound additional relationship to that dark condition in himself with which he had been forever grappling, especially from the time of her rejection of him, when with a vengeance he had been again set back into this condition, this time for good. If there was to be any triumph at last over his dark condition he would have, thus, first to come to terms with this buried love (and the whole scope of destined life that had been associated with it at the time that was lost for good). He had been hopelessly set back into his demeaned condition, with a consequence that has translated over the years into a compassionate intensity of "gazing" at life where the "heart" is not able to enter in because it has withdrawn and is not available—the subject of the poem Rilke had just sent Lou.

Of this poem Rilke says that it speaks of a "turning ... that must come if I am to live" (Snow, *Rilke*, 243), which is to say, if he is ever again to come fully into life. His heart lies within, "painfully bur-

ied-alive", and until now this would have left him no other option of
a life but one: "[h]e had long prevailed by [an artistic] gazing" (242).
That situation can be traced as far back as Rilke's time in Worpswede
where, in the last stages of his immediate partnership with Lou, "looking" and "gazing" first came to mean so much to him. There was to be
the whole of his poetic development beyond that through the period
of *New Poems* right up to the time of the writing of his first Elegies.
Over this greatly protracted period of emotional dispossession, there
had been much anguish: "How long inwardly lacking,/imploring
deep down in his glance[?]"—but, in any case, time for "gazing", he
knows, is now up: he can sense that he has been forbidden "further
communions" (243) along these lines alone. It will devolve upon him
now, he says, to find a way to bring his heart back into "the til now
only won" and "as yet never loved creation". In doing so he will have
thus come into a more properly full relationship with what he describes as the "inner woman" in himself—viz., the elusive Beloved of
whom we have heard so much in Rilke's poems, and above all most
recently (see the end of Volume 2). In the depths of Rilke's heart,
this ideal Beloved is inseparable from Lou; to manage love of the
creation in the terms proposed in "Turning Point", Rilke would have
first to come to terms with his long-buried love of Lou that is yet still
alive in him (where his heart lies, "painfully buried-alive"). How, in a
word, would Rilke come to terms with what has been his own special,
long-lingering form of experience of the death of the Beloved?

Almost exactly a year before, Rilke had produced a poem entitled "Narcissus", which Lou had promptly pasted into her diary
(Snow, *Rilke*, 211). This was during a period when Rilke was visiting
with her, over two weeks from July 9th to the 22nd, 1913. After offering
her exegesis of "Turning Point" at this later time (late July 1914),
Lou brings them back to "Narcissus" by way of elaborating further
on her interpretation of Rilke's present situation and how she sees
the demands it is making on him. The two poems are as different as
the circumstances in which they were written: "Turning Point" was
produced at the time of his break-up with Magda, "Narcissus" when
he was once again in Lou's immediate company. In "Turning Point"
Rilke describes his by now chronic inability to bring his heart to bear
on the ongoing circumstances of his life in the world; in "Narcissus",
once again bestowed actual time with Lou, his heart is momentarily

free to unfold, and cannot be repressed: "And so this: this emanates from me .../... rises incessantly away" (211). There is a "pliant core" in him as in everyone else ("Nothing binds us in") out of which the effusions ("emanations") of the heart must come. In considering his case further, he notes "what forms there" rising up in him now in its "tear-stained signals"; this is on the one hand. On the other hand, he considers what at one time would have formed both in his heart and that of "a woman" *without the tears* but that "*was* [yet] *beyond attaining/(however hard I struggled for it pressing into her)*". In "Narcissus" the focus is not on the "woman" who now continues to live only "inside" him as in "Turning", but the woman out there (and now close by) with whom he was once in a relationship that failed. What was this thought if not an unambiguous, hopelessly wistful acknowledgment of the full love-life with Lou that at one time came so close to materializing for them—and which at the time ought to have materialized—but still was not to be ("was beyond attaining")?

In "Narcissus" this knowledge of the heart again arises, but "tear-stained" with Rilke's consciousness of its irrecoverableness, its one-time impossibility. Momentarily, in the immediate circumstances of his visit, it "lies open" again, finding expression only "in the indifferent/scattered water" of Lou's former evasion of it, which has become *their* irreversible fate, and was *her* death for him. Still he can "gaze" at his defeated love reflected back to him in this "water", and at his forever dead Beloved who, below the "water", lies as in a grave "beneath [his offered] wreath of roses". He is, of course, quite sure that this heart-life that was once theirs "is not loved [down] there" where "there is nothing/but the equanimity of tumbled stones". He is in tears at this grave of *temps perdu*, given over to his life-"sadness", and he is left wondering if perhaps the life-sadness that he feels now was not *already* there in the way he was given to that love-life that was once on the verge of opening up to them, and whether Lou saw this "sadness" in him then as the cause of "fear" or "fright" in her. He is clear about how his sadness translates now into a certain "deadly"-ness or desperation in his "gaze", so that it might *then also* have been *not* a pure gaze of love but of desperation mixed with this love. Here Rilke has descended into doubt about himself, as he had done before, in spite of "knowing" otherwise, as it were deferring to Lou's confirmed view that the impossibility began with him. One way or another that love-life had not been possible in the end, was, by his own admission here, "beyond attaining".

At the time he produced "Narcissus", Rilke was a full one and half years beyond his Duino moment, with nothing more to show of work on the Elegies over this entire time. His visit with Lou at this time, in spite of reviving a deep conflict in him over their former love, had had a reassuring effect that would eventually lift him into further productive work on the Elegies in the late fall of that year (some four months or so later). It is significant, however, and in line with the point of view Rilke expresses at the end of "Narcissus", that his focus in continued work on the Elegies should be in a mode that looks back to what he has lost and how he lost it. Already, back at Duino, he was ready to think that the cause of the failed love between them was the deeper problem of "blood" in him as he presents this in the Third Elegy. Still, he cannot, at the same time, "forget" Lou, as he says in the Tenth Elegy—cannot forget her in her former self back then when the prospect of a full love-life lay open to them. That he cannot forget remains an undeniable constant in his life, whether he wishes it to be so or not. In the meantime, the defeat of that former love-life of which we are speaking created in Rilke a mode of being that has translated into various problematic forms of "gazing" at life. Repressing his heart, he has given himself up to a life of artistic "gazing", which, if powerful and in its intensity, in fact, a form of compensation for blighted love, can only be half of what he could expect of himself. Repressing his heart, and given over primarily to such "gazing", he could not make himself seriously available to another woman. At the same time, defeated love has created in him another form of "gazing" which could show that desperation about love in him that could only frighten or alienate any woman he might have found some hope with. We may believe that Magda would have encountered both of these forms of "gazing" in her brief time with him.

Rilke could not make of himself the poet of the whole of life that he aspired to be, would not be able to break through into that victorious achievement that Lou continued to believe was still within his reach, if he did not first come to terms with a deep imbalance in himself that had made it necessary to find a way also to *free* his heart for creation. Thus the import, at this later time, of "Turning Point". He knew what a forbidding challenge lay before him, knew that he was still far from worthy of taking it on, could only see the victory Lou continued to speak of as a remote ideal. More than Lou was ready to think, he "knew" that, if he were to triumph, above all he would have to reconcile himself, in some seemingly impossible way, to his forever buried love of Lou, that a large part of the "illness" he was suffering from, ever since Lou had rejected his vision of a life for them, was inescapably related to that buried love. All that he had experienced in the meantime, by way of personal kinship, of illness in others and in the world at large, or what he calls "the terrible", and "the common distress" associated with it—all this too he had experienced as a consequence of his defeated love. If he were indeed to break through at last into victory, this still more extended experience of the defeated spirit would also have to come into the equation—hardly an easy or a very straightforward task to perform!

We understand Lou's spoken position *vis-a-vis* Rilke's present situation when we see her concentrating on it without admitting the full impact of his experience of defeat. In time Lou had also come to "know" what Rilke "knew" about their defeated love, but, as I have indicated, she could not admit this without herself folding psychologically, and in the meantime continues in the same role she had always assumed with him. From the time they first met, in the mentoring function Lou immediately assumed with him (very likely from her position of superior age and experience), her concern had always been with the higher unity of art and philosophy. Given Lou's focus in this respect, and from her superior position in the relationship, it was almost inevitable that she would continue to see in Rilke's present struggles, however much they bordered on a complete despair at any time, the germ, even the proof, of the final achievement that was in store for him. Lou's leitmotif throughout the years had been that Rilke could never bring himself to the level of articulation of his suffering that he reaches, in his letters as in his work, if the promise of transcendence were not already showing. Proof of the end-victory lay in the very words he managed to continue to find for his suffering. Lou gives voice to this insistent position most clearly perhaps in the final letter she wrote him at this time[2]:

---

2. We are still covering the period of the letters that went between them from late June to early July 1914.

*you are **not** so lacking throughout in unity as you feel and think "yourself" to be; you suffer yourself as a person blocked, and that piece of happiness which is lodged in this situation remains hidden from you, withheld, even though all its requirements are inside you and **express** themselves; for one **cannot** write … the way you do without some store of happiness (which is just not fully working its way into consciousness!)*

(Snow, *Rilke*, 252)

Still, Lou takes this view to what we will feel is an over-literal extreme where she (wishfully) *morphs* Rilke's "words" with deepest "unities":

*Those **words** with which you articulate this condition … they are nothing if not works, works accomplished, the coming about of deepest **unities** in you.*

How easy it was for Lou to say so while Rilke bore the whole burden of the proof of what she was saying, in a life-struggle that continued terrible for him. What tolerance Rilke could display towards her when she allowed herself to go so far as even to celebrate the great gap in their positions, which she voices as proof that victory was already here:

***You** are in pain; **I**, through your pain, feel bliss.*

(247)

This last aphorism is spoken towards the end of the letter in which Lou has just offered what she clearly considers to be her triumphant reading of "Narcissus", freshly buoyed up by that effort. Her reading is, however, a dramatic mis-reading; it is a moot point to what extent wilfully so. The "melancholy love" of the poem's Narcissus she sees as in fact "mysteriously intensified through the inorganic, non-living medium in which he finds 'himself' mirrored"; "[w]hat is fleeing out of him … gains its full effect only through the dead *materia* in which it comes to a halt so as *thus* to change into its own opposite". Precisely there, she claims, is evidence of the "the *creative* sense dissolving"; "what they [the *materia*] say is dead, is outside, is opposite … [Narcissus'] life *extends beyond* all that", and the "intersect"-ion of the two spheres (of life and death) is the very source of the "erotic melancholy" out of which "the creative person" breaks through into a "new reality". In actual fact, there is no indication whatever in Rilke's poem that such a dissolution process is at work; what Lou would see as the transformative medium of the dead *materia* as she describes it (the world of "tumbled stones" of the poem's underwater grave) is no such medium at all but entirely a dead-end that offers no power of its own/has no role in itself except to reflect Rilke's love back to him hopelessly. Lou is here, in other words, *projecting* into the poem's terms the final synthesizing resolution of Rilke's experience in which she so much believes, which is nowhere, in fact, suggested in this poem.

It is the same with Lou's reading of "Turning Point" where Rilke's by now sterile "gazing" is seen by Lou as already expressing "love", Rilke's "eyes" already "plight[-ing] their troth in a gaze" (245), so that there is *already* for her a mingling of this "gaze", back in "the innermost region" where the heart would work, with the "great love that transforms outside and inside into a completely new union". In fact, a look back at the poem will reveal that the poet's "gazing" lies in a purely antithetical relation to the "heart-work" that he has only now really committed to, once for all, in order to save his life. He is for now nowhere near the creative synthesizing process Lou is looking for. Lou in her letter goes so far as to offer a description of what transpires in the synthesizing realm: "what love does in this union is dark and difficult and glorious, and stands on the side of life; who would dare or even want to guess more than that?" (247-248) And yet Lou has dared and guessed at it: "I hear [even now] your heart-sounds", Lou insists; she can do so she says "probably only because as a woman [!] one somehow is at home in these regions" (246). Out of this intuition she claims she can see already "something in [the poem] as of a newly conquered domain", already "many trails and long wanderings along paths" (246). In fact, turning back to Rilke's poem, all one "hears" about, in contrast with Lou's wishful projections, is that "there was argument in the air … about his still unfeelable heart", that "it does not have love", and that the poet is now exhorting himself to "[b]ehold … the inner woman", whom he can only describe for now, however, as the "as yet *never* loved creation" (emphasis here mine).

Replying to Lou's somewhat artificial optimizing accounts, Rilke is at first, as was his wont, all deference: "You *know and understand.*" He says he is ready to believe that what Lou projects for him will turn out to be true, but he insists in his turn that for the moment he is far from able to see this for himself. He notes how his poems themselves attest to deadening impasse. Of the later poem he says: "God knows how far the poem 'Turning' precedes the onset of those new circumstances [which Lou projects], I am far behind, God knows if such complete turns can still be worked out at all, since the obstinate inner forces continue to abuse and exhaust each other" (248). By these negative "inner forces", of which he will go on to speak almost exclusively in this and his next two letters, Rilke has in mind the depressive, debilitating effects on his spirit of that excessive compensatory "gazing" on the world and on others, that desperate "open"-ness (248) to these, including to the processes of his own body, which in default of his unengaged heart, has left him greatly burdened, "constrained" (250), and indeed deadened in body and mind. Again in reply he notes, as evidence that his is for now quite another situation than the one Lou projects, that if "Narcissus" did speak of what Lou would see in it, he would have since made more progress, when the reverse, in fact, has been true: "Between *Narcissus* and the recent poem ["Turning"] lies a year, a dull year, and when I look back over it, I feel from where I'm standing now, [only] yet another degree heavier, harder to get through to" i.e., "deader" (250).

In sharp contrast with Lou's excited projections of the triumph he is already showing in his work and the altogether certain progress he is making also in personal terms according to her, Rilke's account of himself in the rest of these letters concentrates almost exclusively on those aspects of his condition that are presently making it impossible for him to believe he is coming through, or that he ever will come through. Clearly at this time he had relapsed once again into his old Malte-nature, in spite of the momentary advance he seemed to have made with the Elegies, which yet might not have represented progress. His letters at this time add still more to the extensive data on his depressive tendencies he had produced over years. They are more proof, if any more was needed, that he had known this dimension of the terrible as well as anyone could. Ironically, by entering into a relationship with Magda, he had hoped to pre-empt the recurrence of these fateful tendencies, anticipating that such a relationship would bring a certain stability to his emotional life. He continued to reserve the idea that "a proper loving attitude toward a human being" (248) would only serve to help him. In the meantime it continued to eat at him that, at one time, he *had* known what it meant to *be* in such a relationship, had known difficulty with it but still had found a way to live through it naturally, without suffering division in himself: "O how in my youth I was *One*" (250); he was then in alignment also with what the natural world had to offer him intrinsically: "when I felt the morning's air, it went through all of me ... a piece of fruit ... was already like a word of the spirit" (250) ...

It quite amazes one to see to what extent Lou and Rilke could listen so tolerantly to each other's extensive expositions about his case across the very great divide of their respective positions. In fact, Rilke always fully allowed Lou her say, just as Lou allowed Rilke his, the tolerance working, still more amazingly, both ways. The only display of difference between them in these letters takes the form of a simple begging-to-differ: on Rilke's side, in response to her account: "Perhaps, dear Lou, perhaps. But ..." (249), and on Lou's side: "Yes—and yet!" (252). Rilke's life would run its course, through one condition or another: Lou was, in any case, certain that everything would lead in the end to triumph (or, at least, she would have to maintain this position to help them both along), while Rilke for his part had no choice *but* to let his life run its course, however vulnerable he felt in the meantime to the real possibility that this life might not lead anywhere further. When Lou and Rilke finally met some two weeks beyond their lengthy exchanges, doubtlessly they would have continued to voice their respective positions to each other, but, with the further solace of being in each other's company, they would quite probably have been even more open to what each had to say. Such a course between them could only ground the situation more fully for them both in the long term...

"We Must Die Because We Have Known Them"

In the interval between "Turning Point", produced in July 1914, and the Fourth Elegy, written in November of 1915 and the next major moment in Rilke's poetic career, only a few poems signal themselves, a modest output associated for the most part with the autumn of 1914. One poem of note was written at the time Lou and Rilke met in 1914: "We Must Die Because We Have Known Them."

Something of Rilke's deep melancholy and dismay, even despair, at this time is conveyed by this poem. The poem takes a direction of thought that is determined by his immediate experience: however wondrous women and one's relationship to them may be (and this is conveyed in the poem in wonderfully sexual terms), it is in their very nature to forever elude (their smile is "unsayable", themselves "unattainable"—**Mitchell** 133). This only makes it logical to think that they must therefore at some point be renounced, that one must die not only *of* but *to* them. Rilke could be thought to be exhorting himself here in direct relation to the Magda fiasco, taking the resolve not to drift into such a scape again, but this may be at the cost of a frightful solitude and drifting in which all the old terrors will be all the more free to play themselves out in him: "But the grown man/shudders and is silent …/… [a]s the old sailor is silent,/and the terrors he has endured/play inside him as though in quivering cages."

By the autumn, some three months later, a more many-sided account of his situation emerges. On the one hand there is the poem "To Hölderlin", which gives the impression that Rilke has returned to the ideal point of view on life-as-a-whole of the Elegies. This is an especially impressive poem, Rilke having momentarily found himself again, at least at a certain level, as a reader of Hölderlin, who serves him as a model of creative production at its most successful. In contrast with the "grown man" of "We Must Die" who "wanders pathlessly," in unalleviated solitude all the more subject to "terrors", Hölderlin, as the "most wandering" spirit of all, like the moon moves masterfully in his sphere, above a landscape both "holy" and "terrified" (Mitchell 135)—the terms of Rilke's own concerns. The focus in both poems is on the "landscape" of creative imaginative activity, the creative sphere in which alone the *poet* has his being, one step away from the world that thrusts its impressions into it (hence in both cases it is a "nocturnal" landscape, beyond the world's day[3]). In "We Must Die", the poet, as "the grown man", is not creating because, in his solitude, too much conditioned by the world's "terrors"; Holderlin contrastingly is depicted as being in full command of all the impressions the world has thrust into his creative sphere, including also what is "holy", of which the poet in "We Must Die" shows no immediate

---

3. So the women of "We Must Die" appear to the poet in this nocturnal sphere: cf. "they float and pour down/sweetly transfigured night" (Mitchell 133).

awareness, as *he* continues overwhelmingly "terrified" (such being still Rilke's fundamental position at this stage of his poetic development). Holderlin is thus held up as the ideal poet, one who, unlike Rilke at present, was able to give himself to all that he managed to create out of the world's impressions without attaching himself to any of this. The "compelling image" that Holderlin would have managed to "utter" in any moment he is already oriented to live through, no impression in one kind or the other, "holy" or "terrified", ever getting the better of him:

> *... there was a death*
> *even in the mildest, and you walked straight into it; but*
> *the god who preceded you led you out and beyond it.*
>
> (Mitchell 135)

The great ideal of dispossession and renunciation of Rilke's Elegies, to which he continued to aspire, despite his chronically afflicted condition, has shown up again here: Holderlin could live and create "without any need to hold on ... free of desire". Holderlin even took this tendency to an extreme: his final madness is cited as only additional evidence that in his most essential nature he could only "give away" and "give back" to the universe, as though the "joy" he experienced in creation could not remain "inside" him, "belonging to no one", and to nothing except the "earth".

The distance from Rilke's own condition in this present period is astonishing. On the one hand, there is "To Holderlin", on the other hand "Exposed on the cliffs of the heart", composed contemporaneously with it, in which Rilke's actual present condition is ruthlessly laid bare. The latter poem has links back to "We Must Die": Rilke for his part *remains* at a loss "in the mountain-range of his feelings" (133), which are of a starker kind yet. He has made the denial (137), has renounced for the moment women and the world, and has withdrawn to these "cliffs" of pure self-isolation, alone with his isolated heart. Lying thus beyond illusions, he had thought thereby to remedy his dependency, only to find that the experience is not only sterile but inimical. Here he is "without a shelter", without a comforting influence of any kind, and is all the more exposed to the adverse impressions of the world that continue to reach him. It is Nature's brute day world that, in all its desolate austerity, casts its influence in him here predominantly. Here in this remote world of "pure denial", Nature's animal kingdom might continue to reflect to him the concept of a rounded life, and the possibility of a "full" existence, which *it* has in its own kind, but himself, being human, can only know better than to think life of *this* purely existential sort possible for him. It was only, then, to be expected, though these new developments are in their turn astonishing, that despite Rilke's resolve to renounce love and to bear freer thoughts, he would find himself, in the same period as "Holderlin" and "Exposed", suddenly given up to yet another! relationship with a woman, this time with his former friend and Expressionist painter, Loulou Albert-Lazard, who was also known as Louise.[4] Another poem, written in this same autumn, serves as a token of this event: "Again and again, however we know the landscape of love." It is a straightforward and unembarrassed admission of the inevitability of seeking love again. This is in spite of the general evidence the poem cites of the sorrow and distress of those who have been in love, subjected as these have been inevitably either to the "sorrow" of death or the "abyss" of estrangement from each other when suddenly returned to their isolate selves. Thus the overriding simplicity of the poem's affirmation: "Again and again, however we know the landscape of love... /... again and again the two of us walk together/under the ancient trees, lie down again and again/among the flowers, face to face with the sky" (139). Here Rilke is once again more fully in the day world where human beings also find—love.

It was just as much to be expected, however, that despite the straightforward, honest bravery of this renewed commitment to love, a bare few months into this latest affair the tide would turn once again. Already by the end of January Rilke was again confessing his one-and-the-same complex in an anguished letter to (who else but?) Lou. Speaking of his latest ill-fated engagement, with Louise:

> *What I have gone through is the ever-relapsing fate of these recent years: the entering into a dear heart-felt connection, then ... the painful certainty that every closeness exposes me to violence, then, terror, flight, retreat back into the forfeited solitude ...*
>
> (Snow, *Rilke*, 270)

---

4. **Loulou Albert-Lasard** was a young painter whom he had met briefly in Paris some years before.

With Princess Marie, with whom he continued in a correspondence as always, Rilke is more frank and straightforward:

> ... *there is again a fatality over me ... incorrigible as I am, I again attempted not to remain alone ... it is always the same cruel fact: to be burdened with another life ... and ... the near-impossibility of living ... I cannot see where it will end, I shall have to save myself once more, but I do not want to leave destruction and disaster behind me.*
>
> **(Wydenbruck** 131)

Hers, however, was not Lou's way of responding,

> *Actually I would like to give you a terrible scolding—I believe it would do you a lot of good to be scolded like a baby ...* **Every human being is lonely, and must remain lonely and must endure it and *may not* give way and must not seek help in other people ...**
>
> (133)

Rilke's reply, on the same plane, is that of the apologetic child:

> ... *incorrigible as I am ... I agree with you ... when all this lies behind me I will never again make an attempt of this kind ...*
>
> (136)

To this apology, Rilke, however, adds words that would not have registered with the Princess the way they would with himself or with Lou:

> *I will keep my heart to myself then once and for all time, and ... rejoice that there is room for so much sorrow in it ...*

In the meantime Rilke would have to "save" himself without "destruction" to Louise, and for this inevitably it is Lou who, as the chief orchestrator of his life, would have to step in. Unlike the Princess, Lou was aware of the deeper predicament that would have led Rilke again to "an attempt of this kind", and for this reason treats the matter, in stark contrast, simply as another episode Rilke would have to pass through. However he might err, or need to err, Lou was bound to continue to offer her support and to see Rilke through, also because of her own stake in the course of his life, if for both their sakes he was to come through with a genuine victory over all. That was her faith and her hope. As it is, Lou would indeed win Louise over when Rilke visited Lou with her in early March 1915, associating as they did all together through a full two months. Lou would win Louise over to Rilke's overriding need especially for solitude; she would succeed again, as she had in the past (with Clara, most notably), in making Louise into yet another of her "daughters", as Rilke had wished ("To what extent (if at all) she might find her place among your daughters[!] is, I know, impossible to forsee [they would all have to be referred to Lou!], but if you *were* to grow fond of her, her life would once more enter into a good season"—Snow, *Rilke*, 272). Humbly and generously, Louise did indeed reconcile herself to her situation with Rilke. In a note to her after the visit, Louise thanks Lou: "how beneficial your good words were to me. I very much wish at some point in my life to stand before you not quite so poor, without merely a negative effect" (Snow, *Rilke*, 276), such being the influence Lou could have. Louise would stay by Rilke for another full year, seemingly without destruction to herself and without detriment to his creativity…

***

The positive outcome of this finally therapeutic communal gathering would liberate Rilke and lend him fresh wings in a way he had not known for well over a year. For almost a year the world war (WW1) had been raging, fitfully engaging Rilke in comments that, up to the time of the settlement with Louise, show him for the most part overwhelmed and baffled. By January of 1915, six months into the war, he is speaking of it as "this anomaly" (Greene 127) in relation to the peaceful "life" with which humankind is more essentially identified and to which it is committed. Even so, this "anomaly" has struck at the very root of creative expression; it has silenced Rilke in his vocation as an artist: "I am losing the inner connection with my nature, and this condition leads to a silentness inwardly, and outwardly to an insensibility." No essential expression seems possible: "there is present no inner single-minded impulse" that could issue in "a clean expression" (128). Every ability to write seems inhibited, and if anything is attempted it emerges only as "the noise with which a piece of silence breaks off from the great dumb mass inside me". The effect is general and ubiquitous: "how dumb we have grown; I am sure everyone is so at heart ... there is no one who can draw sounds ... not even to lament,—it is a silence of halted, interrupted hearts" (129).

All this would quickly alter from the time Rilke was, for all intents and purposes, liberated, seemingly once for all, from the effects of pretending to any form of normal, settled-down life with another woman. He felt suddenly freed up, sufficiently to again take the world on in direct relation to himself as an artist, even in such "monstrous" (119-124) times. He is aware of beginning again with possibly less than nothing: "inwardly it is an abyss with oneself living on the edge of it, while down below maybe lie shattered ... all the things of one's former life" (Wydenbruck 142). There is the challenge of orienting himself in the midst of a formless chaos, as one who "cannot manage to find his bearings in a world almost entirely canceled, crumbled, tearing itself to pieces" (Greene 143). As an artist he sees himself as having disastrously failed humankind by not achieving a form of art that would have served to divert it from the need that drives it, in the case of war, to prove itself in "steadfastness, strength, a standing-up-to-life *quand même*" (131). His singular "pain" stems from seeing the extent of "the incurably bad condition that was necessary to force out evidences of whole-hearted courage, devotion, and bigness" (132)—all those impulses, in other words, that humankind continues to require of itself as an ongoing demonstration of its full spirit, here gone amuck. All this his own art and that of others, he believes, should have pre-empted ("While we, the arts ... were unable to transform anyone ... Did we do this so badly, so half-way[?]"). The burden Rilke inherits from this failure is great in proportion to the terrible consequences that were now playing themselves out: "[w]hat weight, what obligation now falls on things that survive a little more" (131).[5]

---

5. A parallel suggests itself with Yeats's own lament during the Irish War of Independence in the period that immediately followed the World War. Yeats is all the more desperate in his dismay as he believes that he and his associates had already created such art, which yet had failed to win his compatriots over: "We too had pretty toys when young .../... habits that made old wrong/ Melt down, as it were wax in the sun's rays .../... Now days are dragon-ridden." From "Nineteen Hundred Nineteen", *The Collected Poems of W.B. Yeats*, Wordsworth Poetry Library, 2008, 175-176.

In spite of the dire inheritance of the times and the proportion-ately desperate challenges they now posed, Rilke continued stubborn-ly to stand by the faith "that continuities [yet] exist that have nothing in common with the progression of history ... [T]he remote past and the distant future will come to an understanding" (Wydenbruck 141). The only question was: would anyone from those times be able again to "participate innocently and calmly in the movement of the great correlations", as he puts it, "or shall we remain cowering timid-ly below, the brand of the times?" Rilke was clearly rousing himself again to the task at hand, however awful the effort required for this appeared. He is once again seeing himself in the light of what he had been capable of only a few years back, which he suddenly considers would have been equal to the present times: "a few years ago ... I might have summoned visions ... which would have survived even a time like this ... for what is it that I am seeking if not the one point ... where terror coincides with [i.e., is matched by] greatness?" (144) By the end of November 1915, he had successfully set up to recover his artistic powers, such as would allow him to at least carry on where he had left off with the Elegies. Having retired to another place in the Munich area, and writing to the Princess, he is signaling a new break-through: "here in this quieter, more remote house I have remembered many things, experienced much inwardly, carrying it forward and re-living it, and was quite close to my work—actually it had already begun; there are two or three things I could read to you" (149).

"Death" and the Fourth Elegy:
A New Self-Emptying

There is a letter by Rilke written some two weeks before this fresh breakthrough that shows him re-living himself in a way that is clearly preparing for it. Because of the direction to their conversation given by one of his correspondents, he had felt it necessary to turn once again to *Malte*, and specifically to "[w]hat is expressed in the suffering that is written into" it (Greene 146). The focus here is on what is *expressed* in the suffering, which brings us back to what Rilke had remarked upon in some depth five years earlier, in his 1910 Good Friday letter to his publisher Anton Kittenberg on having just completed *Malte*[6]. Five years later he notes again how what we experience as "the negative mold" of the contents of that novella, in respect of "agony, disconsolations and most painful insights" (147), implies, in fact, a further "casting" from this of the positive "happiness, assent, most perfect and most certain bliss" we have always been looking for—"most perfect and most certain" now precisely by virtue of having emerged from such a negative. Rilke sees himself as having been in *Malte* engaged in a whole new process of creation that is now inwardly more open to the negative aspects of our experience that have always been known but that have until now always been projected out of ourselves, for example as the gods of ancient myth, so that no reckoning with these has ever been made inwardly.

Over time humankind has systematically separated itself from these aspects of its experience, "eliminating" (148) them as it were by projecting them outside itself, so as to occupy a more livable world, as it supposes, although in doing so it has only put off the reckoning. It is so also with the fear of death: the thought of death has been "pushed out" and thus made into "the contradiction, the opponent, the invisible antagonism", when in fact death is "probably so near us that we cannot at all determine the distance between it and the life-center within us". In this way have we merely put off the reckoning with both death and God, Who, moreover, has now to save us further from ourselves. At some point, Rilke surmises, all that we have projected outside ourselves in the way of negative aspects concentrates itself and re-appears to us "from the outside", it may be also as an outbreak of war, or so he implies: "the strongest, indeed the *too* strong, the powerful, indeed the violent, the incomprehensible, often the monstrous—how should they not, brought together in one place, exercise influence, effect, force, superiority?" (148). Humankind has gone this disastrous roundabout route in spite of the counter-evidence both of Nature and of love: of Nature, inasmuch as "the field is full of death" (149) and only thereby brings forth "a rich expression of life", and of love inasmuch as truly committed lovers are, in the nature of their experience, swept into "an endless consciousness of the whole" so that "being full of life they are [necessarily] full of death". A measure of the highly open-ended nature of Rilke's overall

---

6. The relevant comments are quoted in Volume 2, on pp.276-277.

experience, which was open also to contradiction, is the fact that here Rilke builds on a view of lovers that is utterly positive. Compare with this, the critical view of them (and of himself) he had been taking in his Elegies, although perhaps what he intends by love here is a love that is utterly free of any attachment, in life as in death, even to the other lover. This concept of love we have seen Rilke developing not only in his Elegies but also repeatedly in his letters.

For the moment, however, Rilke's focus is more narrowly on death, and how it behoves us to go out to meet it in our lives; he is offering counsel, and what can read as stark comfort, to his corres-pondent who is "preoccupied" with the issue, having herself suffered various "shocks" (150). One must come to terms also with the fear of death. Tolstoy, Rilke says, can be our masterful guide in this regard. *He* was one in whom there lived "a sense of the whole", a comprehensive "feeling for life" such as "death seemed to be contained everywhere in it". This was Rilke's own end-goal of comprehensive experience to-wards which he was moving as best he could from stage to stage of his life. But within this venture, there would also have to be some way of coming to terms with death as an end-point, "pure death", of which even Tolstoy had a frantic fear. "[P]ure death" being, in comparison with how life naturally unfolded to Tolstoy, an elusive unknown, it was less obvious how this should be dealt with. Rilke's own sense of a comprehensive vision of life and death to which he aspired had him considering also this matter more closely. One day he had suddenly had the experience of an 'active imagination' of pure death as he was walking in a park (Mitchell 233).[7] As the Princess Marie recounts in her *Reminiscences*, published in 1932, suddenly there appeared to Rilke in pure vision the image of "a hand" and "on its level back a cup". This image he was to develop further in his poem "Death"; it is also developed in Rilke's letter to his correspondent: here it appears as "that hideous cup with the handle broken off and the senseless inscription *Faith, love, hope* out of which one is compelled to drink bitterness of undiluted death" (Greene 150). Strangely, this descrip-tion is given, in context, as if Tolstoy himself had offered it, though it was Rilke's own: it is as if Rilke saw himself contributing directly to Tolstoy's own body of knowledge on this subject, as if claiming for

---

7. 'Active imagination': Jung's term for this kind of experience.

his image an authority equal to Tolstoy's offered images of death in his own superior account.

In Rilke's poem "Death", the image of "pure death" is developed both more vividly and more eerily than in the letter. "[U]ndiluted death" has become "a bluish distillate" lying in the cup, while the broken handle makes its presence felt here only through "the line along the glazed curve where the handle/snapped" (Snow, *Rilke*, 141). The further startling image of a cup lying "on the back of a hand" is the aspect that is retained from Rilke's original vision. The inscription on the cup, here "[c]overed in dust", has altered from "Faith, love, and hope", as set forth in Rilke's letter, simply to "Hope". To have addressed the relevant implications for this situation of all three of these virtues would no doubt have involved Rilke in an exposition far beyond the scope of the simpler moral he wished to focus on here. In Rilke's poem there is a "man" who once drank from this cup, "at breakfast", as if this action were simply another like those to which he would ordinarily have been given over the course of his day. This "man" is humankind when it once had a natural sense of how, without holding back, one can give oneself to death as one has given oneself to life, and so find "hope" from all confining existence. Rilke had focused on this imagined ancient aptitude in humankind before (in *Malte*), and had made it the touchstone of a genuinely comprehensive capacity for living. The contrast is with all those for whom such an image of death as Rilke elaborates here only speaks to their fear of death and who consequently turn away from it as from a "poison", degenerating insistently into lives to which they cling with a vengeance, no matter how badly debased their lives have become. We are here back in the world of his social critique to which Rilke had given himself especially from his Paris days but even before (in the *Book of Hours* also). Were it not for the fear of death instilled into the hopeless masses by such an image of death as Rilke focuses here: "Would they keep/chewing so foolishly on their own frustration?/... go on mumbling, mumbling..." At the same time, these many souls "must" be tricked into fear, "must be scared away", or they would otherwise rush madly into death to escape lives they are unable to make good on, being unable to make anything worthy of themselves. "What kind of human beings are they then,/who finally must be scared away by poison?" Rilke asks in utter dismay.

This rather mordant view of general human society will provide the structural pivotal-point of the **Fourth Elegy** which Rilke also wrote at this time. Given the all-pervading spirit of such a society, so inimical to the quest for a genuine comprehensive living—and especially the complete one he has in mind ideally—Rilke believes he ought for now to eliminate his involvement in that society and look for a proper atmosphere for his quest not among these human beings but, rather, among puppets (**Mitchell 351**)! These, by their material neutrality, devoid of all human pretenses, will at least leave him free to wait on the movements of inspiration he is seeking, in order to take his quest forward. The critique itself has shifted to a more ordinary, less degraded, but not for that reason less banal, aspect of human society. Rilke concentrates this aspect in the "dancer", the man who has eliminated all conflict of emotion in life (the inevitable "scenery of farewell"), and all the greater human concerns that follow from this. This "man" moves lightly through life, systematically choosing to impress by his appearance, "costumed" and "made up". Behind this facade he remains in truth but an ordinary, small-minded human being: "hurry[ing] home and walk[ing] in through the kitchen". In this section of his poem, Rilke is taking up again with the theme of romantic conflict he invokes earlier: "lovers/always arriving at each other's boundaries". In this sense, everyone has stood "afraid before his heart's/curtain … the scenery of farewell". This reality of life Rilke's "dancer" has turned his back on, opting rather for the emotionally safer but finally sterile course offered by a world of social pretenses.

In line with his previous Elegies, notably the First and the Second, Rilke pursues in this Fourth Elegy his analysis of romantic conflict still further, no doubt chastened by his most recent experiences with Magda and with Louise. Behind the conflict that inevitably emerges between lovers, this Elegy notes, lies a more fundamental tendency in human nature that always has us feeling, even when still "intent upon one object", the "pull of another". This is "second nature to us", the second nature in which for the most part, in fact, we live our lives, in emotional turmoil. We carry on in this state of dis-unity, allowing ourselves to be impulsively subject to the conflicting directions our lives take, symbolically "[f]lowering and fading" in everything "at once", and also in our deaths for which we are, as a result of fundamental conflict in us, never genuinely ready, always "[l]ate [in our consciousness of it], over-taken", in our destabilized condition remaining un-"forewarn[-ed]" or without any real prescience of death such as would have us living in the full knowledge of it as an event even from the beginning grasped as inevitable. In this fundamental respect we exist in a condition anti-thetical to the great world of Nature where a "majestic power" of existence and a complete "harmony" of instinct obtains in which life and death are perfectly attuned one to the other.

In its aspect of fundamental conflict, human nature stands over and against the majestic, all-encompassing model of harmony that Nature embodies. But, though Nature may have its own power of harmony (at least as a general system), this harmony is of a different kind from that for which human beings would need to be looking. Animals possess this harmony as a matter of natural instinct, in their "blood"; our own "blood" is rather in chaotic turmoil, as Rilke's Third Elegy abundantly gave proof. According to Rilke's terms in the Fourth Elegy, it is for us rather a matter of finding harmony in that "outside" factor that as "background" to our "emotions" forms them and holds the power to unify them. This is not a factor based in in-stinct but a factor based in consciousness. It is equivalent in the poem with the idea of an objective basis for the emotions, what explains and grounds them as a unity. Rilke does not elaborate any further on this idea here; it is as if that prospect remained to be known and is, indeed, the whole *raison d'être* of the Elegies as a whole, which has yet to be truly discovered. However, this idea is the very one Rilke expands on in the letter just quoted. Here, as we have seen, he cites an "outside" realm (originally of mythical gods) to which human beings have consigned all the negative aspects of their lives, an "outside" which would have to be re-appropriated to ourselves and brought into conscious relation to our better natures, if we are indeed to regain or achieve unity of being. Moreover, it is not just the negative aspects that we must re-appropriate, but also those equally intense positive aspects which we renege on in order to occupy a safer sphere of life: love in its pure nature, for example. Any proper consciousness of death we have also banished to this "outside" realm; there is equally a need to come to terms with death in *its* pure condition, if we are ever to fully complete ourselves in our human being.

This is at least the ideal reckoning Rilke is striving to live into more and more fully. But for now, all lies in confusion, and there seems little occasion even for any progress in this quest. The themes of self-division and dissociated existence put the Fourth Elegy directly in line with the first three Elegies Rilke had composed, the First, Second and Third, making it the next inevitable installment in that series, and so quite naturally the Fourth. To the ongoing emphasis on conflict in human nature is here added the choice human beings make for an excision of conflict in human consciousness such as leads to a still more hopeless world of social pretense. In such an oppressive environment, where conflict is almost entirely denied, it is difficult for the poet to find any proper footing that would allow him to carry on with his quest. And so he seeks to alienate himself further, would ensconce himself in a world where all human pretense is neutralised, which for now is this poem's world of puppets. Any proper, genuine development of his themes Rilke believes stands a better chance of being realized for now through the cultivation of a certain neutrality of impulse made possible for him in such a world. He insists that this is at present his only recourse, however austere this context of life may seem: "Here I'm waiting .../... even if someone/tells me 'That's all' [that's all there is to it]: even if [with time] emptiness/ floats toward me .../... I'll sit here anyway" (351-353). One way of understanding Rilke's gambit here is to see in this world of "puppets" the present neutrality of his words in his poem, which at least do not deceive. Some miracle of transforming life may yet arise in the midst of these words in polar reaction to their insistent neutrality and seeming relative lifelessness, these words being a mere appearance that can be expected to fill with reality (Rilke's words being closer to mere appearance certainly than the "half-filled human masks" (351) of social pretense):

> ... I must stay seated, must
> wait before the puppet stage, or rather,
> gaze at it so intensely that at last,
> to balance my gaze, an angel has to come and
> make the stuffed skins startle into life.[8]
>
>   (Mitchell 353)

---

8. Of the puppet Rilke says that "It at least is full" (Mitchell 351), by which he means that it is at least complete in the experience of perfect neutrality it offers in its own kind, without ambiguities, edges, pretenses, etc.

As a route through the chronic self-division in our human nature, Rilke proposes a technique of complete detachment which would focus an extreme alienation in ourselves, bordering on pure emptiness of spirit. Thereby we generate a condition of insistent life-lessness that can bring into sharper relief and, by this means, summon into our presence, as it were by reaction, the full transforming creative life we are looking for: the fullness (*pleroma*) that will arise out of emptiness (*kenosis*) as known to tradition. In fact, Rilke is here building specifically on an *alchemical* model of self-transformation, whereby a complete separation of the elements, the *sevaratio* as it is called, gives way to the *conjunctio*, a new harmonious fullness in the self, leading to ever stronger forms of self-development:

> *Angel and puppet, a real play, finally.*
> *Then what we separate by our very presence*
> *can come together.*

From this consideration, Rilke goes on to project all that will theoretically arise as a development of self in relation to this process:

> *And only then, the whole*
> *cycle of transformation will arise*
> *out of our own life-seasons.*

He considers that this may be the only way to activate the cycle of transformation that pertains to our own existence (Nature, by contrast, occupying its own closed sphere of transformation, which it lives through in quite another way). Over and against this somewhat desperate projection or dream of the breakthrough he is looking for, Rilke bitterly notes the context of his actual reality at the moment:

> *... how unreal, how full of pretense,*
> *is all that we accomplish here, where nothing*
> *is allowed to be itself.*

He is then returned, perforce, to his poem's fundamentally elegiac mode, shifting directly from here to a wistful consideration of how it was in childhood when, momentarily at least, we could really settle into a purely present mode of existence, one that did allow us to live in a world of imaginative possibilities: "enchanted/with what alone endures .../... in the infinite .../... at a point .../... established for a pure event" (355). But that is not how a child "really is", Rilke goes on to imply. The child will grow up to find out that this world of imaginative possibilities must be conjured up out of an existence that brings one in relation to death and the frustration of love, with the threat hanging over it, as a result, of that direction in the elimination of reality and decline into pretense about which Rilke bitterly complains in this poem. How possibly to introduce into the child's world the consciousness that would allow it to know that all this lies before it, so that it may be from its early years predisposed to overcome the odds against fullness of imagination: how to "put the measuring-rod/ of distance in his hand?" It is inconceivable how this may be done without in this process "murdering" innocence; murderers, in comparison, are "easy to understand", for they murder in a world that is already corrupted. The only chance of success, then, would be for the child to have already incorporated "the whole of death, even before life has begun". This possibility only his ideal hero of the Sixth Elegy can embody.[9]

Rilke then works into this Fourth Elegy a pathetic memory of his own case while growing up. He recalls how his father looked on in pained bewilderment at his son's development, since this was taking a strange and seemingly uncharted course, unlike anything he would have considered even reasonable ("You ... who ... searched my unfocused gaze"). Rilke seems more than confident that in death his father has come to understand his son's purposes, at the cost of his own peace showing concern for his son's struggles from beyond the grave, and otherwise supporting him in what Rilke describes as his "deepest hope" (353). That hope bears on Rilke's poetic quest as a whole: as put in this poem's own terms, "that one can contain/... the whole of death .../.../... and not refuse to go on living"—the whole of death, and all those negative aspects of life that bear on it. This concern involves for him more than the courage simply to go on living; Rilke was aiming for something far greater and indeed complete: an account that would reconcile us to the whole meaning of life in relation to all the forces of death as he would have experi-

---

9. See the final passage he was to write for this Elegy when at Muzot: ll's 32-41: "Wasn't he a hero inside you, mother, didn't/his imperious choosing already begin there, in you?"

enced these for himself.[10] Already from his "small beginning" Rilke recalls also how the women who had him in their charge could only inspire him to embrace the more universal, "cosmic" implications of the love they bore him, forcing him, in time, to turn away from them towards his greater purpose. Both father and women are thus called to witness that it was inevitable that Rilke should be considering the extreme course he is on at present; they have borne witness to the fact that his life as he was growing up already pointed to this. His present resolution is seen by him as a matter of making good on his life also on account of the pained bewilderment he would have caused them: "Am I not right? .../... Father/... And you, dear women/... am I not right/to feel as if I **must** stay seated, must/wait" ...

***

Right, as it turned out, he was, and in the case of the Fourth Elegy there had been a genuine symbolic advance on what were to become the first three Elegies which were already written. How the Fourth fits into the Elegy sequence as an advance would not become clear, however, until almost six years later, when Rilke finally produced the Fifth Elegy, the very last Elegy to be written. By that point, the groupings among all these Elegies had been formed. It becomes clear only then that while the First, the Second, and the Third constitute a unit outlining what may be roughly formulated as *the description of the problem*, the Fourth, Fifth, and Sixth (the hero Elegy) evoke something like an intermediate stage characterized by *the will to overcome*, however pathetic the evidence of such will may be, oriented, however brokenly, towards unity. This set of three is in turn followed by four other Elegies that fill out the sequence by offering extraordinary forms of *resolution of the problem*, to the extent, at any rate, that one can speak of a resolution in the case of formulations that are intensely relative in the face of a problem that remains largely ongoing. In the meantime, the Fourth Elegy was to stand apart, on its own, for a full six years.

---

10. These "forces of death" involving, in addition to all the negative aspects of life-experience that bear on death, pure death itself. In relation to all of this, Rilke sought to conceive of the life-forces as such, which for him included also life beyond the grave.

What Rilke would have made of this Elegy at the time it was written can only be guessed at. When he wrote it, it looked like he was again in the midst of a whole new moment of production. The orientation towards inspiration created by his most recently conceived technique of self-emptying (*kenosis*) inaugurates a fresh movement in experience that seemed to be opening up a whole new dimension to his artistic quest. Some form of new venture into an alchemy of the spirit seems to be implied. However, his forced enlistment into the war, some few weeks into this new period, would put an end to all that. Just how fully Rilke experienced his creative breakthrough at this time, before he was called up, is measured by what he very sadly declares to his publisher after a month in service:

> *a fortnight before the muster here ... I was in a rapid ascent of work, a fore-storm of work, some curious single poems, the Elegies, everything mounted and flowed ... the freest prospects were ahead, when the gray army cloth fell before my clarified vision ...*
>
> (Greene 153-154)

Again he had owed this breakthrough to Lou's intervention in his confused life. She was keeping him on track, according to her plans for him, which could be said to date as far back as his Russian days, when she had diverted him from his own plans for himself and for her. She had followed him as far as this, whatever he would have gone through or might have to go through now. She would continue to be there for him, but it is significant that over the next three years, until as far along as their meeting again in the after-war chaos of Germany in the spring of 1919, Lou should withdraw into the background of his life as never before. One can say, indeed, that over this period Rilke was, for the first time in their association, almost altogether on his own, not seeking any recourse to her, while submitted as never before to forms of alienation from himself that threatened the very basis of his creative life. This was quite another kind of alienation than the one he was actively looking for at the time of the writing of the Fourth Elegy. Rilke's time in the army (briefly as a soldier-in-training, then a war archivist) provoked in him a trauma that re-awakened that other great one from his youth suffered when in military school, the parallel extending to the life-promise that had been squelched in both cases: in the past just when Rilke was coming into his best youthful

forces, in the present just as he had come into his own again as the
writer of the Elegies:

> *With the fatal resemblance of its circumstances to that most dif-*
> *ficult stratum of life at the military school, it* [his army time[11]]
> *has, as I am only now properly realizing, inflicted on me some-*
> *thing like what a tree would have to undergo that found itself*
> *upside down for a while, with its crown buried below in the bad*
> *and stubborn soil ... To which must be added that this crown*
> *just at the instant of being buried stood full of new sap, ready to*
> *blossom and to bear ...*
>
> (Greene 157)

The War Years

Rilke found himself as alone with the trauma of his army experience as he had been in his experience when in military school.
The account above is to be found in a letter to his publisher written
almost a full year beyond his release from the army, which in the
meantime had been arranged by friends. Both levels of trauma, recent
and revived, would very much have colored Rilke's ongoing experience of the war. Three months later he is writing his publisher again:

> *You yourself will often have thought with concern how heavi-*
> *ly it* ["the weight of the time"] *presses on my own mind and*
> *spirit and distorts all that I inwardly possess. If I turn up my*
> *most fruitful memories—I hardly know one that is not as though*
> *scratched out and canceled ...*
>
> (Greene 159)

A month beyond this, in a letter to another friend, he is still harping
on this same disastrous effect on him of "the time":

> *... today's air ... confutes me in the inmost recesses of my mind,*
> *even far into my memories—how much that is beautiful and big,*
> *how much that I have felt and thought, opens up, when I try to*
> *recall it, like a page crossed and criss-crossed out ...*
>
> *... everything ... has become invalid, been retracted ...*
>
> (Greene 163)

---

11. Rilke refers to this time as "the Vienna interruption".

What could a poet be without his fruitful memories (or "emotion rec-
ollected in tranquility", as Wordsworth had put it)? With a complete
relevance that might not have fully registered with his publisher, Rilke
had spoken of himself as a "mind dispossessed" (157). The process
of dispossession that was now taking place in him was at quite another level from the more general experience of dissociation he had
been through in the first year of the war, when he was also struggling
with his relationship with Louise.

Among the most significant of all the experiences Rilke would
have over the course of his personal and poetic life, and among the
most decisive, was the one he had at just this time. By now the war
had been raging for over three years, and Rilke would find a whole
number of ways of engaging with it as "these terrible, incomprehensible world-conditions" (164), "this predominating inhumanity"
(167), "this entangling in so much doom and horror" and "prosti-
tuting of human destinies ... subversion and destruction" (178) etc.
It would have been too easy to go under in such circumstances: the
very basis of Rilke's poetic mind, as we have seen, had been assailed.
Then, from some still more profound depth there suddenly set in the
great reaction to all this of the unconquerable universal artist:

> ... *these terrible, incomprehensible world-conditions ... have*
> *caused me to grow inwardly numb ...*

> ... *But when I think how much salvation and relief will be*
> *implanted in my spirit the moment the great healing process of*
> *this wounded world can be begun ... I foresee a point of time at*
> *which, in an irresistible reaction of dispossessed humanity, all*
> *things and all people will again strive toward us and concur with*
> *us, more strongly, more passionately, more unconditionally, than*
> *was the case in those so remarkably tense years before 1914.*
>
> (Greene 164)

Rilke was recovering here that profoundest sense of "obligation" with
which he had already countered the effects of the war two years before when suddenly he was personally more free to engage with these,
at the time of his "liberation" from Louise:

> ... *every day the war still lasts increases the obligation of human-*
> *ity toward a great better-intentioned common future, for what*

could be more productive of obligation than the suffering aug-
mented beyond all measure which must join millions of people in
all countries more closely together.

... over and over again I have had to conquer infinite hopeless-
nesses, but now one may hope indeed to be near those decisions
through which the spirit will be restored to its own particular in-
fluence.

(Greene 165)

Rilke would return to his experience of imaginative dispossession during the war again and again, bearing witness to a titan-
ic struggle in himself the outcome of which was far from assured.
Another six months later, to a promising young poet of the time in
whom he had great hopes and who was serving at the front, Rilke
does not sound hopeful:

What might, under the violent and extraordinary conditions of
your present life, make you desirous of getting letters, is surely
only the assurance, which flows from them that intellectual and
spiritual continuity has not been given up in this land of ours.
*And it is just **that** for which I cannot produce the least evidence.*
On the contrary, where I am concerned, all general circumstances
and the most difficult personal ones have worked together to inter-
rupt all flow in me and to separate me from the nourishment that
otherwise, even in the worst days, rose up to me imperceptibly
from unerring roots. The more I felt this fatality, the more I began
to look about in the disastrous events of the time, but this very
orientation made me more and more miserable. For where for us
here is this visible in this desperate world?

(Greene 170)

Still, there is a paradoxical ring to Rilke's words here, who almost
appears to be confirming that this young poet expectations are rightly
conceived, in spite of all evidence to the contrary. Then, three months
later, Rilke comes to an irrevocable decision, as expressed to his publisher; in this decision he is committed to reversing the impact the war
will have had on his poetic memory:

The longer the confused interruption lasts, the more I see that
my task lies in carrying on the past with absolute constancy of

purpose and in inexhaustible remembering; though the conditions
out of which I grew may have come to an end, I believe I have
understood their mandate so timelessly that I can look upon it
even now as inviolable and final.
(Greene 171)

Coming to this decision would stand Rilke in good stead in the
midst of the cultural turmoil that would engulf Germany as the war
at last wound down, and also in the aftermath of this when the severe task of re-organizing Germany was undertaken in great earnest.
Rilke re-affirms his position at this time in a letter to an old friend:

I long for people through whom the past in its large lines continues
to be connected with us, related to us; for how much the future ...
is ... going to depend on whether it falls in with the direction of
the deepest traditions ... (and not out of negation) ...
(Greene 177)

Rilke saw a rising threat in some parts of the radical youth of this
time:

The continued and inextricable wrong of the war has called up
more and more young people of contradictory mind, who think
to deduce the future more cleanly out of the negation of the past.
(Greene 174)

Late in the fall of 1917, some many months earlier, Rilke had wilfully
decamped to Berlin where he stayed for all of two months "seeing
over and over again people of all sorts, in order to take instruction
from them in current events and changes which, even if I have to
breathe among them, remain for me a theme indescribably inflected"
(Greene 422). Rilke bravely undertook this mission in defiance of
his deep characterological aversion to the chaos of social experience.
All this seemed to him important enough: "a theme indescribably
inflected". It is at this time, less than three months after this experience, that he is lamenting to his young poet-friend that he can see
no evidence of an understanding of cultural-historical continuity in
the current discussion, and that this has only made him "more and
more miserable" (170). A year later, with the end of the war, Rilke
was taking part in large political gatherings in the streets of Munich,
in which political options for Germany's future were being voiced by

many opposing parties. On this wide basis of experience, Rilke could only re-affirm his understanding of what "revolution", among other options, should really be about:

> *I understand by revolution the conquering of abuses for the benefit of the deepest tradition, and from this point of view I look upon today and tomorrow with the greatest concern ... My inclination is now more than ever to do what I really **can**, quite against the call of the time which would like to seduce everyone away from his real ability into a political dilettantism.*
>
> (Greene 184)

Dilettantism would soon give way to the real thing: in the spring of 1919, military-political struggles between left-oriented, 'socialist' and right-oriented, 'white' factions would play themselves out in the streets in the form of civil war. Several months later Rilke is re-capitulating these events that put an end to any more broad-minded and balanced evolutionary process of change:

> *... evil and vengeful impulses ... destroyed the cleaner future of this forward drive, joyful at first, but later desperate and finally totally senseless ... [T]he unswerving intellectual could side ... neither with those who drove ruthlessly ahead nor with those who met the often criminal outbreaks of this insanity with old and no less unjust and inhuman means ...*
>
> (Greene 196)

Both sides had dispossessed themselves of those "subtle, secret, tremulous transformations out of which alone will proceed the agreements and unities of a more clarified future". According to Rilke, it was a sad commentary on the unreal forms political solutions will assume in relation to the depths of ongoing human life lived among those "great correlations" that link past, present, and future according to incontrovertible evolutionary laws of their own. By the same token, it is an extraordinary testimony to Rilke's commitment to the experience of his times that, given the option of leaving Germany as he could have long before the civil war broke out (he had been invited to lecture again as of old, in Switzerland), he should have decided to stay put in Munich at the risk of his own life. Things came to a head one early morning in May when soldiers of the 'white' army invaded his apartment, accusing him of being a 'bolshevik'. His 'aristocratic' associations, which were also noted and extensive, in spite of his own leftist sympathies, are what saved Rilke from then being taken, and possibly even shot. That Rilke could have lost his life there and then, and so profound a cultural life-struggle gone to waste![12]

Short of fighting at the front, there is no part of the experience of his times that Rilke had not exposed himself to (this included a thoroughly critical scrutiny also of the unconscionable and deceitful rhetoric of the war-time press over all those years). He could certainly have said with justice that he had taken the measure of it all, and it remains to be seen to what extent this experience was to inform his later production of the Elegies. It had always been his purpose to wish to experience "everything" so as to be able to offer eventually a genuinely complete artistic rendering of human life in his time. In this respect his aspirations were somewhat 'god-like,' as if Rilke might come to share in a god's perspective also on this additional and still more intense "terrible" of human experience that the war had brought. Not long after the war broke out, he had had a vision of such a prospect, over which we shall be left wondering greatly:

> *Perhaps that is what is meant by the terrible war, perhaps this experiment is going on before some unsuspected observer—if it is conceivable that there are unconfused eyes, the seeing, experienced eyes of the investigator who is examining this like a hardest sort of stone, and confirming the existence of a further degree of hardness of life under up-boiling death.*
>
> *... for somewhere in space there will surely be places from which this monstrosity still appears natural, as one of the rhythmic convulsions of the universe which is assured in its existence, even where we go under.*

                                          (Greene 124)

Shoring Up Against the Ruins

The end of the war had Rilke, naturally, examining himself again for what he could actually manage to come through with artistically, beyond the terrible war years. The initial assessment was not

---

12. Lou herself was present in Munich at this time, visiting Rilke.

exactly auspicious, although there is an indication that he had done much to protect himself against the attacks of the war on his inner being.[13] Closing himself off even from himself, he was, however, unable to say where he now stood with himself exactly, whether he still had it in him to seriously attempt again those great "world-relationships" to which he had dedicated his whole life hitherto (Greene 186):

> *I do not really know whether I have survived. My inner self has shut itself up more and more. As though to protect itself, it has become inaccessible even to me, and so I do not know now whether in my heart's core there is still the strength to venture upon world-relationships and realize them, or whether only a tombstone of my former spirit has quietly remained there. I still do not know, and have not been able (for how long) to give myself the slightest proof of inner activity.*[14]

> (Greene 186)

Rilke may have been at a serious loss with himself at this time, but even so, could still know what his task would be: "to confirm confidence toward death out of the deepest delights and glories of life: to make death … more distinct and palpable again, as the silent knowing participant in everything alive" (Greene 188). It was over this same month that he notes also the "deepest obligation" the war had laid upon him: "to give up nothing of what mankind had previously gained and acknowledged after honest search" (189). This obligation he continued to feel, despite the appalling distress over himself. In this period (early January to early February 1919), Rilke was on the verge of contending with all of the political violence that would hit Munich throughout the spring months, culminating in the visit by the 'white' forces to his apartment in mid-May. In fact, Rilke was only really able

---

13. In early 1920, one year later, he is still expatiating on what was a purely negative technique of resistance: "During almost all the war years I was, *par hasard plutôt*, waiting in Munich, always thinking it must come to an end, not understanding, not understanding, not understanding! *Not to understand*: yes, that was my entire occupation in these years, I can assure you it was not so simple! (Greene 214)

14. "[T]he intersection point of my forces has lost its starriness, has fallen out of the great constellations that used to shelter and support it in spiritual space."

to free himself for himself for the first time after he had at last left Germany for Switzerland in early June of 1919.

His main task from that point onwards was, naturally, to find a proper refuge for himself ("the most protected solitude"—213), so as to begin the long process of re-making himself in relation to what he had been before the outbreak of the war. However, it was only after being in Switzerland a full year and more that he would actually begin to find himself again. This was in the fall of 1920. At first it took the form of a gratuitous visit to Geneva, where Rilke lingered beyond his actual plans at the time. He had continued in touch with the Princess with whom he had formulated the idea of settling down to work in a remote corner of her estate at Lautschin. However, he kept putting off his return there, very likely because he knew these arrangements were not what he really needed, though they might have to serve as a last resort. Would returning to the old places really ignite in him the inspirations he required, to set him on that difficult new course of production he was now bound to? Duino, for its part, had been largely destroyed in the war and survived in his memory only as the shadow-symbol of a former breakthrough now well beyond him. It would have somehow to be replaced by a new setting, a new Duino that would rise again out of the ashes. He was lingering on in Switzerland while he knew himself still estranged from any real inspiration, had stopped over in Geneva because it recalled Paris to him (224), and it was there that a most fateful and deep-set passion now emerged between himself and a woman-friend he had met briefly once when in Paris, Baladine Klossowska, whom he was later to affectionately name his "Merline".[15] She was to be the most crucial figure in his life as he approached the last stages of his writing, perhaps in the end a critical figure without whom he could not have finally come through. She would turn out to be as crucial to Rilke in these last stages of his writing as the Princess had been at the time of Duino, and Lou on the long, circuitous path he had taken before and after this time. Both the Princess and Lou had remained stalwart supports throughout the years, but by this point both had fallen into the background of Rilke's immediate concerns. He had broken through the war as his own person, dependent for any further success in writing on himself, and now

---

15. A painter, **Elisabeth Dorothée Klossowska**, née Spiro, had taken "Baladine" as her artistic name.

also the relationship he had chosen to have with Merline. This was a passionate emotional relationship of great pathos and inspiration to him and unlike anything he had known with any of the women he had attempted a life with after Lou—hard as it may be to believe this…

The last stage of Rilke's writing begins, as a matter of now certain progression, in fact, with a short six-day visit to Paris from Geneva, which had also not been intended. Here, in late October of 1920, he was to announce himself restored: "for the first time since the dreadful years I am feeling the continuity of my existence again … here, here: *la même plénitude de vie, la même intensité, la même justesse même dans le mal*" (226); "only now have I the hope again of carrying on, really continuing my work" (228). And as destiny would have it, on his return from Paris the refuge he was seeking had suddenly come into his lap: a gift-offering from friends: "then Schloss Berg offered itself … was offered me (to me, alone!) as an abode for the winter" (228/230). By late December, he is speaking of "everything that fills my mind to overflowing" (240) to which he feels the "obligation" to render full justice by shoring up the "strength to put it by in obedient and significant form", thus committed to "this bringing to completion at last of interrupted and imperiled tasks".—And just then a "fatality", as Rilke describes it (244): much as she had wished to support him in his solitude, Merline had fallen seriously ill from the ordeal of their separation, and Rilke felt he could not but defer to her in her need ("to which I had to concede the right on the spot to tear me forth and away"). The effect on him was "exactly like that time in Munich when I was just beginning to reflect and pull myself together,—and I was called up … something just as relentless"—as relentless, certainly, if not quite as severe. Even so, it is an extraordinary reflection on the strength of his character by this time that not only did Rilke make himself available to Merline, despite the extreme disappointment of being separated from his work, but after this should have simply picked up the pieces from where he had left off, ready to look for yet another fitting refuge for his work—for his allotted time at Schloss Berg had run out. It was then that Merline discovered, in their now relentless search for a new abode for him, the Château at Muzot that was to become one of the most celebrated shrines to the triumph of modern poetry on record.

Merline was to be in her turn relentless on his behalf, making the Château as ready for his solitary habitation there as could be, in spite of the most unpromising physical conditions in which they found it. Another benefactor had made it possible for Rilke to stay for as long as he wished—a significant improvement on the limited terms of stay at Schloss Berg, which in any case, Rilke now conceded, would not have allowed him the full expansion of spirit he needed: "the period granted was after all still too short to allow me to complete what I had so spaciously begun" (250). And so he was now set up, despite many hard difficulties in adjusting to the severe requirements of the place. Notwithstanding, by late September (259) he is seriously wondering if he can, in fact, hold out at Muzot, is still in doubt that he can find there the proper conditions that he needs to once again enter into the inmost sanctuary of his art. A great weight of responsibility now lay upon him and upon his art. All the adversity he had been through in those many recent years, both personal and on a world scale, would have to go into the words of the Elegies that he now desperately needed to get on with, for such words alone could be his justification:

> [N]early ten years' silence lays upon the words with which I want
> to break it an extraordinary responsibility: those words ... are
> made of the stuff of the indescribable hindrances that have been

*put upon me through the years (and especially since 1914), and they will be heavy and massive by nature ... [F]rom now on but one thing, something final and valid, **the one thing that is needful**, would give me the right to speak.*

(Greene 261)

"[W]ords heavy and massive by nature" will recall Rilke's equally austere commitment to writing a "massive prose" in the case of *Malte*. The work Rilke now expected of himself would have to be pursued on the same plane of weighty, ponderous creation. In the meantime, "a very stable confidence" would be required "to believe in the mending or salvation of so much that is damaged" (267). Even by December, he is confessing that "the destructive influences of recent years ... are still there", that he was still "being shaken" by these; and by early January he is admitting to a "heart ... diminished, beside its ... greatest task", a direct result of "the bad years" (282). This is one month before he would actually come through. And only *five days* before his final triumphant outbreak, he thinks himself still far from making good on his experience and achieving that "turning" he has been expecting of himself for so long. The dire process of dismantling the effects of the bad years continued in him:

*I am far from this good turning, **still**; to "liquidate", so to speak, the obstructions of the war years, to loosen stone by stone from the ring of wall that seemed to separate me as much from what was past as from everything that might yet have come, is **still** my modest occupation, I don't know for how long ...*[16]

(Greene 287)

---

16. Emphasis mine.

II

The Sonnets to Orpheus and the *Elegies*

How, we may ask then, *did* Rilke finally come through?

Of course, a great poet embarked on a "massive" project would never give away in his letters what would have been boiling over deep inside him, out of that dark embryo of creative transmutation to which alone his unconscious had access, even when he was to any degree aware of it. All this he would do well to reserve for himself, while the results of work had yet to show. But in this case Rilke was not able to say at all how the great Sonnets he suddenly found himself working at, of which there were twenty-six written in a mere four days, could have materialized just then, when there had been no directed conscious preparation made for them. Rilke's whole preparation at this time had been geared towards continuing with the Elegies. They had been and were his whole concern. It is well-known that thoughts of the death at 19 of Vera Knoop, a childhood friend of Rilke's daughter, Ruth, played a significant part in the production of these Sonnets, but Rilke had no conscious forewarning whatever that any of this would bear down on him just then.

Over the previous two months Rilke happened to have written Vera's mother twice. Naturally there would have been a shared consciousness of Vera's death in the correspondence between them, and some notes written by the mother accounting for the course of Vera's illness as this led to her death had been copied by her and sent to him, as it happened, at just this time. He was very impressed by these, "so manifoldly moving, affecting, overwhelming to me" (Greene 284). His focus at this time is on "this excess of light in the heart of the girl" in which

> *became visible, so infinitely illumined, the two extreme limits of*
> *her pure intuition: this, that suffering is an error ... that drives*
> *its wedge, its stony wedge, into the unity between heaven and*
> *earth—, and, on the other hand, this united oneness of her heart,*
> *open to everything, **with** this unity of the existing and enduring*
> *world, this assent to life ... belonging to the here-and-now—ah,*
> *in the here-and-now only? No ... into a much more than here-*
> *and-now ...*
>
> (Greene 284)

In his letter two months earlier, in speaking of "time and age" in relation to himself, he claims to live in a sphere in which all boundaries of time are overstepped, including those between

> *... life and death! How open the roads are to us from one to the*
> *other,—how near, how near to the almost-knowing-it,—how*
> *nearly expressed in words, this something in which they suddenly*
> *become one ...*
>
> (Greene 266)

The Sonnets to Orpheus
"First Part"

The Argument in Sonnets 1-9

Even so, Rilke did not at first have any idea of what was prodigiously overtaking him when he suddenly began to write his Sonnets to Orpheus, twenty-six of which appeared over four days, between February 2nd and February 5th 1922. As for this set of poems, they appeared in an interval just before Rilke at last turned to his main project as intended: the completion of the Elegies. The catalyst and doorway for the emergence of the Sonnets was, clearly, a drawing of Orpheus that Merline had framed and put up on a wall in Rilke's study sometime before she left him to his solitude at the Château.[17] In this drawing Orpheus sits on a small rocky earth-mass that could be a throne, intoning on his lyre, a single, thick-set tree rising at his back at some point straight up, while a number of animals have gathered round to listen.

---

17. A drawing by Cima da Conegliano.

In the first lines of **Sonnet 1**, Rilke has masterfully interior-ized and conflated the images of song and tree. In the poem the tree now ascends *as* the song that is heard *in* the ear and given full scope.

'Orpheus' by Cima da Conegliano

Simultaneously, this song emerges *as* the tree. Both suggestions are al-ready there in the drawing, if one looks closely enough, but their full symbiotic development could only have been actualized in a poem such as the one that had come to Rilke. Suddenly there has been "pure transcendence" (Mitchell 411): we have here moved beyond Nature as we know it abstractly or even in its form as a species of life (as *nat-ura naturata*); by virtue of this song—learned now from Orpheus who is the one who sings through him—the poet has entered into Nature as a living principle (*natura naturans*). Nature does not here stand on its own, as its own manifestation only; suddenly we are given in this "song" the identity of Nature and Self: Nature has manifested in and through the Self, and what has sounded, moreover, has sounded out of the very "silence" that installs itself as both a prelude to and conse-quence of sounding. It is out of such a silence that "a new beginning" has come. Absorbed into the "stillness" that emerges in the midst of this "silence", all the usual "[b]ellow, roar, and shriek" of animal life has grown "small", and all this from a pure "listening" that has been conjured up in it, and not as the result of any "dullness" (dull interest) *or* "fear", which are its usual responses to an unusual sounding. Among human beings also suddenly a "temple" has been created in their "hearing" where before there had been but "makeshift" efforts to hear any such thing "out of their "darkest longing", i.e., longing for such a revelation from the midst of their terrible, sorrowful lives. Too often nothing is heard among human beings except mechanical motions out of the world's empty spaces, in spite of their desperate expectation of some revelation ("an entryway that shuddered in the wind"). Or perhaps too caught up in the darkness of their lives, what revelation will have come to them will have reached them unprepared for it, with an effect more like nausea or terror of an uncanny happening.

It is easy to imagine Rilke in his study at Muzot, when at last deep into the solitude he had been seeking for so long, consciously or unconsciously taken with the drawing Merline had put up for him there. In the sudden depths of a new silence experienced in the midst of this remote environment, this inspirational song then comes to him out of answering depths in himself, without *any* expectation that this level of song would be emerging or that it would turn out so extraordinary as inspiration. **Sonnet 2** puts us still more in mind of an inspiration that was truly out of the ordinary in any sense for the most part known to poetry hitherto. It is the transcendent level of the poem's actualization that astounds. Out of the unitary source of "song and lyre", human and natural spheres, Self and World—"this single joy", as the poem puts it—a being now reveals herself who is described as "almost a girl" (413), and she has "made herself a bed" inside the poet's "ear"; there she sleeps "the world"—"trees", "distances", "meadows"—"all wonders that had ever seized my heart". The "Turning" that Rilke had so desperately hoped for eight years earlier would appear indeed to have taken place here (see above p.345). From mere "gazing" on the world, however artistically rich this experience could turn out to be as rendered by the poet at one time, he has gone on to "do" the centralizing "heart-work" (Snow, *Rilke*, 244) that has at last related such "gazing" to the unitary power in the world that is at one and the same time without and within. Rilke then comes forward in his own detachment from this experience, whose transcendent evocations he has grasped and continues to harness. He has begun to address the "[s]inging god", who has thus spoken through him and revealed this "girl" who "sleeps the world". He asks him about her own beginning, and how it was that her sleep at that time could have been "so perfect that she had no desire/ever to wake" (Mitchell 413)—unlike humankind, perhaps, which once awoke at the time of the fall. When this girl "arose" with the world, she continued to sleep...

Who is this "girl", then, we will wonder? Of course, we will suppose it must be Vera, or some version of Vera, on whom Rilke had been thinking in the immediate period before the Sonnets came through. Be that as it may, the poet asks the god not about Vera but about this girl's "death", and where *that* can be, now that *she is sleeping the life of the world*. If Vera *is* present to the poet here, she has merged with and become this girl. This is a "theme" the mystery of which the poet hopes the god will declare before his song, which has presently taken the poet over, "consumes itself". That it is assumed it will is a measure of the poet's additional detachment and finite place in relation to this "transcendental" development. In fact, already the song is giving sign of slowly fading, and it is as if the poet were making every effort to hang on to it before it does: "Where is she vanishing? ... A girl almost ..."—this girl who is the light that illumines Nature from within, that "through her green veils shone forth radiantly". It remains to say what we are to make of this girl, who in the last analysis is the Eurydice of these poems...

Already in **Sonnet 3** the poet is much aware of his limited powers in relation to the god who is fitfully inspiring him. It is "[s]imple" for Orpheus, the god, to "enter through the lyre's strings", but not so for a man, whose "mind is split" (415). This division in human nature is viewed in the poem in relation to our experience of love. At "the crossing of heart-roads" a "shadow" inevitably falls, "crossing" in one sense giving way to "crossing" in another, a fated meeting of hearts to contradiction between them and terminal frustration. This intrinsically "shadowed" world cannot allow for the building of a "temple" of "hearing" such as concerns the "song" of the poet. This the poet has learned from the god himself ("as you have taught it"). "Song" is *not* "loving" in any romantic sense, *or* "the passionate music" that is compelled by it, where "music" signifies any and all expression of such love, including all artistic expression. All of that has a beginning and an end however passionate, is finite, cannot be repeated as itself, as compared with the infinite (unchanging) continuum of inspiration on which "true singing" draws.

Such inspiration has no beginning or end, even if, given human-kind's tendency to division, it breaks through only fitfully. Here Rilke is returning to the idiom of the Elegies, in declaring that "[s]ong ... is not desire/not wooing any grace" that is to be "achieved": in "achiev-ing" grace in this compelling way, one loses it. "[T]rue singing" can only be "reality", in the following sense: we become "real" by al-lowing the "wonders" of creation to "pour" into us: "the earth, the stars". This can only happen for humankind every so often, when we are suddenly made worthy of the experience: when we suddenly and momentarily find ourselves living in "a gust inside the god", a "wind" that is blowing through. We note especially the identity established here between the creation "pouring" into us and this "gust" inside the "god" into which we have entered. Nor is there any creed or passion-ate manifesto associated with this experience: "true singing" is about "nothing". It is purely the power out of which the creation manifests in its own purposes which are leading us on. These purposes cannot be appropriated or tied down to human intention or profit.

In **Sonnet 4** the poet goes on to address those who have had this occasional extraordinary experience of "reality", whom the poet designates the "tender ones" by virtue of their openness to the possi-bility. They are open to "the breath that blows coldly past" (417), re-gardless of the momentariness of the revelation: they "walk now and then" into this "breath" without any concern that it will have turned "cold" behind them, when the moment of revelation has passed. In this moment these "tender ones" have become the "blessed ones". They have been made "whole" in this moment, but in this wholeness only "*seem* the beginning of hearts", being without romantic inten-tions, "bows" and their "targets" rather than the "arrows". The focus has altered here from that in the First Elegy (written ten years previ-ously), where the "arrow" of romantic intention is still in play, still "*endur[-ing]* the bowstring's tension" (Mitchell 333), even if it is there already seeking to be "released" from the limits of subjective desire and to become "more than [merely] itself". Likewise does the "wind" now constitute something other than what it is in the First Elegy. It blows through the "blessed ones" at the profoundest inward level of

Nature as creation; in the Elegy it is a more outward experience of Nature, even if a "voice" can be heard within it: there it is "a wind full of infinite space", that space representing potentially freedom from romantic care but still a realm that has yet to be inwardly harnessed.

The difference in focus points to a profound shift in experience in Rilke over the intervening years. Even so, one is inevitably returned, in this Sonnet, to "suffer[-ing]"; even the "blessed ones" have only a fitful experience of wholeness, and are soon returned to the "heaviness" of their earthly lot. Nature may manifest in its wholeness from time to time, but there remains the additional direction Nature takes towards material decay on account of "the earth's own weight" ("heavy are the mountains, heavy the seas"): this must be suffered, but will turn out to be an indispensable feature of the whole cycle of creation. The blessed ones continue to be aware of this direction in heaviness even in their moment of blessedness, "tear-bright" as they are in that moment, yet smiling the "more eternally" for their consciousness of their mortality. In this poem the direction towards decay and death appears as a feature of experience still hard to live with, but the poet hints at the hopeful vision he reserves ("Don't be afraid to suffer"): there is in the meantime always the prospect Nature offers, in its outward material dimension, of release, Rilke being momentarily returned to the more outward focus of the Elegy: "But the winds ... the spaces." But might he not have in mind here multiple possible other "winds" and "spaces" along the lines of that more inward inspirational "wind" into which he has lately come?

If we assume that the elegiac mood of the end of Sonnet 4 carries over into the beginning of **Sonnet 5**, then the opening lines of that poem are explained:

> *Erect no gravestone for him. Only this:*
> *let the rose blossom each year for his sake.*
>
> (Mitchell 419)

The impulse to erect a memorial implies a mournful sense, carried over from the previous Sonnet, that the god who can manifest does so only rarely and is for the most part removed from our experience, otherwise as if buried. To this the poet counsels that it is more meaningful to honor him by continuing to acknowledge that he makes himself present in "the rose" that "blossom[s] each year". Perhaps we have not reached that degree of devotion yet, and so need to understand better that it is "*[h]is* metamorphosis/in this and that", his reality that is present beneath the appearance. What the god, Orpheus, accomplishes in this respect depends on an energy and drive that carries him "beyond our life here"; it involves an "overstepping" that he must "obey". Wondrous natural life only appears as such because it has metamorphosed out of another realm which, if no less wondrous, is not life but death. The god commands this other realm as well, and we are in no position to follow him there beyond his metamorphic manifestation in Nature. Between these two realms "[h]e comes and goes". It is even said that he himself is "afraid to disappear" but nevertheless "*has* to vanish".

Sonnet 6, working in tandem with Sonnet 5, now drives the point home: "both realms are the source of his earthly power" (421). It is in this poem that the other realm is formally identified as the realm of "death". It is only in relation to this realm that Nature accomplishes its wondrous, lyrical manifestations of life, and it is the god, Orpheus, who reaches into this other realm, for

> *He alone who has known the roots of the willow*
> *can bend the willow-branch into a lyre.*

"[D]well[ing]" as he does in both realms, and passing between them, the god knows what the "roots" know of the mineral world and its material death; he knows the spiritually creative counterpart of their transforming process, and because of *this* is in possession of the secret of the wondrous manifestations of life.[18] "[M]eadows in spring" (Sonnet 2), the "blossom[-ing]" "rose" (Sonnet 5), all manifestations of the "pour[ed]" out "earth" and "stars" (Sonnet 3): all are made possible by virtue of the god's metamorphizing power won from his complete relationship to the processes of both life and death. It devolves upon us, then, to seek to identify with Orpheus, he who moves between both realms. To this end Rilke theorizes a wondrous metamorphic relationship between *two* practices. Into the practice of seeking "the clearest connection" with what is "seen" in our world— by doing the rational-imaginative work that permits of such a "con-

---

18. For more on this theme, see Elizabeth Sewell, *The Orphic Voice: Poetry and Natural History*, Yale University Press, 1960, in which Francis Bacon, Wordsworth, and Rilke are featured.

nection"—we are to incorporate a complementary "magic of earth-smoke and rue", which we shall seek to make quite as "real". It is by way of this "magic" that we shall strive with Orpheus "to mix death into everything seen", allowing the god to "settle/under the calm of the eye's lowered lid"—"lowered" towards the underworld, so as to open itself in its vision also to the influence of death. "True singing" (to quote again from Sonnet 3) shall then be the coordination of these two practices resulting in metamorphosis, "song" thus become "reality".

Via this route then, or one like it, we arrive at last at the "true image", the metamorphic creation of "true singing", of which it is said that "[n]othing can trouble" its "dominance", for the influence of death itself has been incorporated into it. All wondrous lyrical manifestations of life are instances of such "true" images, if only we can develop the discipline that will lead to knowledge of this. The unitary basis of such manifestations is the focus of **Sonnet 7**. When Orpheus is taken hold of by his godhood (suddenly in "the god's paradigm grip") he comes into the correlative in spirit of Nature's creation:

> *All becomes vineyard, all becomes grape,*
> *ripened on the hills of **his** sensuous South.*
>
> (Mitchell 423)

From here, in one direction, there is a further wondrous lyrical creation, representing an apotheosis of the human spirit, as it reaches into an immortal sphere: "pressing out/a deathless, inexhaustible wine". In the other direction, there is a full ripening of Nature that becomes our god's offering to the sphere of the dead out of which Nature's creation and his own creative spirit initially emerge: "holding far into the doors of the dead/a bowl of ripe fruit worthy of praise". All spheres, higher and lower, are in this way brought into a unity, which is the unity of creation. There can only be "praising" where there is such unity, defying, on the one hand, the challenging evidence of "decay in the sepulcher [even] of kings" and, on the other, the equally challenging "shadow" of seemingly random misfortune inflicted by the "gods". In the terms in which this overall situation is set forth in **Sonnet 8**, where "praising" maintains its "clearest connection" to the unity of creation, "the stream of our complaint" is itself "kept clear"

(425). Or at least this is what one would ideally expect of oneself in association with "Lament" as her own budding deity, where she walks "in the realm of Praising". Slowly there "dawns" in her then

> ... *the bright*
> *sense that she may be the youngest sister*
> *among the deities hidden in the heart.*

And while "Joy *knows*, and Longing has accepted" that reality is unity, and "only Lament" is "still" in the process of "learn[ing]" this, yet every so often the lesson bears fruit for her also, as "she suddenly/lifts a constellation of our voice/glittering into the pure nocturnal sky"...

While these Sonnets only make their appearance on the literary scene a full five years after the end of the Great War, there is no doubt that to a great extent they served to express Rilke's intention to bring the tragedy of that time into a finally positive framework, one that would *actually* have reconciled himself and his readers to all that had been suffered over many years. Except for the fact that he did not witness the horrors of the war first-hand, not having served at the front, Rilke shared in these horrors as much as many a civilian in his day would have, as we have seen. He had overseen the deaths of many loved ones in the lives of his friends and associates, and had himself borne the deaths of his own friends.[19] "Don't be afraid to suffer" is now Rilke's exhortation in Sonnet 4, addressing humankind's natural tendency to want to despair over decay and death, death and decay—it hardly needs saying in relation also to the recent events of the war. In the meantime, as these Sonnets bear witness, death is overcome: it has been shown to lie in the all-capable hands of a god who overcomes death by incorporating it into the ongoing manifestations of life. It is a testament to the extraordinary capability of the human spirit that we ourselves are in the position to share in this final meta-

---

19. Among whom was the young poet at the front to whom Rilke had written back in 1918—Bernhard von der Marwitz. He would die of war-wounds in a field hospital two months before the war ended and nine months after Rilke wrote him (see above pp.373-374). His death was a personal blow to Rilke who felt he had lost "a close friend"; "I regarded this relationship as a possession not yet entered upon, the future productivity of which seemed to me... precious...my hopes...left in a lurch" (Greene 175). Von der Marwitz' journal was published in 1924, and his letters and war-diaries in 1931.

morphizing power of this god, from whom we learn, as pronounced
by Rilke in **Sonnet 9**, that

> *Only he whose bright lyre*
> *has sounded in shadows*
> *may, looking onward, restore*
> *his infinite praise.*
>
> *Only he who has eaten*
> *poppies with the dead*
> *will not lose ever again*
> *the gentlest chord.*

(Mitchell 427)

We may only come into this capability every so often, only every so
often come into a direct perception of the "image upon the pool". It
is enough that we have had the experience and have grown firm in our
knowledge of it, which will bring calm: "Know and be still." It is the
"calm" that is in turn the precondition for a renewed experience of
the "image" (see Sonnet 5). In the meantime we have come into the
sustaining knowledge and certainty that

> *Inside the Double world*
> [of life and death]
> *all voices become*
> *eternally mild.*

We will note, then, what are, in fact, two levels on which these
first nine Sonnets come across. There is in the first instance the fully
actualized Orphic experience into which Rilke has come in the first
two poems of this group, which are nothing short of miraculous.
Beyond these poems Rilke then shifts into what could be described as
a form of theorizing about the experience, so long as we bear in mind
that this is an extraordinary form of theorizing that continues to be
intimately interwoven with the experience that has just materialized.
However we are to theorize a practice or discipline that would open
one up to such an experience, there is no doubt that Rilke had himself
come into such an experience in these Sonnets. The outpouring of
these Sonnets, which came upon Rilke so unexpectedly, did not find
him mentally unready or ill-equipped for elaborating on the experience. It is a pure mystery how this was so, for although Rilke's letters

in many places and over many years convey his preoccupation with how life is intimately involved with death, there is no indication of a process of development in regards to this phenomenon that can be so closely traced as to explain the advanced position of theorizing readiness into which Rilke had come by the time his Orphic experience broke in on him. Especially highlighted in these first poems is what could be described as Rilke's advanced doctrine of "the true image" fully incorporative of the influences of both life and death.[20] Such "true images" include the wondrous manifestations of Nature which inherently mediate at once both of these influences. Yet these are in turn made the more wondrous by the Orphic lyrical dimension which we, when harnessing the spirit of Nature, are in the position to introduce into them additionally. All such "true images" bear on the archetypal reality of the Orphic "paradigm", are also a sounding and a revelation: the sounding, in every instance, of the "tree" of Orphic "song" of Sonnet 1 and the revelation of the "girl", Eurydice, of Sonnet 2, she who is said to be "sleep[ing] the world" of "all wonders" that can "seize" the "heart". An experience of such "true images" is, moreover, how we are finally reconciled to all suffering we will have known, for in the last analysis the conquest of destruction and death has been incorporated into them (on which more below).[21]

Applications of the Argument in Sonnets 10-16

The intense Orphic atmosphere of these first nine Sonnets is, then, momentarily loosened in **Sonnets 10 and 11**, where Rilke suddenly turns to subjects that might have occupied him in the days of

---

20. I use the term "doctrine" here by way of acknowledging Rilke's claim, in the case of "true images", to a fully established truth, as distinct from a "concept" such as Rilke elaborates later in the case of "the valid symbol", in Sonnet 11, as I show below.

21. Not that "true images" are limited to the manifestations of Nature; included among these are also what will have been created in the way of human artefacts, as for example, in Sonnet 6, "finger-ring, bracelet, and jug"—ancient Egyptian practice, for one, making of these as much a feature of the realm of death as the realm of life; Sonnet 7 picks up on this allusion, explicitly invoking "the great kings of Egypt in their tombs" (Mitchell 580). The Orphic devotee, we hear additionally, is one who passes equally between "graves" and "rooms".

New Poems, and to a treatment of them that might have come straight out of that work. For a moment Rilke has turned his attention to what lies outside the Orphic experience proper. To the doctrine of "true images" Rilke now adds his concept of "valid symbols". These are more narrowly symbolic expressions, whether fashioned by us or derived from Nature, from which the lesson is learned, on the one hand, of cheerful faith "wrestled from doubt" (in Sonnet 10) and on the other, the necessity of our divided nature as a basis for an inspirational creativity (in Sonnet 11).

In a first form of the case (in Sonnet 10), Rilke's subject, a favorite of his, are the Roman sarcophagi, some of which are "flow[n] through" with "cheerful water … like a wandering song" (Mitchell 429), while others, set in gardens, lie "open wide" to Nature's life, "like the eyes of a happily waking shepherd". In both cases, "doubt" that there is more to life than our mortal destruction has been overcome. One will have lived through "the hesitant hour" in which doubt appeared to rule: there has been "long knowledge of what it is to be mute", an expression that very likely gestures to the sense of dispossession and dismay that the war horrors had brought upon all, and in which Rilke himself had shared. But something else to be known has emerged "*after*" such "long knowledge" and from the very process of doubt itself: knowledge of doubt, rooted in the consciousness of death, has brought knowledge of faith, in life: an ongoing openness to life, and a cheerful wandering of spirit that continues: "*[b]oth* [knowledge of doubt and knowledge of faith] are formed by [involved in] the hesitant hour", at that point where a "deep calm" has come into it (cf. Rilke's concept of "calm" as brought to bear on death, in Sonnet 6).

In a second form of the case (in Sonnet 11), Rilke directs our attention to a certain constellation in the starry heavens, two stars jointly called "The Rider" on account of a concept of horse and rider that is suggested between them. An application is made from this symbol to our own case in our experience of an inspirational creativity. Just as a horse must "bear" the rider who "drives and halts it", there is in us a "rac[ing]" power of expansive creative experience that must at some point be "reined in", if there is to be any proper control of ourselves in this experience (Mitchell 431). There will be a "path" and "new expanses", but also a "turning point" conveyed by "a touch" of the rider's hand for purposes of renewed focus; otherwise there would be pure (mindless) infinity. In this experience of creative meaningfulness, we demonstrate our fundamentally divided nature. Both aspects of our nature work together at some point, but only because these are fundamentally "separate, utterly", opposed, and yet complementary, symbiotic. And we draw a lesson from this: "gladly let us trust the valid symbol", gleaned by us in this instance (as distinct from the humanly constructed sarcophagi in Sonnet 10) from a picture that Nature offers. The impression of a "starry union" in the association between two stars suggestive of horse and rider, as conveyed by the single concept "Rider", is a "fraud", for in fact division is the basis of their associative "union". Likewise are we guilty at the other pole of what is described as "this pride of earth", this antipodal illusion of completeness in our own nature as if we were only and always a unity, without division. We thrust this concept of unity onto the stars (hence "Rider" for two stars, and for horse and rider) without our being aware in this process of the levelling distortion we have introduced into our concept of Nature and of ourselves.

Thus doubt is as much a part of our experience as faith, division as much as unity, highlighting an understanding that prepares us for the still greater associative antinomy of death and life. "[F]or a moment", we carefully recognize, outside the region of actual Orphic experience of the association of death and life, what are "the valid symbols" of our existence, in human artefacts as well as in Nature, and it is "all we need" while we wait on a renewal of that experience. Such "valid symbols" are, in the meantime, distinct from those other "symbols" alluded to in **Sonnet 12** "where[in] we *truly* live" (Mitchell 433), which are the "true images" already elaborated on. This is when the god, Orpheus, "joins" us, when we have our "authentic" time, beyond our cultural practice of orientation in the cultivation of valid symbols (in this latter case what could be described as an Orphic culture in preparation). In Sonnet 12, Rilke returns in memory to the Orphic experience that was actualized for him in Sonnets 1 and 2; returning to this experience, and building on his suddenly developed theorizing power, he realizes that in that moment he was in a condition of "pure readiness" for the experience and "pure relationship" to it: that is what made the experience possible. He evokes what it felt like to be disposed to the experience:

Far away, antennas hear antennas
and the empty distances transmit …

To be *ready* to "hear" in this way is as much as one can do, for we are otherwise "unaware of our true status"; that is, we cannot pretend to have the knowledge that would allow us to activate the experience for ourselves, cannot actually know ourselves at the level from which, from its own source beyond us, the experience emerges that will suddenly come upon us. In the meantime there *is* a "starry music" that remains "unheard", and it is so that it may be "protected" from "the ordinary business of our days". Our crude ways of life can have no access to this music, for it would then be defiled. It is equally the case that not all of a farmer's "work and worry" can by itself determine "where the seed is slowly/transmuted" that will eventually bear fruit: it is "[t]he earth" that "bestows". With this double focus, on stars and earth, Rilke returns (by analogy) to the main parameters of the Orphic experience as such, concentrated, as that is, as we have seen in Sonnet 3, in that sphere where both the earth and the stars are "poured into us", if only for a time.

In **Sonnets 13 to 15**, Rilke turns his attention in some detail to the productive phenomena of the earth, working his way into these in order to penetrate their nature as best he can. He is here at some distance from these phenomena but nevertheless indicates a significant understanding of them on the basis of the Orphic experience he has had. In Sonnet 13 his focus is specifically fruit: "[p]lump apple, smooth banana, melon, peach,/gooseberry":

How all this affluence
speaks death and life into the mouth … I sense …

What he "senses" is observed from the pure experience a child will have in tasting fruit. Rilke imagines himself into this experience, where a "miracle" takes place, and, beyond "words", "discoveries" are made pertaining to the feeling of something being freed from the fruit into which the child has bitten (Mitchell 435). We then enter a closely imagined experience of what "'apple' truly is" in its real nature, "dar[ing] to say" what this is. This is still not the Orphic experience as such, but a close and progressively deepening imagination, supportive of it, pursued from this side of the experience. It is a measure of the varied range of levels at which these Sonnets come across, which are not simply one unitary thing, for Rilke would not pretend to have the Orphic experience for longer than he actually does. But he may yet sing, and dance, around it. In the case of the apple there is in its "sweetness" at first something "thick, dark, dense", which then grows "clarified, awake, and luminous": the former experience communicates the influence of the earth, the latter that of the sun, and so "doubly-meaninged" together, a unity in duality. "Oh knowledge, pleasure—inexhaustible", Rilke adds: a deliberate apposition of terms, as if to suggest an identity that is yet not quite, cannot be, a strict identity.

Rilke is at a rather greater distance from Nature in **Sonnet 14,** in spite of the impressive pronouncement with which it begins: "We are involved with flower, leaf, and fruit" (437). This statement makes for a somewhat awkward transition in the Sonnet-sequence. Not before the end of the second quatrain do we come to understand that the statement is meant to convey, specifically, the sense of our *material* involvement in this production, as a species, as a consequence of laying our corpses into the earth, which in time feed it, right down to the freeing of the marrow over a great period of time. Hence the early emphasis in the poem on the reality of an "ancient cycle" and that in Nature's production we are not dealing with "just the language of one year". The question is then raised as to whether the dead contribute to this process "willingly", or with some "jealous[y]" of the living as the ones who profit from their "heavy" work as "slaves" to the process. Alternatively the poet offers a picture of the dead as in fact not "slaves" to us, but rather the actual "masters" in this process who willingly, and in their "sleep (recalling, perhaps, the "sleep" of the girl of Sonnet 2) "grant" us their "riches". The poet clearly implies that the latter is the proper view to be taking of the role the dead have in this process.

There is much in the way of speculation here, even if the matter *is* settled from the first as far as this poet is concerned, who has lived out much and intuited much about the process of life and death. How could the dead be resentful in creating, in the case of the fruit Nature finally produces, something so richly compounded of "speechless strength and kisses" ("kisses" bearing on the moment when the fruit reaches our lips)? But why, then, have gone into the idea of the jealous resentment of the dead, whom the poet goes so far as to picture with "clenched fist ... threaten[-ing] us"? Was this by way of addressing lingering doubts in his readers that among their dead, from the war, would be those who had been cheated of life? Or is this merely a rhetorical gambit on the part of the poet, the gratuitous projection of a false idea structurally designed to allow him to finally triumph with his own view? One way or the other, one feels that the range in theme and method suddenly falls outside the scope of the rigorous focus on Orphic experience the sequence has maintained until now and on its relevant coordinates in the careful practice of an imaginative thinking supportive of that experience. But why should the poet not reserve the freedom to acknowledge himself also an entity who occupies his own sphere of limitation (limited either by the throughts of others or his own rhetorical needs) beyond the strict Orphic paradigm, seeing as we cannot, in all honesty, always be its rigorous devotees?

The poet is also in the position to correct himself. **Sonnet 15** takes up as if the poet has recognized for himself the limitation of the view taken of the experience of tasting fruit with which Sonnet 13 ends. "Inexhaustible" is how he had put it there, and yet this experience is exhaustible:

> *Wait ... that tastes good ... But already it's gone.*
> (Mitchell 439)

So Rilke now traces the experience further, into the sphere where the fruit is consumed, where it continues to have another life, as for example in the girls who are inspired to "dance the orange". There is more to the fruit than its as yet unconsumed "sweetness", as celebrated in 13, for this fruit also struggles "against its own sweetness", towards decay, though saved, as it were, by us who have eaten of it. In us, in the girls who dance from "joy" inspired by this fruit, "[t]he sunnier landscape" of Nature finds it "homeland", and on yet another level—the level of the expression of the human spirit—this fruit is now "peel[ed] away/scent after scent". We are reminded of the symbolic value of the "deathless, inexhaustible wine" that is produced from the grape in Sonnet 7, representing what the human spirit adds to Nature as lyrical creation, expressive of the full range of Orphic experience in the sphere of life. And so are we exhorted to lyrical creation in Sonnet 15:

Create your own kinship
with the supple, gently reluctant rind
and the juice that fills it with succulent joy.

From the focus in the preceding three Sonnets on what "the earth bestows", for the most part in the form of fruit, Rilke in **Sonnet 16** shifts his attention to the mutual relationship between a man and his dog (see Mitchell 582 note). This poem is also narrated from the sphere of limitation: the relationship between master and dog is the inverse of the Orphic one in which animal life is won over and marvellously transformed by man's "song". The man, in this poem, occupies his own sphere of limited aesthetic creativity, which cannot reach down to the paranormal sensitivity characteristic of the dog in its sphere. There is an unbreachable gap between master and dog, trapped as they both are in their opposite worlds. On our side, we may "make the world our own", though *we* are "perhaps its weakest, most precarious part". There is a level of human creativity, a level on which we re-create the world in ourselves, that is still far from expressing us in a full impregnable (Orphic) strength or unity. On the other hand, more immediately than we do, a dog can sense the presence of the "the dark forces that lurk at our side," which would appear to include "the dead" (Mitchell 441), and the dog, in its turn, tends to "shrink away" from any fuller contact with these forces such as a "magical spell" might accomplish (this disposition in the dog lying at the other extreme from the action *we* are exhorted to undertake by seeking a connection to death through "the magic of earthsmoke and rue", in Sonnet 5). Thus there is (for the most part) a mere aesthetic power of creating in man, on the one hand, and a paranormal over-sensitivity to the dark otherworld in a dog on the other. Each being is pictured in its own form of weakness. But a compassionate relationship between master and dog is yet possible. The man has *his* higher purpose as this has been revealed to him, in contrast with the dog. Still, this man (the poet, who is projected in this role) would ask *his* master, Orpheus, to cherish the dog as being itself a feeling part of the creation as given, and to reach out sympathetically also to it. For as Rilke put it once (Mitchell 582): "they touch me so deeply, these beings who are entirely dependent on us, whom we have helped up to a soul for which there is no heaven."

No doubt it will surprise (and even confound) us to discover that the poems from this second group concern themselves to such an extent with the sphere of limited existence *vis-à-vis* the Orphic ideal. Only Sonnets 14 and 15 can be said to be working actively in the spirit of Orphic experience, but even so are themselves limited in their approach to it. Surrounding these two Sonnets are others that show the poet acknowledging his place in a world that stands outside the sphere of Orphic experience properly speaking but that yet yields many points of contact with it, as the poet continues to abide by it. Sonnet 12 ("Hail to the god who joins us") constitutes a key link back to that experience. In the meantime, that the world offers many "valid symbols", and that "the earth bestows" and we may "dare" to say what or how it bestows, has kept the poet properly oriented towards the experience. At the same time, the poet indicates his attentiveness to spheres of existence (as in the case of the dog) and points of view (that the dead may be jealous of us) that show a significant alienation from the Orphic sphere and yet continue to engage the poet's compassion and consideration. The reach of his concerns stretches that far, as it should if one is to honestly come to terms also with the world in its *present* limitations, which continue. The further link to the Orphic sphere is what finally transforms the poems from this group that could read like they were expressions of the same asystemic approach to distinct subjects that once characterized Rilke's *New Poems*: from the Roman sarcophagi, to a pairing of stars, to the apple, ideas of the dead and their relation to the fruit we eat, the orange, the dog, etc. It is as if Rilke were at this point bringing his earlier work to a *form* of completion in the further relation to the Orphic. And so, also, with the method of *The Book of Hours*, which is making a comeback of its own in the next group of eight poems from Sonnet 17 to 24.

Tying Up Themes in Sonnets 17 to 24

In **Sonnet 17** Rilke specifically brings back the "Ancient One" who had figured largely towards the end of the first part of *The Book of Hours* ("The Book of Monastic Life"). There He is the Original Source of the universal songs the poet at that time said he could hear, in contrast with the insistent deafness to them of his contemporaries.[22]

---

22. As discussed in Volume 1 of this study, p.69.

The influence of the Ancient One is not just felt in the present; it stems from an origin deep in the remote past and has been available ever since. Only, it has been systematically disregarded by human beings over the course of history, who have lived for other things: warfare and preoccupation with the hunt, subservience to hereditary truths, betrayal among brothers, the lyrical attractiveness of women as an end-goal: all of which has generated a congestion of self-proliferating intentions that has left no one free ("none of them free") and aspiring to more and more, at last to breaking-point (the analogy is with a growing tree: "branch upon branch" of human perversity). Only in the case of the poet's discovery of the Orphic ideal, at this late point in time, has history at last reached its proper and lasting goal:

> *Yet this*
> *top one bends finally*
> *into a lyre.*

(Mitchell 443)

The opening address in **Sonnet 18**, "Master, do you hear[?]" (Mitchell 445), puts us in mind again of *The Book of Hours* when Rilke's Master had been the God of those times. Rilke had then had a dream of bringing the course of history to completion around the inspiration of his God with Whom he was so intimately connected then. Over much time, and the whole course of evolution in experience that we have traced in Rilke's life since that time, this God has given way to the god Orpheus as the poet's now main adressee. (We shall return to the implications of this shift below.) It is this Orpheus whom Rilke now involves in his longstanding concern, traceable as far back as *Hours*, with where the world has come in its ongoing obsession with the machine.

Focus on the opposition between machine and Orphic lyre is an important one and well-taken, but it will seem to us precipitated when one considers that Rilke was still so young in giving us and developing the Orphic experience. No doubt we would wish to have more of *this* experience, to be given more sense of *it* and of its coordinates, before larger applications were made to the expanding contemporary craze for a more and more elaborate mechanics. When the Sonnets came through over these few days, Rilke gave still more expression to this concern with the machine than in the Sonnet-sequence as Rilke would finally offer it, and as we have it today. Happily, he revised his original outpouring of Sonnets so as to remove what would surely have struck us as one poem too many devoted to this concern, replacing this with a poem on a theme intrinsic to the Orphic[23], and he would, equally happily, at a later time add yet another Sonnet, not in the original stream that had poured out from him, but also on a theme closely linked to the Orphic.[24] Was Rilke in his original and more extended concern with the machine in these Sonnets deliberately attempting an artistic parallel with *The Book of Hours*, as a way of rounding out his artistic production as a whole, aiming thus at a still more comprehensive unity than what the Sonnets might constitute in themselves? Suddenly yet *another* ambitious project seems to be showing its head here! What we take to have been a spontaneous outpouring in the case of these Sonnets, beyond the control of Rilke's consciousness, turns out to have been not altogether so spontaneous—except, clearly, for the first few Sonnets that came upon him. At this point, I would count only the first group of nine as spontaneously Orphic; a more deliberate artistic effort is already showing in the second group, from Sonnet 10 onwards, until we reach the even more deliberate (and at one point artificial) effort that shows through from Sonnet 18 onwards.

Sonnet 18 ends with (for Rilke) the rather strange point that the machine can "remain" and also be "praise[d]"—perhaps to say that the authentic human spirit will prevail against it notwithstanding, since we are its creators: "all its strength is from us" (an optimistic view). This point is immediately counterpoised in **Sonnet 19** by a renewed foregrounding of the power of Orphic song to "soar" above all that is "changing" and "passing"; as accomplishment, it transcends time: "falls home/to the Primeval" (another invocation of *The Book of Hours*). As an expression of the sphere of change or limitation, there is "grief" that cannot be "possessed"; "love" that cannot be "learned"; and "death" whose mystery could never be fully "revealed". No other consolation can come in relation to these except for the "hallow[-ing]" and "heal[-ing]" power of Orpheus's "eternal song". The question may be asked to what extent Rilke is actually mediating this song in this poem (and on what basis one would be justified in being sure of this); or is Rilke simply invoking this song

---

23. Thus the original Sonnet 21 on the machine was replaced.

24. What is now Sonnet 23.

in a more limited though admittedly powerfully gnomic way, having at some point shared in it? He would be quite justified in doing this, since it cannot be denied that he *has* shared in this "song". In Sonnet 5 Rilke had grandly proclaimed that "[i]t is Orpheus once for all/whenever there is song", but how freely can this claim be extended: to what extent of manner of song? for it cannot be to all song, without distinctions. Another issue is raised where Rilke pronounces on grief, love, and death as finally intractable realities that cannot be brought under our control through any reliable understanding possible to us. Grand as this sounds, and it has a real air of finality to it, it is yet reductive: the question at issue is begged. It may perhaps be the case that these realities cannot be finally known, but we have not yet reached the point to say that it is so. What's more, if Rilke had listened to himself in these Sonnets, he would never have continued with his Elegies, for that grief could be possessed, and a proper form of love learned, and the mystery of death revealed, even by way of a desperate hope, is the whole basis on which the Elegies were conceived, and were to be further developed.

Rilke's entirely unexpected and still very young experience of Orphic song precipitates him in the Sonnets in an assertive confidence for which he cannot quite yet have made himself ready. One has only to compare with this the assertive confidence with which Rilke addresses the God of *The Book of Hours*, which did have time to mature and for which he did have time to prepare. **Sonnet 20** begins with another address to the Master Orpheus that reminds again of Rilke's former address to his God: "But, Master, what gift shall I dedicate to you[?]" But Rilke's familiarity with Orpheus here does not strike us as being as intense or authentic as his familiarity with his God heretefore. It is too young a relationship to be so, and it is almost as if Rilke were in this line rather mimicking his former relationship to his God; he is re-activating for a fresh purpose that former model of address here. As it happens, the material of this Sonnet takes us back literally to Rilke's time in Russia. Thus we have the narration of a moment, experienced back then, when a hobbled horse bounded free from its confines and galloped on awkwardly, towards a meadow: in spite of its handicap, once again "in his stallion-blood" this horse was "feel[ing] the expanses" (Mitchell 449), having overcome limitation. In his memory Rilke further attributes to this horse in this moment its own level of immersion in the all-encompassing power of Orpheus: "He sang and he heard—your cycle of myths was completed in him." It is all to the point that here Rilke is offering a revisionary view of his former experience, bringing it into focus now for the first time, since he did not see it as such then, as its own memorable expression of the Orphic spirit. It is *this* revised picture of the horse that he is offering as a "gift" to Orpheus. Thus another "valid symbol" has been produced, this time out of Rilke's memory, out of what is now seen to have been, in *that* far-off moment, a "true image" of Nature, in the Orphic sense of what is actually true.

There would seem to be a more or less deliberate if still loosely conceived attempt across this third group of Sonnets (from 17 through 24) to tie things up not only in the context of the Sonnet-sequence as given thus far but also in relation to Rilke's former production in *The Book of Hours*. More and more the Sonnets take on a form that resembles the basic method of that earlier work. Thus one poem follows upon another in a spirit of continuous address to the Master and as an elaboration on the scope and range of the world he reigns over, just as in the case of Rilke's former production dedicated to his God. In the context of the Sonnet-sequence, a significant further association of themes is taking place. Thus in Sonnet 20 Rilke re-activates his focus on the "valid symbol" as compared with the "true image". And now in **Sonnet 21** he brings back the theme of the Earth, not so much for what it bestows, as for how it bestows it. With that, the poem also brings back the Ancient One of Sonnet 17, for it is from Him that the Earth, in its aspect as Spring, has learned the lesson of its production.

What we have as Sonnet 21 is the poem with which Rilke happily replaced the original that again had gone (once too often) into the theme of machines. The new poem was added (on February 9th) in the interval between the time Rilke more or less completed his Elegies (February 7th, 8th, and 9th) and the time he took up again with the Sonnets to produce an entire "Second Part" (February 15th through the 19th). This was an interval in which, clearly, he stepped back from both the first Sonnets and the recent Elegies to consider what additional adjustments might be made to all of this (an interval that straddled six days). Thus, most of the 10th Elegy was rewritten during this interval (on February 11th); another new poem, as Sonnet 23, was also added to the Sonnet-sequence (on February 13th), and a new Fifth Elegy (on February 14ᵗʰ) written to take over from the poem that had stood in its place until then. All of which goes to show that Rilke was by then very much acting in a deliberate mode *vis-à-vis* his production at this time.

Rilke's study at Muzot

Sonnet 21 was composed when Rilke thought he had at last completed the Elegies: they could now be thought of as a whole (though he would go on to rewrite the 10ᵗʰ and re-place the "Antistrophes" that had stood in the 5ᵗʰ position). The newly produced Sonnet 21 reflects some of the strength of what had just been momentously achieved, and indeed it has much in it in the nature of a "true" celebration—in a rigorously Orphic sense. The first stanza of the poem is easily referred to what we can only think was Rilke's feeling of ecstatic release from a burden he had been carrying for so long[25]:

> **Spring has returned.** *The earth resembles*
> *a little girl who has memorized*
> *many poems ... For all the trouble*
> *of her long learning, she* [at last] *wins the prize.*
>
> (Mitchell 451)

---

25. As he put it to Lou two days later, on the 11ᵗʰ: "It really had been like a mutilation of my heart that the Elegies were not—here" (Greene 292).

Rilke had come back to the Sonnets with a confidence that suddenly precipitates him, and we along with him, into another actual Orphic experience—or so this poem reads. We had been through the winter of the spirit with the Ancient One, He who lies at the root of all things, past and present, and we had "loved" Him in that winter (so it proves), and we emerge now with the Earth in spring, She who has learned His hard lesson for Herself:

> *Her teacher was strict.*
>
> *What her teacher taught her, the numberless Things,*
> *and what lies hidden in stem and in deep*
> *difficult root, she sings, she sings!*

The Earth has learned Her power of production (as Orpheus has) from the Ancient One, and we are made privy to Her knowledge:

> *Now, whatever we ask about*
> *... she knows, she knows!*

Consider Rilke on the finally-appeared Elegies[26]: "They are, they are"; the close affinity with Rilke's life-mood at this time is all-telling. In realizing all this for himself, Rilke has realized this *for us*: *we* are still only "catch[ing] up" to what the Earth literally "knows", but Rilke has learned for himself that that soul is "[t]he happiest" who, like Her, "will win". Already deep into the completion of his Elegies and suddenly given over to this Sonnet (the morning of the day the 9th Elegy was written, the last to be completed over those days), Rilke had indeed reached the "happiest" point in his life since he had first set off on his hard life-quest under Lou's command. At last Rilke's long suffering or agony had converted into happiness; dreadfulness or horror had bred bliss...

By replacing the original Sonnet 21 with what we now have as Sonnet 21, Rilke in effect saved this third section of the sequence, which at this point had fallen quite flat with its overdone insistence on the machine-theme. The new Sonnet 21 adds weight to this section (from 17 to 24) first and foremost by bringing us back to the Orphic experience as such, but also by its bulk, being the only other poem in this section, along with 20 and 24, that is not what could be described

---

26. From the letter to Lou of the 11th. See n.25.

as a mini-Sonnet. Five of the eight poems in this section have but three rather than five feet: 17, 18, 19, and 22, 23, the creative tension of the sequence having clearly loosened by then.[27] Sonnet 23 is also a later addition; it was clearly intended to reinforce the somewhat too light effect of Sonnet 22, which (without its link back to the original 21) now stood on its own. **Sonnet 22** ties in with Sonnet 19 by returning to the contrast between "what is passing" and "what lasts" (Mitchell 453). Opposing himself to the modern tendency to be driven in time and to suppose that passionate undertakings are the way to "the truth", Rilke quietly notes that in fact "all things already rest", are already perfected, and to find the secret of *this* mystery is rather the way: in "darkness and morning light,/flower and book". The Orphic truth that lies buried in these actualities, which require, rather, deep thinking on, is the real object of our quest. However, before Rilke could shift from Sonnet 22 back to the theme of the machine in Sonnet 24 (in the original stream the two poems followed one on the other), Rilke would need to add a transition poem, **Sonnet 23**. Here the subject of misplaced passion and ambition, which is concentrated in the theme of "flight", receives further treatment, in relation *specifically* to "the boyish boast/of how much machines can do" (Mitchell 455). A far richer texture of associated themes was thereby created across these poems. What we gather from these several happy interventions on Rilke's part, as he looked back on how to bolster the effectiveness of the Sonnets in this third section, is just how good he was as an editor of his work. This we have noted about him before.

  Sonnet 23, like the also later-added Sonnet 21, is itself a marvel, another, but the best of the mini-Sonnets of this third section, being perfectly adapted to its place in it. The Sonnet turns out to be one uninterrupted sentence, and its accomplishment lies in the way Rilke, at a pivotal point, by a masterful control of rhythm, draws the misplaced, ambitious spirit of "flight" of his contemporaries into his own sure stream of experience, actively demonstrating that where

---

27. Sonnet 9 is also a mini-Sonnet, being the only other such Sonnet among the first twenty-six, but in this case the "mini"-form quite properly conveys its actual oracular content. The mini-Sonnets among those from 17 through 23 cannot boast such a content but are more in the nature simply of "conduits for the stream", to adapt Rilke's descriptive term for them in a letter to Vera's mother at this time (Mitchell 585).

all self-seeking is abandoned an instrument of expression is created that bears one into its own powerful sphere of "pure destination" (Mitchell 455), where it is now "caressed by the winds/streamlined, agile, sure". From what constitutes, at this still point of creation, a perfectly balanced state of rest, "overwhelmed with gain", such an instrument allows one then to achieve as "being" what before was merely grasping desire, opening one to potentially more and more unhindered creativity. Such is the gift of being among the "sublime/ unwooing gods" whom Rilke will go on to invoke in **Sonnet 24**, which ends this section. It is precisely because they are "unwooing" that the gods create the possibility of a perfectly free exchange of "being" with us. In the meantime, however, they leave humankind free to pursue their own perverse notions of power as demonstrated in the contemporary lust for the machines that are fast draining what is left of the human spirit ("[w]e ... keep losing what small strength we have"). Rilke having replaced the one poem too many in this section on the theme of the machine, we are now in the position to accept his development of this theme more readily, now that it has been more carefully referred back to the Orphic experience by which it is being measured. While not the complete or near-complete expression of this experience that Sonnet 21 proved to be, Sonnet 23 also bears on this experience, inasmuch as it has taken us to that point of "pure destination" where we find ourselves again poised for the deeper "hearing" that heralds the onset of the Orphic experience as such (cf. the "pure readiness" of Sonnet 12). [28]

Concluding Poems: Sonnets 25 and 26

What we have as the "First Part" of *The Sonnets to Orpheus*, comprising the first twenty-six Sonnets, is, in fact, far more a work of deliberation than we might have supposed especially if we had paid heed to Rilke's comments about how the whole was "given" to him and arose as a purely "spontaneous" event, to which he gave himself

---

28. The structure of the third section (excluding 17) thus breaks down as follows: Sonnet 18, the machine, counterpoised by Sonnet 19, Orphic song; Sonnet 20, the valid symbol, horse; Sonnet 21, the earth (later added); Sonnet 22, what forever remains vs. the flight; Sonnet 23, again flight vs. being (later added); Sonnet 24 the gods vs. the machines (also 18 and 23 less obtrusively).

in a pure "obedience".[29] What we make of the evidence of a deliberate creation in these Sonnets in finally assessing their import and
value relative to the Elegies is a matter I enter into a few pages hence.
One cannot deny the purely spontaneous emergence of the first few
Sonnets right up to and including Sonnet 9, even where Rilke shifts
into a theorizing mode about the experience he has had/is having.
But already in the second group of these Sonnets, from 10 through
16, a more deliberate imaginative practice has begun to show itself,
while in the third group, from 17 through 24, still other more obvious
levels of deliberation are in evidence. Two of the Sonnets from this
last group were very consciously (and happily) added *after* the original stream of Sonnets was written; moreover, even in the original sequence before these revisions were made, we find an overly deliberate
attempt to continue too insistently with the machine-theme, which
is precisely what led Rilke to revise. Then again, he felt the need to
fill out the sequence as it stood after the replacement of Sonnet 21,
sensing that this third part still needed a final transition poem, a function duly supplied by the addition of Sonnet 23.[30] I have also cited
evidence that appears to show Rilke at some point distracted by the
idea of seeking a structural correspondence between these Sonnets
and *The Book of Hours*. Rilke's distraction by *The Book of Hours* may
even explain his over-absorption in the machine-theme, which is a
prominent feature in that earlier work, not to mention his return to
the "flight"-theme also prominent in that work. There would appear

---

29. "In a few days of spontaneous emotion, when I actually intended to
take up some other work, the sonnets were given to me"—from a letter to
Vera's mother, Gertrud Ouckama Knoop, written soon after these twenty-
odd Sonnets were composed (Greene 289). In a letter to a friend over a year
later Rilke remarks "I could do nothing but submit, purely and obediently,
to the dictation of this inner impulse" (Mitchell 575). Also around this time,
in another letter, he describes these Sonnets as "the most mysterious, most
enigmatic dictation I have ever endured and achieved; the whole first part was
written in a single breathless obedience" (Mitchell 576).

30. There is evidence that over a month after these first twenty-odd Sonnets
were written, Rilke was still debating whether to insert the new 23 where we
have it today, and that the thought of doing so is recent (see Mitchell 585).
However, the very close continuity in the "flight"-theme between 22 and this
23 is an indication that the decision was, for all intents and purposes, already
taken at the time 23 was written.

to have been some impulse to link the two productions, these Sonnets and the *Book*, in some parallel form that would serve to round out and complete the pattern of his *oeuvre* as a whole. Rilke had been at the time of *The Book of Hours* very much committed to the idea of a life-work that would be about "coming to completion"—however we finally understand this intention, about which more in due course.

Sonnets 24 through 26, with which the "First Part" ends, themselves belong to the original stream of Sonnets, and they are fully worthy poems, if perhaps not so spontaneous creations. Nor are they oracular. They are deliberately interrelated poems. Sonnet 24 ends with the point that contemporary obsession with the machine is sapping us of what little strength we have left, but as **Sonnet 25 and Sonnet 26** now insist, in the Orphic sphere everything is different. There was no strength lost in the case of the girl Vera even when she knew she was dying (the subject of 25) or in the case of Orpheus himself even after he was murdered (the subject of 26). We are thus brought back explicitly to the main point of reference in these Sonnets. Moreover, these last two Sonnets were, clearly, very consciously designed to round out the whole group of twenty-six. The second-to last Sonnet about Vera, Sonnet 25, links us back to the second Sonnet, where the sleeping girl is spoken of, and the last poem about Orpheus, Sonnet 26, links back to the first where Orpheus initially makes his appearance.[31]

In the course of producing these many first Sonnets, Rilke at some point became aware ("little by little") that the girl Vera had, in fact, served as a catalyst in this production, being herself an exemplary case of the inalienable interassociation in our human fate of the processes of life and death, death and life.[32] In **Sonnet 25** the

---

31. Rilke's claim otherwise, that the Vera poem just happened to appear in this spot—"*Without arranging it this way ... it happened* that only the next-to-last poems of both parts explicitly refer to Vera, address her, or evoke her figure" (Mitchell 576)—is belied by the structural fact I have just cited of exact correspondence between the first two poems and the last two poems of the First Part. He had already been deliberate in placing the Vera poem as the second-to-last in the First Part; it can hardly be thought that, after this, it was "without arranging it" that another Vera poem found its place likewise as second-to-last in the Sonnets' Second Part.

32. See Mitchell 575: "I understood only little by little the relation of these

poet again dedicates an image, this time to the "sublime unwooing gods" of Sonnet 24 (the "them" of Sonnet 25). This is the image of Vera as the "beautiful companion of the unsubduable cry" (Mitchell 459), faithful as she was to the new form of life that emerged from the ineluctable process of her dying, from the time she was struck with a lingering illness. "[G]rieving" from her fate, yet "listening", she opened herself thereby to the "unearthly music" that then "fell into [her] altered heart". Here was the Orphic influence directly at work, or so the poet conceives of it now. Though flowing "darkly", yet Vera's "blood ... burst out into the natural pulses of spring", like a microcosmic facsimile of the yearly fate of the Earth, as rendered in Sonnet 21: "[a]gain and again interrupted by downfall and darkness,/ earthly, it gleamed". It is again a case of the poet, in his present, making a valid symbol out of a formerly true image, which has thus been recovered from time. Yet this is but an account of the life that emerged from within the process of dying: when death comes at last, with its "terrible pounding", nothing more can be said or known from this process, and no further consolation can be had. This is where the fate of Orpheus himself breaks bounds, for he was both to know death *and* to return to us from it, singing and playing on.

Sonnet 26 thus takes the account of death and life further. The Sonnet is a very competent dramatization of Orpheus's legendary fate, depicting how a "swarm of rejected maenads" attacked and killed Orpheus, and how even from this "pure destruction" there "arose [his] transfigured song" (Mitchell 461): "their hatred could not destroy your head or your lyre". Precisely because of his god-like power to survive death, "in trees and in birds" he is "singing still", and "[o]nly because you were torn and scattered through Nature/ have *we* become hearers now and a rescuing voice". The question remains to be decided, however, just how and to what extent "a rescuing voice". We will note also that this poem may come across as a deep proclamation of faith, but it does not in itself offer us an actual Orphic experience, as some other poems in this Sonnet-sequence do. It is, moreover, a highly deliberate poem, very carefully chosen to end this sequence of twenty-six, and is not a purely "dictated" outpouring. More locally, in the context of the last section from Sonnet 18

---

verses to the figure of Vera Knoop."

onwards, it functions as the final installment in Rilke's argument on behalf of the "gods" set over and against the contemporary craze for "machines". I will be returning to this Sonnet in particular to consider other aspects of its significance, especially as regards its application to the course of Rilke's personal destiny and the influence this bore on his poetic achievement in the long run.

Transition
to the late Elegies

A very great deal has been made, over the years, of the vatic and oracular impact of *The Sonnets to Orpheus*, ever since this work was first published in the spring of 1923, but as for its "First Part" which we have now covered, the achievement is far more varied and multi-leveled than these characterizations suggest. These poems come across at many levels. It goes without saying that they are all marvellous poems, but there is far less vatic and oracular content to them than we suppose and far more in the way of a deduction of imaginative principles *derived* from the Orphic experience, which, as such, may be strictly limited in fact to the first two poems of this sequence only. There is the oracular Sonnet 9 and other very near-approaches to the Orphic experience in Sonnets 21 and 23 (both later additions to the original stream of Sonnets). There is, thus, the Orphic experience proper, and oracular pronouncements arising out of it, but for the most part elaborations of imaginative principles either deduced from or thematically related to the Orphic experience, which is to say significant theorizing arising from it, at one level and another, some of this theorizing more intimately related to the Orphic experience, some of it less so. These first twenty-six Sonnets are a composite production in yet another way, inasmuch as in the second and third groupings, as we have seen, Rilke returns respectively to the thematic dispositions of his *New Poems* and the continuous method of *The Book of Hours*. It is as if the techniques of these two earlier works were being re-invoked and brought into line now with the new direction in Orphic vision, as if Rilke were, indeed, bearing thoughts of proceeding to the integration of his work as a whole. I have cited evidence that suggests that Rilke became at some point distracted by the comparison with *The Book of Hours*, driven to take over some of its themes again in a way that became too mechanically deliberate, so that he was forced to replace at least one superfluous poem on the "machine"-theme with a new poem more in the Orphic line, and to introduce yet another new poem to bear out more fully the "flight"-theme also taken over from that earlier work. In addition to much deliberate artistic development of the Sonnets' main theme in the second grouping of the "First Part", there is evidence, thus, also of over-deliberation in the further expansion on the theme in the third grouping.

We have been misled by the idea, which we have assumed in part from Rilke himself, that as the products of a mysterious "dictation" the Sonnets are all of one piece (one continuous "stream" of spontaneous inspiration, as it were), vatic and consistently oracular. Rilke himself misleads us, for example where he speaks of these poems as constituting "the most mysterious, most enigmatic dictation I have ever endured and achieved ... written down in a single breathless obedience" (Mitchell 576).[33] Alluding to the "spontaneous" emergence of these poems, which were very suddenly and unexpectedly written out over a mere three days, Rilke speaks of the production of these poems simply as "the stream" (Mitchell 585).[34] There is a need to introduce numerous important distinctions into this account, and to discriminate closely among the many varied poems from the "First Part" of these Sonnets. (We shall see what the "Second Part" is about in due course, in the end a still more composite production.) There is *one* sense, which we will easily accept, in which one can speak of "the stream" of poems written out over these days, and of "a single breathless obedience" to this process: Rilke did not *stop* writing over this time, and he got *all* of those poems written out; (except for, one imagines, some sleep) he did not interrupt his work: referring to the whole of his production in this period including the Elegies, he at least *says* that "There was no thought of eating"—Snow, *Rilke*, 331. That is one sense in which one can speak of a "stream" of poems and

---

33. To what extent Rilke's words could be misleading may be further measured by the exuberance of the following statements written a full year later. With both the First and the Second Parts in mind, "the structure of the whole", he says, was "based entirely on inner dictation" (Greene 326); "the whole first part was written down ... without one word being in doubt or having to be changed" (327).

34. As for his reference to a "spontaneous" outpouring of poems, see n.29.

of Rilke's "single, breathless obedience" to writing them in that moment. There is a *second* sense to these terms, however, encouraged by Rilke, that suggests that he was merely a conduit, or medium, for *all* of these poems, which we shall not find to be the case, in fact. One is bound to acknowledge that the first nine poems in the "First Part" are such a "stream" and that Rilke was acting out of a pure "obedience" in the case of these, but, as we have seen, a careful process of artistic deliberation (which eventually gets out of hand) sets in already with Sonnet 10 and continues through the rest of this "First Part" over seventeen poems. In other words, these poems are not consistently vatic or oracular at all.

We will be disposed, then, to make of these Sonnets a more profound and a greater achievement than they actually are as a whole, and on this basis among other things be inclined to profess their final superiority to the Elegies (as Walter Kaufmann for one believed). In any case, the Sonnets cannot claim for themselves the status of those "words ... heavy and massive by nature" with which alone Rilke felt he could finally vindicate himself in his artistic production as a whole.[35] It is the Elegies rather than the Sonnets that, in this respect, constitute an answer to *Malte*. That does not mean, on the other hand, that the Sonnets did not play a crucial, and indeed indispensable, role in Rilke's final achievement, as we shall see. If Rilke had not settled with himself in his depths in the way the Sonnets finally bear witness, it is arguable whether he would have finally come through with the Elegies in the way he did. We are on a more promising track with the Sonnets, however, in seeing them as, on the whole, a secondary achievement in the context of Rilke's main purposes, *even if they are also an indispensable stepping-stone* to the final Elegies. In this respect they have a role comparable that of *The Life of Mary* in relation to the first Elegies. Rilke was quite right, and un-misleading, on that point:

> *In the same way as the "Marien-Lieben" came into being in the vibrant leisure-hours before and after the first great Elegies (in Duino), so this time a series of ... sonnets presented themselves, entitled the "Sonnets to Orpheus" ...*
>
> (Wydenbruck 216)[36]

---

35. See above pp.380-381.

36. From a letter to the Princess Marie towards the end of February, by which

How Rilke Pulls Himself Together

We have seen[37] that *The Life of Mary* signals Rilke's return to that great Mother-theme in which he was utterly absorbed back in his Florence days before Lou virtually compelled him to go in another direction. Rilke's absorption in that theme at the time involved him in a close association with his spiritual forbear, Novalis, with whom he shares the same prophetic vision of a creation to be brought to completion by the modern artist under the inspiration of the Mother. As we have seen, the Angel who out of the Bora spoke to Rilke when at Duino is Novalis's (and Rilke's own) prophetic Angel, with whom Rilke's old Self remained interwoven, though it had been left behind. Only an inspiration from without, coming to him out of the Bora and his abandoned past, could save Rilke from the otherwise unfathomable artistic impasse into which he had fallen by that time. Rilke had momentarily displaced the effects of Lou's repression in him. He regresses further through a deliberate sycophancy with her at this time and *by way of this very process* (as Jung would have shown was possible) achieves re-integration with his old Self.[38] Thus could the Angel with whom he was implicitly associated of old now speak through Rilke. But though his old Self is in this way momentarily renewed, sufficiently to allow him to recover inspiration for himself, given where he has come to by this time he can only turn away from this Angel. He is by then in a state of self-division that spills over into the extended meditation those first Elegies give voice to on the seemingly impossible contradictions in human nature that bind us to earthly limitation. He is pursuing his own way now, from the sphere of limitation, but related back in his explorations to all that the Angel yet represents of the possibility of transcendence. From this point onwards he must find his way further on his own. It will be for him to complete the pattern, for at no point will his Angel be visiting him again.

There is an extraordinary *inverse* parallel to these earlier developments during Rilke's time at Duino in the later situation at Muzot. There the *Sonnets* suddenly come through, signaling yet

---

time all the late poems were written.

37. In Volume 2, p.292ff.

38. All this was covered in Volume 2.

another miraculous breakthrough after an even longer period of impasse (of not two but six years and more). Rilke's subject at this time is not the Mother, but Rilke and Lou themselves, and in place of the transcendent reality of Novalis and the Angel there is Orpheus and Eurydice. As Rilke has had to find his own way since Duino, his inspiration now emerges not from without but from within, and not from the outer elements of the Bora, but from the inner elements of the Orpheus-drawing Merline had put up on the wall of his study at Muzot. At this time Rilke again steps back in order to spring forward (*il recule pour mieux sauter*). He returns to his old Self lost in love to the lost Lou, the other main feature of his abandoned past, and now at last fully comes to terms with this loss, thus re-integrating himself in a yet fuller way. The result is that now, in place of self-division, there is (near-complete) self-integration. *He has accepted that his former love should die and yet retains his commitment to that love even so*: hence the peculiar form of the phrase in the Sonnet that finally acknowledges this event (from the "Second Part", Sonnet 13): "Be forever dead in Eurydice", dead "in", not dead "to". Having, in the second half of the war years, achieved inner independence from Lou at last, as we have noted, Rilke proceeds to this final resolution of his situation with her. In this way he achieves a final independence, and is at last his own person again, free to create as himself and for himself, if still out of that alienated world-experience (the inverse of the prophetic life) that he has had to make his own. The Sonnets at first and then the final Elegies follow from this release. To reach this point he had, first, to free himself from himself at a still deeper level than the one he had managed in the Duino moment. Two Sonnets bear directly on this great psychological event in Rilke's life at this later time: Sonnet 26 of the First Part, and Sonnet 13 of the Second Part (the former Sonnet the last from that Part, the latter appearing just about halfway through the other). Sonnet 26 from the First Part depicts the death by which Orpheus achieves power over death: his head continues to sing and his lyre to play beyond this death. To the extent that Rilke now shares in Orpheus's surviving power of song, *he himself must have been through the same death*, at one level or another, and the key to understanding this death is in Sonnet 13 from the Second Part, in those cryptic words spoken by Rilke to himself that seem to sound as though from an otherworld:

Be forever dead in Eurydice—more gladly arise
into the seamless life proclaimed in your song.

We recall how at Duino Rilke had first to undo the deep repressive influences of Lou on him, of many years, in order to be able at last to break through with the inspiration that, overtaking him from his old Self, finally got him going again, this after a significant period of impasse and drought that had lasted two years. By the time of Muzot, after another long period of tribulation, in this case lasting some six years (from 1916-1922), one must speak of something deeper than impasse and breakthrough: here there was to be a final reckoning, of sorts, inclusive of the whole of Rilke's experience to date, after an accumulation of still deeper setbacks that had threatened to engulf for good any such possible reckoning. In the case of these setbacks (the "hindrances" of the war, principally) Rilke was strenuously working at dismantling that "wall" of adversity they had created around him, "stone by stone" as he says, so as to meet up once again and at last with himself in all the poetic powers he knew he still reserved (see p.381). But once that was done, Rilke would still have had to come to terms with himself, free his spirit more fully than he ever had, if his life and work were indeed to come to have the authority of completeness that alone, he says, would justify him. What this meant was that beyond undoing Lou's repression, as he had to a significant degree by now, having achieved independence, it devolved upon Rilke to complete himself by settling at last the one thing that remained unresolved in him: his continued attachment to Lou as they had once been, bound to each other in a complete hopefulness that, yet, at the time was buried, as it were, alive, when Lou opted for another life and another mission for him. He had *per force* assumed that mission, had been given no other choice but to do so, and he had assumed it, though in the meantime was left broken and incomplete, alienated from himself, and in a deep portion of himself as disturbed as ever. He had had one hope of fully undoing this disturbance, and it had been denied to him, and he had come to see at last that if he were ever to resolve this disturbance he would have then to cling to that hope, swear himself to the lost Lou, and, like Orpheus "[b]e forever dead *in* Eurydice" (Mitchell 487)—dead *in* the lost Lou. It is because he had indeed, somewhere in the depths, achieved this terrible resolution, which could only be in these terms, at some point beyond Rilke's consciousness that he had so determined it, that there arose suddenly the triumphant *Sonnets to Orpheus*.

Rilke had now let his love of the lost Lou die—and she was now the dead Eurydice, and he had fully accepted this, but in letting this love die he had *in that same act re-embraced it*, and the result was the emergence of an entirely new power of transfiguring song we have rarely known, such as the one Orpheus, though beheaded, yet lived to sing, his lyre playing on along with him. The beheaded Rilke, forever dead *in* Lou, yet lives and sings, his lyre playing on, and all *because* of the new transcendent life he has willed, whence his miraculously triumphant artistic power has arisen. From Rilke's newly re-created sense of self arises, then, first, a new Orphic creation in the *Sonnets*.[39] Orphic creation, as we have seen, is experienced at the level of the interassociation of death-in-life and life-in death, both in the form of our natural existence as well as in our lyrical-artistic life. In these *Sonnets* a whole new Orphic *culture* stemming directly from this creation is *also* being worked out, somewhat precipitously, even haphazardly (by the time Rilke gets down to writing the Second Part to the *Sonnets*, as we shall see, Rilke has had somewhat more time to think all this out). Everything in an Orphic culture is oriented towards the circumstances when an Orphic creation may be made possible. However, only one attitude can finally bring such creation to realization, and it is signaled in a clause in Sonnet 13 presented in direct apposition to Rilke's cryptic directive, "Be forever dead in Eurydice": namely, "Be ahead of all parting, as though it already were/behind you." Rilke was not here advocating an insouciance or deliberate detachment in our relationships, but on the contrary championing so complete an engagement in love it makes one perfectly ready for, and accepting of, the experience of separation, loss, and death that

---

39. This is, in the last analysis, the true significance and power of the Sonnets as achievement, and it is a great one: that in them is born this finally all-resolving Orphic inspiration and creation, which is what spills over into and justifies Rilke's final ordering of the Elegies, as we shall see. Otherwise as an *artistic* achievement *overall* the Sonnets do not compare with the massive stateliness and philosophically more comprehensive range of the Elegies. (See above, and also below, for my assessment of the more relative value of the Sonnets as achievement.)

is bound to come, before any of this happens.[40] It is not in the end a giving up of love but rather a complete living with it *as it is*, right through the loss of it. This is an exceptional attitude, and Rilke has had to learn it in the hardest possible way.

Especially would these last quoted words—"Be ahead of all parting"—bear on that time early in their relationship when Rilke was, in fact, *not* ahead of parting from Lou, not just later when they finally separated but from their earliest point of "parting" when the clear prospect of their taking up as a couple, mutually devoted to their love and life of work together, had been cast aside by her. He had never accepted that fate; in fact, one can say that it was because of his continued devotion to the lost Lou over all this time that all had turned out so disturbingly terrible for Rilke in the precise way in which he had experienced this: all of this terrible had taken its distinctive coloring *from* this hopeless devotion. For Rilke thus to speak the lesson and exhortation he now pronounces in his poem with integrity: "Be ahead of all parting", he would have had to come to terms with what he experienced as his own personal tragedy. He would have had, at some depth of his being, to go back and undo the events associated with it, and this he does by at last letting the old hope die, letting the lost Lou die:

Be forever dead in Eurydice.

But here precisely is where Rilke's Orphic power emerges: he does not die "to" her but "in" her, i.e., *remains* with the lost Lou, and from *this* additional, perverse movement of spirit has possessed himself of new formidable forces of "song" that, surviving death, are what give Rilke his power to disarm "destruction". One will note that what is involved is no renunciation of love, but on the contrary a still deeper and fuller, perverse embracing of an original love that dispossesses death, and so now also all "parting" that can ever be known. The embracing of such love is a pure act of the poetic will.[41]

---

40. Cf. "I will not say that one should love death; but one should love life so magnanimously, so without calculation and selection that spontaneously one constantly includes with it and loves death too ... which is in fact what happens also, irresistibly and illimitably, in all great impulses of love!" From a letter to the Countess Margo Sizzo, dated January 6, 1923 (Greene 316).

41. Such will as perhaps is only available to the strong, revisionary spirit Rilke

It is an act *all the more* embracing of earthly possibility. At the same time, it is in the course of this act that Rilke is fully attacked and "beheaded" by the "maenads"—he is overcome by all that the world's terrible forces have in the meantime gathered against him—having by his act opened himself to a comprehensive "destruction" that is in some sense final. In the meantime Rilke had accepted what Lou had determined for them, had accepted the limitation she had put on them. In short, he had accepted his beheading—though only by thus resisting it all the more perversely, salvaging the love that was once spurned, dismissed, ignored, and abandoned ...

The Late Elegies:
The Seventh, Eighth, Ninth,
the Tenth revised, the Fifth

It is only another way of formulating the great life-lesson he had learned that Rilke incorporates into his revived work on the Elegies, which also follows from having finally come to terms with himself. It is now his purpose to be ahead of all parting, beyond every impulse to fix down or possess. It is the point from which the Seventh Elegy (the next Elegy he was to undertake) begins: the time when one sought to press one's own suit, *in life as in love*, has come to an end:

> *Not wooing, no longer shall wooing, voice that has outgrown it*
> *be the nature of your cry.*

Rilke's principal artistic commitment had always been and still was to the Elegies. There had been a first irrepressible outpouring of *The Sonnets* (the "First Part"), and a second act (the "Second Part") was in store. However, it does not appear that Rilke had any notion that there would be more Sonnets after the first twenty-six. His main purpose, for which he had scrupulously prepared over years, was to complete the Elegies, and no doubt he would not have let these new Sonnets so encroach on his purpose as to continue to make room for

---

had already proven himself to be. I use "revisionary" in the sense established by Harold Bloom of a strong re-making of reality. See *The Anxiety of Influence: A Theory of Poetry*, New York/Oxford: Oxford University Press, 1973, 2nd edition, 1997.

them much longer than he had. He risked being diverted from his main purpose, and the sense that a limit would have to be put on work on the Sonnets may account for a tailing off of the original intensity in the third grouping of these Sonnets. Then come the two Sonnets that suddenly put a cap on this sequence: a moving poem about the tragic fate bravely lived out by Vera Knoop who serves as a model of openness to life and to death, followed by a competent Sonnet on Orpheus's final fate that holds a great secret to Rilke's daring evolution in love in his own depths.

It was now time to get on with the Elegies, for which he had very much prepared. No doubt Rilke, throughout the lost years, would have been in the process of reviewing what he had already written in the way of Elegies, even more so, one must think, as he neared his goal of resuming with them, now set up to do just that. He had thus far written six Elegies: what would become the 1st, 2nd, 3rd, 4th, 6th (as yet to be quite fully rounded out) and 10th. This last from the first he thought of as the one that would end the sequence, the run of the argument to date being thus as follows:

1st Elegy:

"What we need is to renounce our attachments in love—and yet, we can't."

2nd Elegy:

"We long for permanence, in spite of impermanence, in spite of transience."

3rd Elegy

"In spite of our enslavement to passion (blood)."

4th Elegy

"If only we could experience a complete alienation; then, spilling into that complete emptiness would be fullness, the fullness of spirit without attachment."

6th Elegy

"The hero of old was capable of just that: a perfect detachment and thus a perfect control of every experience that engaged him."

10th Elegy

"In the meantime, how precious the painful conflict in us that will one day lead to jubilation. This jubilation will then be all the more ours since it will have emerged through our grief, through our pain."

It is debatable whether it was yet clear to Rilke when at Muzot that, in the end, there would only be ten Elegies, but there was a certain structure to those already produced that would suggest this. The first four Elegies in the sequence just narrated imply a downward spiral with some form of possible release from this pattern hinted at in the Fourth Elegy. In the Sixth Elegy we have a narration of the ideal hero and his complete integrity in his experience. This opens the door to a positive upswing or upward turn, and it is just this opening that Rilke has found in what was to become the **Seventh Elegy**, with which he now resumes. This Elegy suddenly displays an overwhelmingly positive spirit that is also overwhelmingly real. Rilke is suddenly writing now on the other side of alienation and tragedy. The "cry" with which he now identifies in this Seventh Elegy (or would identify—it is not quite clear how relative this is) is a very different thing from what it was in the First Elegy:

> The First Elegy:
>
> *Who, if I cried out, would hear me among the angels'*
> *Hierarchies?*
> > (Mitchell 331)
>
> The Seventh Elegy:
>
> *Not wooing, no longer shall wooing, voice that has outgrown it,*
> *be the nature of your cry.*
> > (Mitchell 369)

It very much looks like Rilke's "cry" or "call" in the Seventh Elegy is intended to be in direct, inverse relation to what he would "cry out" in the First. In the later case we are now considering, it is what we might describe as the "cry" of a form of new emergence from suffering that, on a now rather different level, continues all the same.

In the First Elegy, as we have seen, Rilke had acknowledged how, even while we know there is a need to detach from and transcend our possessive ways in respect of love and of life, we cannot do so. We find ourselves always still sadly implicated, and this leads us to want to cry out to—no one, for no one is there to really console us in this dire "need": "not angels, not humans"—not even "the animals" (Mitchell 331) that know better than to be implicated as we are. Only the outer world of Nature, being always the same neutral entity, can serve as a proper sounding-board, of the type that can allow us to continue in our pain without judgment, and even with sympathy. This fundamentally sympathetic aspect of Nature, always duly reflecting our condition back to us, whatever this may be, is the never-denying/nothing-denying constant between the First Elegy and the Seventh. For the first time Rilke, in the Seventh Elegy, would "cry out as purely as a bird", without any expectation of a return on his emotion; Nature, he implies, would as ever be there, quite as purely, to reflect this experience back to him (Mitchell 369). At a certain level of its experience, the bird nearly forgets "that he is a suffering creature"; suddenly he can "fling" out into the world a "heart" made momentarily "single" by his consciousness of an emotion free of any impulse to possess. The male reference in the presentation of the bird here emphasizes with all the more force that this is Rilke's own case. Rilke writes that he "would" now "be wooing, not any less purely". Yet, though he would renounce "wooing", he has, nevertheless, returned to the concept here. This highlights a certain division in him that continues, in spite of the euphoria of this moment; this division is already, in any case, implied in the consciousness (the bird is also otherwise said to have) of a "suffering" that continues. One notes also the insistently *conditional* form of Rilke's expression throughout this section, emphasizing that this is now the poet's deepest wish, but a speculative wishing all the same: "you would cry out as purely as a bird", "you would be wooing, not any less purely" etc.

Thus is the elegiac point of view consistently maintained throughout these poems: there is an ongoing consciousness of division and conflict that is never denied—but there is now real possibility. Acting on the basis of a pure motivation such as the poem considers, Rilke "would" at last engage the sympathetic response of that elusive Beloved ("the silent lover") who continues to lie within the depths of creation waiting for a proper form of emotional expression to reach Her (and who is "still unseen" though "slowly awakening" to what She is now "hear[ing]"). Everywhere around Her, Nature would already be responding to his newly fashioned "cry": "Oh and springtime would hold it—, everywhere it would echo/the song of annunciation." "Springtime", as this poem presents it, will put us in mind of the Sonnet, "Spring has returned". It is the same "song of annunciation" of that Sonnet that we hear in the Elegy. However, that Sonnet was written two days later (see pp.405-406), out of a greater sense of self-integration. Coming away from what he had already written as Sonnets, Rilke was already a re-created being, but it does not appear as if, when he wrote this Elegy, he fully grasped the implications of his new-found transformation. He had at last absorbed his lesson, but this lesson had not yet quite fully registered with him. "Springtime" in this poem, not to mention the "summer" into which it unfolds, with all of the many different subtle splendors that are rung on Rilke's lyrical instrument in unison with these seasons, directly expresses the personal transformation Rilke has been through, but, significantly, in this Elegy Rilke is still in a *conditional* relationship to this transformation. That does not make Rilke's expression of himself in the first part of this poem, in the last analysis, any less Orphic expression than it is in the Sonnets, but a presently limited understanding of such expression only very recently experienced by Rilke ends up necessarily serving a different exposition. And it is just as well, for the Elegy form, which recognizes that we continue to live at the mercy of ourselves in spite of hope, would not have accommodated recognition of the full achievement Orphic expression finally represents.

To account for Rilke's situation after this fashion is to recognize that he was at this time in the midst of two productions that were proceeding, more or less, simultaneously. That the "Second Part" to the Sonnets would emerge almost as soon as the Elegies were completed, even if Rilke did not plan this, is an implicit testimony to this dual fact. Fresh from the achievement of the first many Sonnets, it must have taken great resolve on Rilke's part to shift his attention to the very different idiom of the Elegies. The orientation is very different. The Seventh Elegy, unlike the Sonnets as a whole, does not look back to "the great void where all things begin" (Mitchell 487), the Orphic sphere of the dead earth and of death. It comes to a focus rather in the thought of how we are in the process of making the visible creation over into an invisible world, and in the transformational effects of artistic expression in general as distinct from the basis on which Orphic expression specifically proceeds. Rilke's exposition in this poem is finally oriented more towards the struggling civilization he is addressing generally in the Elegies than towards Nature's promise in the hands of the Orphic artist.

Thus the shift in the poem's next section from a self-transforming Nature to the "disinherited ones" (Mitchell 373), those "many" who "no longer perceive" what "was formerly prayed to, worshipped, knelt before". They fail to appreciate that "temples" were once the outward expression of real "extravagances of the heart", being the visible manifestation of an *inner* movement towards "the invisible world", and that it behooves us now, as then, to continue to "build" these temples "inside ourselves". Failing to see this, many consequently live in an unredeemed continuum of time where not the past, nor the future, nor even the present is brought into any distinct focus. Contrasting with these are those who have "truly experienced" even "one earthly Thing" (371). They have thereby been proven in "being". Those girls who died young, who, along with the elusive Beloved, would also be responding to the poet's pure "call", would understand with him that it was enough that they "truly" were just once, even in "a barely measurable time between two moments". In this other sphere of time they would have reached that point where a transformed nature, transformed from within, would have made itself purely "visible", if even for a trice of time, and thus served as an offering to the invisible world. This is the process of our evolution here on earth:

> *Our life*
> *passes in transformation. And the external*
> *shrinks into less and less.*

The Elegies as a whole have been very much about this desired and also elusive process of transformation, even if they do not trace this process back to its source as the Sonnets do. In the first part of the Seventh Elegy we are given the transforming process in (nearly) full colours, without any attempt subsequently to trace the experience to its source, though its *effects* and the evolutionary purpose that is said to lie behind it are here powerfully conceived. The evidence of still-standing monuments, which are the visible manifestation of this transforming process, in the meantime remains an important source of inspiration, and it is our task to continue to "preserve" these. We are not to be discouraged by modern attitudes that, on the one hand, are unable to "perceive" (373) the achievement behind these older monuments, and on the other, have thrust out their own material structures that themselves belong merely to "the realm of concepts, as though [they] still stood in the brain" (371). We live in the midst of such, and other "reservoirs of power" (the steam engine, for example), which are merely mediated, untransformed nature, the external world perpetuating itself. Older monuments as expressions of a veritable transformation of the external—the poet cites, pre-eminently, the Sphinx and Chartres—stand, contrastingly, as evidence of "a miracle" (373) of nature, and are a tribute to what humankind can accomplish. They have been fashioned out of a process that has defied both "Fate, the annihilator" and the "great" outer "spaces" of the world, which "since thousands of years" have continued to dominate over us in spite of our accomplishments, not to mention, in the case of more recent monuments, the alienation of spirit that has taken over the modern city abandoned to its own decay (and so a cathedral can be cited for its "surviving thrust ... from a fading or alien city"). "Be astonished, Angel" the poet cries out, as he returns to the central addressee of these Elegies, that alien Being who stands aloof in the purity of its own invisible world beyond contradiction, and who yet must recognize that such visible monuments of the *human* spirit give evidence of an inner movement in and towards its own invisible sphere. There has been a transformation of what is merely external into the monumental artistic achievement by virtue of an invisible transforming power that has been tapped into within, and this points to the fact that all is a passing from the invisible to the invisible by way of the visible. It is not our purpose, in any case, to project ourselves wholesale into any invisible world, as if it were even possible to do that, being as we are as yet not fully transformed beings; we are, rather, to continue to be transformers of the visible in this world, as we must.

From an initial position of great dismay in the early Elegies, where the Angel overbears Rilke's spirit by its terrible unapproachability and seeming indifference to his conflicted plight, Rilke has progressed by now to an expression of great confidence in his existence in relation to this same Angel. It is a measure of the distance

Rilke has travelled also from Novalis's Angel who *transformed* into Rilke's terrible Angel early on (see above, pp.302-306). No longer is Rilke's attitude towards his terrible Angel a deferential one, for Rilke has learned to understand and to accept his own mission. Every occasion on which he has risen to creative heights now sees him eddying back towards the human scene he is in the process of transforming, thus effecting a "current" (Mitchell 375) of human experience against which the Angel "cannot move", for the Angel is now held back in its own sphere. So the Seventh Elegy concludes. It is Rilke's turn to hold the Angel at a distance, and there is even a threat voiced against it, rather as a swimmer, who is or could be drowning, will threaten one who would help him, to warn it both of the danger of being taken down with him and as a defense against the confusion its outside intervention would create. It is as if Rilke had become even somewhat arrogant and contemptuous of the Angel's station, seeing as it is so far beyond what can properly concern the human scene. This new attitude contrasts with the torment he once knew when wondering if the Angel could ever be reached and be of any help:

> *Ungraspable One, far above.*
>
> > *Don't think that I'm wooing ...*
> > *... For* [now] *my call*
>
> *is always filled with departure.*

What, then, has become of that great "song of annunciation" with which this Seventh Elegy begins? Rilke has been diverted from it, once again, by the thought of how human beings continue to struggle with their understanding of what there is to make of life on earth. It is this, the fundamental impulse of these Elegies, that has Rilke eddying back into general human experience in spite of the extraordinary advance in creative vision he himself has made. There is the additional case of his presenting the vision into which he has come, by way of this "song", as a conditional accomplishment, as if he were emphasizing what could be happening for all of us even as it is happening for him, at once conditional and real. Hence the use, typical of these Elegies, of the ambiguous "you" in Rilke's address in this poem, by which he refers at once to himself who has been there and to all the rest of us who will not have been but could be...

The **Eighth Elegy** continues with this process of eddying back, or "departure", the note on which the Seventh Elegy ends. As if in counterbalance to the evidence of advance and accomplishment the Seventh Elegy records, Rilke now gives his attention to what it is in human nature that has us turning away from the prospect of "truly being" (371). That which explains our balking before the challenge of our being is the isolated consciousness in which we lie ("our kind of consciousness"—379); this is distinct from consciousness in the "natural world" which "with all *its* eyes ... looks out/into the *Open*" (377), as this is known to plants, flowers, animals. To this world belongs also the child before it is rudely "shaken" (377) out of such consciousness; Rilke even includes, among these, lovers: they too have a peripheral view of this "Open", in spite of themselves, since for the most part they only see each other: "As if by some mistake it opens for them/ behind each other" (377). In contrast with consciousness that looks out into the Open, for *us* "[a]lways there is *World*": for our part we are "spectators always, everywhere,/turned towards the world of objects, never outward". We find ourselves forever "re-arrang[ing]" this world which is always "break[ing] down", and "ourselves" along with it. In this poem Rilke returns to that exposition he had given, more than six years before, about a fundamental tendency in humankind to "eliminate" all that is real, to thrust it all outside and beyond itself: the thought of death and of God pre-eminently. At the time, Rilke had made the point that contrastingly Nature knows "nothing of this removal" (Greene 149).[42] The paradox is that, in pretending to eliminate death from our consciousness, it turns out that "[w]e, only, can see death" (Mitchell 377). Inevitably we find ourselves oppressed by it from the other side. The animal, for its part, lives "[f]ree from death" just because it is fully immersed in Nature's sphere where life and death already commingle: thus an animal "has its decline in back of it ... God in front" and so "moves/already in eternity". The animal's experience, in contrast with humankind's self-conflicted life, is of "all time and itself within all time, forever healed" (379).

What, then, can it mean for humankind to be so self-isolated, and how are we, given our limitations, to find a way of "truly being"? The Eighth Elegy does not answer this question but leaves us pondering the problem of our fundamental separateness in consciousness.

---

42. See above pp.361 and 365.

It is an incontrovertible fact: in our consciousness we are turned away from Nature in its fullness of being. Rilke speculates that if an animal in its full being were to be suddenly possessed of our consciousness it would wrench us around in turn and drag us into the stream of its own full life. However, this could not be *our* way of truly being: this could not solve the problem of *our* being. An animal remains what it is: "it feels its life as boundless", whereas we begin from the other end: "spectators, always, everywhere". Even so, Rilke claims to have found a crack even in the animal's consciousness:

> *For it too feels the presence of what often*
> *overwhelms us: a memory, as if*
> *the element we keep pressing towards was once*
> *more intimate, more true ...*

Thus Rilke postulates a "first home" in Nature from which even the animal has been to a degree separated. *We* stand at the extreme other end of what is in fact a continuum: from gnat, through the bird-world, toward the animal, and finally ourselves, a greater degree of separation from Nature distinguishing each of these categories in turn: the gnat being that creature that lives its whole life still in the "womb", that "first home" of Nature, whereas we have come away from it more than any other creature. Much of the Eighth Elegy has thus taken the form of a philosophical disquisition on Nature in this straightforward, elementary, 18th century-like way.[43] In spite of a general decline from fullness among all creatures, yet even we find ourselves "pressing towards" an element other than that of our separated consciousness. At the same time, subject as we are to our consciousness, being naturally constituted in this way, we keep turning back from that venture forward, upon ourselves:

> *so that*
> *no matter what we do, we are in the posture*
> *of someone going away.*
>
> (Mitchell 381)

---

43. It is Rilke's most prosaic Elegy, but, even so, it was Lou's favorite Elegy, perhaps just because of its straightforwardly philosophizing manner, being without much significant poetic elaboration.

Even at the moment of death, "which shows him [her] his [her] whole valley/one last time", there is a turning back upon the isolation of oneself, the greater prospect of what lies Open before one being even in that last moment either obscured or denied.

"[S]o we live here, forever taking leave", Rilke concludes in this Elegy. And this has become Rilke's definition of fate:

> *That is what fate means: to be opposite,*
> *to be opposite and nothing else, forever.* [44]
>
> (379)

Significantly the **Ninth Elegy** begins with this same focus on fate but from a broader perspective, returning to the point made in the Seventh Elegy of what can, nevertheless, still be known by way of "truly being"—as that earlier Elegy puts it: "[f]or each of you had … a barely measurable time … when you were granted a sense of being" (371). The implication in the Ninth Elegy is that it is possible to spend an even more significant period of time than we do in a state of being, "serenely in the form of a laurel", as a poet or any creative artist will. [45] If we *can* spend such time in a state of higher being, Rilke further speculates:

> *… why then*
> *have to be human—and escaping from fate,*
> *Keep longing for fate?*

What, then, explains the undeniable impulse that has us consistently turning back from our experience of a higher being to a more fundamental existence where fate reigns? The answer, Rilke finds, is:

> *… because truly being here is so much; because everything here*
> *apparently needs us …*

---

44. It should be clear that by "taking leave" Rilke does not mean, here, that readiness to accept "departure", in this case having to do with renouncing possession, that he elsewhere in these Elegies idealizes and makes into the most important disposition when cultivating our attachments in life as in love. See above p.428.

45. That the laurel is of a shade "darker than all other green" (383) makes it into a symbol of that higher lyrical-artistic realm beyond Nature that concerns Rilke so much, in which Nature finds itself further transformed.

The answer is that it is a matter of our truly being *here*. After every occasion of an accomplishment in being, we are returned to an existence that continues to require our power to transform it, for always there is more to transform. And *that is why* we are inherently constituted so in our consciousness, which has us always turning back upon ourselves, back to the sphere of fate. It is here especially that a creative effort is required of us, to overcome "Fate the annihilator" in the way the Seventh Elegy had boasted it is in humankind's power to do. *Our* mission, the purpose of *our* existence, lies precisely in this strenuous effort to overcome fate, transcend ourselves, and along this route transform the things of the earth, again and again.

And only "[o]nce for each thing": that is all that is needed. To have transformed each thing "[j]ust once", from within, in our consciousness, implies that "even if only once" with each thing, we "have been at one with the earth", in the way *we* are meant to be (as distinct from how the animal is meant to be). A strangely qualified comment follows: such acts of uniting with the earth, with the consequence of transforming it and through which we have our being, "seem beyond undoing". It is clear from many accounts that Rilke thought such acts *in fact* "beyond undoing"[46]; that is to say, they have a permanence that literally survives time: that is the whole basis for claiming that the whole of the visible world is to be transformed, and finally transposed to an invisible world. Rilke's reticence about this essential fact here (re: "seem") is a measure of the point of view from which he is generally addressing his readers in the Elegies. Generally we are only *in the process of* understanding all this, inevitably tentative in our approach to what is being presented, and so Rilke must lead us along. If not yet a reality for us, it is because we *believe* such acts are "beyond undoing" that, at one moment and another, "we keep pressing on, trying to achieve" that singular transformative act of being by which, uniting with the earth, we see things through into a world of invisible permanence. We *are* in the position to achieve this, in spite of where we start from, even though our starting-point is not advantage but disadvantage, our "hands" being "simple", our "gaze" "overcrowded", and our "heart" "speechless".

---

46. Most famously in his letter of November 13, 1925 to Witold von Hulewicz (see Greene 372).

We may then have the wish, in realizing it, to bestow this achievement in transformative being upon someone. We will feel that we are now *in the position to* bestow, having come a long way from the time when we were in conflict with ourselves and in dire need of support, as highlighted in the First Elegy: "Whom can we ever turn to/ in our need?" (Mitchell 331). Again the question is raised: "Whom can we give it to [this achievement in being]?" (385) Not to Rilke's Angel, "not the unsayable one" who occupies a sphere beyond the processes and things of the earth; *we* occupy our own sphere. Still the idea may be that "we would hold on to it all, forever" (383): Rilke's comment on this is that we cannot take the whole process of our experience into "that other realm", beyond death. There are aspects of this process that cannot be transposed there: in the first place, "what [physically] happened here", second, what "the art of looking" is all about, on which we also depend in this process, for this is laboriously learned and without the instantaneity of "that other realm". That realm is, moreover, already perfected in the "unsayable", and it will therefore have nothing to gain from receiving all the unsayable elements that have figured in this process of our achievement, such as "[t]he sufferings … the heaviness,/and the long experience of love"— all of the informing emotional constituents of the experience. What *would* make an impression on that other realm, on the other hand, is what it is in our unique power to mediate/accomplish, which is, precisely, *to say*, to have spoken "the word" (385) *through which* all has been transformed here. Rilke offers the analogy of someone who is returning into a valley from some mountain-retreat: among the things he will bring back with him, what would impress others, is "not a handful of earth, unsayable to others" but rather something distinctly voiced and seen: "some word he has gained, some pure word,—the yellow and blue/*gentian*".[47]

---

47. This earth, Rilke assumes, is itself unsayable: it is the dead earth into which the human imagination cannot venture directly (Rilke had remarked on this inevitable limitation for us, if not for the god Orpheus, in Sonnet 12 of the "First Part"). This is not to say that the Orphic artist is not otherwise immersed in the whole intertwined process of life and death. The sphere to be traced from dead earth through to the gentian and beyond (into the "wine" of the invisible—cf. the "deathless, inexhaustible wine" of Sonnet 7, for wine could also be made from the gentian) marks the limits within which we are exhorted to "[p]raise this world to the angel" (385)—"praising" being the

There remains, in the meantime, an unbridgeable gap between that other "ungraspable"[48] and unknowable invisible realm of the Angel, and the more distinctive, fully known invisible realm *we* are in the process of creating out of our own unique experience on Earth. In this respect, Rilke's Angel is being *left out* of the process; the Angel is now itself compelled to look down on *us*, "astonished" at what *we* have accomplished and are in the process of accomplishing. In this way is this our own human world, the one we are in process of bringing into being, set over and against that other of the Angel's. The reader will note that this "Angel" is by now far from being Novalis's Angel or what was Rilke's own Angel, potentially, early on, from which point everything begins for him, but is rather what this Angel has turned into: the symbol of a standard of unified existence pretending to lie beyond humanity's suffering, in a condition that has fully absorbed life's terror and beauty as it exists untransformed or wholesale—a forbiddingly unreal unity, which no human beings could possibly attain to. Unlike this Angel, we belong to the Earth, which we are in the process of slowly transforming, and ourselves along with it, *in its own* sphere from a visible condition into an invisible one:

> *Earth, isn't this what you want: to arise within us,*
> ***invisible?** Isn't it your dream*
> *to be wholly invisible someday? —O Earth, invisible!*
> *What, if not transformation, is your urgent command?*
>
> (Mitchell 387)

What may be described as the position to which Rilke is led after everything is that "we are here in order *to say*"; "*[h]ere* is the time for the *sayable, here* is its homeland" (385). Everything depends, in the end, on what is said or spoken as being, and on each thing of *this* world being given being. "Speak and bear witness": "[t]hings" will know when "you are praising them" (387) for they "look to us for deliverance". However, for this to happen it is necessary that we "say them *more* intensely than the things themselves/ever dreamed of existing" (385); most importantly, one must say how "innocent" and "happy" they can be. Thus are even "suffering, heaviness, and the

---

defining and overriding expression of the Orphic artist at all times.
48. See p.428.

long experience of baffled love" made innocent as these are spoken: "even *lamenting grief purely* decides to take form" (387), in this way "blissfully escap[ing] far beyond the [mournful] violin". It is to be understood, of course, that a thing can also be part of a complex of things, as the experience of lamenting grief imports. With this position that Rilke has at last assumed, the heavy, suffering case of Malte himself has been answered. By *saying* experience, suffering converts at last into happiness, horror into bliss. It is significant that the solution Rilke should finally settle into (that it is a matter, in the end, of articulating experience) should be, more or less, the same position Lou had projected for him when Rilke still stood knee-deep in his own baffled suffering. The difference, of course, is that it is Rilke who is at last fully living out this solution, whereas Lou had only ever projected it, for him and for them both by implication, Lou being by moments a sympathetic, by moments a somewhat insouciant, bystander...

***

By the time Rilke completed the Ninth Elegy, there lay before him a more or less full array of Elegies: the first four, as we have said, marking a downward turn in spirit, another four, from the Sixth through the Ninth, an upward swing; as for the Tenth, it had always been thought of as the one that would end the sequence. Not that there could only be ten Elegies, but Rilke would appear to have stopped at this number, and he would surely have remarked that only one other poem would now need to be written, to link the poems of downward import to those of upward import. That poem would be the linchpin connecting the Fourth to the Sixth. Promptly, then, Rilke produced the **Antistrophes** to satisfy this requirement, on the very day the Ninth was completed. The name itself, "antistrophe", conveys its function here: according to the OED, "the returning movement, from left to right in Greek choruses and dances [cf. the upward swing of the Elegies of the second half], answering to the previous movement of the strophe from right to left [cf. the previous downward swing of the first half]".

The Fourth Elegy had ended with Rilke's prized thought of an ideal childhood in which the impulse "to go on living" (Mitchell 355) would be from very early on reinforced by a prescient knowledge of

death, which would already be incorporated into it. In this respect
the child would be like the "hero" of old who was already made so
"inside the mother" (367) as celebrated in final additions Rilke was
also now making to the Sixth Elegy: this "hero" of his who was previously described by him (when in Ronda) as "sung" into "the storm of
his onrushing world/...his darkened voice, carried on the streaming
air". (365). Rilke's thought along these lines serves to console him
in his own fateful understanding that in his own childhood he knew
nothing of the sort, which has put him at a great disadvantage in later
life. This is how he sees the fate of boys and of men generally. Women
have survived better, as the Antistrophes relate:

> *The breaking away of childhood*
> *left you intact. In a moment,*
> *you stood there, as if completed*
> *in a miracle, all at once.*

> (Mitchell 405)

This is why, although, like men, themselves "grief-filled",
women are "nevertheless/able to bless like the blessed". By contrast,
men "afflict" (407) themselves. Men, boys, are "as if broken from
crags", "like pieces of rock/that have fallen on flowers", while women
are themselves the "flowers .../loved by all roots" (407). One could
say that they reflect in themselves the wholeness of Orphic creation,
and they are indeed pictured as "Eurydice's sisters/full of holy re-
turn/behind the ascending man [Orpheus]". However, no more than
Eurydice herself do her sisters make it back with Orpheus, and one is
left wondering how Rilke could have allowed himself such an image
after the tremendous evolution in Orphic experience he has just borne
witness to in his Sonnets. It is a gratuitous image, inasmuch as Rilke
by now knew too well that Eurydice never does return, except in the
highly paradoxical sense in which he paints his experience of this
possibility in his Sonnets (see above, p.418ff). There is wilful distortion in this image, considering the point Rilke had reached in his poetic experience by this time. The intention *was* to suggest a nurturing
power in women that compares relatively with those ancient mythical
mothers who fully supported their hero-sons through the worst. The
supporting power of women today is, in comparison, only relative:
they are "almost protection", for much harm has in the meantime

been done, but the "thought" of them *will* occasionally offer a place of rest to "the solitary man" in his life of continuous restlessness.

How effective, then, are the Antistrophes as a linch-pin between the Fourth Elegy and and the Sixth? The relativity in the role women play in the life of the poet (as in the case of other men) properly acknowledges the deep limitation that continues in the poet's situation as conveyed in the Fourth Elegy. At the same time the association of these women with the ancient mothers of heroes duly supports the upswing in hope the poet is striving after in the Sixth Elegy in defiance of his situation. Even so, is this somewhat abstractly thought-out sequence enough to prepare for the outburst of complete positive spirit that takes us over in the Seventh Elegy? Has there been enough expression in "the will to overcome" to justify the sudden proclamation of a solution to fate that the Seventh Elegy so proudly introduces? Rilke may also have been uncomfortable with the gratuitous use he makes of the Orphic legend in the Antistrophes, to smooth over the direction in hopefulness that is needed to move effectively from the Fourth Elegy through into the Sixth. However that may be, five days beyond his writing of the Antistrophes, Rilke would replace them with another full-fledged Elegy, which was to become the Fifth (we have been speaking of the Fourth Elegy and the Sixth on the basis of how they were finally presented, but if the "Antistrophes" had been left to stand, titled as such, the numbering would, of course, have been different). Could the Antistrophes have, in any case, quite held their own in this long series of massively discursive presentations which we are offered as for the Elegies themselves? Much as the Antistrophes seemed structurally the right addition, lying as they would have between the first four Elegies of downward swing and the following four Elegies of upward swing, they were in the end somewhat too slight to assume a proper place in this massively ongoing production (beautiful as these lines are in their own right). The Fifth Elegy would, in the meantime, provide what the Antistrophes could not: that still deeper grounding in the will to overcome which, across the Fourth Elegy, the Fifth, and the Sixth, was needed to prepare adequately for the final expression in triumphing spirit that we find overall in the Seventh, Eighth, and Ninth. We will turn to the Fifth Elegy below.

We are focusing at present on the period between February 9th, when Rilke completed the Ninth Elegy, and the 15th when he carried on with the "Second Part" of the Sonnets. This was clearly, as I have said, a period during which Rilke was looking back on what he had written by way of Sonnets and Elegies and considering improvements. We have already noted his replacement of the 21st Sonnet from the First Part, the great poem "Spring has returned", and his addition of another Sonnet which became the 23rd, respectively on February 9th and February 13th. Rilke would not get around to the Fifth Elegy until the 14th; on the 11th, he was engaged in re-writing the **Tenth Elegy**. By that point he was clearly not satisfied with what he had written as the Tenth, even though it had been written with the intention that it would end the sequence. The original Tenth belonged to another time when Rilke had quite another sense of where the Elegies would carry him and how they would end. The original (the larger part of it) is thus replaced, to reflect a greater faith in immediate possibilities than was anticipated at that time.

The first fifteen lines of the original Tenth Elegy were written when Rilke was at Duino; the rest over a year later in Paris in the autumn of 1913. The original Tenth thus belongs among what I have (for convenience) called the Elegies of the downward swing. These are basically mournful poems, weighed down by a baffled sense of the irresolvable dilemma of life's conflicting demands. As we have seen, the Tenth Elegy was the poem in which Rilke had confessed to his hopeless love of Lou, by which he continued to be weighed down; it describes how at one time "he kept sobbing long ago, for her" (Mitchell 403), and how still at this later time he cannot "forget her". All that had changed, had been through a metamorphosis, by the time Rilke was into his final Elegies at Muzot. These final Elegies had brought forward too much of a new positive spirit to accommodate a shift back to that old mournful setting. Inevitably Rilke would have to re-write. Unfortunately he retained the first section of it, which was no less anachronistic with its immersion in "hidden weeping", "nights of anguish", "hours of pain" etc., so typical of a former time. He would have done better, as I believe, to make a whole new beginning with his re-writing of the Tenth at Muzot from the point of that line that reads:

> *But how alien, alas, are the streets of the city of grief*
> (Mitchell 389)

The startling contrast between the glorious new emphasis on "super-abundant being" at the end of the Ninth and this additional fresh focus on what yet continues on "the streets of the city of grief" would have made for a more coherent and a dramatically effective transition.[49]

With this focus on "the city of grief" we are returned to one of Rilke's most enduring concerns, thinking back to his great novella *Malte*, where an antidote to the problem of the city seemed direly urgent. Rilke had made much progress since then. The situation of the city is still intensely conceived: the tendency of basic human society is to seek release from its empty forms of life, on the one hand through "gilded noise, the bursting memorial", and meretricious religion, and on the other through "all sorts of attractions" that are a far cry from religion and tending to degeneracy. In the midst of this unreal scene, suddenly "the view becomes *real*": "children are playing", "lovers are holding hands" (391), and another scene is narrated in which one young man is pictured taking a fancy to a young girl whom Rilke transforms into an allegorical figure of Lament: "But he leaves her, turns around,/looks back, waves ... What's the use? She is a Lament" (391). Fanciful love, even when it faintly recognizes what is "of noble descent", cannot reach to the depths required to bring one into a meaningful relationship to Love in its association also with realities that belong to Sorrow and to Death.

Only those "who died young", Rilke insists, can ever have truly known Love in its association with the world of Lament. Whereas for others Lament would in time have altered Love, for those "who

---

49. It may not be too fanciful to suggest that with its clear relation in mood to the first Three, the original Tenth Elegy had basically the function of a Fourth Elegy. It certainly falls in with the mournful setting of that group, but if it had been given that function, as the Fourth, the Elegy-sequence as a whole would no doubt have had to take another form. There would have been far more to overcome by way of a life-problem, which would likely have entailed a longer sequence of poems. That is if the intention had been in the end to succeed in surmounting the problem. As it was, the original Tenth Elegy was intended to be the last in the sequence. This suggests a more pessimistic sense of what the Elegies would finally be featuring as a whole.

died young" the reverse is true: Lament (which continues to figure by virtue of a death) appears in association with a Love that has never altered. That is the wonder of Rilke's presentation in this concluding Elegy: "glorious" is how he would describe this poem to Lou on the same day he wrote it (Snow, *Rilke*, 321), and he was right. Suddenly, and we are startled to discover this, it is the young man of the previous part who is pictured, in death, being led by one of these Laments through the world from which they derive (presumably there is one such Lament for every soul). As it is, we do not realize that it *is* this youth who has died until we are well into this journey through this other realm. What is this youth if not a structural embodiment of human consciousness as Rilke has presented this over the course of these final Elegies? Inclined as it is in its initial nature at first to turn away from reality, human consciousness continues nevertheless to press forward in search of it, to an extent beyond even its own will. Rilke's focus specifically on those who died young is his way of insisting on what is *purely* possible as an experience of reality, since for the most part, because of our embroilment in the world generally, which intensifies especially with time, for the rest of us the tendency will have been to distort or disfigure this reality.

Beyond death, Rilke's youth is led into another realm that is the archetypal setting of this our world, which is fundamentally a world of grief. It is the substance of this other realm that at once underlies our visible world and is in turn shaped by our transformations of this world, being the world "the endlessly dead" (395) inherit. This is a world of mythical-historical time, where the constructs of time survive in archetypal form: thus we journey back in time, in the first place through a sphere that embodies the creations of medieval and classical culture: "temples" and "castles", surrounding which are "trees of tears", "fields of blossoming grief", and "herds of sorrow" (393). A middle ground then appears, marked by "a startled bird" and "its solitary cry", out of which "the graves of the elders" suddenly show, who once "gave warning", was it of the decline in the experience of reality that was to take place with advancing time? For moving still farther back in time, there now appear human constructs that once embodied the reality of this archetypal world more powerfully and directly; they now survive as virtual replicas of themselves in this world, as "brother[s]" to those others. Thus "the sepulchre" of the Pharaohs in ancient Egypt, which is overseen by the "regal head" of the Sphinx, has its counterpart here: its "human face" "lifted" "to the scale of the stars", in this place "forever". There then follows a most haunting description of an owl's sudden shadowy appearance from behind this face, its "slow downstrokes" throwing another dimension over it that is captured in the youth by a "new sense of hearing" that adds itself and indeed serves to complete his vision, as if he was now reading it "as upon a double/unfolded page". Rilke was here re-creating an experience of his own that he had had when in Egypt sitting before the Sphynx some ten years earlier. He had recorded this experience in a letter to Magda during their courtship[50]:

> ... *and now, upon my hearing, which had grown very acute in the hours-long nocturnal silence, the outline of* [the Sphynx's] *cheek was (as though by a miracle) inscribed.*
>
> (Mitchell 574)

It is as if Rilke were now imagining his own experience in that former time being imprinted as reality in this other realm.

From this famously constructed face, so powerfully measured on the vast scale of the stars, we move on to the stars themselves, which in this realm of pure, transformed reality are "the *new* stars of the land of grief" (395). They are stars that reflect, if they do not embody, especially the content of human experience, and they are now listed in hermetical fashion: the Rider, the Staff, Garland of Fruit, Cradle, Path, The Burning Book, Puppet, Window, all of which are offset at the other (southern) end by the Mothers. Goethe intuited and named the Mothers in the depths of the Earth: in naming them (or "saying" them, as Rilke would have put it) did he *re-create* them, so that they now take their own place as a constellation in this farther realm? And what of the new poetic tropes of human creation arising out of more modest spheres than the depths of the Earth, all other items like those randomly listed above (Cradle, Window etc.), and which have also been spoken, in Rilke's own work as in the work of so many others? Rilke imagines each of these, as a Thing transformed, also assuming its individual form of constellation amidst these "new stars".

---

50. A letter dated February 1st, 1914.

The Lament who is guiding the dead youth through this other realm now directs his attention to its veritable centre, which takes the form of a "ravine" from which rises "the fountainhead of joy". This is the "joy" that at last rises from "the land of grief" *and that also courses through our world*. As we know it, "[a]mong men[,]/it is a mighty stream". An English reader will be reminded of Coleridge's poem, "Kubla Khan":

> *And from this chasm, with ceaseless turmoil seething,*
> *A mighty fountain momently was forced:*
> *Amid whose swift half-intermitted burst*
> *Huge fragments vaulted like rebounding hail…*
> *And mid these dancing rocks at once and ever*
> *It flung up momently the sacred river.*

Coleridge experienced this landscape as an already full-shaped poem that had been dictated to him in his sleep. Never averse to a dictation of his own work (at least in its initial stages), Rilke sets this landscape in the sphere of Death, who has been seen as the brother of Sleep …

In the end, Rilke's dead youth must make his own way "up the mountains of primal grief", alone. They are the mountains from which "sometimes even/among men you can find a polished nugget of primal grief/or a chunk of petrified rage" (393)—one thinks of Solon or of Oedipus? "Yes, that came from up there". The mountain has often been imagined as a symbol of the spiritual world. Dante climbed his mountain all the way up to his one God. In the landscape of Rilke's dead youth are to be imagined not one mountain but many mountains, mountains belonging to quite another, a new universe of endless possible worlds. And from these worlds a message comes to us from the endlessly dead which may be transcribed into symbols: the symbol of "catkins hanging from the bare branches of hazel-trees", the symbol of "raindrops that fall onto the dark earth in springtime"; their message: "a happy thing *falls*" (395). In their experience of a joy that finally lies beyond grief, the dead do not bask in glory but rather find themselves falling back upon our world and giving back to us all that they have learned as a displaced experience of our own. With this finally elusive, not to mention highly cryptic, content had Rilke at last fashioned the virtual end-point of his Elegies…

***

It would appear that in the very moment Rilke put down his pen, having just finished off the Tenth Elegy, and having before him what he believed were his "Ten" Elegies (the "Antistrophes" at the time seemingly figuring as one of these), Rilke wrote both Lou *and* the Princess to announce the good news, one almost thinks at the same sitting. Parts of his letters to them contain the same text. In the letter to Lou we find these words:

> *At this moment, now, Saturday, the eleventh of February, at six o'clock, I lay my pen aside after the last completed Elegy, the tenth … All in a few days. It was a hurricane, as on Duino that time: all that was fiber in me, tissue, framework, groaned and bent. There was no thought of eating.*
>
> (Snow, *Rilke*, 331)

And in the letter to the Princess:

> *Ten! My hand is still trembling with the last, great one … At this moment, Saturday, the eleventh at six in the evening … All in a few days, it was a nameless storm, a hurricane of the spirit (as that time at Duino) every fibre and tissue in me was strained to breaking-point—I could never think of food. God alone knows who nourished me …*
>
> (Wydenbruck 214)

"But now it is done. Done. Done." So Rilke informs the Princess. And to Lou: "They are. They are."—But, then, not quite yet done, for three days later, on the 14th, Rilke undertook to replace the Antistrophes with what at last came to be the Fifth Elegy…

With that (almost) unerring editorial sense that he displays throughout his poetic career, Rilke would surely have seen, on reviewing the whole of the Elegy-sequence now with some detachment, that the Antistrophes had not done the job. For the reasons given above: that a stronger middle section was needed—among the Fourth Elegy, the Fifth, and the Sixth—to properly tie over the basic life-problem, as set forth in the first three Elegies, to Rilke's dramatic expression of a solution to the problem, as given beyond the Sixth. To set things on a more even keel, Rilke now handily produced the **Fifth Elegy**, focusing on material and a subject that had claimed his attention for some time, ever since he had spent a full four months in the company of a painting by Picasso that was in the possession of a friend, having settled into that friend's apartment alone, where the painting hung.[51] *La Famille de Saltimbanques*, as it was called.

Rilke's narrative description in his poem builds on the scene of this painting quite closely. More was needed to ground the theme of *the will to overcome* in a properly *human* reality: on the one hand, as conceived in the Fourth Elegy, there was the poet's creation of a pure space of alienation protected from the world's false influences, the better to be properly inspired to act; on the other, in the Sixth Elegy, the invocation of an idealized hero who from antiquity had proven himself fully capable of overcoming limitation. Here were two opposite poles of a spectrum that was now to be filled at its mid-point, through the Fifth Elegy. Odd as Rilke's focus might seem, though no more so than his fetishistic focus on puppets in the Fourth Elegy, the extraordinary display of will-power of a travelling family of acrobats, as pictured in Picasso's painting, provided the opportunity to do this.

---

51. The painting was owned by Frau Hertha Koenig (Mitchell 561). Appropriately, the Fifth Elegy was dedicated to her.

The will to overcome is here masterfully lived out by a group of human beings who are not any less emotionally unfavored than the rest of struggling humanity. They are, as much as anyone, held in the grip of iron necessity. This is not just because of the unending displacements to which they are bound, from the itinerant life that is imposed on them, but in the very nature of their livelihood, which consists in being forever at the mercy of threatening physical laws in the midst of their high-flying leaps and difficult hard landings instantly commanded and endlessly repeated. They are described as

> ... *wrung out*
> *by a never-satisfied will (for **whose** sake)? Yet it wrings them*
> *bends them, twists them, swings them and flings them*
> *and catches them again; and falling as if through oiled*
> *slippery air, they land ...*
>
> (Mitchell 357)

This demand on the will is brought into focus especially in the youngest and lightest male member of the family, who must continue to perform through ever-intensifying pain from his landings. In spite of this, he is still able to muster for his audience, through the physical tears that are forced into his eyes from the "pain", a "smile" (359) that is ever so strangely genuine. Strange as it is to say, his is no less an achievement for Rilke than the wonderful accomplishments of art that he had celebrated in the Seventh Elegy and offered the Angel as evidence of humankind's own form of triumphing spirit.

How much of Rilke was in his description of this young boy, who, before seeing his performance through, would share "a loving look" with his "mother", herself a member of this troupe, and who is said to be "seldom affectionate"? The characterizations Picasso's painting offers Rilke are worthy of the attention he had bestowed upon his material in *Malte*, to which one could say Rilke has momentarily returned. There is the old weight-lifter, the grandfather, who is far beyond being able to perform now and who in his enormous shrivelled skin is as if widowed from his old self. There is also the other son, the eldest of the three children, who is all neck and anomalously pictured with the face of a nun. And, then, the much younger daughter who, in the midst of this life of strenuous performing, is yet "a display-fruit of equanimity" (361). They have forged this life as a family, straining to satisfy continually an audience on which they depend and who are ambiguously pictured caught up in the blossoming "rose" (357) of the players' intricate tectonics (born of pain and the pounding of dust), but otherwise pictured as "unconscious/gaping faces", their "specious" half-smiling finally wrung out of them, and whom, the suggestion is, it hardly seems worth satisfying. For *this* the family has at last bent iron necessity to their will. Once they were "far from mastery", hard as it is for the poet to imagine this, with everything "falling apart", but "suddenly in this laborious nowhere" there came into being that "unsayable spot" where "the difficult calculation" became "resolved" (361). Such has been their achievement in will-power.

One member of this family who is not commented on by Rilke is the father, pictured in Picasso's painting in the costume of Harlequin. He appears to be looking over at the mother who sits to herself in the far corner of the painting as if working out the next stage in this family's wanderings, where they are to perform next. Might it have been the father's gaze that prompted Rilke's thought of the confounded "lovers" (363) in the last part of his poem? His thought runs as follows: what, then, if lovers were to find in themselves, and in their own "high-flying" acts of daring, final "mastery" over their *emotional* life in a way that would correspond to what these acrobats prove themselves in on a *physical* level? In a very daring act of his own, Rilke imagines as an audience to this hypothetically imagined emotional achievement the dead themselves, whom the poet says would at the sight of such love throw down their own "forever saved up ... coins of happiness" in recognition of the exploit. Rilke had just come from writing the end of the Tenth Elegy (some three days earlier) wherein he speaks of the dead as lying happily beyond our tragically incomplete (and misdirected) world. At the end of the Fifth Elegy, written subsequently, he boldly wrests the dead back, referring them again to this our world as a place where there might be or might have been completeness of passions won.

The dream of love, and the hope in that dream, are thus once again powerfully deferred to. Not that Rilke had not moved beyond the dream: he had, "no longer wooing". It is simply, or not so simply, that in proceeding, as he now had to, to supply the fifth Elegy, he would have had to go back to an earlier stage of the emotional process. It is a wonder that he could do so with such *panache* (a measure, no doubt, of his great exuberance at this point). He naturally qualifies his rethinking of the idea of a complete love in this world by immediately noting that such love is impossible: such love these lovers "could never bring to mastery here". It is all the more extravagant of Rilke, then, that in this context he should walk back his most advanced idea of the dead, as recently articulated in the Tenth Elegy, so as to suggest that they might here be turning their attention to the miracle of love on earth as freshly conceived. At the same time, there may have been more to Rilke's backward-leaning gesture to love of this kind, when we consider that although he had indeed consigned his lost love of Lou to death, he had, as we saw, concurrently held fast to it. As it is, when reading through the sequence, one has the impression on reaching the end of the Fifth Elegy of a significant new turning-point. On the one hand, the claims on us of such love as is here so dramatically rendered, up to now a key focus in the Elegy-sequence, are again duly acknowledged, as far as they could be, while, on the other hand, more than ever in this sequence the understanding that such love is impossible opens the door to the later acceptance that it can "no longer" be a case of "wooing".

Before either Lou or the Princess had written back to Rilke in reply to his news that the Elegies had been completed, he had thus suddenly produced another Elegy, the Fifth, and what's more was now freshly absorbed in the production of what would turn out to be twenty-nine! more Sonnets, written over the course of the three days that followed the writing of the Fifth. Literary history has rarely, if ever, seen production on such a dizzying scale, especially as Rilke was so very quickly shifting ground from one context of writing to another. From the ending of the Tenth Elegy, he could, in three days, move to the ending of the Fifth, this being a complete inversion of the imaginative direction of the other, and from that back in turn, with hardly a day's interval, to the first of his new Sonnets of the "Second Part" to focus, once again, on Orpheus and his highly precious world of inwardly mirrored realities, another wholly different context still. What finally unifies this highly diversified production, taken, as it is, to an extreme in each direction, can surely only be divined at best…

The Sonnets to Orpheus
"Second Part"

Another Inwardness in Sonnets 1-7

One must imagine Rilke resuming work on *The Sonnets*, the day after composing the Fifth Elegy, with a very great confidence and freedom, unlike anything he had known before. His great Elegy-sequence, on which he had been focused for a full decade, was now complete, and all the Elegies had fallen fully into place! His great life-*oeuvre* had at last been fully rounded out. He had hardly had time to think about it, but from the evidence of the first Sonnets written for the "Second Part", Rilke would appear to have indeed entered a state of deepest inwardness and stillness (deepest satisfaction), finding himself in a profoundly inward space that we too feel, along with him, could be mirroring "the strength and purpose of how many worlds[?]" (Mitchell 471)—like the flower in Sonnet 5 of this "Second Part" that actually mirrors these many worlds. Sonnets 2, 3, and 4 prepare the ground for 5 where this intuition of an inwardness that could be reflecting all worlds comes to expression. Rilke began with Sonnet 2; Sonnet 1 would not be added until the very end of his production of the "Second Part".

A quick reference in **Sonnet 2** to how his page can catch some brushstroke of "the master" Orpheus, allows us to fathom Rilke's focus in this poem on "mirrors" which likewise reflect the "pure" images and impressions they receive from human beings in the outer world (465), as do also fireplaces: "How much was once gazed into the charred/slow-dying glow of a fireplace[?]". *Poems* are such mirrors and fireplaces. A daily range of experience is suggested whose import is eventually summarized: the pure smile of girls in the morning as reflected in mirrors; only a reflection of that smile later in the faces of these girls, their faces become, over the course of the day, mirrors; then the "gaze" into the "slow-dying glow of a fireplace" in the evening: a daily pattern referred, in the end, to a totality of losses over time: "Who knows what losses the earth has suffered[?]" However, it is the poet's already established association with his master Orpheus in the "First Part" of *The Sonnets*, of which the new Sonnets are a continuation, that allows him to proclaim confidently in the face of these losses: "One who, with sounds that nonetheless praise,/can sing the heart born into the whole."

Rilke's quick reference in the first line to a poem as a mirroring reality of its own sets us up to understand that by "mirrors" in Sonnets 3 and 4, he means primarily his own poems. The analogy with the way mirrors work gives him a range of corollary functions derived from mirrors that allows him to characterize closely what his poems are doing. Rilke would in the end produce what became Sonnet 1 in order to throw a more emphatic light on what was but a bare suggestion of analogy between mirrors and poems in Sonnets 2, 3, and 4 when these were written. At the time he no doubt already understood that his focus was really poems and not mirrors, but **Sonnet 1** establishes this context conclusively. Here he characterizes the poem as "a counterweight/in which I rhythmically happen" (463). We may understand this point with reference to the Elegies where Rilke associates the separate isolated consciousness with a counterbalancing will to "press forward" notwithstanding to an engagement with the world, as discussed above. A poem is itself an ideal ground for this venture. At the level of the poem there is a "[c]omplete interchange of our own/essence with world-space", for the poet as well as for us. And the poet remarks further: "How many regions in space have already been/inside me." In fact, there might be no limit to what might be experienced in poems.

In **Sonnet 3**, Rilke describes what poems are and can do with reference to mirrors. In the first place, it may look like they are "filled with nothing but sieve-holes" (467), though it is only "as if" they do: more to the tantalizing point, they are "fathomless in-between spaces of time": though fathomless, they can still be referred to what may yet be fathomed. At a certain point a poem, like a mirror, is "unenterable", although Rilke still acknowledges, in somewhat occult fashion, that "[a] few seem to have walked straight into your depths". In the Orphic context of these poems, the understanding is that the depths of a mirror or a poem are like death. Eurydice passed beyond into those depths, and she was in the position also to attract Orpheus thither. Somewhat strangely, as it may seem, Rilke's mythical subjects here are actually Echo and Narcissus ("she lets/Narcissus penetrate"). Yet the association of Narcissus with Orpheus is legendary: they have been seen as embodying the same "refusal to accept separation from the libidinous object (or subject)".[52] Such a characterization will invoke for us again how Rilke finally resolved the tragic problem of his own attachment to the lost Lou. Rilke, as another Narcissus, and like Orpheus, has also penetrated through to these inner depths of libidinous association, having in his own psychological terms braved death, to the point of reflecting these realities also in his poems, having, as these poems attest, come under the direct inspiration of Orpheus.

There is something fantastic in these developments, and they may even seem to us impossible: they will seem to us based in unreal, romantic claims only. **Sonnet 4** almost seems to take on these doubts, with its utterly unembarrassed acceptance of the unicorn as a mythical reality created by the power of love. It is from the "assurance" this "beast" acquires, precisely from "the thought" in those who love it "that it might be", that its legendary horn is produced (Mitchell 469). Only until then was it the "one that never was". The unicorn finds itself in time "inside the mirror" (poem) where it is received by the "virgin" (the beloved) who, herself embodying its power, from inside this world (poem) holds yet another depth of mirror to it (the allusion here is to the famous tapestry entitled "Sight" in 'The Lady and the Unicorn' series housed in the Musée de Cluny). All is possible to inwardness. The most dramatic *inner* developments may "open" to us, if we can only be "receivers" of them (471). It is no less the case with the "many" other *outer* worlds to which we may "open" through a yet more developed inwardness. **Sonnet 5** takes us in this other direction, focusing now on the flower, the anemone in this case, and its dramatic power of "infinite acceptance" of what is outside itself. More than any other flower (so Rilke had noticed[53]) the anemone could be so "overpowered with abundance" of what is outside it, so opened up to the day's experience, it would sometimes fail to retrieve its petals and close itself at night. So the poet might fail to close himself at night (as may indeed have been literally the case with Rilke at this time). The flower, like the mirror, is a trope of the poet and his poem, and as itself a "valid symbol", at the other extreme from the mirror— not drawing inward but opening to all that is without—it rounds out

52. See, e.g., Herbert Marcuse, *Eros and Civilization*, Boston: Beacon Press, 1966, 170.

53. See his letter to Lou dated June 26th, 1914 (Greene 248). This phenomenon Rilke had noticed once when in Rome.

Rilke's perception of all that he feels he might himself give proof of through the medium of his poems. His poems offer evidence of his having given himself both to the inner depths as well as to the outer spaces, in an especially rich abundance that, theoretically, could know no bounds.

In spite of their continued invocation of what has been Rilke's Orphic experience, these opening Sonnets would appear to be concerned with inwardness in its broader effects and at a more self-involved level than is strictly entailed by that experience. It is as if Rilke were exploring more closely the nature of the medium through which the experience was given, namely his own inwardness as such, which might be infinite in its applications. As Sonnets 2 through 5 have shown, in his inwardness he might be giving expression to infinite possibilities of representation. As for inwardness itself, it appears to be built upon nothing but the "light" of consciousness, like the rose of **Sonnet 6**, "the full, the numberless flower .../... wearing gown upon gown/upon a body of nothing but light" (473). And yet, its "fragrance" has mystified us for "hundreds of years", and "we have never known what to call it". In **Sonnet 7**, the focus is on flowers that have been picked and now lie "on the garden table, from edge to edge, exhausted" (475). The poet is falling out of his intense focus on his own inwardness, to take up his place again in the midst of the human scene, which from within itself reserves its own limited power to revive one (as in the "girls" of this poem with their "sensitive fingers that are able to do/even more good than you guessed" in keeping the picked flowers fresh for a time). A kinship with the flowers that grow naturally, to blossom in the fields—i.e., a more essential inwardness—is thus maintained, even if distantly and for a shortened time only ... Beyond Sonnet 7, through to Sonnet 17, Rilke will return to the more circumscribed manner to which we had grown accustomed in the "First Part": circumscribed, that is, by his Orphic theme, and its various coordinates...

Tying Up Themes in Sonnets 8-29

First he reconsiders in **Sonnet 8** his treasured theme of childhood with its "joy that belonged to no one", in comparison with which "*[w]hat* in the [greater] world [of adult society] was real?" (477). As for that world, and its "judges" (**Sonnet 9**—479), its "machine[s]" (**Sonnet 10**—481) and its "rules of death" (**Sonnet 11**—483): as in the "First Part", to these Rilke opposes "true mercy" (9), pure "existence" (10), and that extraordinary "[w]ill[-]transformation" (12) that, as we have seen, the "Earth" (**Sonnet 15**—491) accomplishes and the Orphic devotee along with Her. Here are, once again, the typical oppositions developed in the Sonnet sequence as a whole. In **Sonnet 16** Orpheus himself makes a fresh appearance, healing us even in the midst of our conflicted nature: "Over and over by us torn in two,/the god is the hidden place that heals again" (493). In **Sonnet 12** Orpheus is implicitly present as the power of "*Will*-transformation" working in league with "Knowledge" who, as Eurydice, leads him "enchanted through the harmonious country/that finishes often with starting and with ending begins" (485), this "space that the two pass through" being "a child or grandchild of parting". Underneath all this is the great reference-point of the relationship between Rilke and Lou. It is at this juncture that we are given that great central **Sonnet 13** in which we are exhorted, now that Rilke has proof of the possibility, to "Be forever dead in Eurydice", and "*ahead* of all parting" (487).[54] It is now our mission to transform "Things", say them and see them through from the visible into the invisible, to "sleep" with them, and finally to "stay" among them, as we shall one day forever, in death: cf. "all those silent companions in the wind of the meadows" (**Sonnet 14**—489)…

What Rilke gives us in the rest of the "Second Part" freshly repeats his most cherished concerns as embarked upon in the "First Part", with the hard-won wisdom of the completed Elegies also occasionally spilling over here, as for example, where Rilke celebrates the advances humankind has made over time in spite of all, in **Sonnet 24**: "we the endlessly dared—how far we have come!"/"We one generation through thousands of lifetimes …/… who are more and more filled with the child we will bear" (509). A *combination* of themes is featured in the "Second Part" of *The Sonnets*, some of which are more intrinsic to the Elegies, some to the Sonnets themselves. Thus the theme of being "turned away" and "dismissed" from our best "moments" of creative inspiration in **Sonnet 23** echoes the focus of Sonnet 4 of the "First Part" where Rilke had brought forward

---

54. See above for discussion of this Sonnet's theme, p.418ff.

those "tender ones" and their merely fitful experience of wholeness from which they are soon banished, falling back into "heaviness". Notwithstanding, we remain still integrated in the whole, "because we are the branch, the iron blade/and sweet danger [i.e. both what we create (the branch) and the difficulties which bring forth creation (iron blade and danger)], ripening from within" (507). Still, the poet insists, along with Orpheus "we praise", through the whole of our dualistic situation: we are exhorted to remember that "what seems so far from you is most your own". More in line with the Elegies, on the other hand, is the view expressed towards the end of the "Second Part", in **Sonnet 27**, that "[a]s who we are ... we still matter .../... as a use of the gods" (515). Then again, something of both of these works is conveyed in **Sonnet 25** where Rilke re-visits the theme of spring and how it "always took you" (511): "what has so often/come to you/is coming once more", though "you .../... never took" it. There is a significant contrast here with Rilke's euphoric profession in the Ninth Elegy that "even one" of the Earth's springtimes "is already too much for my blood" (387). In the Sonnet Rilke is reaching out to those who are wilfully depriving themselves of this experience, which paradoxically is yet so close at hand as "[e]very hour ... grows younger" (511). It is a measure of the extreme range of expression that characterizes Rilke's poems over the mere fortnight in which all (Sonnets and Elegies) was being set down. Among the last five Sonnets to be written, Sonnet 25 is an indication that, as in the Elegies, it was as much Rilke's concern here to stay linked to our own ongoing struggles as it was to prove to us just how much has been possible for him. The sequence's third-to-last **Sonnet 27** is still settled in the same sphere of limitation as is brought into focus in Sonnet 25: cf. "[a]s who we are ... we still matter"...

There is, at the same time, the impulse in Rilke especially in this "Second Part" of *The Sonnets* to press impossibilities. We are to imagine, along with him, that it is an aspect of our creative task to "sing" our way into "the gardens ... that you never saw" (**Sonnet 21**—503), those "blissfully watered gardens" where hang "the exotic fruits of consolation" (**Sonnet 17**—495). The moral behind cultivating the impossible impulse: "[a]void the illusion that there can be any lack/for someone who wishes, then fully decides, to be!" (503) It is how the unicorn itself came to exist: "with the thought that it might be" (Sonnet 4—469). One must also be ready to admit and confront the paradox that "all things are far", indeed "incomprehensively" so, as much the things that are "right here" as in the "vaster" "distances" (**Sonnet 20**—501), and that precisely the language of what is "far" is what we need to learn (cf. Sonnet 23: "what seems so far from you is most your own"). The overriding themes of both the Elegies *and* the Sonnets are summarized in **Sonnet 22**, where "fate" is opposed by natural-creative "overflowings" and social "frenzy" by "abundances" (505). We shall also be able to "say" how persistently "fate" can be endured, and at last "praise" this accomplishment, in the case of lives that no one has yet really ventured to "see", as in the finally very moving **Sonnet 19,** on mendicancy. As for the general calamity of social life, from the time childhood is appropriated to it, our purpose will be to "compose the criers" by bringing them around, from their "cries … become unreal" to that "clear stream" of reality that carries "the head and the lyre" (**Sonnet 26**—513). There is, in this respect, the shining example of the afflicted Vera, the "dancing girl" of **Sonnet 18**, who re-appears climactically in **Sonnet 28**, the second-to-last Sonnet of this sequence, where she is presented as once "stirred to total hearing just when Orpheus sang …/… [y]ou knew the place where once the lyre arose" (517). And to Vera's "friend" in **Sonnet 29**, which ends the sequence, who may perhaps continue to be troubled by her loss, Rilke's exhortation is as strong as ever: "[m]ove through transformation" (519); she is to add herself to the Earth in *Her* transformation of Herself (cf. Sonnet 13). Thus when the day comes when it will be her turn to pass into death, she will continue to "whisper to the silent earth: I'm flowing./To the flashing water say: I am"…

✳✳✳

After the Storm

The Princess Responds

Rilke had suddenly launched into the "Second Part" of *The Sonnets* over the days when both Lou and the Princess received his letters announcing the completion of the Elegies and were responding to this (both replied on the same day, the 16th). Rilke wrote the "Second Part" largely from the 15th through the 17th and the 19th, carrying on with it right up to the 23rd. In his letter to the Princess he had not only dedicated the Elegies to her; he had made them her "property" (**Wydenbruck** 214). That distinction seemed only too fitting as it was she who had been his one great, necessary support after *Malte* and in the time of Duino. Also, in the highly distressing and long, uncertain period before Muzot, the Princess had continued to hold her garden-house at Lautschin for him as a possible refuge for the writing he was desperate to resume, even when over many months he kept putting off his commitment to the place. She had remained his most stalwart support through the whole of that time, and when Rilke completed the Elegies at Muzot, they had known each other for well over ten years. As was to be expected, the Princess was ecstatic over the news of the Elegies; she was brought to tears (215), and she received the information that the Elegies were to belong to her with the deepest pride and gratitude. It is a testimony to the deepest regard in which Rilke held the Princess that he should then offer to have her at Muzot in order to read the Elegies to her himself. This he did three months later. On her visit to Muzot and Sierre in early June, he read her all the Elegies on one day, and on the next day all of the Sonnets. He and the Princess would meet again on a few other occasions. This is unlike in the case of Lou whom Rilke would not meet again. In fact, after Lou's visit to him in Munich in the spring of 1919, during the days when the political turmoil reached his own apartment, they would never again meet.

Lou Responds

In spite of this distance, Lou's response to the news of the Elegies opens up a still deeper sphere in Rilke's life, going back to his earliest days as a poet over twenty years before, when they first met. At the news of the Elegies, Lou was also brought to tears (**Snow, Rilke**, 332), her first response on receiving some of these being primarily laudatory: that Rilke had achieved poetry of the highest order. It is poetry especially distinguished by the fact in it "things of mute presence … are being rescued", and "inexpressibility … has become word" (333)—a "primal text", as she characterizes it. In the meantime, she if anyone would be able to imagine how Rilke must appear these days:

how you must look now: just as in those days long, long ago,
when the brightness in your eyes and your cheerful stance would
sometimes make one imagine a boy; and whichever hope moved
you then, whatever it was that you were asking of life, absolutely
and intensely as your only need and necessity—is now as if ful-
filled.

Rilke had sent Lou copies of the Sixth Elegy, the Eighth, and the
Tenth. Lou then received Rilke's further news that the Fifth Elegy had
also been written and also many more of the Sonnets. He promises
copies of the other three Elegies Lou had yet to receive: the Fifth,
Seventh, and Ninth, and in the meantime sends her some of "the
most beautiful" of the Sonnets (334). Reacting in turn to this additional good news, and with some of the Sonnets now before her, Lou
becomes still more expansive. This is in her own, impersonal way, as
a philosopher of life, all the while as she involves Rilke intimately in
musings she assumes he shares: "—ah, Rainer, all this is like a dream,
this glorious certainty that life *is* in such glorious order" (335). Here
Lou was echoing Rilke's use of "glorious" in speaking of the Tenth
Elegy, but it is the Sonnets he had just sent her that are more on her
mind in this letter.

Reaching Homeland

She quotes from Sonnet 17 of the "Second Part", which speaks
of those "forever blissfully watered gardens", where "trees" are
"flown through by angels", as the poem says (Mitchell 495). She cites
this material as confirmation of the glorious order from which our
own world is derived: this "primal spring", as she puts it, through
which alone the "gates of the coming seasons" are "fl[u]ng open"
(Snow, *Rilke*, 335).[55] These gardens, for which Rilke in his poem is
still looking and still only, if magnificently, speculating about, she assumes are indeed a veritable expression of this order. Of this group
of Sonnets that she has received, which distinguish themselves especially by their "limitless manner of experiencing", she claims she

---

55. Lou's insistent emphasis on spring both here and elsewhere in her letters
of this time makes one wonder if she had not also received Sonnet 21 of the
first Part, which begins "Spring has returned". See above.

can say "what it all comes to": "inward thanking", by which alone is given "proof of ... the actuality of God". On one side, there is God's gift to Rilke; however, only by "the creative person's gesture of giving back" (336) is His actuality confirmed through that person's "power of unveiling, of verifying". Quoting further from Sonnet 13 of the Second Part, she insists that only that person in this way truly "adds himself" to God and "joyously erases the score": only in this way is atonement reached. Here Lou was quoting from the Sonnet high-lighted by the line "Be forever dead in Eurydice" ("surely the most glorious sonnet", she adds). Could Lou really have failed to see that Eurydice was herself whom Rilke had lost? Eurydice and Orpheus both are re-written in God's name, their story transformed into an expression of *His* order. In short, Lou would refer Rilke's work to *her* philosophy of life. Rilke's achievement, in her view, has justified God: in the meantime, Rilke will have, as it were, seared off all that in him-self had over years clouded his ends. It is not that he will have found himself "anew", but that "all the negativity will have disappeared", dropped away from him, as it were, to reveal him as he always was. In other words, he will see that all the obstacles he had put in his path were only self-created. Lou ends her letter with this long parenthetic declaration, as a postscript:

(It is certainly no "loving oneself anew" that you will feel for yourself; rather in a new way all the negativity will have dis-appeared, all the "being unable to love oneself", all the taking offense at oneself, all the scuffling against oneself, to which one so often submits in moments of despair as to a sin against oneself.)

Nothing much had changed—at least on the surface: Lou still had the same old view of Rilke that she had always had, and was, moreover, still to the last pretending to tell him what he will be feeling...

Nothing had changed very much except this: that Lou had been given at last what she had always been hoping for. Part of the third and last letter Lou wrote at this time is a complete expression of this fulfilled hope. That part of her letter is a response to the Ninth Elegy which she had at last received. The other part of her letter, which we shall look at first, is a response to the Fifth Elegy; as an application of that poem to Rilke's case, this part is nothing less than a *tour de force* of pseudo-biographical interpretation. Her letter begins with this response: Rilke's case has been on another level exactly like that of the Saltimbanques, as one who

> ... *all the while kept working over and over at achieving mastery in every inward exertion, and felt only the failures—who, like the Saltimbanques, until they do succeed, are perpetually only* **exposed***, wrenched, sent reeling ...*

(Snow, Rilke, 337)

This is the only reading of the poem Lou could have: "Only *thus* could I let the Fifth speak to me, as saying something I have known from your most long-ago emotions." Among other things, she speaks of a "'widowed' self-robbed existence in one's own skin" (Rilke's "self-robbed existence in [his] own skin"), with reference to the painting's depiction of the old grandfather. And thus is every detail scrupulously applied to Rilke's case: even the "almost bull-like self-concentrated strength (of neck and nun)" of the oldest child acrobat. It is as if Lou could not let Rilke's case go, and of course there is a reason for all this, as this study has amply shown. Otherwise Lou's response does properly acknowledge the essential function of this poem, which *is* to highlight the will to overcome, in defiance of the disadvantage and extreme vulnerability one will also feel in one's situation in life. As we have seen, in the context of the Elegy-sequence as a whole, this poem especially marks a significant impulse forward toward resolution of the problem of existence as depicted in the sequence's first four Elegies.

In the second part of her letter, Lou turns to the Ninth Elegy and its climactic depiction of having reached "homeland"—as we have seen, the great achievement of this poem. It is for her "the most powerful" Elegy (338), for the reason that here the odyssey of her life as lived with Rilke has reached its goal. How significant that Lou should refer this poem's "homeland" to *herself*. "Yes, these are the gardens of my most secret homeland from far, far back; childhood and youth and all existence have always stood in the midst of them." Rilke had given her at last her dream of fulfilment; it is as if his whole enterprise had served principally to unite them in this final justification of the creative life after which she had so much hankered and that had at last been achieved:

*I can never tell you: how much this means to me and how I have
unconsciously been waiting to receive what is **Yours** as also **Mine**,
as life's true consummation.*

In the aftermath of Rilke's Florence days, as we have seen, Lou had
indeed taken over Rilke's poetic enterprise, virtually dictating the direction he would take for the rest of his poetic life. It had come as an
ultimatum to him at the time: *that* life with her, or else nothing to do
with her and he would have to go his own way. A whole other order
of life and love between them had at that moment been sacrificed, as
Rilke knew only too well, and he would never forget that this was so:
his whole life had been an effort to come to terms with this primordial
tragedy. In the meantime Lou had missed the whole point of Rilke's
creative struggle in relation to this love between them. Or perhaps it
only appears that she had…

Lou had always had her own way of assessing her situation with
Rilke, from the time of their first separation, and it had become the
dominant way of understanding between them. Rilke had let her have
this way of understanding it. It had always been for her the problem
of Rilke's willed, or self-created, failure: a "self-robbed existence"
from the start. I have made the case throughout this study that it was
quite otherwise, that, in her own role at the most crucial moment
in their life, Lou had failed that one love between them that alone
offered Rilke any chance of redeeming himself from a condition imposed upon him from his youth. A great unhappiness followed for
Rilke from this moment that would last him all his life. I believe that
at some point Lou recognized this failure, of which she had been
guilty, but it was a deep and desperate psychological need of hers to
have to think otherwise, that Rilke's unhappiness was his own; hence
the continual emphasis, *right through this final great moment* of achievement and celebration, on Rilke's self-created unhappiness. She had *to
continue to deny* what she otherwise I believe intuited, that the offense
he took at himself was not of his own making, but was the inevitable
consequence of having been rejected by her. In the meantime she is
revelling in the knowledge that she had been right, proven right in
thinking all along that Rilke would come through with what she had
designed for them.

There is a reason why the Ninth Elegy made such an impression on Lou: it is the poem in which Rilke finally reaches for himself, and so for them both, the end-goal of triumphant creative expression that Lou had always held up as the ideal of personal achievement and life in God. As we have seen, it is the poem in which Rilke sounds most like her: the poem in which, in its final idealization of what is sayable, her own ideas are finally confirmed and have become his own: "*Here* is the time for the *sayable, here* is its homeland" (385). In the period of the *Book of Images* and even in the composition of the *New Poems* Rilke was still entertaining the idea that he could return to himself after Lou, but once plunged into *Malte*, and on discovering that he had not been able to disentangle from his suffering, he had had to accept that there could be no other way for him, that he had been irreversibly marked by the direction their life had taken, and that Lou's enterprise had inevitably become, and would have to be from thereon in, his enterprise. However, we have seen how Rilke finally reaches his end-goal: only by a quite extraordinary act with respect to his love of the lost Lou that at last frees him fully for this task, and which he encapsulates with reference to what takes place between Orpheus and Eurydice. When Lou speaks of Rilke's having "erased the score" she was quoting from the very poem in which Rilke's great pronouncement is made: "Be forever dead in Eurydice." Lou appropriates the Orpheus myth back to her myth of herself, back to her God, the God of the *Book of Hours*. And yet, it is very hard to imagine that she would not have seen for herself that *she* was this lost Eurydice of whom Rilke is boasting he had at last come to terms.

Rilke had restored her to what she had been, in spite of herself, restored her with reference to the form their youthful love had taken. Paradoxically it is how he finally manages to satisfy her deepest wish for his achievement: in her words, "Yes, these are the gardens of my most secret homeland from far, far back; childhood and youth ..." Once, when they had first met, he had brought her back there, and now he had brought her there again. How extraordinary are the terms in which she describes herself in her experience of Rilke's final poems: "This is the essence: one becomes passionate again over all this, becomes young, enraptured, partial, happy, dead serious" (Snow, *Rilke*, 338). We can refer ourselves to the young girl in Gustav Moreau's painting of Orpheus, which serves as the cover image for this book.

It is as if Lou had indeed re-assumed her identity as a young girl, but uncognizant (or not readily cognizant) of the fact that her Orpheus could only be singing to her, and his lyre playing, because *he had died in her*, necessarily driven to the extreme of his beheading as the condition of his satisfying her in her deepest wish. Greater love for her had no man had. He had indeed re-created her, but in the meantime had had to give up the life that once lay in store for them that would have taken another form of relationship. He had had to give up himself as he was then, in those days when, in his Florence revelation, he was filled with the vision of how his life would unfold with her, he in his own creative way she in hers, and so knitted together in life and love. There he lay before her now at the other end of their life in association with each other, sacrificed at last to her ends and yet retaining to the last the image of what they were, which he had salvaged. It was his own achievement, if an achievement for them both; it was he who had seen it all through in the face of the worst obstacles that had been put in his way as the result of a broken life and a broken-off love. He was not, on the other hand, any the less satisfied with what he had achieved in Lou's image, and perhaps all the more so because of the dire sacrifice he had made...

God, Orpheus, the Angel

None of this would have fully reached Lou's consciousness, though I believe it was what Rilke had made of it all in his consciousness. It is my belief that Lou did recognize all this for herself, in some part of her only secretly admitted however, for there was an undeniable need in her to stick to the script of which she had always been the master of ceremonies. Her description of how she transforms around her reading of Rilke's final poems ends with her referring everything back to her God:

> *... one becomes passionate again over all this, becomes young, enraptured, partial, happy, dead serious, in short a creature of God the Creator.*

Yet it is Orpheus, not Lou's God, who is the prime mover behind Rilke's final poems. This bias in Lou's cosmological view is what also drives her to associate the primroses, in which Rilke was basking after his poetic exploits, with Rilke's Angel, rather than with Orpheus, Rilke's new Master by that time:

> *And now ... the Saltimbanques have caught up with you, have **arrived** where you are, so that your meadows with the first prim-roses became their carpet, spread out by that Angel of yours with the deepest smile (as **a springtime everywhere**) ...*

Here Lou was elaborating on Rilke's communication to her that some days after all his writing was done he entered for breakfast one morning to find a bowl of the first primroses set on the breakfast table, presumably disposed for him there by the housekeeper who had become familiar with his ways? or it may have been Merline?[56] Admittedly Lou had received but a few of Rilke's Sonnets by then, but more familiarity with them would probably not have altered her view that this carpet of triumphant achievement had been rolled out by the Angel. By now Lou did have all of the Elegies before her; she had not had much time to look all this over, but then is not likely even from them to have altered her basic view. That view is of an Angel that she assumes Rilke continues to idealize as his (and her) own, when in fact his view of the Angel, in the Elegies at least, has altered profoundly. As we have seen, in the end it is *this* world of ours here that Rilke would champion to the Angel of the Elegies, as opposed to that world that is the Angel's own beyond this one, by which Rilke was once greatly oppressed.

The evolution Rilke's Angel undergoes in the Elegy sequence as a whole would be worthy of a full-length study all to itself. That study would doubtlessly thrive on the many ambiguities in Rilke's presenta-tion. Here only general indications can be given. There is no question that Rilke is initially in awe, and indeed stands in some terror, of the Angel-figure that he invokes in the first two Elegies. Soon enough, however, the sense of the immense distance of its world from his, and ours, has taken over, and it is as if this Angel has withdrawn to its own sphere and reverted to being, very simply, an unknown factor. It has no presence whatever in the Third (the 'blood') Elegy, and by the Fourth has turned into a mere *type* of existence, set over and against the puppet as its type of existence at another extreme. The context of

---

56. See Snow, *Rilke*, 336.

the Fourth Elegy is the extreme alienation from virtually all human life in which Rilke finds himself by that point. The Angel has no presence at all also in the Sixth (the hero) Elegy and the Eighth (the 'consciousness') Elegy. In three of his Elegies, then—the Third, Sixth, and Eighth—Rilke has taken up a position very much in his own sphere and in his own world (of struggle), beyond any reference to the Angel. A dramatically new attitude towards the Angel is then pronounced in the Seventh Elegy. Here the Angel is for the first time directly addressed on Rilke's own terms—Rilke has won through to that degree of confidence about it. He addresses this Angel now out of his newfound sense of having at last much in this, our own, world to be proud of, over and against the remote world the Angel inhabits: "Be astonished, Angel"/"Don't think that I'm wooing" (373, 375). This form of address is also imported into the Fifth Elegy where Rilke signals the achievement represented by the young Saltimbanque's "smile" by proudly saying: "Oh gather it, Angel .../... Set it among those joys/ not *yet* open to us" (359). We must remember that the Fifth Elegy was the last to be written, and it continues to convey that finally freed form of relationship to the Angel Rilke had first introduced in the other final Elegies, notably the Seventh and the Ninth. In the Ninth Elegy, the Angel is at last reduced to a third-person reference: "Praise this world to the angel .../... He will stand astonished" (385). It is the strongest sign yet of the distance from the Angel Rilke has assumed from his by now established position in *this* world, to which he has fully committed. In the Tenth Elegy there are two final references to "angels" and "an angel". In the latter case this angel reads like a relic from *The Book of Hours*: it is *any* angel who would soon "stamp out" the degenerate ways of those who take "solace" in a life engrossed in the "market" economy. In the case of the other reference, to "angels": this is from the first twelve lines of the final Tenth Elegy, which we recall were taken over almost entirely as is from the original Tenth. This reference, to the prospect of at last offering "jubilation and praise to assenting angels" (389), constitutes also the relic of an older time, which I have argued Rilke would have done better to leave behind. His perspective on life at the time of his writing when at Muzot had altered radically from those very early, still much disturbed days at Duino, some ten years earlier, when these lines of consolatory hope were somewhat too valiantly thrown off.

Rilke's Angel, as it appears to him initially in the first two Elegies, one can say slowly withdraws from view over the course of the Elegy-sequence, and has been displaced by the end of it. The direct form of address Rilke later assumes in relation to it, and which is characteristic of the final Elegies, should not beguile us into thinking otherwise. Paradoxically, it expresses a form of ironic superiority, given the strong position Rilke has by now assumed in our own world here; the address is made to a Being who has, in the meantime, ceased to be present as it once was. One can say, indeed, that it only ever had any presence in this form in those first two Elegies, becoming from thereon in itself a mere relic of Rilke's past encounter with it. By the time we reach the end of the Elegy-sequence, our view of the Angel is that it has been an emissary of an otherworld from which Rilke has, substantially, turned away. By the Tenth Elegy, as we have seen, he is elaborating a picture of an otherworld, the world we inherit in death, that no longer bears on any such Angel-Being. It is presided over rather by a mythical race of Laments, not by hierarchies of Angels. It seems to have been Rilke's purpose here to give us a beyond that is precisely "*not in the Christian sense*", as he would put it later, not a beyond "whose shadow darkens the earth" (Greene 374), but rather one that constitutes "a whole", incorporative of "a purely earthly, deeply earthly, blissfully earthly consciousness".[57] In his letter Rilke describes this as a consciousness that "things of our intercourse … should be understood and transformed", in keeping with what he presents in his late poems. Such consciousness is none other than the Orphic consciousness that Rilke has come into in this late period, of which *The Sonnets* is the titular record. Such consciousness is the decisive element also in the production of the final Elegies, beginning with the Seventh Elegy where Rilke breaks out with his "song of annunciation". It is in the Ninth Elegy, we recall, that Rilke presents his elaborate view of how we have been called to see the Earth through from its visible form into an invisible one.

Not that Rilke does not remain attached to this Angel-figure in his life, in spite of the great distance he had finally taken from it certainly by the time he was composing the last few Elegies. As we have seen, this Angel is, initially, Novalis's Angel in whose like Rilke had once had his own profound interest, although by the time of the

---

57. These accounts from the letter to Witold von Hulewicz cited in n.46.

Duino moment Rilke had stepped so far away in his own terrible existence, this Angel could only appear to Rilke as a terrible reality. It had become a figure on whom Rilke projects the burden of his own by then terrible existence. To what extent Rilke's continued attachment to the Angel-figure became from there misplaced can be seen from the following. Three full years after the whole Elegy sequence was completed, in 1925, he would give expression to an elaborate theory, as to how such an Angel can be so constituted, that makes one wonder where Rilke would have found support for such a theory. In what has become a famous letter, the Angel is conceived as having at one time *itself* lived through the world of visible things that we know, with all its terrors and ecstasies, and *already* achieved the transformation of these things. Hence its peculiar rejection of us when we come close to it, for we have as yet to transform these things, mired still in these terrors and ecstasies, without the progression that the Angel has known already:

> *The angel of the* **Elegies** *is that creature in whom the transformation of the visible into the invisible, which we are accomplishing, appears already consummated* ... [It] *"is that being who vouches for the recognition in the invisible of a higher order of reality.— Hence "terrible" to us, because we, its lovers and transformers, do still cling to the visible.—All the worlds of the universe are plunging into the invisible as into their next deepest reality; a few stars immediately intensify and pass away in the infinite consciousness of the angels—, others are dependent upon beings who slowly and laboriously transform them, in whose terrors and ecstasies they attain their next invisible realization. We are, let it be emphasized once more, in the sense of the* **Elegies***, we are these transformers of the earth* ...

(Greene 375-376)

Rilke might as well have been speaking here of any Being other than what is recognized in Christian tradition as an Angel, and for this reason perhaps he would (wilfully) have his Angel into an Angel of Islam:

> *The Angel of the Elegies has nothing to do with the angel of the Christian heaven (rather with the angel figure of Islam)* ...

(375)

It is also in line perhaps with the Islamic conception of the afterlife that Rilke now gives this Angel the functions that in the Elegies clearly belong rather to the race of Laments:

> *For the angel of the Elegies all past towers and palaces are existent, **because** long invisible, and the still standing towers and bridges of our existence **already** invisible, although (for us) still persisting physically.*

Rilke has here projected back onto the figure of the Angel, who has been so carefully dissociated from any such function in the Elegies, all the attributes with which he had there imagined a whole new race of otherworldly Beings whom, grandly and in original fashion and in a way more fitting of our human experience, he denominates the race of Laments—Rilke having passed on to quite another *mythical* understanding of our teleological destiny…

Rilke was in those later years making of the Angel of the Elegies more than it can bear, *and it is a measure of a great fault-line in Rilke's thinking about it.* How haunted he was by this Angel if he could still pursue his attachment to it to such wilful lengths, in spite of all the evidence in the Elegies of his growing estrangement and final separation from it. We shall return to this haunting below. The Elegies take Rilke into what is in fact another, new *mythic* territory, where the Laments preside. It is territory as yet only tentatively intuited and explored but whose reality is already intimately conceived. Rilke is motivated therein by what is not any Angel-oriented purpose but rather a new *Orphic* impulse. This impulse suddenly breaks into the Elegies from the time he has come back to them at Muzot (it breaks through with the Seventh Elegy), and it puts a cap on them in a way quite other than what we can have expected. Rilke did not expect to put a cap on them in this way either. I have indicated how masterfully Rilke assimilates his new Orphic impulse into his ongoing exposition in the Elegies, so surrendered as he is by then to this impulse and yet working it so fruitfully into this other, his main work of this time.

The Elegies had been put together over a very great period of time (ten full years). They are in this respect unlike anything Rilke ever wrote. They were finally compiled in three distinct phases—a fourth if we set the Fifth Elegy apart from the other final Elegies by virtue of its being added later—and in each if these phases Rilke was writing in a significantly different idiom, and with a significantly different level of concern at the time. The First, Second, Third, and Sixth, and the original Tenth belong to a first phase; the Fourth to a second phase; the Seventh, Eighth, Ninth and revised Tenth to a third phase, the Fifth Elegy to a fourth phase. The Elegy sequence as finally realized is thus a highly constructed work that *reaches us from several distinct levels of experience.* How do we finally assimilate it? It should be easy enough to see that, in spite of the greatly extended period of composition associated with it, and the significantly varied range of levels and styles that result from this, the first six Elegies have been masterfully made to cohere, even if among them is also the Fifth, which was written last and bears something of the impress of Rilke's altered spirit in his final phase. As we have seen, as a replacement for the *Antistrophes* that were originally set in its place, this Fifth Elegy serves to reinforce the sequence, by more properly bridging the gap between the first four Elegies and those that follow the Sixth. With the final addition of this Fifth, and thus a firmer grounding in the theme of the will to overcome, it was at last made possible for us to effect along with Rilke that leap into positivity he finally takes, especially with the Seventh Elegy, albeit at a level that also startles us with its sudden new enthusiasm stemming from Rilke's newly discovered Orphic spirit.

Completion, and Hauntings

In this same letter from which I have been quoting[58], Rilke offers to review what we can accept turned out to be the main landmarks of his artistic production, working his way back from the final achievement of the Elegies:

> *They* [the Elegies] *reach out infinitely beyond me. I regard them as a further elaboration of those essential premises that were already given in the* **Book of Hours***, that in the two parts of the* **New Poems** *tentatively played with the image of the world and that then in* **Malte***, contracted in conflict, strike back into life and there almost lead to the proof that life so suspended in the*

---

58. The famous letter written to Witold von Hulewicz, Rilke's Polish translator, written over three years after the completion of the Elegies.

bottomless is impossible. In the **Elegies**, *starting from the same postulates, life becomes possible again, indeed it experiences here that ultimate* **affirmation** *to which young Malte, though on the difficult right path "des longues études", was as yet unable to conduct it.* **Affirmation of life-AND-death appears as one in the "Elegies"** ... *I am amazed that the* **Sonnets to Orpheus**, *which are at least as "difficult", filled with the same essence, are not more helpful to you in the understanding of the* **Elegies** ... *[T]he new elegies and their conclusion were preceded, in a few days, by the* **Sonnets to Orpheus**, *which imposed themselves tempestuously (and which had* **not** *been in my plan.) They are of the same "birth" as the* **Elegies**, *and their springing up, without my willing it, in connection with a girl who had died young, moves them even closer to the source of their origin: this connection being one more relation toward the center of that realm whose depth and influence we share, everywhere unboundaried, with the dead and those to come.*

(Greene 373-374)

It is perhaps understandable that Rilke should here pass over the *Book of Images*, that masterly work in its own kind in which he is striving hard to return to himself after his willed separation from Lou, if, in the end, to no effect. The main pattern of his life, which had him caught up with Lou by an iron necessity, had been forever established. Nevertheless, I have made an extensive effort to show what a masterly work this is, and how it has its own distinctively worthy place in the whole picture of Rilke's progressive achievement as this finally comes across to us. (See Volume 2 for my study of this rather special, wondrous *Book*.)

On other points we will also have questions and seek to introduce qualifications. Rilke is confident that in the *Elegies*, which were to appear over twenty years later, is to be found "a further elaboration of those essential premises that were already given in the *Book of Hours*". No doubt he is right, but only in a certain very broad sense, for the terms of Rilke's quest had shifted radically, and often, over those many years of interval between these two polar works. Over the years Rilke had been through many major shifts in his poetic allegiances, as we have seen. Thus, from his initial, profound fealty to the Christian visionary projections of Botticelli and of Novalis (which were to mark him for the rest of his life) he moves on, first, to Russia's (and Lou's) God; then, to the all-consuming work ethic of Rodin in *New Poems*; thence through a complete alienation from God in *Malte*; suddenly back to Novalis's Angel at Duino, only to thrust this Angel *away* from himself, as he would have to by then; in order, finally to find, many years later, his true home with Orpheus and the Laments. In what apprehensible terms can the *Elegies*, given these very greatly varied developments over many years, be finally said to be associated with such a remotely different world as that of the *Book of Hours* or for that matter the world of the *New Poems*?

There are a number of attempts by Rilke in *The Sonnets*, as he is reaching conclusion, to reconsider and recover some relation to his earlier works, by way of an impulse to round things out and to offer a picture of completion. I have pointed out the various forms in which he alludes back to the *Book of Hours* and the *New Poems* in his composition of *The Sonnets*. Still, all this is a far cry from Rilke's grand purpose of one day bringing the whole creation "to completion" through his poetic work, as conveyed at an early stage of his career in the *Book of Hours* (we looked at this grand purpose in Volume 1). Among other things, the idea of completion there had had a direct relationship to the God whose creation Rilke was serving at that time. That God had been through a great number of crises since, and in the end, in Rilke's poetic world at least, gives way to the god Orpheus. More to the point of completion in the sense in which this finally figures in Rilke's work, it is a matter of the deepest aesthetic judgment whether the *Elegies* with their miraculous informing Orphism do, in the end, provide an answer to *Malte* and the dark depths of its "impossible" world. There is a question as to whether we can fully assent to Rilke's encapsulating view of the chief informing experiences that account for these works, termed, in Rilke's *Malte*-phase and echoed over the years by him and by Lou, "dreadfulness" and "bliss" (variously "horror" and "happiness"):

> *To show the identity of dreadfulness and bliss ... this is the true significance and purpose of the **Elegies** and the **Sonnets to Orpheus**.*
>
> (Mitchell 551-552)[59]

---

59. From a letter to the Countess Margot Sizzo-Noris-Crouy, written on April 12th, 1923.

Can it really be the case of an *identity* of dreadfulness and bliss in either the *Elegies* or *The Sonnets* taken as a whole? Surely there can only be a certain relativity of dreadfulness and bliss in these works. One might think there is more of dreadfulness than of bliss in the *Elegies*, and only a balance (not an identity) of both in *The Sonnets*. But the matter could well be experienced otherwise: for example, the last four Elegies are almost entirely written in a positive spirit that is perhaps worthy of the exclusive term "bliss", although in these Elegies there is also much significant reference back to the dreadfulness of human suffering, which continues. What formula does that finally leave us with? Locally one can speak of an identity of these terms only where the Orphic experience is purely given, as at various points in *The Sonnets*. It may also be assumed behind the song of annunciation in the Seventh Elegy. However, even in the case of *The Sonnets*, as I have shown, there is much derivative work (nor is it altogether the purely spontaneous creation of legend). I have tried to show that for the most part this work develops what is more properly described as an Orphic culture *derived from* the Orphic experience, and as such comes across to us at some remove from any actual representation of an identity of dreadfulness and bliss. What there is to say about dreadfulness and bliss may be equally applied to Rilke's view that an "affirmation of life-AND-death appears **as one** in the *Elegies*" (my emphasis). Certainly it appears "as one" in the key Sonnets that give us the Orphic experience directly, but only in such instances, and there are very few such instances. It appears "as one" in the song of annunciation. But, otherwise, "affirmation of life-AND-death" is, rather, a broad faith in these poems. Apart from this, it may be said to be an *overall* effect of Rilke's artistic work taken as a whole. In this Rilke will have accomplished a very great deal indeed, but only in a highly qualified sense satisfying He whom he calls "the God of completeness" (Greene 361), who is altogether changeably served along the way.[60]

And so, also, with the debate as to the relative greatness of the *Elegies* and *The Sonnets*. Relative, indeed. I have made my own case for supposing *The Sonnets* the inferior work in the context of Rilke's ends. Miraculous as they are in part, *The Sonnets* have not in the end that

---

60. In a letter to Professor Hermann Poggs, dated October 21st, 1924.

"massiveness" of execution and expression that Rilke himself had seen alone could answer the full depth of Malte's despair. The *Elegies*, on the other hand, do possess this "massiveness" to set alongside *Malte*. From the first, Rilke thought of *The Sonnets* as work supportive of the *Elegies*, crucially instrumental in their inspiration but yet finally secondary as achievement. Hence he speaks unambiguously of (the "First Part") of *The Sonnets* as composed in the "fore-storm" (Greene 291) to the *Elegies* (otherwise translated, "in the squalls that announced the storm"—see Snow, *Rilke*, 331). It was only after Rilke read the whole of the Sonnet-sequence to the Princess in one sitting, when she visited him in Sierre, that he was left with a greater impression of it:

> *And the sonnets, which at first I took rather lightly compared to their elder, august sisters, the **Elegies**, have really been vouchsafed me in their full meaning by you, Princess, through the wonderful manner of your listening. Believe me, it needed only your reception to round off the achievement that was there, completing it richly and joyfully for me.*

> (Wydenbruck 218)

Three years later he is speaking of the Sonnets as having, as the Elegies had, "imposed themselves tempestuously"[61] (Greene 373), as an intrinsic part of the *one*, great "storm" of that former time. Historical distinctions had, by then, receded from him. Everything had by now been fully integrated into the *one* miraculous event of his writing when at Muzot.

With *The Sonnets* and the *Elegies*, Rilke had, indeed, at last established himself in a world that had fully consolidated, after a very long struggle; and this was, in the end, at the other extreme from Novalis and his world with which Rilke was once identified. Thus Novalis and Rilke become, in the end, mighty opposites. Where Novalis finally goes the way of (a highly complex) renunciation of the world, Rilke goes the way of a deeper and even a perverse immersion in it. We may take a measure of this final difference between them with reference to phrases from *The Sonnets* (respectively Sonnet 24, and 12 and 13, from the Second Part). For Rilke "the child [humankind] will [even-

---

61. In the letter to Witold von Hulewicz.

tually] bear" in historical time (24) turns out to be quite other than the one Novalis was anticipating when he ecstatically proclaimed: "Who does not feel the sweet shame of being with child?" Rilke had himself once identified with this historically nascent (Christ) child and the Mother of this child in his Florence days, but, as we have seen, he had been compelled to go quite another way. In the end, his child is not the once-and-forever, all-saving child of the Virgin Mother and Her God, rather that earth-transforming "child" (12) of historical-creative evolution born of the "parting" (12 and 13) that is also a uniting of the dead Eurydice and Orpheus, the Beloved Lou and himself, as Rilke had finally and momentously conceived of this (as above, p.419). Novalis would have seen in his opposite surely a formidable even a necessary proponent of all that in the world continues to need addressing, if only because it *is* the tragic world humankind continues to live in and to struggle with, as Rilke's own life had fully borne out. There was much to say on behalf of this continued struggle, as Rilke was more than amply to show, and there is no doubt that in the end he had acquitted himself masterfully in this enterprise. But it was at the extreme cost *of continuing haunted*. For Rilke was to *remain* haunted, by Novalis *and* by his proclaiming Angel to whom Rilke continues attached in the depths ambivalently and in the end anomalously—by Novalis and his Angel, though also by a young girl whom (unlike Novalis in his story) Rilke had never been able to give up. And he was to continue ill, shortly after to be dragged down to death by the blood that had continued to torment him throughout his struggle to find his way to what had seemed his impossible goal. Rilke died of leukemia, four years after completing the Elegies, in 1926, just past his 51st birthday.

Orphic Aftermath

Finally, in coming away from Rilke's work in its last stages, we are left with the question of how his Orphism, the crowning point of his poetic vision, will have fared subsequent to his achievement. In fact, beyond *The Sonnets* and the *Elegies*, Rilke did not, as a poet at least, undertake or find himself carrying on on that plane, nor did he give himself any further to the elaboration of an Orphic culture such as we find already quite developed in *The Sonnets*. Strange to say, he is almost altogether silent on such a promising and prospective culture in his letters. Not that we do not find there some allusion to the basic aspects of such creation and such culture, as where Rilke insists on the necessity of thinking of the Beyond in strict relation to what he forcefully describes as "a purely earthly, deeply earthly, blissfully earthly consciousness; we must introduce what is *here* seen and touched into the wider, into the widest orbit" (Greene 374). However, in the context of a more general focus on "poetic creation", in which he says he finds himself "intitiated into the fabulous wonders of our depths", his most pressing concern is with "marvelling" as such, and he goes on to confess that "my greatest, my most passionate marvelling goes to my own achievement, to certain activities in Nature" etc. (343). Here too the reference remains general and is spoken by Rilke as but another humble reader of his work by then. In the meantime, Rilke's poetic production one could almost say had ceased; it had become, after the Elegies and the Sonnets, only occasional at best, as his uncollected poems from this time illustrate.

As other texts we have been looking at show, Rilke was very much intent on establishing the parameters within which his work should finally be understood, but his purpose in doing so is to provide a proper picture of the contours and effect of his work as a whole. As for the Elegies and the Sonnets specifically, he is often mystified, even baffled as to what to say about them. He speaks of them as "my difficult books" in which one finds "endless inevitable difficulties", "points of departure ... often concealed (340), "lyric totals" that leap beyond illustrating "the figures that were necessary for the result" (330), and "darkness ... of such kind as to demand not illumination but submission" (328). The impression one has is of a poet who, having brought such extraordinary works into being and at such great pains, would very simply have to relapse and fall back into himself. Rilke speaks of "a strange situation for the person who brings them forth to feel beside him *such* essence of his own existence in its indescribable outweighing" (340). Relapse is inevitable from there:

> *The actuality of such poems stands out singularly above the flatness and incidentalness of daily life out of which nevertheless this greater, more valid thing was wrested and derived—**how** one scarcely knows oneself; for hardly is it done before one belongs*

again in the general blinder destiny, among those who forget, or
know as if they didn't know … Thus every big artistic achieve-
ment, into its last possible success, is both distinction and humili-
ation for him who was capable of it.

(Greene 340)

Rilke credits "the poetic word" as possessing unto itself a "freedom" not available to us as ourselves, and this leads him to propose that poetic works may only have their rightful place, in the end, among other poetic works, testifying to a higher order of existence among them that has yet to be really understood:

The poetic word of course has about it an atmosphere of free-
dom that is wanting in us; it has no neighbors, save in turn other
equivalent formations, and between it and them a spaciousness
may evolve similar to that of the starry sky: enormous distances
and the unpredictable movements of a higher order for which we
lack any comprehensive view.

(Greene 340-341)

If this proposition about poetic worlds were fully true, however, there would be no need to feel that outside conceptions of our place in reality ought to be challenged. That Rilke felt he had to continue to challenge a good number of these is itself testimony that there was more to a poetic world than only its own inherent laws as to what is real and possible. There were ways of thinking about religion, and especially about the Christian experience as we have seen, and even about God, that would need to be surmounted if one were to be able to properly create or approach and assimilate such poetic worlds as Rilke's own late work gives voice to. These worlds, both in their creation and in the way they should be received, require a whole other education in how we are to think, principally about our experience of the natural, the earthly world itself. We are thus brought back to where we start from, in *this* natural world, which needs to be fully accepted for all that is comprised by it. This becomes the basis for at last rejecting the concept of a Mediator between us and the natural creation, which Rilke especially associated with the Christian religion:

The strong, inwardly quivering bridge of the Mediator has sense
only where the abyss is granted between God and us—, but this

very abyss is full of the darkness of God and where one experiences it, let him climb down and howl in it (that is more necessary than to cross it). Only to him for whom the abyss too has been a dwelling place do the heavens before him turn about and everything deeply and profoundly of this world that the Church embezzled for the Beyond comes back; all the angels decide, singing praises, in favor of earth!

(Greene 325)

Needless to say something else would need to be interposed between us and this abyss, if one were not to go the finally futile way of the pure schizophrenic. Thus Rilke duly recognizes the equally absolute need to "waken counterweights" to the abyss, in one's own "consciousness" (Greene 343)—hardly a simple achievement this, in relation to the abyss itself, though Rilke had, as for himself, managed just that, in his own way and at his own level at any rate.[62] [63]

Such are the considerations, then, that absorbed Rilke beyond the writing of *The Sonnets* and the *Elegies*. They could be said to be a roundabout way of serving Orphic culture in the last analysis, but they were not a continuation of it as such. Such considerations make of Rilke in his last phase more generally a man of letters than someone who was concerned about any continuity in the Orphic stream of creation. Of course, for some time he did not know it was to be his last phase, though soon enough he will have had some intimation of this. Only a little more than a year after producing his great poems, his health had become a more serious concern than it ever had been, and within two years of that, by the fall of 1925, he was more or less diagnosed as chronically ill. His condition at this later time had been much exacerbated by his insistence on returning to his beloved Paris where he had sojourned for a full eight months. One year later he was dead.—Will Apollo have silenced him?[64] The question of what future

---

62. Rilke speaks of such "counterweights" specifically in the context of how to deal with "mediumistic happenings" whose reality he was fully ready to credit—in a letter to Nora Wydenbruck, written on August 11th, 1924.

63. My extensive discussion above will have helped the reader to take the measure of the problematic anomaly of Rilke's reference here to angels "singing praises in favor of earth".

64. This is the last feature of the Orpheus story as it has come down to us from tradition.

Orphic creation and Orphic culture have had and could have beyond Rilke, I must leave to those who will have since and in future times decided this matter…

In this study I have had my own purposes: to provide an extensive commentary on Rilke's work that is very closely linked to the details of his life from stage to stage and to bring out thereby an overall pattern to his life and work that may be usefully compared with what Rilke himself had to say about this. Almost all of Rilke's poems, between *The Book of Hours* and *The Sonnets*, have been commented on in detail, with specific attention given also to the figure they create among themselves in the context of the volume to which each group of poems belongs. Especially have various aspects of Rilke's life been brought forward that have not hitherto been given the attention they must assuredly get if we are indeed to bring both the life and the work into proper focus: most notably the intensely paradoxical and, indeed, problematically involuted relationship between Rilke and Lou, hitherto not quite fully properly viewed, as well as Rilke's further revisionary relationship to Novalis as his great poetic precursor, with the crucial bearing this relationship finally has on the problem of the Angel-figure in Rilke's life and work. Finally I have sought to establish what the full basis of that miraculous Orphic creation can be said to be to which Rilke committed himself at the last, and on which all Orphic poets following him would need to rely to continue in this stream:

> *Be forever dead in Eurydice.*
>
> *only the won-back heart   can ever be satisfied*
> ....
> *heavier by the weight   of where it has been.*[65]

It was enough for him to have broken that stream open, at some cost to himself; it would be for others to carry on in this stream, helped to a more favorable course by his account of the rudiments of an Orphic culture that he also provided to support it.

---

65. The last two lines quoted, from a poem written in August 1926.

Appendix

A Note on
"the magic of earthsmoke and rue"

I have spoken above (see pp.393-394) of Rilke's theoretical *readiness* when the experience of the Sonnets suddenly and unexpectedly came upon him. There is one instance, however, in which Rilke, for all his theorizing aptitude, does not rise adequately to the occasion, and this is in the phrase "the magic of earthsmoke and rue" (see the commentary on Sonnet 6 of the "First Part", pp.390-391). Richly evocative though the phrase may be, one has only to attempt an elucidation of it to realize after some time that it does not clarify itself; nor is it likely that an extra-literary commentary on any of the known forms of such magical practice, either in tradition or in Rilke's day, will explain what Rilke intended by it. Perhaps what he intended by this phrase was simply the *general* point that reality must be found not just in the rational-imaginative sphere (re: "the clearest connection"), but also in the seemingly irrational sphere. What complicates our reading of Rilke's phrase is the fact that while earthsmoke and rue are known to be "herbs used in summoning the dead" (Mitchell 579), Rilke's focus here is emphatically *not* on summoning the dead, a practice which he seems to be dismissing in Sonnet 6 (we are not to "draw back the dead" to what we take to be our "single world" here), but rather on our extended involvement with them in *their own* real world. There may be, as I show below, a psychological application to the phrase, but this too will not fully explain the process of magical involvement with death Rilke is alluding to here. "Rue" (in light of the traditional associations of this plant with such an idea) invokes the general sense of regret or mourning, mourning over ourselves perhaps because of our failure to understand our place in the whole complex of life and death. The use of earthsmoke could, in turn, be referred to the fact that "the Greeks and Romans used the juice [of this plant] to clear the sight" and that "they noted that while doing so it would make the eyes water as smoke would". (See *The Dictionary of Plant Lore*, by D.C. Watts, Elsevier Publishing Company: 2007.) The upshot of the reference to "earthsmoke and rue", taken as a whole then, would be that *mourning or sorrowing clears the sight* and thus marks its own path to "the clearest connection" with what is "seen" that is also invoked as a necessary culture in this poem. In a letter written three years earlier Rilke associated earthsmoke with "patience" (Mitchell 579); the term in this sense connecting further with rue as "sorrow", one ends up with the added idea of "patience in sorrow", the kind of patience in sorrow that leads in the end to "clear sight". Rilke's path through his life had been very much marked by his idealizing at every turn the virtue of patience in his own sorrowing. See, for example, from his letters, some two years before the Sonnets appeared: "often in life things seem to depend only on the longest patience" (Greene 233); *and only five days before*: "nothing is really as necessary as patience" (Greene 287). Also, towards the end of the same month in which all of the Sonnets were written, Rilke speaks of having been "permitted the patience, the long patience, for what has now been reached (Greene 294).

BREAKDOWN OF CHAPTERS